# Job Search Magic

**INSIDER SECRETS FROM AMERICA'S CAREER AND LIFE COACH**

Susan Britton Whitcomb

jist
Works
America's Career Publisher

# Job Search Magic

© 2006 by Susan Britton Whitcomb

Published by JIST Works, an imprint of JIST Publishing, Inc.
8902 Otis Avenue
Indianapolis, IN 46216-1033
Phone: 1-800-648-JIST     Fax: 1-800-JIST-FAX     E-mail: info@jist.com

Visit our Web site at **www.jist.com** for information on JIST, free job search tips, book chapters, and ordering instructions for our many products! For free information on 14,000 job titles, visit **www.careeroink.com**.

Quantity discounts are available for JIST books. Have future editions of JIST books automatically delivered to you on publication through our convenient standing order program. Please call our Sales Department at 1-800-648-5478 for a free catalog and more information.

Acquisitions and Development Editor: Lori Cates Hand
Interior Design: designLab
Page Layout: Trudy Coler
Cover Designer: Aleata Howard
Proofreader: Paula Lowell
Indexer: Kelly D. Henthorne

Printed in the United States of America
10  09  08  07  06        9  8  7  6  5  4  3  2

Library of Congress Cataloging-in-Publication Data

Whitcomb, Susan Britton, 1957-
Job search magic : insider secrets from America's career and life coach /
Susan Britton Whitcomb.
     p. cm.
Includes index.
ISBN 1-59357-150-X (alk. paper)
1. Job hunting.  I. Title.
HF5382.7.W485 2006
650.14–dc22

2005032560

We have been careful to provide accurate information in this book, but it is possible that errors and omissions have been introduced. Please consider this in making any career plans or other important decisions. Trust your own judgment above all else and in all things.

Trademarks: All brand names and product names used in this book are trade names, service marks, trademarks, or registered trademarks of their respective owners.

ISBN-13:  978-1-59357-150-4
ISBN-10:  1-59357-150-X

# Dedication

*Keep your face to the sunshine and you cannot see the shadow.*

*—Helen Keller*

*To Jean Gatewood and Judy Santos—whose gifts and goodness bring light to my path and strength for the journey.*

# Acknowledgments

Sincere appreciation goes to those who contributed insider tips, insights, and industry knowledge for the writing of this book:

Dana Adams, Microsoft Corporation

Lou Adler, Adler Concepts

Reginna K. Burns, AT&T

Freddie Cheek, Cheek & Cristantello Career Connections

Gerry Crispin, *CareerXroads*

Mary Ann Dietschler, Abundant Life for U

Kirsten Dixson, Brandego

Christine Edick, A Career Coach 4 U

Dean Eller, Central California Blood Center

Meg Ellis, Type Resources

Debra Feldman, JobWhiz.com

Julianne Franke, The Right Connections

Sheila Garofalo, SFC Consulting

Dr. Charles Handler, Rocket-Hire.com

Beverly Harvey, Beverly Harvey Resume & Career Services

Barry Hemly, Corning, Inc.

Mike Johnson, Corning, Inc.

Valerie Kennerson, Corning, Inc.

Martin Kimeldorf

Kate Kingsley, KLKingsley Executive Search

Louise Kursmark, Best Impression Resume and Career Services

Murray Mann, Global Career Strategies

Mark Mehler, *CareerXroads*

Don Orlando, The McLean Group

Dr. Dale Paulson, Career Ethic/Allegiance Research Group

Jean Hampton Pruitt

Pamela Ryder, Wyeth Pharmaceuticals

Kevin Skarritt, Acorn Creative

Dr. John Sullivan, San Francisco State University

Eileen Swift, Swift Graphic Design

Peter Weddle, Weddles.com

Gwen Weld, Microsoft Corporation

Judy Wile, New England Human Resources Association

Deborah Wile-Dib, Executive Power Coach

Michael A. Wirth, Talent+, Inc.

This book came to life because of a terrific team at JIST Publishing. A huge thank you goes to editor Lori Cates Hand, who had the vision to take the

*Magic* series further. She truly has the "magic touch" when it comes to development and editing. This, paired with her moral support and patience along the way, has been priceless to me. In addition, a big thank you to Trudy Coler, Aleata Howard, Amy Adams of designLab, Paula Lowell, and Kelly Henthorne for behind-the-scenes work with expert production, design, desktop publishing, proofreading, and indexing.

Special thanks go to Sandi Tompkins, my friend and "sister," who also happens to be a crack editor. Her editorial guidance helped make the author review process that much smoother. Heartfelt thanks go to my colleagues Judy Santos, Christine Edick, and Wendy Enelow for reading chapters and offering insights based on their expertise in coaching, career change, and job search strategy. Career coach and assessment expert Nancy Branton of CareerLifePotential.com was instrumental in mining volumes of information on career assessments for chapter 3; job search expert Beverly Harvey of HarveyCareers.com shared her in-depth research on online job search to make chapters 10 and 11 as current as possible; and careers expert Louise Kursmark of YourBestImpression.com made terrific contributions to chapter 17 on salary negotiations.

To my "bone marrow" buddy Jean Gatewood, once again, a huge thank you for supporting me in all my endeavors—you keep me focused on the Big Picture. And, to my husband Charlie, thanks for always carrying a pen so I can record my epiphanies and helping me stay grounded as I lunge at life! Finally, to the Lord, who equips and allows me to deliver the message that every human being is uniquely gifted and infinitely important, I am truly grateful for this life-work.

## Contact the Author

Thank you for selecting *Job Search Magic* from a shelf full of career books. The author welcomes your comments about this book. E-mail to let the author know what you found helpful, what you would like more information on, or what could be done to make this book stronger. Also, feel free to share how this book helped you find the *magic* in your work-life. Please be sure to mention this book's title in your correspondence.

Susan B. Whitcomb, CCMC, CCM, NCRW, MRW
Whitcomb Career Strategy
Fresno, CA
E-mail: swhitcomb@careerandlifecoach.com
Web site: www.CareerAndLifeCoach.com

# About This Book

This resource is for career-minded job seekers who need insider secrets that will make them stand out from the competition, as well as for career changers who want to be enthusiastically engaged and radically rewarded in their work-life. Although it's titled *Job Search Magic,* this book is not about using incantations, spells, or sleight-of-hand to trick an employer into hiring you! It is, however, about finding the *magic* in your work-life.

No, work won't be 40 hours a week of unending bliss, but there can be many magical moments along the way. In the job search journey, the magic comes when you step beyond your comfort zone and, having obeyed your intuition, set into motion serendipitous events that amaze and encourage you. In your career, magic happens when you lose track of time because you absolutely love what you do. Or it comes in those occasions when others appreciate and acknowledge you for your contributions. Magic is often signaled by goose-bumps and frequently associated with "ah-ha" moments—insights when you realize you're truly proud of who you are, what you do, and how you make a difference. This book is about helping you realize, package, and communicate your value so that you can have the magic!

*Job Search Magic* is divided into five parts. Part 1 establishes the all-important foundation for job search success. Chapter 1 reveals 10 often-overlooked secrets that will empower you, expose limiting beliefs, and set the stage for your job search. Chapter 2 will give you a structure and system as you create a job search plan. Chapter 3 helps you target positions that will be a Magic F.I.T.™. After all, what's the use of sailing through a job search if it lands you a job that isn't a good fit?

In chapter 4, you'll catalog a series of SMART Stories™; these success stories will help you provide employers with hard evidence of how you can deliver a return-on-investment (ROI) to the company by solving problems or serving needs. Chapter 5 then walks you through the steps to create a memorable career brand—that unique combination of skills or competencies that employers are willing to pay a premium for! Branding is one of the hottest trends in career management.

Hear this! All of the insider tips and strategies shared in this book are nearly useless if you don't (or won't) believe in yourself. Chapter 6 will infuse you with that make-or-break "I CAN" mindset, teaching you how to *I*nspire yourself daily, *C*ontrol the controllables, *A*ct now, and *N*ever give up!

In Part 2 of *Job Search Magic*, you'll create a killer résumé and other career marketing documents. Chapters 7 and 8 walk you through easy steps to outline and plug in keywords to your résumé, while chapter 9 will help you unearth accomplishments, the linchpin of a winning résumé. Chapter 10 covers e-résumés, cover letters, and other pieces of the puzzle.

Part 3 contains a wealth of job search strategies for both targeted/active searches and traditional/passive searches. Chapter 11 explains why it's important to uncover opportunities in addition to openings and offers a straightforward seven-step process for conducting a "new economy" search. You'll also see "magic words" scripts that will help open doors to more than a dozen types of networking contacts—the people who can help tip the job search scales in your favor. Chapter 12 will help you leverage the seven venues in a traditional/passive search, including online searches, résumé posting, résumé distribution, recruiters and agencies, classified ads, direct inquiry, and career events.

In Part 4 of *Job Search Magic*, you'll find important secrets for acing the interview. Chapter 13 covers online prescreening and telephone interviews, while chapter 14 offers a foolproof method for connecting with interviewers, clarifying what they need, collaborating on how you can meet those needs, and closing with professionalism and confidence.

Behavioral and competency-based interviewing continues to be used heavily by human resource professionals and hiring managers. Chapter 15 explains how to recognize behavioral interview questions, reveals the top 50 competencies most desired by employers, and coaches you on how to deliver a SMART Story™ that packs a powerful punch. In chapter 16 you'll learn how to respond to frequently asked questions (FAQs), industry-specific questions (ISQs), and illegal and awkward questions. With helpful sample responses, you'll learn how to be positive, precise, and pertinent so that the employer knows beyond a shadow of doubt that you will contribute to his or her bottom-line productivity and profit.

Part 5 of *Job Search Magic* equips you to enter into salary negotiations as a confident optimist. With a clear picture of your "reality," "comfort," and "dream number" salary ranges, you'll find in chapter 17 the secret to negotiating with power and integrity so that you can receive what you're worth!

Finally, chapter 18 will prepare you for those first critical few weeks on the job. Here, you'll learn 10 tips for making a fantastic first impression with your boss, your boss' boss, coworkers, customers, and clients. Setting the stage for success is critical. The more successful you are in your new job, the easier it will be to succeed the next time you need to interview!

Be sure to scan appendix A. It includes "Magic Tips" from industry-leading career coaches, counselors, and job search strategists, all of whom are members of Career Masters Institute. These tips cover all facets of your job search. Also see appendix B for worksheets to help you write your resume.

An important feature of this book is the tips found at the end of most chapters. The "10 Quick Tips" will give you a quick overview if you're in a hurry, while the coaching tips will help you take charge and move your career forward with commitment, intention, and momentum. If you're ready to do something awesome for your career, read on!

# Contents

## Part 1: Career Foundations.......................................1

**Chapter 1**   **Getting at the Heart of Job Search Success** .......................3

What vs. How ...............................................3

10 Secrets to a Successful Search ...........................5

Chapter Wrap-Up ..........................................21

**Chapter 2**   **Getting Your Job Search Plan Together** ......................23

Five Phases of a Job Transition ............................24

Plan A—Create a SMART Goal .............................28

Plan B—Give Yourself Options .............................43

Job Search Resources and Budget ..........................44

Your Support Team ........................................45

Chapter Wrap-Up ..........................................47

**Chapter 3**   **First Things First: Focus on the Magic F.I.T.™** .................51

Why Job Seekers Jump at the Wrong Opportunities .................52

Identify Your Magic FIT™ .................................55

Using Online Assessments to Discover Your Magic F.I.T.™ ..........83

Coaching Questions to Decide on the Best Career Direction .........93

Finalize Your Magic F.I.T.™ ..............................95

Create Your Focus Statement ..............................96

Chapter Wrap-Up ..........................................97

**Chapter 4**   **Capture Your Value with "Smart" Success Stories** .............101

Conveying Value to Employers .............................102

Inventorying Your Success Stories .........................105

Questions to Elicit Success Stories .......................107

Using the SMART Format to Answer Behavioral
    Interview Questions ...................................108

Writing Your Success Stories .............................114

Chapter Wrap-Up ..........................................119

**Chapter 5**   **Communicate Your Value Via a Career Brand** .................121

How Can a Career Brand Help? .............................121

The Elements of Your Brand ...............................122

Verbal Branding—Creating Your Sound Bites ................123

Visual Branding—Look and Act the Part! ...................137

Chapter Wrap-Up ..........................................146

**Chapter 6**     **Manage the "Buoy Factor"—How Mindset Can Sink or Support You . .149**

The Buoy Factor . . . . . . . . . . . . . . . . . . . . . . . . . . . . . . . . . . . . . . . . .150

The "I CAN" Mindset . . . . . . . . . . . . . . . . . . . . . . . . . . . . . . . . . . . . .150

Gauge Your Buoyancy . . . . . . . . . . . . . . . . . . . . . . . . . . . . . . . . . . . . .151

Inspire Daily . . . . . . . . . . . . . . . . . . . . . . . . . . . . . . . . . . . . . . . . . . . .156

Control the Controllables . . . . . . . . . . . . . . . . . . . . . . . . . . . . . . . . . .164

Act Now . . . . . . . . . . . . . . . . . . . . . . . . . . . . . . . . . . . . . . . . . . . . . . .174

Never Give Up! . . . . . . . . . . . . . . . . . . . . . . . . . . . . . . . . . . . . . . . . . .177

Chapter Wrap-Up . . . . . . . . . . . . . . . . . . . . . . . . . . . . . . . . . . . . . . . .182

# Part 2: Resumes and Career Marketing Documents...185

**Chapter 7**     **The Blueprint for a Magic Résumé** . . . . . . . . . . . . . . . . . . . . . . . .**187**

Two Tried-and-True Winning Formats: Chronological
   and Functional . . . . . . . . . . . . . . . . . . . . . . . . . . . . . . . . . . . . . . . .187

Selecting Category Headings . . . . . . . . . . . . . . . . . . . . . . . . . . . . . . . .195

Putting It All Together . . . . . . . . . . . . . . . . . . . . . . . . . . . . . . . . . . . .208

Chapter Wrap-Up . . . . . . . . . . . . . . . . . . . . . . . . . . . . . . . . . . . . . . . .209

**Chapter 8**     **How to Write Great Keyworded Copy** . . . . . . . . . . . . . . . . . . . . . .**211**

Keywords . . . . . . . . . . . . . . . . . . . . . . . . . . . . . . . . . . . . . . . . . . . . . .211

The Objective or Focus Statement . . . . . . . . . . . . . . . . . . . . . . . . . . . .214

The Qualifications Summary . . . . . . . . . . . . . . . . . . . . . . . . . . . . . . . .220

Professional Experience . . . . . . . . . . . . . . . . . . . . . . . . . . . . . . . . . . .223

Skills . . . . . . . . . . . . . . . . . . . . . . . . . . . . . . . . . . . . . . . . . . . . . . . . .226

Education, Credentials, Licensure . . . . . . . . . . . . . . . . . . . . . . . . . . . .227

Affiliations and Other Supporting Material . . . . . . . . . . . . . . . . . . . . .228

Chapter Wrap-Up . . . . . . . . . . . . . . . . . . . . . . . . . . . . . . . . . . . . . . . .229

**Chapter 9**     **Accomplishments: The Linchpin of a Great Résumé** . . . . . . . . . . . .**231**

Words to Woo Employers . . . . . . . . . . . . . . . . . . . . . . . . . . . . . . . . . .232

Strategies for Presenting Accomplishments . . . . . . . . . . . . . . . . . . . . .235

Where to Find Material for Your Accomplishments . . . . . . . . . . . . . . .242

Impact-Mining: Probing Questions to Unearth Hidden Treasures . . . .245

Sifting Through the Accomplishments You've Gathered . . . . . . . . . . . .246

Use Impact Statements to Portray Yourself as the Right Fit . . . . . . . . .246

Finalizing Your Résumé with Formatting, Editing, and Proofing . . . . .247

Chapter Wrap-Up . . . . . . . . . . . . . . . . . . . . . . . . . . . . . . . . . . . . . . . .250

**Chapter 10**     **E-Résumés, Cover Letters, and Other Career Marketing Documents . .253**

Creating ASCII Plain-Text Résumés . . . . . . . . . . . . . . . . . . . . . . . . . .253

Creating an ePortfolio . . . . . . . . . . . . . . . . . . . . . . . . . . . . . . . . . . . .257

Getting on the Blog Bandwagon . . . . . . . . . . . . . . . . . . . . . . . . . . . . .258

Cover Letters and Other Correspondence . . . . . . . . . . . . . . . . . . . . . . .261

Chapter Wrap-Up . . . . . . . . . . . . . . . . . . . . . . . . . . . . . . . . . . . . . . . . .268

## Part 3: Job Search Strategies . . . . . . . . . . . . . . . . . . . . . . . . . . .271

**Chapter 11**   **Tap the Hidden Job Market with a Targeted Search** . . . . . . . . . . . . .273

The Difference Between Openings and Opportunities . . . . . . . . . . . .273

Determine Your Search Strategy—Targeted or Traditional . . . . . . . . .276

Seven Steps to a Targeted Search . . . . . . . . . . . . . . . . . . . . . . . . . . . .278

Chapter Wrap-Up . . . . . . . . . . . . . . . . . . . . . . . . . . . . . . . . . . . . . . . . .314

**Chapter 12**   **Cover Your Bases with Traditional Search Strategies** . . . . . . . . . . . . .319

Why People Continue to Use Traditional Search Strategies . . . . . . . . .319

The Seven Venues of a Traditional Search . . . . . . . . . . . . . . . . . . . . . .320

Chapter Wrap-Up . . . . . . . . . . . . . . . . . . . . . . . . . . . . . . . . . . . . . . . . .335

## Part 4: Interviews . . . . . . . . . . . . . . . . . . . . . . . . . . . . . . . . . . . . .339

**Chapter 13**   **Pass Online Prescreens and Telephone Interviews with Flying Colors** .341

Navigate Online Prescreening Tools . . . . . . . . . . . . . . . . . . . . . . . . . .342

Ace Formal Assessments . . . . . . . . . . . . . . . . . . . . . . . . . . . . . . . . . . .346

Make a Great First Impression in Telephone Interviews . . . . . . . . . . .347

Chapter Wrap-Up . . . . . . . . . . . . . . . . . . . . . . . . . . . . . . . . . . . . . . . . .354

**Chapter 14**   **The 4 *Cs* of Interviewing—Connect, Clarify,
                 Collaborate, and Close** . . . . . . . . . . . . . . . . . . . . . . . . . . . . . . . . . . .357

Phase 1: Connect with the Interviewer—How to Create the Right
 Chemistry . . . . . . . . . . . . . . . . . . . . . . . . . . . . . . . . . . . . . . . . . . . . . . .358

Phase 2: Clarify *What* Needs to Be Done . . . . . . . . . . . . . . . . . . . . . .366

Phase 3: Collaborate on *How* to Do the Job . . . . . . . . . . . . . . . . . . . .370

Phase 4: Close with Professionalism—How to Wrap Up and Win . . . . .372

Measure Your Performance in a Post-Interview Analysis . . . . . . . . . . .377

The 4 *Cs* in Second and Subsequent Interviews . . . . . . . . . . . . . . . . .379

Sample Follow-Up Letters and "Leave-Behinds" . . . . . . . . . . . . . . . . .379

Chapter Wrap-Up . . . . . . . . . . . . . . . . . . . . . . . . . . . . . . . . . . . . . . . . .385

**Chapter 15**   **Score Points in Behavioral Interviews** . . . . . . . . . . . . . . . . . . . . . . .391

How to Spot a Behavioral Interview Question . . . . . . . . . . . . . . . . . . .392

What Employers Look for in Behavioral Interviews . . . . . . . . . . . . . . .392

How Employers Use Competencies to Develop Interview Questions . .395

Mining Job Descriptions for Competencies . . . . . . . . . . . . . . . . . . . . .396

Linking Competencies to Your SMART Stories™ . . . . . . . . . . . . . . . . .397

Why SMART Stories™ Are Critical in Behavioral Interviews . . . . . . . . .398

Chapter Wrap-Up . . . . . . . . . . . . . . . . . . . . . . . . . . . . . . . . . . . . . . . . .402

Chapter 16    **Ace Frequently Asked Questions, Industry-Specific**
              **Questions, and Illegal or Awkward Questions** ..................405
              Frequently Asked Questions ...................................406
              Master Your Industry-Specific Questions (ISQs) ................430
              Field Illegal and Awkward Interview Questions ..................431
              Chapter Wrap-Up .............................................440

# Part 5: Salary Negotiation and Job Success.................443

Chapter 17    **Negotiate Your Salary: The Secrets to Knowing and Receiving**
              **What You're Worth** .........................................445
              Preparing for the Salary Dance ...............................446
              How to Deflect Salary Questions Until the Offer ................450
              When an Offer Is Made .......................................452
              How to Initiate a Counter-Offer ..............................456
              Negotiating Additional Elements of Your Compensation Package ....458
              Get the Offer in Writing and Think It Over ....................459
              Chapter Wrap-Up .............................................462

Chapter 18    **10 Tips for a Great Start in Your New Position** ...................469
              Your Results ................................................470
              Your Relationships ...........................................473
              Chapter Wrap-Up .............................................476

Appendix A    **Magic Job Search Tips** ......................................477

Appendix B    **Worksheets to Catalog Professional History** .....................509

              **Index** .....................................................520

# Part
# I

# Career Foundations

Chapter 1:   Getting at the Heart of Job Search Success

Chapter 2:   Getting Your Job Search Plan Together

Chapter 3:   First Things First: Focus on the Magic F.I.T.™

Chapter 4:   Capture Your Value with "Smart" Success Stories

Chapter 5:   Communicate Your Value Via a Career Brand

Chapter 6:   Manage the "Buoy Factor"—How Mindset Can Sink or Support You

# Getting at the Heart of Job Search Success

*"Success is not the key to happiness. Happiness is the key to success. If you love what you are doing, you will be successful."*

—Albert Schweitzer

When it comes to job search, most people are concerned with the *how-to*. How do I tap the hidden job market? How do I use keywords to make my online résumé stand out? How do I answer tough interview questions? How do I negotiate salary?

Granted, the *hows* are important. But the *whats* should be answered first. The *whats* include knowing who you are, what you were hardwired from birth to do well, what you're passionate about, what will make you happy, and what kind of legacy you want to leave the world.

Answering the *how tos* without first answering the *whats* is putting the proverbial cart in front of the horse. However, getting at the heart of job search enables you to put first things first. When you do, you'll be able to focus clearly and gain new ground.

## What vs. How

To determine the *whats* for your career, look to some profound questions. Martin Luther King, Jr., certainly understood the power of questions: "Our questions in life are everything. The questions we ask on a daily basis will shape our destiny as

clearly as the skeleton shapes the body." Your answers to these questions can shape your career destiny:

- What is your purpose here on this planet…what do you really want to do with your life?

- What is the one significant career goal you want to accomplish?

- What career dream do you keep postponing? Or, what thoughts keep surfacing that you're embarrassed to voice for fear your family or friends will think you're crazy? (The test of time is often a good clue to career direction. If something keeps "calling" you, it's worthy of exploring further.)

- Whose career do you secretly envy? Whose career do you sincerely admire?

- If you had it to do all over again, what work would you choose?

- What are the top three things about your career that you want to be different this time next year?

- What are the *non-negotiables* you need in order to feel satisfied in your work? For instance, the ability to influence policy, freedom to schedule your own work hours, ability to work with fun people, and so on.

- What insights about you do your friends share with you? For instance, "You know, you'd be really great at _____?" or "Have you ever thought about becoming a _____?"

- What problems do you love to fix? What need is your heart drawn to helping?

- What aspects of your work do you procrastinate on? (These provide clues as to what you're *not* drawn to!)

- When your career eventually comes to a close, what accomplishments will you look back on with gratitude and pride?

## Career Magic Is Found in the *Whats*

Knowing the *whats* will create magic in your career. Once the *whats* fall into place, the *hows* of your search will come more easily. The *whats* lead to a passion-driven career… an *Occupassion*™ rather than an occupation. *Occupassion*™, a term coined by Steve Gallison, a career counselor from Baltimore, Maryland, and Career Masters Institute member, combines occupation with passion so that your work is supercharged with motivation. Passion generates motivation.

Some of you already know the answers to the *whats* in your worklife. Others are at a crossroads where it's time to reevaluate what is most important—the things that matter in your twenties will be different than those in your thirties, forties, fifties, sixties, and beyond. For those in search of answers to the *whats*, you'll find ideas and exercises in Part 1 of *Job Search Magic*. Parts 2 through 5 will reveal the *hows*.

As you may have surmised, *Job Search Magic* looks at careers from a holistic, life-work perspective. If you think career and life are two separate issues, consider these sobering numbers. Over the span of a 50-year career, clocking 40- to 50-hour workweeks, you will devote 100,000 to 125,000 hours to your job. That's more time than most people spend sleeping, and it's likely more than can be spent on home-life and recreational activities. With this in mind, forget the hope of work-life balance, which many experts believe is the wrong focus. Instead, pursue work-life synergy, which means choosing work that will energize you. When you're doing lifework, life on the whole is more fulfilling, financially rewarding, and fun.

### Are You Satisfied?

Surveys from the past three years by the Conference Board's Consumer Research Center indicate that approximately 50 to 60% of people are unhappy with their jobs. The culprits for job dissatisfaction are rapid technological changes, rising productivity demands, and changing employee expectations.

The key to greater job satisfaction, productivity, and performance is aligning your work with your passions and with employers who offer a good organizational-culture match. Greater productivity and performance doesn't just benefit the employer—it also positions you as a more appealing and valuable professional.

Now that you know the importance of putting the *whats* before the *hows*, let me share some important insights before you tackle your transition to a new job or new career.

## 10 Secrets to a Successful Search

There are some lesser-known secrets that are key to a successful search (and a successful career). I refer to them as the Pivotal P's:

| | |
|---|---|
| Secret #1: | Visualize the Right **P**icture |
| Secret #2: | Pursue **P**urpose |
| Secret #3: | Embrace the **P**rocess |
| Secret #4: | Offer **P**rofit |
| Secret #5: | Keep **P**erspective |
| Secret #6: | Commit to **P**ersistence |
| Secret #7: | Be **P**repared |
| Secret #8: | Enlist **P**artners |
| Secret #9: | Go **P**ublic |
| Secret #10: | Create a **P**lan |

Apply these secrets, and you'll find job search and career management an empowering experience. In discussing them next, you'll see there are some common themes and crossovers.

# Secret #1: Visualize the Right Picture

To obtain the perfect outcome, you must first have an unwavering belief that you can, indeed, achieve it. Picture yourself successful, deserving the satisfying work that you want, making the money you need, and living the lifestyle you desire. In my work with thousands of job seekers over the past two decades, I continually see people aim lower rather than higher. They resign themselves to less than the best, and yet they hold secret dreams of doing something truly great. Others have shared these observations. Author Marianne Williamson penned this stirring challenge to envisioning success:

*"Our deepest fear is not that we are inadequate. Our deepest fear is that we are powerful beyond measure. It is our light, not our darkness, that frightens us. We ask ourselves, 'Who am I to be brilliant, gorgeous, talented, and famous?' Actually, who are you not to be?… Your playing small doesn't serve the world. There's nothing enlightened about shrinking so that other people won't feel insecure around you… As we are liberated from our own fear, our presence automatically liberates others."*

## Don't Settle

Don't play small! Don't settle for average when awesome abundance is there for the taking. For those who think awesome abundance is not available, here are some figures that offer hope. As the United States ages, analysts have noted a growing labor and skills shortage that started almost imperceptibly around 2004–2005. This is predicted to increase to a shortage of 14 million postsecondary workers and seven million noncollege workers by 2020, according to an article in the American Society for Training & Development's *T+D* magazine, January 2005 issue. This will give workers a lot of leverage. So please, dream big! Envision WILD success. You have a finite amount of time on this planet, with just ONE life to live. Live it with vision, optimism, and action.

## Envision Your Ideal Work Environment

Steven Covey, in his bestselling book *The Seven Habits of Highly Effective People*, gives evidence of the importance of visioning success. Covey identifies Habit #2 as "Begin with the End in Mind." He explains that all things are created twice: first in the mental world, and second in the physical world. Most endeavors that fail, fail in the first creation. Take the time to daydream or meditate on your desires. Mentally rehearse things in detail! What does your ideal work environment look like? What smells or aromas do you notice? What do you hear? With whom are you interacting? What work activities are you enjoying? What papers, computers, or products are you touching? What gives you a sense of pride? What kudos are you getting? What new contacts are you making? What hours do you work? What does your commute look like (if any)? How are you dressed? What kind of lifestyle and

free time does your position allow? How and with whom have you celebrated landing this new position? And, what kind of future advancement opportunities will come as a result of this position?

Some job seekers get stalled because they can't envision the end result clearly and insist on knowing all the answers before making a move.

### Don't Expect ALL the Answers in Advance

A recent issue of *Fast Company* magazine was devoted to design. Several famous product designers were interviewed, including innovators from Ideo, the company behind the brilliant idea for the folding screen on laptop computers. Interestingly, designers conceptualize new ideas only after they've analyzed market needs. Then, they build a prototype to elicit feedback that helps work through the problem to be solved. The act of focusing on the prototypes brings about more improvements, with the final product multiple iterations away.

The correlation to careers? If you cannot clearly see your final destination, analyze the market to find a need you can fill, and envision yourself filling that need. Then, start building—take a related class, taste-test the career with a night job or volunteer work, talk candidly with people in your chosen field, take a position that is a good stepping stone, or rethink your working identity. The simple act of focusing on your new career will bring about improvements. Your final career may be multiple iterations away, but you won't know that until you start building.

## Envision the "Big Picture"

While on the subject of picturing success, why not also explore the Big Picture? Your part in the Big Picture is like a thread in a beautifully woven tapestry. Without your contribution, the picture won't look as rich and the tapestry will have loose threads. If you're not doing what you were designed to do, two things happen: first, you won't be fulfilled; and second, the needs of other people may not be met. When their needs aren't met, they will be delayed or detoured in doing what they're supposed to do. We are connected by bonds we cannot fathom.

I can hear some of you thinking, "I'm just an ordinary person. I don't plan to make a big impact." You don't have to be famous to have a long-term impact on peoples' lives. Mitch Albom's *The Five People You Meet in Heaven* (Hyperion) weaves a tapestry about 83-year-old Eddie, who led what he saw as a disappointing life working as head of maintenance at a seaside amusement park. An accident at the park closes the door on Eddie's earthly life and opens the door to heaven, with revelations that his life impacted others far more than he could ever have dreamed. (I won't spoil the story by telling you how!) The same is true for your life. Whether maintenance mechanic or managing director, paralegal or programmer, category manager or commodities trader, your lifework has the ripple effect.

quite quickly? Do you encourage others? Remember facts and figures? Design strategy? Bring logic to a discussion? Envision the future? See better ways to do things? Create new ideas? In chapter 3, we will look more closely at creating a Magic F.I.T.™ to help you really hone in on career opportunities that match your nature.

## Assets

Assets include the knowledge, skills, and values you bring to an employer.

- **Knowledge** includes information, facts, data, experiences, and so on that are gained over the course of your education, career, and life.

- **Skills** are proficiencies and expertise that are honed through on-the-job practice.

- **Values** are the things that are important to you in your career. They might be tangible or intangible; for instance, economic rewards, independence, social interaction, intellectual challenge, personal development, or creativity. A clear sense of your values will help you in evaluating different opportunities and making wise career choices.

Be who you were meant to be! Look to your **D**esigned **N**ature and **A**ssets—your career DNA—to give you purpose, identify your value, and help you find the ideal place to practice your Occupassion™.

### A Job or a Career?

Throughout this book, the terms *job* and *career* are used synonymously. Some people much prefer *career*, as it implies ownership of work that brings financial reward and fulfillment—career conveys something you "want to do." *Job*, on the other hand, may imply an unwilling servitude—something you "have to do." The reality is that the world uses the term *job* frequently and so, throughout this book, I use the terms interchangeably. If *job* doesn't conjure up positive images for you, I encourage you to think of it in light of this acronym:

*J—Journey*

*O—Of*

*B—Becoming*

Your *JOB* is, indeed, a journey—a place where you can become more of who you were meant to be.

## Secret #3: Embrace the Process

The unwelcome truth about process is this: Quality and quick are not synonymous when it comes to your career. Anything of value requires an investment. Like

You make a difference both now and in the long-run. Think legacy. Look past the distractions, busyness, confusion, and frustrations to the Big Picture. The choices you make today put you on a trajectory that will intersect thousands of lives. Intersect them for the good! This brings us to the next Pivotal P.

# Secret #2: Pursue Purpose

The bookshelves at your local bookstore are full of titles about living (and working) with purpose, authenticity, and intention. These aren't new topics. More than 400 years ago, Shakespeare penned, "That at each man's birth there comes into being an eternal vocation for him, expressly for him. To be true to himself in relation to this eternal vocation is the highest thing a man can practice." Shakespeare recognized that life purpose was linked to eternal vocation (or the modern-day term, *career*). If you've been wondering about your highest purpose, look to the work that you have been gifted to do. In it, you'll find significance and security. Purposeful work is the secret to shifting from drudgery to dream job.

In broad terms, *career purpose* can be defined as

**Being radically rewarded and enthusiastically engaged in work that adds value to others.**

Here's how that definition breaks down:

- **Radically rewarded**—This is your carrot! What are the payoffs for you? Beyond compensation and benefits, your carrots may include recognition, responsibility, intellectual challenge, personal growth, a sense of community, contributing to a cause, job security, special perks, and so on.

- **Enthusiastically engaged**—Passionately pursue your talents and interests! Find the sweet spot—work that is comforting, feels good, comes naturally, causes you to easily lose track of time, and occasionally makes you think, "I cannot believe they pay me to do this!"

- **Adds value to others**—Implicit in the definition of work is the performance of some action that achieves a result. That result should always, always, always meet a market need and add value to others, whether it be helping people, improving processes, enhancing products, or impacting profit.

Some wrestle with the question of "what's my purpose in life?" Here's a simple answer: Your purpose in life is to live a life of purpose. Your career gives you the perfect stage on which to act out that purpose. As you ponder purpose and fulfillment, consider these questions:

- What do you want to accomplish through your work?

- What impact do you want to make?

- What do you want to be remembered for?

The secret to finding your purpose lies in tapping into your "career DNA." You learned in school that DNA is the molecular basis of your heredity. In other words, it's the root of your innate, or natural, talents. For our purposes, I'll refer to DNA in a career-management framework, with the letters standing for your **D**esigned **N**ature and **A**ssets. Let's look at the significance of each of those words.

## Designed

You were uniquely designed with a thumbprint, a voice pattern, and an iris that does not match any other human being on this planet (even the eyes of genetically identical twins have iris barcodes as different as unrelated eyes). That individuality makes you distinctly valuable and grants you the ability to create a career like no other.

You were designed with a purpose. That purpose gives you value. Value gives you bargaining power. Bargaining power gives you confidence. Confidence is integral to success. Tap into your designed purpose and you will unlock your passion. Purpose produces passion!

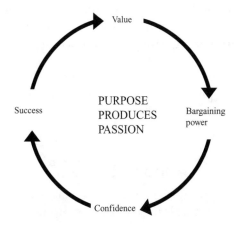

**Figure 1.1: Tapping into your designed purpose.**

## Nature

From birth, you have exhibited certain preferences and personality traits. In fact, if you look back into your childhood for clues to what you'd be good at today, you will likely find some interesting evidence. Everyone has those clues. As an example, Grandma Moses, the Vermont artist who gained notoriety after picking up her paintbrushes at the age of 80, actually showed very early signs of her artistic skill. A child of six who loved to draw, she would go out to her family's vineyards and pluck grapes from the vines to experiment with blending colors. Her homemade paints had to be put aside for plowshares, as the demands of farm life in the late 19th century left little time for artwork. (For more inspiring stories in this vein, see *Now, Discover Your Strengths* by Marcus Buckingham and Donald O. Clifton [Free Press, 2001].)

Your distinctive nature makes it easier for you to do certain things better than others. So, what have you always done well, or what new thing have you picked up building the home of your dreams, it takes time to craft the perfect career. It's a process. The perfect career won't materialize instantaneously. Anyone who has built a new home will tell you that it takes time (usually longer than expected) to go from designing plans and breaking ground to moving in. And once moved in, it still takes time to find just the right furnishings, housewares, and decorations to make the home uniquely yours. Finally, there are the subsequent home-improvement and repair projects to keep things maintained and updated.

You will encounter a similar process in building your dream career. It takes time to design a career blueprint and build according to plan. The argument could even be made that job search competence is more important than any other career skill, because if you can't unearth opportunities and make others aware of your value, you won't have a career. You're guaranteed to find insider tips and strategies throughout this book to boost your job search IQ. Once hired, you'll add to your skills, industry knowledge, and network of contacts. As time passes, you'll challenge yourself to stretch beyond comfort zones, learn new skills, and take on new challenges. This continual construction will keep your career fresh and lead to interesting projects and rewarding promotions.

While coaching people in career transition, I occasionally hear the question that I sense many are afraid to voice: Is there really an employer out there who will want me and appreciate me? Your answer to that question will be fundamental to your career success. If you doubt there's a positive answer to the question, look to the ancient wisdom of King Solomon, who offered the timeless quote: "there is a time for every season."

What season are you in now? It might be a season to teach or to learn, to grow or to rest, to move on or to wait. Process helps you develop a continual awareness of what needs to be in place for you to be your best. As you embrace the process, perhaps one of these career situations sounds right for you at this time in your life:

- **Bridge job or stepping stone:** A stepping-stone position is not a dream job, but it might lead to one. Perhaps your industry has encountered steep declines and opportunities aren't plentiful. Maybe you just need to remove yourself from a toxic employment situation. Either way, a transitional position might be just the ticket.

- **High yield:** Looking for big rewards based on a significant investment of time and energy in your career? If you are a fast-tracker, you might be ready for a pressure-cooker position where you can stretch and challenge yourself to the extreme.

- **Incubator:** You might have recently endured a significant loss, illness, or setback. If so, an incubator position might be the place where you can heal and regain your strength. Incubator positions do require that you perform work of value, but the work might not be particularly challenging. Incubator positions are temporary and can serve a purpose for certain seasons of your life.

**Life balance:** Life-balance positions appeal to those who previously sacrificed quality of life by pouring themselves into jobs that required 60, 80, or even 100-hour work weeks. Typically a lesser-paying position than what you've come from, a life-balance position can offer less tangible but more meaningful payoffs. It might even include a flex-time or job-sharing arrangement.

**Lobster:** Ever wonder how a lobster can grow to be so big? It has to shed its shell periodically. You might feel cramped or stifled in your current position. If so, it might be time to find a place where you can grow.

**Circuit rider:** In the 1800s, a circuit rider was a clergyman on horseback who would spread himself among multiple towns. The concept of dividing time among two or three companies might be appropriate for you, especially if you're working in an industry that is cash-strapped and cannot afford a full-time arrangement.

**Free agent:** Similar to a circuit rider, a free-agent position allows you to move quickly between or within companies where your skills are in highest demand. Reminiscent of workers in the film industry, where work is project based, free agents typically accept work by the project, as opposed to a traditional, open-ended employment situation.

**Site seeing:** Do you like what you're doing but perhaps just need a change of scenery? A site-seeing position is one that allows you to do similar work but with different surroundings or people. Sometimes a simple change of scenery can do wonders.

**Portfolio:** A portfolio position allows you to use and further develop a variety of special skills. This type of position is especially appealing to those who thrive on variety and a spontaneous, flexible approach to life and work.

**Destination:** A destination position is one that you've been aiming at for a number of years. This type of position is typically at the top of the career ladder for your functional area.

It's obvious that up and ahead are not the only options when it comes to a new position. Instead, in embracing process, your goal should be progress, not perfection. Progress includes anything that is right for you at this juncture in your life. With all these different options in mind, there *is* an employer out there who will benefit from your career DNA.

## Secret #4: Offer Profit

Here's a universal hiring principle: If a company perceives that you can add more profit to its bottom line than other candidates, you will be hired. Every employer (even a not-for-profit organization) wants a strong return-on-investment when hiring. Too many job seekers think that companies are flush with cash. The reality is that the companies rely on employees to generate cash. Unfortunately, the term *profit* makes some people uneasy, conjuring up images of greedy executives

pillaging corporate coffers and employee retirement funds. Those who know me well know that I don't worship the almighty dollar, but I do respect it (and advocate conscientious capitalism) and see the connection to employment. If an organization does not generate profit, there won't be money to pay you. No profit, no job.

An often-used codeword for profit is *value*. Truly successful professionals understand the importance of delivering value. Epitomizing this principle is Dr. Ivan Misner, Founder and CEO of Business Network International (BNI), the largest business networking organization in the world. In 1985, the then-28-year-old business consultant had a vision that led BNI to grow from infancy to its now impressive reach in 22 countries. The formula for BNI's success is the "givers gain" philosophy—an unselfish attitude of helping others (providing value), which promotes profitable and lasting relationships.

The perspective of providing value will shift the emphasis of your job search from "who will hire me?" (a position of powerlessness) to "where can I contribute the most value?" (a place of power). The latter position gives you more confidence and choices. Value differentiates you from the cattle call of candidates.

Being conscious of contributing to the bottom line and communicating value in the job search is critical. You'll learn how to do this in chapter 5 through your career brand—a visual and verbal montage that will attract projects and people who are a perfect match.

---

### Value = Profit

In the employment marketplace, value means working in a manner that will make your employer a better, stronger, more productive, and ultimately more profitable company. Gwen Weld, former General Manager of Staffing for Microsoft, related the story of a candidate who impressed the Microsoft interview team because of his competencies of courage, conviction, and passion for technology. These competencies, coupled with his substantive skill and absence of ego, led Weld to extend an employment offer. Says Weld about the candidate, "he would make Microsoft a better Microsoft."

As a bottom-line contributor, how will you make your new company a better company?

_____

_____

---

## Secret #5: Keep Perspective

Perspective is different than the Big Picture mentioned in Secret #1. Whereas the Big Picture involves a long-term, purpose-driven view of how your life intersects with your corner of the world, perspective involves a personal, in-the-moment assessment of your attitudes and beliefs. Attitude determines outlook, and beliefs drive behavior.

Why is perspective important? Employers want employees with positive perspective. What hiring manager in his right mind would hand a job to someone with a poor perspective when he could have someone with a positive perspective? What is your perspective on work? Is it, "life's a __itch and then you die"? Or is it, "Work is a playground where I can learn, grow, have fun, bring value, and be fulfilled?" The first option brings you down, while the second brings energy and hope.

Here are some perspectives, or beliefs, you can adopt to ensure career success, especially in an uncertain economy or industry upheaval:

- ✦ I, and I alone, am responsible for my career success. I recognize that no one else will take charge of this for me.

- ✦ Even though I work for (or will soon work for) a company, I have the mind-set of an independent contractor (see Secret #10, Create a Plan). As such, I am solely responsible for marketing my services (networking), delivering a work product that satisfies needs, and producing profit for my customer (employer).

- ✦ Everything that comes my way—from being picked for a great project or a coveted promotion to getting the unwelcome news of a demotion or lay-off—can work out for good IF I am open to learning and growing.

- ✦ I am a career commander—actively in charge of perpetually building my personal brand, strengthening my network, and expanding my value to employers.

It's easy to maintain positive perspective when things are going well—it's quite another story when things don't seem to be going your way! And yet, that's exactly when you do need positive perspective. Perspective finds a different frame for difficult circumstances. It transforms futile thoughts into constructive beliefs, as these before-and-after examples show:

## Before

✦ *All of this "find-your-passion" stuff is a bunch of baloney. I'll just tough it out and keep doing the work I've been doing, even though I don't love it. Besides, I have no way of breaking into that new industry I've been thinking about pursuing.*

## After

✦ *Part of the reason I exist is to use the talents I've been given. If that's so, then I can be confident that the right opportunities will open up and the right people will cross my path so that I can move ahead.*

Or, this perspective on mature age:

## Before

✨ *My age is going to be a huge disadvantage for me. Why would anyone want to hire someone nearing retirement?*

## After

✨ *This job search is an opportunity to target employers who value experience and wisdom. At the same time, it will prompt me to get up-to-speed on current technology and other business trends so that I stay fresh and increase my value.*

Or, this perspective on job loss:

## Before

✨ *I didn't deserve to be let go from my job. I can't believe they chose to keep that recent college graduate over me! I trained him, so I know how little he knows! I feel like I've been stabbed in the back. I will never forget or forgive them for what they did to me. My life is a mess. How will I pay my bills?*

## After

✨ *What's done is done. Yes, the layoff was handled poorly and, yes, I feel angry and betrayed. I'm taking steps to acknowledge my feelings, forgive them, forgive myself for the places where I could have done better, and move on. I am committed to seeing the good in this. The one thing I'm truly grateful for from that whole experience is _____. I won't burn my bridges because I don't know when I might run into a former co-worker. This is also a chance to take a hard look at what value I offer and what steps I can take to increase my value, which can lead me to an even better-paying position.*

This last example is an important one if you've experienced an unplanned job loss. Specialists who regularly handle layoffs and provide career services to displaced workers know that the first place to start is with emotions. Be aware of and own the feelings, forgive those who have hurt you (intentionally or unintentionally), forgive yourself if needed, find something to be grateful for and hopeful for, and make choices that will allow the situation to turn out for your good.

Check your perspective on a regular basis. The minute you reveal frustration, anger, bitterness, pessimism, and so on, you lessen your appeal to potential employers.

---

## Reframe Your Perspectives

What perspectives do you need to reframe so that they *help* rather than *hinder* you?

_____

_____

_____

_____

_____

_____

---

# Secret #6: Commit to Persistence

*"Nothing in this world can take the place of persistence. Talent will not; nothing is more common than unsuccessful men with talent. Genius will not; unrewarded genius is almost a proverb. Education will not; the world is full of educated derelicts. Persistence and determination alone are omnipotent. The slogan 'press on' has solved and always will solve the problems of the human race."*

—Calvin Coolidge

Persistence is key to success. It trumps circumstances and motivates you to overcome whatever might be lacking in your candidacy. Persistence is initiative in action. It chooses wisely and takes action, especially during rough times. Commit to persistence!

## Persisting Through Disturbances Takes You Higher

Coach Shandel Slaten of TrueLifeCoaching.com tells a vivid story about how disturbances are often the impetus to push through self-imposed ceilings. She writes, "I recently went paragliding and hit the top of a thermal. I was begging my guide to take me higher so I could see more and he said 'We've hit a ceiling—we're looking for a thermal disturbance so we can gain altitude.' He pointed out the folks below in the same predicament. I carefully watched as they found their entry point (yes, disturbance) and were bounced around a bit. But next thing I knew, they were at eye level. Then he said 'okay, here we go' and the turbulence rocked us, but only for a moment compared to the smooth, calm air we hit as we rode the thermal up to higher altitude."

"It is the same experience as you try to gain ground in your career or life. If you want to go higher, see more scenery, and sustain altitude, you must understand the role that ceilings play. They are natural speed brakes for you to enjoy the journey and scenery at each level, but they often must be broken through. When it is time to go to the next level, you must step out of your comfort zone and usually experience some turbulence. Do not confuse the sudden jerk as a setback. It may be exactly what is needed to prepare you for the adventure that lies ahead. Perspective is key to having the patience and persistence required to conquer self-imposed ceilings."

I don't want to overemphasize the turbulence that lies ahead for you, but the reality is, there *will* be some bumpy air! Expect it, and welcome it as preparation for the adventure that lies ahead. Challenge yourself to use different language and ways of thinking to describe your turbulence. When you do, you'll no longer see it as a problem, but a "place of possibility." It is no longer a setback, but a strengthening exercise. It's not a chance happening, but a challenge to make good choices. Without these so-called problems, we would have no opportunities to move forward.

What are your "places of possibility?" Check off any that you relate to:

### Personal "Places of Possibility"

☐ Not enough time

☐ Lack of focus

☐ Limited finances

☐ Family commitments that prevent me from devoting more time to my career

☐ Lack of support and fear of criticism from family members, friends, or colleagues

☐ Lack of confidence

☐ Too shy or embarrassed to ask for help

☐ Too independent or overconfident to think I need help

### Professional "Places of Possibility"

☐ Frustrated by too many (or too few) options

☐ Unsure of the best job search processes

☐ Not enough contacts in my target field

☐ Missing the "right" experience

☐ Lack the right degree or training

☐ Skeletons in my career closet

☐ Relocating to a new area where I do not know anyone

Every challenge is an opportunity to prepare you with the knowledge, skills, and tenacity to be more equipped and empowered. Every problem is perfectly timed, meaning that it has arrived because it will allow you to learn something or apply new knowledge that will make you stronger and better equipped for what's next. That means your current situation—even an unplanned period of joblessness—is an opportunity to flex new emotional or intellectual muscles. Make the conscious choice to take charge and move forward. Commit to persistence, and you'll find profound confidence, power, and success.

## Secret #7: Be Prepared

You can control your success. How? Control the controllables (those things you can be in charge of). In real estate, the maxim is "location, location, location." In job search, it's

★ Preparation

★ Preparation

★ Preparation

Preparation is non-negotiable. How do you prepare? By doing your "due diligence" (a term that describes how business leaders thoroughly verify facts or examine operations before committing money to an investment). Preparation starts with knowing your strengths and value proposition. In networking and interviewing, it means taking the time to learn the key concerns and trends within the industry, the company's strengths and weaknesses, any problems the prior incumbent experienced, how the position fits in with the company's entire strategic plan, and how the company will tangibly measure your success in the next 60, 180, or 360 days and beyond. (Part 4 of *Job Search Magic* will equip you for this task.) When it comes to interviewing, preparation also means practicing your delivery in front of a video camera or, at the least, a tape recorder. No matter what the circumstance, be prepared. As Henry Hartman said, "Success always comes when preparation meets opportunity."

## Secret #8: Enlist Partners

Partner with people for the course of your search. Choose people who believe in you, genuinely want you to succeed, and respect you thoroughly. Don't go it alone! You've heard it said that job search is a contact sport. It's true, as you must connect with employers. But job search is also a team sport. You need people on your team who can be a sounding board, support structure, and safety net for you during this time.

Who do you need on your team? Maybe some of these types will help:

- A goal-oriented accountability partner(s) who will hold your feet to the fire on job search tasks and celebrate with you when you've gotten closer to your goal

- Well-connected colleagues who know virtually everyone

- A savvy researcher who can help you uncover important company information

- A trusted friend(s), whom you can be transparent with when you hit a low spot

- A job search group where you can help one another stay focused

- An experienced career coach or job search expert who has strategies that will fast-forward your progress (Some job seekers don't have an extensive group of people to call on, either because they haven't made time to keep their network alive, they are new to an area, or they are introverted and prefer fewer, but typically deeper, relationships. If you fit into any of these categories, it can be especially helpful to enlist the support of a career coach or job search expert.)

You may even consider adding to your team someone who you aren't able to speak with, yet whose opinions you trust. For instance, one client called on the wisdom of his father who had passed away recently. Whatever or whoever you need, enlist partners in your search. We are stronger when people believe in us.

## Secret #9: Go Public

Get your name out there. Anonymity will not win you any job offers. Too often, job seekers are afraid that talking with other people about themselves will appear pushy or self-centered. And yet, in job search, you must talk to people to find out what they need and how your skills can be of help. If you relate to this way of thinking, challenge yourself to rewrite that belief. If you keep secret your talents and abilities, you are doing a disservice both to yourself and your potential employer.

Wherever you go, do what you can to get on people's radar screens. For instance, when attending an association meeting, ask to help hand out name tags. When taking a class, offer an occasional intelligent comment or insight and introduce yourself to the presenter during a break. When reading an interesting article, e-mail a thank-you to the author. Look for radar-screen opportunities!

## Secret #10: Create a Plan

Finally, create a plan! You might not think that planning is a secret to job search, and yet when asked "How will you get there?" far too many cannot articulate a well-orchestrated plan. The fastest path to failure is to skip planning. Remember the dream home analogy? You'd never start building without a blueprint that specified layout and dimensions, a budget, a schedule for the various tradesmen, and so on. All of that requires planning. To make your dream job a reality, there are two kinds of plans to consider: a macro plan and a micro plan.

## The Macro Plan—Plan to W.I.N.!

At the macro level, you'll address three key elements. Together, they spell W.I.N., which means you must be a **W**isdom Worker, **I**ndependent Contractor, and **N**ever-ending Networker:

* **Wisdom Worker**—A wisdom worker is someone who is committed to continual learning. Wisdom workers are hungry to master knowledge about their industry, company, and competitors. They add to their "hard skills" (such as functional knowledge and technical skills). And they stretch personally to enhance "soft skills" (such as self-discipline, teamwork, and interpersonal skills). Wisdom workers are always challenging their comfort zones, pushing through the fears associated with going beyond current boundaries.

* **Independent Contractor**—Futurists and trend watchers, such as Bill Bridges in his book *Jobshift: How to Prosper in a Workplace Without Jobs* (Addison Wesley Publishing Company, 1995), accurately pointed to the conversion of the traditional, "permanent" job to a contractual, temporary assignment. When referring to Independent Contractor here, I'm not suggesting you go the self-employment route (although that may be appropriate for some, given the trend toward contractual or outsourced jobs). Instead, I'm urging you to adopt the attitude of an independent contractor or a solo-preneur (a term used to describe a one-person entrepreneurship). Independent contractors think in terms of opportunities and projects, rather than openings and permanent employment. They analyze what the market needs and adjust their skills to be in demand. Independent contractors focus on results, realizing they can never rest on their laurels. And finally, independent contractors maintain the mindset: "If it's going to be, it's up to me."

* **Never-ending Networker**—Your relationships and connections will make or break your career. Who needs to know about you and trust you in order for you to land your dream job? Who are the hiring managers and potential co-workers at the top five companies where you'd love to work? If you've already built a strong network, kudos. If you don't have one, it's never too late. Begin now. Start by joining or stepping up involvement in your industry's professional association. A world-class network of people who can help you, and whom you can help, will ensure that future job searches are swift and painless! Beyond this, networking connects you with people who keep you informed and excited about work, consistent with the old adage: As iron sharpens iron, so one man sharpens another.

Personify these three elements, and you'll thrive in today's and tomorrow's marketplace.

### The Micro Plan—Plan an Orchestrated Campaign

At this second level, you'll address the specifics of your job search. A micro plan provides a framework and focus, strategy, methods to measure your progress, daily to-do lists, and a timeline. More than anything, a plan lets you *take control*. Here are some pieces of the plan to consider:

- Big-picture goals and bite-sized goals, along with timelines for completion
- A contingency plan, or Plan "B"
- A support team of partners to help encourage, equip, counsel, challenge, and inspire you
- Analysis of your motivated skills and interests
- Strategies for packaging and positioning yourself
- Identification and research of target companies
- Networking activities
- Résumé and career marketing documents
- Interview preparation to prove you can do the job, be a good fit for the company, and add to its bottom line
- Daily and weekly activities, along with systems to measure your progress
- Rewards to celebrate small-step successes along the way

# Chapter Wrap-Up

There you have it: the secrets to success. As you visualize the right picture, pursue purpose, embrace the process, offer profit, keep perspective, commit to persistence, be prepared, enlist partners, go public, and create a plan, *you will be unbeatable*. Depending on your circumstances, you will need to concentrate on some secrets more than others. Checkmark those that you'll make your top priorities.

- ☐ Visualize the Right **P**icture
- ☐ Pursue **P**urpose
- ☐ Embrace the **P**rocess
- ☐ Offer **P**rofit
- ☐ Keep **P**erspective
- ☐ Commit to **P**ersistence
- ☐ Be **P**repared
- ☐ Enlist **P**artners
- ☐ Go **P**ublic
- ☐ Create a **P**lan

---

**Actions for Focus**

What action will you take to stay focused on your top-priority secrets?

_____

_____

_____

_____

_____

---

In the next chapter, you'll find helpful information on creating the plan for a well-orchestrated campaign. Subsequent chapters may contain familiar information if you read previous books in this series, _Résumé Magic_ and _Interview Magic._ Highlights from those books have been updated and woven into _Job Search Magic,_ along with fresh, new "magic tips" (see Appendix A) courtesy of members of Career Masters Institute, the foremost training, development, and professional networking association serving the career and employment industry.

If you're cramming for a crash course in career transition, review the 10 Quick Tips found throughout or at the end of many of the chapters.

Now, let's move forward. It's time to gain new ground!

# Chapter 2

# Getting Your Job Search Plan Together

*"It takes as much energy to wish as it does to plan."*

—Eleanor Roosevelt

Y ou may be familiar with the movie *What About Bob?* starring Bill Murray and Richard Dreyfuss. Murray plays Bob Wiley, a troubled but lovable therapy patient who has phobias about everything. Bob makes great progress with noted psychiatrist Dr. Leo Marvin (Dreyfuss), thanks to the advice found in the doctor's latest self-help book, *Baby Steps*. The book title is a fun metaphor for taking small steps when approaching any goal, whether it be conquering fears or tackling an important project, such as a career move.

Without a plan, your job search may seem overwhelming or beyond your control. Yet, the very act of creating a plan puts you back in control with the simple steps to reach your goal. Plans make dreams materialize. They move desires from your head and heart to your hands and feet. To make your dream reality, do the following:

- **Write About It**—Put pen to paper or start a file on your computer and detail your goal and action steps. Develop a purpose statement for your career. Describe your future success in full-sensory detail. Write a letter dated several months in the future congratulating yourself on your new position and the focused work you accomplished to get there.

- **Talk About It**—Share your vision with people who wholeheartedly support you. Practice describing your passion and value to networking contacts and employers. Learn how to strike up conversations with strangers who can share their mutual interests, ideas, tips, and leads.

- **Act on It**—Get moving! Results come when you put yourself in motion.

Big dreams are realized in small steps. Your first small step is to develop a plan. Before you do that, let's get an overview of the phases of your job search.

# Five Phases of a Job Transition

The five phases of your transition can be described by the memorable vowels A-E-I-O-U, as table 2.1 shows.

### Table 2.1: Five Phases of a Job Transition

| Phase I: Analyze | Phase II: Express | Phase III: Investigate | Phase IV: Orchestrate | Phase V: Uncover |
|---|---|---|---|---|
| Career success starts with self-analysis and market analysis; commit to one or two targets for the focus of your search. | Package strengths and bottom-line value through a career brand, including résumés, verbal networking scripts, and interviewing responses. | Identify a large list of target companies; research and target specific companies in a phased approach; learn TOP (Trends, Opportunities, Problems/ Projects), identify contacts, and investigate how to add value to the company. | Blend targeted/ active and traditional/ passive search strategies; in addition to résumé posting, make 20 to 30 contacts daily to get to the 5 to 10 people who have the authority to hire you; continue with Investigate Phase. | Uncover employer's priorities, needs, and motivation to hire; clarify key deliverables of target position; prove you can do the job in the interview. |
| Duration: A few days for Career Hunters; weeks and possibly months for Career Explorers (see "Are You a Career Hunter or a Career Explorer?" later in this chapter) | Duration: One or two days with focused effort | Duration: A few hours to get you going; continue with weekly research | Duration: One to two weeks to gain momentum; this phase continues throughout your search | Duration: Depends on company that's hiring—in rare cases, firms hire in a few days; many take weeks; and some take months |

Let's look more closely at each phase in your job transition.

# A = Analyze Phase

The first phase of a transition requires that you do some career reconnaissance to analyze the right career F.I.T. (detailed in chapter 3). Here, you'll inventory and analyze your functional skills and strengths, industry interests, career and life values, personal definition of career fulfillment, career identity and drive, career beliefs, personality, preferred work environment and company culture, and so on. In the Analyze Phase, it's essential that you come to a greater awareness and understanding of what you are hardwired to do and what values are most critical for you. This first phase also includes analyzing market conditions to determine what companies/industries would benefit most from your skills. Based on this analysis, come to a commitment about one or two ideal targets. This will be the focus of your search.

**Duration:** The Analyze Phase may last just a few hours or a few months, depending on whether you're a Career Hunter or a Career Explorer.

## Are You a Career Hunter or a Career Explorer?

Career Hunters have completed the F.I.T. analysis and know *what* they want to do and *where* they want to do it. They are now on the hunt for specific opportunities that are a good match. Career Hunters are simply in a different place in their professional journey than Career Explorers. And, all too often, people think they are Hunters and jump into a job search without a careful analysis of the best F.I.T. The end result is a frustrating position that is an occupation rather than an Occupassion™.

Career Explorers (also known as career changers) are taking the time to analyze the best F.I.T. (Functional skills, Industry/Interests, Things that matter, and so on) before they hunt for specific opportunities. Explorers are still getting clear on the *what* and *where*.

As an Explorer, how much time should you budget for the exploration process? I'd love to tell you that you'll have an epiphany in the next 24 hours, but that doesn't seem to be the pattern. A few weeks or several months is more realistic to uncover a totally new career direction (not bad, given the grand scheme of things). If you accomplish it in less time, wonderful.

Good career managers should go through the Career Explorer process every few years when they can stop and take stock of new skills, passions, priorities, and opportunities.

## E = Express Phase

Next, express yourself! Package your strengths into a career brand, which is the essence of what makes you unique and valuable. In the Express Phase, you'll create profit-oriented marketing materials that support your brand. The written materials will include traditional and online résumés/portfolios, networking letters, inquiry letters, thank-you letters, business cards, and so on. Your verbal marketing messages will include S.M.A.R.T. Success Stories, a Verbal Business Card, your Three-Point Marketing Message, and well-delivered interview responses (all of which are covered later in the book).

**Duration:** With laser-focused effort, the Express Phase can be completed in a few days (the better part of a day each for development of a résumé and verbal branding elements). If you have limited time to devote to your search, this phase will take longer. Be aware of the tempting trap of tweaking, untweaking, and retweaking your résumé. Of course it needs to look good, and you can revise your résumé as you become aware of new information based on your research. But, many job seekers put far too much time into the résumé, thinking it alone is the silver bullet for getting the next job. In doing so, they waste precious time that could be better spent connecting with people.

## I = Investigate Phase

In the Investigate Phase, you'll research and target specific companies. Start with a large list of companies, say, 50 to 100 to start. Investigation involves research on the company or department's TOP issues (**T**rends, **O**pportunities, **P**roblems/**P**rojects), identification of internal and external contacts, as well as analysis of how you can add value to the company. Investigation includes both reading (print material, online resources, and company and competitor Web sites) and talking to people who are in-the-know. This information is then woven into your future written communications (e-mails, letters, and résumés) and verbal communications (networking exchanges and interviews).

**Duration:** Although the Investigate Phase continues throughout your search, you can get immediate traction here in just a few hours by uncovering TOP issues on one of your target companies.

## O = Orchestrate Phase

Like an orchestra conductor who uses his musical score to direct many musicians all at once, you will use your job search plan to orchestrate many activities simultaneously. That means blending together targeted and traditional job search activities (see chapters 11 and 12), such as networking in person and online, developing relationships with decision makers, submitting résumés, working with recruiters or agencies, meeting with a job search group, and following up with contacts. Remember that the bottom-line result you want from all this activity is relationships with 5 to 10 people (typically in positions a level or two above your target position) who have openings, or who have the authority to create openings based on opportunities and needs in the company. Practice perseverance here—it may require 20 to 30 conversations every day, for days on end, to get to these decision makers.

The calendaring system mentioned later in this chapter will be important during the Orchestrate Phase because it will keep you focused on daily and weekly activities. In addition to posting résumés, your activities during this phase include making 20 to 30 contacts daily to yield the 5 to 10 ongoing relationships with decision makers who need you and have the authority to hire you. Throughout the Orchestrate phase, you will continue with activities from the Investigate Phase.

**Duration:** This phase continues until you have secured an acceptable offer.

## U = Uncover Phase

The Uncover Phase involves informal and formal interviews. Your goal in these business meetings is to uncover what will motivate the employer to hire you. Hiring motivators typically center on the following:

- **Competencies:** Can you do the job better than others and quickly get up to speed?

- **Chemistry:** Will you fit in and will you stick around?

- **Compensation:** Can we afford you?

You must uncover the hiring manager's priorities and demonstrate that you can deliver on those priorities. This strategy will make your prospective boss look good (always a good thing) and add value to the company's bottom line. Value is the key driver in a hiring decision.

**Duration:** This phase may take several weeks or months, depending on the company's interview process. Some companies put candidates through 10 to 20 interviews with a variety of managers and supervisors.

### Action Step

Grab a calendar! It's very important that you sketch out timelines and general steps for your search. Without timelines, it's hard to stay focused. Use a calendaring system that works best for you, whether it is software such as Microsoft Outlook, Act!, or Franklin Covey PlanPlus™ that interfaces with Microsoft Outlook, or a low-tech system such as a pocket day planner or a calendar dry-erase board.

Refer to the Five Phases of a Job Transition earlier in this chapter and pencil into your calendar a timeline along with the general steps you will complete

*(continued)*

*(continued)*

in each phase. For example, in the Analyze Phase, you might write that you will spend approximately two weeks on completing assessments, analyzing market trends, and identifying a clear focus for your search. In addition, write into your calendar a weekly meeting time (preferably with one of your accountability partners). At these meetings, evaluate your progress on each step for the week, congratulate yourself on the ground covered each week, and make adjustments to the upcoming week's schedule.

Now, let's focus on getting your job search plan together.

# Plan A—Create a SMART Goal

Front and center to any plan is a "gotta have it" goal—one that is truly exciting, enticing, and meaningful. This goal should align with the SMART acronym. Used widely to create great goals—whether for big-picture, lifetime goals or for immediate, short-term goals—SMART stands for

S = Specific

M = Measurable

A = Attainable (or Achievable)

R = Relevant (or Realistic)

T = Time-specific

Following is a description of each of these components as they relate to job search. After reviewing them, you'll have a chance to write your own SMART goal using the blank form (My SMART Goal) that appears near the end of this chapter.

## Specific

Write your job search goal in present tense, as if it were true today. This will help internalize the goal. Believe you deserve the new position and act as if you are already enjoying it! For instance, a Web developer might state his goal this way:

🪄 *I have a great position in Web development with a prestigious tech firm, where I am creating amazing Web sites!*

If you're not yet clear on your next move, consider this kind of a specific goal, again written in present tense:

🪄 *I loved completing the career discovery process. I have uncovered how to make a living at something I'm passionate about. Now I'm ready to target opportunities that will be an ideal fit.*

## Measurable

A measurable goal has a result that can be evaluated on either a success-failure rate or some sort of graduated scale. The following examples describe a measurable goal using a graduated level of attainment, from exceptional to unsatisfactory:

- **Exceptional:** *I will accept a position as Web Developer with salary in my "dream" range.*

- **Expected:** *I will accept a position as Web Programmer with salary in my "comfort" range.*

- **Could do better:** *I will accept a Web Programmer or Developer position with a company not on my target list; or, I will accept a different position that will be a stepping stone to my desired position.*

- **Unsatisfactory:** *I will accept a position with a salary below my "reality" number.*

## Attainable (The 10 Job Search Factors)

An attainable goal is one that is reasonable given various factors. In job search, there are 10 factors that affect attainability: skill set, industry experience and education, motivation, social skills, support systems and network, search strategy, computer skills, target salary, amount of time available for your search, and potential obstacles. The latter can include anything from conducting a long-distance search to being handicapped by a history of job hopping.

The following examples illustrate how one job seeker used the 10 factors to evaluate whether his goal for a technology job was attainable:

- **Skill Set:** *I have 80% of the skills, education, and experience needed for my target position. I have a solid knowledge of Internet technologies and programming (C/C++, Perl, PHP, Python, ColdFusion, ASP, Visual Basic & VB.net, SQL, Java, JavaScript, and HTML). I need more hands-on time with PHP. I could get up to speed quickly.*

- **Industry Experience and Education:** *I have five years of experience developing and maintaining department-level applications, components, Web and desktop clients, and back-end data services. I'm currently working for an advertising agency, building Web sites for their clients. I did work on one Web site for a technology start-up, but I don't yet have experience working inside technology companies. I don't have a four-year degree, but I do have my IWA Certified Web Professional (CWP) Site Designer certification and am working on certification as a Microsoft Certified Application Developer (MCAD). I'm also looking into the Sun Certified Web Component Developer for the Java 2 Platform certification.*

- **Motivation:** *I am determined to get this position and willing to work hard to get what I want. My parents instilled a really strong work ethic in me, and I don't expect things to be handed to me on a silver platter.*

✦ **Social Skills:** *I've been told I'm a bit of a recluse, which may affect my networking and interviewing.*

✦ **Support Systems and Network:** *My significant other supports me completely in making this move. I also have a buddy who promised to be my accountability partner. I know quite a few people who have ties to my target companies.*

✦ **Search Strategy:** *I have five specific companies that I'm targeting, and may add more later. Since I'm in the tech field, I'm using primarily online methods for my search (e-portfolio, blog, online networking), and will also do face-to-face networking through one of my professional associations.*

✦ **Computer Skills:** *I have above-average computer skills and all the equipment I need to work at home.*

✦ **Salary:** *I researched www.salary.com and am realistic about my salary goals.*

✦ **Time Availability:** *I'm putting in 60-hour workweeks on my current job and I have a 1-year-old, so I can only devote a few hours a week to face-to-face networking. I will do a lot of my online networking in the evenings.*

✦ **Potential Obstacles:** *I have a couple of tattoos and body piercings, which might put some people off if I have to interview with traditional corporate types.*

The stronger you are in each factor, **the faster your search will be.** Likewise, if you come up short in some areas, it will take longer to get where you want to go.

## How Attainable Is Your Goal?

Table 2.2 will help you assess each of the factors that affect goal attainment. Using a scale of 1 to 10 (1 is low/false, 10 is high/true), circle a rating for each factor and then total your scores. Get a reality check on your scores by asking a trusted colleague to also rate you—compare your scores and calmly explore any differences.

### Table 2.2: Assessing the 10 Factors That Affect Search Success

| Factor 1–10 | Rating (1 = low/false; 10 = high/true) |
|---|---|
| 1. **Current Skill Set:** Do you have the majority of the skills employers want for your target position? Can you get up to speed quickly? Are your skills above average? (This is especially important if the number of total openings for your target position is limited.) | 1 2 3 4 5 6 7 8 9 10 |

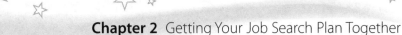

| Factor 1–10 | Rating (1 = low/false; 10 = high/true) |
|---|---|
| **2. Industry Experience and Education:** Do you have recent, hands-on experience in your target position? Do you have the number of years of experience most employers are looking for? Is your target industry hot and hiring? Are you experienced in your target industry? Have you researched your target company thoroughly? Are you familiar with its competitors? Do you have the degree or certifications required for the position? | 1 2 3 4 5 6 7 8 9 10 |
| **3. Motivation:** Do you *really* want this career change? Are you willing to make some sacrifices to get what you want? Do you have an accountability mentality (in other, words, "if it's going to be, it's up to me") vs. an entitlement mentality (in other words,, "the world owes me because I've been dealt some hard blows"). Are you resilient, with a strong "buoy factor" (see chapter 6)? | 1 2 3 4 5 6 7 8 9 10 |
| **4. Social Skills:** Are you personable and well-groomed? Do you have good communication and relational skills? Are you reasonably self-confident? Can you clearly and persuasively articulate your target and your return-on-investment in networking and interviewing situations? | 1 2 3 4 5 6 7 8 9 10 |
| **5. Support Systems and Network:** Are you enlisting the support of others during your search? Do you have a goal-oriented accountability partner? Can you tap into a reasonably strong professional and personal network, or can you resurrect one quickly? Do you know people in the industry? Do you know how to build reciprocal networking relationships? Is your spouse, partner, or family behind you 100 percent in this transition? Are you familiar with the benefit of working with a career coach during this critical time? | 1 2 3 4 5 6 7 8 9 10 |

*(continued)*

*(continued)*

| Factor 1–10 | Rating<br>(1 = low/false; 10 = high/true) |
|---|---|
| **6. Search Strategy:** Do you have a clearly defined position target and company target, giving consideration to geographic area, company size, organizational culture, and so on? Are you using the wisest job search strategy for your situation? Are you working smart as well as hard? Are you leveraging time and not just being busy? | 1 2 3 4 5 6 7 8 9 10 |
| **7. Computer Skills:** Are you proficient with the technology needed for the target job? Do you have a computer and Internet connection at home for job search activities? | 1 2 3 4 5 6 7 8 9 10 |
| **8. Salary:** Is your salary goal in line with market realities and current salary surveys? | 1 2 3 4 5 6 7 8 9 10 |
| **9. Time Availability:** Can you devote 30 to 40 hours or more each week to your search if you're unemployed and 10 to 15 if you're employed? | 1 2 3 4 5 6 7 8 9 10 |
| **10. Potential Obstacles:** Are you free of any of these potential obstacles: a long-distance search; poor employment record; disability; appearance; "silent" discrimination for reasons of race, sex, religion, or age; language barriers; criminal record; health problems; heavy smoker; emotional problems; anything else? | 1 2 3 4 5 6 7 8 9 10 |
| **Total your points** (100 possible): | _____ |

Although there may be some gray areas in scoring, this quick assessment will give you an idea of whether your goal is attainable. If your total score is in the 80 to 100 range, you should be set up for a relatively smooth and quick search. If your score is in the 50 to 80 range, concentrate on the factors that need shoring up. If your score is below 50, change your target to a "bridge" job if you want to be in a new position quickly. To fast-forward your progress, see "Strategies to Enhance Your Candidacy and Shorten Your Search" later in this chapter.

## How Long Will the Search Take?

That's the million-dollar question! Be assured of this: The higher your score in the "10 Factors That Affect Search Success" (table 2.2), the greater your appeal to employers. The greater your appeal, the faster you'll be hired!

The two most common factors for screening applicants are functional skills and industry experience. If you don't score high in these two areas, your search can stall in a hurry. Figure 2.1 illustrates how the combination of functional skills and industry experience affect the length of a search.

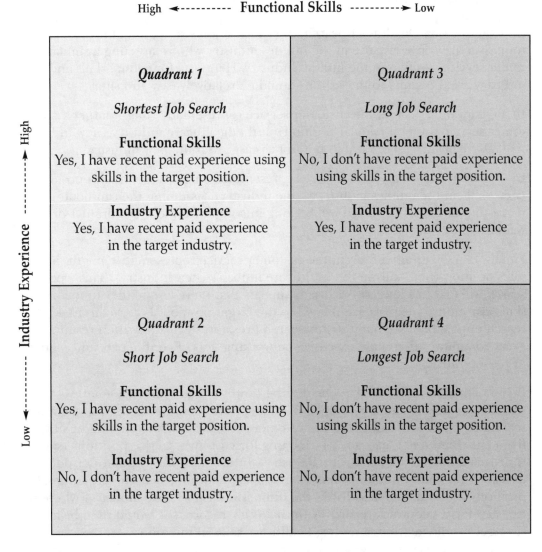

High ◄--------- **Functional Skills** ---------► Low

Industry Experience ◄--------- High / Low ---------►

*Quadrant 1*

*Shortest Job Search*

**Functional Skills**
Yes, I have recent paid experience using skills in the target position.

**Industry Experience**
Yes, I have recent paid experience in the target industry.

*Quadrant 3*

*Long Job Search*

**Functional Skills**
No, I don't have recent paid experience using skills in the target position.

**Industry Experience**
Yes, I have recent paid experience in the target industry.

*Quadrant 2*

*Short Job Search*

**Functional Skills**
Yes, I have recent paid experience using skills in the target position.

**Industry Experience**
No, I don't have recent paid experience in the target industry.

*Quadrant 4*

*Longest Job Search*

**Functional Skills**
No, I don't have recent paid experience using skills in the target position.

**Industry Experience**
No, I don't have recent paid experience in the target industry.

**Figure 2.1: Length of job search related to functional skills and industry experience.**

Which of the four quadrants does your search fall into?

* **Quadrant 1 Search, the Shortest Search:** Targeting a similar position in the same industry.

* **Quadrant 2 Search, a Short Search:** Targeting a similar position in a different industry.

* **Quadrant 3 Search, a Long Search:** Targeting a different position in the same industry.

* **Quadrant 4 Search, the Longest Search:** Targeting a different position in a different industry.

An example of a Quadrant 1 Search, the shortest job search, might involve a customer service representative in the utilities industry who is targeting a similar customer service position in the utilities industry. Here, the functional skills and industry are the same, so the search should be relatively easy and short.

In a Quadrant 2 Search, the customer service representative might target a customer service position (similar position) in the healthcare industry (new industry), also typically a short search but not as easy given the new industry.

In Quadrant 3, the customer service representative might target a sales position (new skill) in the utilities industry (same industry). Assuming the candidate has no history of sales, this search will be long in comparison to a Quadrant 1 or 2 search.

Finally, in a Quadrant 4 Search, the customer service representative might target a sales position (new skill) in the healthcare industry (new industry). This type of search will take the longest because it appears that there are neither functional skills nor industry experience related to the target position. Is a Quadrant 4 search impossible? No, but it definitely requires a strategically written résumé, great communication skills, extensive networking, lots of confidence, and plenty of perseverance.

If your situation is classified as Quadrant 4 (and you can't afford a lengthy search), it's wise to aim at a bridge job, or stepping-stone position, to shorten the search. In the case of our fictitious customer service candidate, she might shift from Quadrant 4 to Quadrant 2 by looking for customer service positions (same functional skill) in the healthcare industry (different industry) that offer potential to move into sales. Another option would be a Quadrant 3 Search, targeting sales positions (new functional skills) in the utilities industry (same industry) where she can develop a sales track record. With that track record, she would then be a stronger candidate when targeting healthcare sales in the future.

Of course, there are factors beyond skills and industry experience that affect the length of a search. Not surprising, deficits in any of the 10 factors listed in table 2.2 can slow down a search. Fortunately, there are strategies to bolster your scores in each area.

## Strategies to Enhance Your Candidacy and Shorten Your Search

To boost your appeal and shorten your search, consider some of the following strategies (these are not exhaustive, of course, and some strategies will work for more than one area). Identify any low scores from table 2.2, and then review the magic strategies for the corresponding factor. Skip over any factors that are already strong for you.

### Factor #1: Skill Set

Do you have the majority of skills employers want for your target position? Can you get up to speed quickly? Are your skills above average? (This is especially important if the number of total openings for your target position is limited.)

Magic

### "Magic" Strategy

Learn to counter objections about not matching the employer's wish list of requirements. Find out what needs to be done and demonstrate how you'd do it. Some candidates may have more experience than you but perhaps not the innate ability or track record.

When you're targeting a promotion but lack specific experience, point to your potential and track record of success in taking on new challenges.

If you need to take your skills from average to above-average, look to above-average performers and make them role models for your new performance standards.

If you are targeting a new functional area and meeting resistance, consider entering the target company in a position similar to your current position, with the intention of making a move into the new functional area after you've proven your potential.

### Factor #2: Industry Experience and Education

Do you have recent, hands-on experience in your target position? Do you have the number of years of experience most employers are looking for? Is your target industry hot and hiring? Are you experienced in your target industry? Have you researched your target company thoroughly? Are you familiar with its competitors? Do you have the degree or certifications required for the position?

Magic

### "Magic" Strategy

Overcome the paradox of "we can't hire you without the experience." Get experience by volunteering for projects or taking a part-time position.

If you don't have the right degree or certification, tell the employer you are taking steps to get it. Pay for the training yourself if needed—don't wait for the employer to foot the bill. Consider online courses. If funds are tight, ask a colleague to mentor you or check out library books and undertake a self-study crash course.

If your target industry is shrinking, consider looking into a different industry.

Get up to speed on your industry by joining and participating in industry associations (you can find associations online at www.asaenet.org).

Start preliminary research on your target companies and learn about their TOP issues and key internal and external contacts (see chapter 11 for more on learning TOP issues).

### Factor #3: Motivation

Do you *really* want this career change? Are you willing to make some sacrifices to get what you want? Do you have an accountability mentality (in other words, "if it's going to be, it's up to me") vs. an entitlement mentality (in other words, "the world owes me because I've been dealt some hard blows"). Are you resilient, with a strong "buoy factor" (see chapter 6)?

*Magic*

### "Magic" Strategy

If motivation is low, find the right carrot (an appealing career target or an improved lifestyle based on the new position). If your goal isn't thoroughly enticing, there won't be sufficient motivation. If the goal is right but you're still not taking action, examine potential fears that might be blocking you. For instance, are you afraid of what people will think about you if you're more successful? Are you afraid of the physical, emotional, or financial sacrifices it might take to get where you want? Are you afraid you might fail?

Don't be embarrassed if the answer to any of those questions is yes. It's human nature to have fears! This familiar acronym for FEAR can de-power many an apprehension in your life: **F**alse **E**xpectations **A**ppearing **R**eal. Expose the fear—shine a light on it—and determine whether it is a valid concern. If the fear is unfounded (a false expectation that appears to be real), banish its paralyzing grip. If it's a valid concern, put strategies in place to manage it. And, be sure that you're not mistaking adrenaline for fear. Adrenaline is your friend—it arrives when you need to be "on" for networking and interviewing.

Beliefs are another common block to motivation. What thoughts hold you back? You may believe that if you don't have contacts inside your target company, you won't be able to get a foot in the door. You may believe that it's not truly possible to have a career you love or that you don't deserve success. Maybe that little accusatory voice inside your head is telling you that there just isn't enough time to do all the things needed for an effective job search.

Whatever the belief block, break through it with these A-B-Cs:

- **Awareness:** Be aware of what's happening. For example, "Hmmm, I notice that my nervousness about networking is causing me to procrastinate."

- **Beliefs:** What bully-like beliefs are underlying the issue at hand? Here's an example: "That old negative voice in my head is trying to tell me I'm no good at networking." Banish that belief and write a new truth for your

"belief bible," such as this: "The truth is that I genuinely care about people and want any interaction with them to be valuable. I am learning that I can be an effective networker, especially with these new strategies I've learned."

**Choices:** Choose to be proactive, emphasizing small-step victories to gain momentum. For instance, "I will use my new networking skills to connect with five new people this week."

Momentum is one of the surest paths to motivation. Break tasks into small steps that will give you traction and bring some quick wins.

## Factor #4: Social Skills

Are you personable and well-groomed? Do you have good communication and relational skills? Are you reasonably self-confident? Can you clearly and persuasively articulate your target and your return-on-investment in networking and interviewing situations?

*Magic*

## "Magic" Strategy

A little extra likability goes farther than a little extra competence in making someone desirable to work with. (See the sidebar at the bottom of this page.) To improve social skills, Dale Carnegie's *How to Win Friends & Influence People* (Pocket, reissued 1990)—the grandfather of all people-skills books—is a great place to start, but you'll also need feedback from a supportive yet honest human being. Enlist help from a socially competent friend, colleague, mentor, or coach, and be open to new ways of relating to people.

Get honest feedback on how people perceive you. For a nominal fee ($14.95 at the time of this writing), you can go to www.ReachCC.com and use the 360° Reach tool (www.ReachCC.com/360register), which allows you to e-mail colleagues, clients, managers, employees, friends, or family and gather anonymous feedback about your professional reputation or brand.

If it's a matter of improving your presentation skills, audiotape or videotape yourself in a mock interview. Ask for constructive criticism from someone who is well-versed in making presentations or public speaking.

---

### Competent Jerks, Lovable Fools: The Likability Factor in Career Success

The June 2005 issue of *Harvard Business Review* featured an article titled "Competent Jerks, Lovable Fools, and the Formation of Social Networks." Harvard researchers were curious about how work partners are chosen. The bottom line to their research revealed that when people in an organization need help getting a job done, they prefer to choose a congenial colleague over a more capable one.

*(continued)*

*(continued)*

The researchers, Tiziana Casciaro and Miguel Sousa Lobo, conducted a series of social network studies at four organizations that reflected a wide range of attributes (for-profit and not-for-profit, large and small, North American and European). They asked people to rate all company workers in terms of how much they personally liked each one and how well each did his or her job. The two criteria—competence and likeability—produced four archetypes, which they grouped into these caricatures:

- **The Competent Jerk,** who knows a lot but is unpleasant to deal with;
- **The Lovable Fool,** who doesn't know as much but is a delight to be around;
- **The Lovable Star,** obviously the most preferred, who is both competent and likeable; and
- **The Incompetent Jerk,** who is neither competent nor likeable.

Not surprisingly, everyone wanted to work with the Lovable Star and no one wanted to work with the Incompetent Jerk. More interesting, though, were people's preferences when faced with choosing between a Competent Jerk and a Lovable Fool. Casciaro and Lobo noted that "feelings worked as a gating factor.... If someone is strongly disliked, it is almost irrelevant whether or not she is competent; people won't want to work with her anyway. By contrast, if someone is liked, his colleagues will seek out every little bit of competence he has to offer."

Like it or not, likeability is a business reality. A little extra likeability goes a long way!

## Factor #5: Support Systems and Network

Are you enlisting the support of others during your search? Do you have a goal-oriented accountability partner? Can you tap into a reasonably strong professional and personal network, or can you resurrect one quickly? Do you know people in the industry? Do you know how to build reciprocal networking relationships? Is your spouse, partner, or family behind you 100 percent in this transition? Are you familiar with the benefit of working with a career coach during this critical time?

## "Magic" Strategy

Give yourself permission to ask for help, and then receive it! Make requests from those closest to you. Be ready to enthusiastically yet rationally explain why you have chosen your new career goal.

Ask your support people what they need in return for helping you—in many cases, their reward will simply be seeing you happy! Limit your time with people who overtly or passively discourage you from pursuing your goals. Hire a coach to help you get farther faster.

### Factor #6: Search Strategy

Do you have a clearly defined position target and company target, giving consideration to geographic area, company size, organizational culture, and so on? Are you using the wisest job search strategy for your situation? Are you working smart as well as hard? Are you leveraging time and not just being busy?

### "Magic" Strategy

*Magic*

First, get clear on what you want. Next, work smart! Spend priority time on activities that will yield the greatest reward. These activities are typically face-to-face networking and researching for interview preparation.

Also, take into account how companies normally hire for your target position. If they typically use recruiters, be sure that working with recruiters is a major component of your search. If they use employee referrals, face-to-face networking should be your primary strategy.

Work smart! Don't fall into the trap of devoting the majority of your time to searching online and posting résumés. Balance this isolating behavior with live human interaction—that means face-to-face or telephone contacts with people who can lend insider insights and advice, be a great reference for you, and influence a hiring decision in your favor.

### Factor #7: Computer Skills for Job Search

Are you proficient with the technology needed for the target job? Do you have a computer and Internet connection at home for job search activities?

### "Magic" Strategy

*Magic*

The basic computer skills needed for job search are the ability to access a computer easily (preferably from your home), create and store résumés in MS Word and plain-text formats, receive and send e-mail with attachments (résumés), search and respond to job postings, research companies and contacts, and network online.

If you don't have a home computer setup, local libraries provide free access to computers and the Internet, as do some colleges. Avoid using your current employer's computer system for job search.

Sometimes the fastest way to remedy out-of-date computer skills is to ask a tech-smart friend to tutor you. Yes, you could take computer classes, but some informal how-to lessons will often give you exactly what you need in less time.

### Factor #8: Salary

Is your salary goal in line with market realities and current salary surveys?

### "Magic" Strategy

*Magic*

Be realistic. Research salary ranges at www.salary.com (see more in chapter 17) and talk with people in-the-know to be certain your salary makes sense. If your

target salary is too high, you'll price yourself out of the market. Too low, and employers will not respect your value.

### Factor #9: Time Availability

Can you devote 30 to 40 hours or more each week to your search if you're unemployed and 10 to 15 if you're employed?

### "Magic" Strategy

The most precious commodity of the 21st century is time. For those conducting a search while still employed, consider an alternative workweek (four 10-hour days as opposed to five 8-hour days). One of my favorite resources for negotiating a flexible work schedule is Pat Katepoo's www.WorkOptions.com. Here, you'll find free tips and low-cost proposal templates for presenting the business case to your boss for fewer or flexible hours on the job. And, take a hard look at your schedule to evaluate the activities that are not absolutely essential. What can you let go of or postpone for a later time?

If you can devote full-time effort to your search, treat it as a full-time job. Go "to work" every morning, set daily goals for yourself, and act as if you will be evaluated by a boss for your performance each day.

Establish boundaries with friends! They may think, "Oh, she's unemployed and must have plenty of time on her hands, so it won't be any trouble if I ask her to help with _____." The hours spent on your job search are just as important as clocking in with an employer. If necessary, set up a log to ensure that you put in six to eight hours per weekday on your search.

Create a routine for your day—devote high-energy time (often in the morning) to important tasks such as face-to-face or telephone networking. Save less-important activities for other times. Job search can be emotionally draining and physically tiring, so be kind to yourself. For example, if you don't thrive on meeting strangers, don't schedule cold calls at 3 o'clock in the afternoon, especially if that's the time of day your body usually needs a serious nap.

### Factor #10: Potential Obstacles

Are you free of any of these potential obstacles: long-distance search; poor employment record; disability; appearance; "silent" discrimination based on race, sex, religion, or age; language barriers; criminal record; health problems; heavy smoker; emotional problems; anything else?

### "Magic" Strategy

Don't be discouraged if you have obstacles—they may impede progress but they won't prevent it. The first step with any obstacle is to acknowledge that it exists; only then can you establish a strategy to counter it.

Are you conducting a long-distance search? If so, do plenty of pre-work before making a trip to network or interview (identify target companies, talk to your current local network for leads on contacts in the new area, research opportunities, post résumés, and e-mail and make phone calls to target company contacts). Next, plan a one- to two-week trip to the target area. Set up meetings based on the results of your pre-work. Write a script with a logical explanation of why you're moving to the new area, as people will be curious or concerned that you won't put down roots and stay long. Here are a few reasons that will make people more comfortable: you're returning to your roots, you visited the area several times and loved it, it's the bastion for your industry, your spouse's family is from the area, or the area is known for its quality of life and you're family-oriented.

Strategies for the remaining potential obstacles (poor employment record; disability; appearance; race; sex; religion; age; language barrier; criminal record; health problems; heavy smoker; emotional problems) can be found in chapter 16.

As we wrap up the "A" in the SMART acronym, remember that an Attainable goal directly affects your length of search and degree of success. Don't ignore any of the 10 attainability factors. Those who proactively address these issues are better off than those who passively bury their heads in the sand!

## Relevant

Relevant goals are aligned with your purpose and the Big Picture of your life. This example shows how the job seeker's goal has been a long-term desire and is aligned with his natural talents:

> *For the past 10 years, I have wanted to be part of a Web development team at a leading tech company. From as far back as I can remember, I have been fascinated by technology. I sense that my purpose is to use my technical skills to create Web experiences that inspire, educate, and empower people.*

## Time-Specific

Your goal needs a realistic deadline. For example:

> *I will accept an offer within 90 days.*

### Action Step

To help clarify your goal, write about it using the following form. The wording doesn't need to be perfect at this point. It's more important that you move the ideas from your head to paper. Seeing your thoughts written out helps you commit to the goal. Remember to write the first section (Specific) in present tense, as if it were already true. If you need ideas, refer back to the examples for each of the SMART elements.

# My SMART Goal

**Specific:** _____

_____

_____

**Measurable:**

Exceptional: _____

_____

Expected: _____

_____

Could do better: _____

_____

Unsatisfactory: _____

_____

**Attainable:**

Skill Set: _____

_____

Industry Experience and Education: _____

_____

Motivation: _____

_____

Social Skills: _____

_____

Support Systems and Network: _____

_____

Search Strategy: _____

_____

Computer Skills: _____

_____

Target Salary: _____

_____

Time Availability: _____

_____

Potential Obstacles: _____

_____

**Relevant:** _____

_____

_____

_____

**Time Specific:** _____

_____

_____

# Plan "B"—Give Yourself Options

You may be thinking: "I was just told to dream big, and now I'm supposed to think about a Plan B? Doesn't that send a subtle message that Plan A might fail?"

Not so. Life is unpredictable, and there are variables beyond your control that may affect your success with Plan A. Better to prepare an alternative now rather than later, when you may be disappointed and not thinking as clearly.

Plan B oftentimes works out for the best. A business development client of mine who was targeting an executive position with a Texas-based company was disappointed when his Plan A didn't work out. He went to Plan B, which involved transitioning from part-time consultant to full-time executive for an East Coast company. A few months later, he was accepted to the Wharton Executive MBA Program at the Philadelphia campus. The employer in Plan B was located in an area much closer to the campus, freeing up dozens of hours in commute time for this rigorous academic program. Although Plan B wasn't his first choice, it worked out well.

Think of Plan B as creating options—options give you the freedom of choice and control. Write your Plan B (and even a Plan C) here:

| **My Plan B Goal** |
| --- |
| |
| |
| |

| **My Plan C Goal** |
| --- |
| |
| |
| |

# Job Search Resources and Budget

A job search plan requires that you take stock of your resources and create a budget. If you were planning a vacation, you'd make sure you had the right clothing and enough cash. On your job search journey, make sure you have the right resources and financial reserves to get you through. Resources include computer setup, résumé stationery and envelopes, networking business cards, note cards for follow-ups and thank-yous, a calendaring system, professional wardrobe, and so on). Note that business cards are a must in your networking, and you can obtain them free at www.vistaprint.com.

Take a look at your monthly budget and adjust for necessary job search expenses. If finances are of concern during this time, see "Finances" in chapter 6 for ideas on getting an emergency loan, simplifying your lifestyle, and bringing in part-time income.

# Your Support Team

Job search is a team sport! You learned this in chapter 1, and it's driven home as one of the factors that affect goal attainment in chapter 2. Support is critical. Please do not attempt your transition alone. You might think that this book will give you all the support you need. It is definitely one form of support, but it's not enough! *Nothing* replaces the powerful synergy created when human beings connect. Pull out the stops when it comes to enlisting support.

Do you have trouble asking for help? If so, chances are you don't want to be a bother, or you perceive asking for help as a sign of weakness. If you adopt either line of thinking, it does only one thing: It prevents you from being your best. The truth is that two (or more) are better than one—you are stronger with support.

## Who to Enlist

Who should you recruit for your support team? In the My Support Team box that follows, jot down names that come to mind. If you can't fill in each space right away, try this "antenna exercise" (aptly named because it puts you in a heightened state of awareness). In your notebook or computer, outline the following categories and leave space to fill in names later. Next, say these words aloud: "In order to use my talents and be of value to this world, I need help from these types of people. In the hours and days to come, I will become aware of who they are." Carry your outline with you and be ready to fill in names and ideas. You'll be surprised at what will come to you.

---

### My Support Team

A goal-oriented accountability partner (more than one is okay) who will hold your feet to the fire on job search tasks and celebrate with you when you've gotten closer to your goal (choose someone with a style that works best for you—you may want a gentle but firm friend, or a military-like commando, or an enthusiastic cheerleader who keeps reminding you that "You can do it!"):

_____

_____

---

*(continued)*

*(continued)*

Well-connected colleagues who know virtually everyone (these should be a few people whom you know fairly well; later, you'll identify a longer list of networking contacts):

_____

_____

A savvy researcher who can help you uncover important company information (this may be your local librarian):

_____

_____

A trusted friend(s), with whom you can be transparent when you hit a low spot:

_____

_____

A job search group where you can help one another stay focused (these are often sponsored by churches or affiliated with quasi-governmental or community groups—if you can't find one in your area, start your own!):

_____

_____

Outplacement assistance (typical in larger corporations, outplacement is offered to employees affected by a RIF [reduction in force] and paid for by the corporation; if you get an outplacement package, take advantage of it. If you have the option of selecting your own outplacement services, select a career expert experienced in career transition and job search):

_____

_____

A professional career coach or job search expert who has strategies that will fast-forward your progress (consider some of the "Magic Tip" contributors found in appendix A—a trained coach is well worth the investment, supporting you as a catalyst, strategist, collaborator, resource person, cheerleader, and more):

_____

_____

To enlist your accountability partner's support, you could say something like this: "John, I've always respected your opinions and admired what you've accomplished in your career. Because of that, I wanted to share with you some plans that I'm excited about. I'm focusing my next career move on a position in Web development at a leading tech firm in the Valley. To help keep me on track, I'm looking for people whom I can meet with weekly, either by phone or for a quick coffee—coffee's on me! During those times, I'd report on my progress for the past week and share what I plan to do in the coming week. I thought of you because you're goal-driven and focused. I recognize your time is valuable, so we'd keep the meetings short. I'd like this to be a win for you as well. I'm hoping I can provide you with insider information I come across while doing my company research. (Or "What would you need to consider this as a worthwhile investment of your time?" Then wait for a response. It's likely that a family member or friend won't expect anything in return.) Is this something you'd be interested in exploring further?"

## Be Courteous

Remember that people feel good when they help others, so you're providing them an opportunity to feel good. Just be mindful to limit two things:

- **Time:** The amount of time you'll need from them; and

- **Pressure:** The extent you look to them for answers or emotional support.

Don't look to just one person for too much time, too many answers, or too much emotional support.

# Chapter Wrap-Up

Your plan should be taking shape at this point, making hopes and dreams become the new reality. Remember to break tasks into small-step phases if things look overwhelming.

## 10 Quick Tips for Getting Your Job Search Plan Together

1. **Big dreams are realized in small steps.** The first small step in any job search is to develop a plan.

2. **In your plan, understand the sequence of a job search and outline timelines according to these five "A-E-I-O-U" phases: Analyze, Express, Investigate, Orchestrate, and Uncover.** Analyze your skills and the market and settle on one or two targets for the focus of your search. Express your skills in résumés, verbal scripts, and interviewing responses. Investigate by assembling a list of 50 to 100 companies and identifying their TOP issues and key contacts. Blend targeted/active and traditional/passive search strategies (in addition to résumé posting, make 20 to 30 contacts daily to get to the 5 to 10 people who have the authority to hire you). Finally, uncover the employer's priorities, needs, and motivation to hire; clarify the key deliverables of the target position and prove you can do the job.

3. **Front and center to any plan is a "gotta have it" goal.** This goal should align with the SMART acronym, meaning it should be Specific, Measurable, Attainable, Relevant, and Time-Specific.

4. **There are 10 factors that affect attainability in a job search: your skill set, industry experience and education, motivation, social skills, support systems and network, search strategy, computer skills, target salary, amount of time available for your search, and potential obstacles.** Using a scale of 1 to 10 (10 is high), rate yourself on each of these 10 factors. Shore up any areas needed to speed up your search. If your score is below 50, change your target to a "bridge" job if you want to be in a new position quickly.

5. **The two most common factors for screening applicants are functional skills and industry experience.** If you don't score high in these two areas, your search can stall in a hurry.

6. **Motivation is another big factor to success.** If your goal isn't thoroughly enticing, there won't be sufficient motivation. You must first find the right carrot. If the goal is right but you're still not taking action, examine potential fears or beliefs that might be blocking you. Break through limiting beliefs with the A-B-Cs: Awareness, Beliefs, and Choices.

7. **After creating a SMART goal, give yourself some options by identifying a Plan B or Plan C goal.** It's a matter of putting the proverbial eggs in several baskets. Better to prepare an alternative plan now rather than later.

8. **Create a budget for your search,** taking into consideration the cost of distributing your résumé through online vehicles, membership in professional organizations, networking expenses, travel expenses, relocation expenses, hiring a career coach, and so on. Take stock of your resources (from printer cartridges and résumé paper to a professional wardrobe suitable for interviewing).

9. **Job search is a team sport.** Assemble your team with people like these: a goal-oriented accountability partner (more than one is okay) who will hold your feet to the fire on job search tasks and celebrate with you when you've gotten closer to your goal, a few well-connected colleagues who know virtually everyone, a savvy researcher who can help you uncover important company information, a trusted friend(s) with whom you can be transparent when you hit a low spot, a job search group where you can help one another stay focused, outplacement assistance (if available), and a professional career coach or job search expert who has strategies that will fast-forward your progress.

10. **To keep your plan on track,** write into your calendar a weekly time to evaluate your progress, congratulate yourself on the ground covered each week, and make adjustments to the upcoming week's schedule.

## Magical Coaching Questions

If you haven't already done so, by what date will you have sketched out your SMART goal, your job search plan, and timelines for the A-E-I-O-U phases? To whom will you be accountable?

_____

Which of the 10 factors to job search success is your strength? How will you leverage this strength in your search?

_____

_____

Which of the 10 factors to job search success can you focus on improving? What action will you take to do so?

_____

_____

What motivates you? How will you build this motivation into your daily routine?

_____

_____

What fears or limiting beliefs might block your success?

_____

_____

Address each issue with the ABCs (Awareness, Beliefs, and Choices) noted earlier in the chapter.

Awareness: _____

Beliefs: _____

Chioices: _____

_(continued)_

*(continued)*

What is one action step you can take today to boost your job search momentum?

_____

_____

_____

# First Things First: Focus on the Magic F.I.T.™

*The best vision is insight.*

—Malcolm Forbes

Are you suffering from fish fever? Fish fever is an ailment peculiar to Alaskan bear cubs who manage to go hungry despite standing in the middle of rivers thick with salmon. While studying the starving cubs, wildlife biologists observed them lunging indiscriminately after any airborne fish that appeared in their paths. Their fishing strategy yielded minimal success. The biologists came to the conclusion that the cubs were too immature to focus on just one target. In comparison, the nearby mother bear would choose a fishing spot that offered promise, hone in on one fish, and then strike. Her fishing strategy yielded frequent success. Mama bear's target fish was usually underwater, less noticeable than those jumping about, but more promising in the end.

Too often, I see job seekers with symptoms of fish fever. One opportunity pops up that looks appealing (for example, "I want to be a pharmaceutical sales rep") and the job seeker pursues that direction. Then another opportunity comes into sight ("I want to broker loans") and the job seeker pursues this new direction. And then another opportunity, and another. Like the hungry bear cubs, these job seekers end up losing their catch despite the many opportunities at their feet.

Although it's wise to be on the lookout for interesting opportunities, the key to successful job search and interviewing is to be *discriminating* about which opportunities are right for you. To be discriminating, you must know what you want. Hiring managers and recruiters *expect* you to have self-knowledge about your functional strengths, interests, passions, and motivators. AT&T's Director of Talent Acquisition, Reginna K. Burns, offers supporting advice: "Step 1 in the job search process is really about understanding yourself—your skills, your values, your priorities—and what kind of work you want to do."

# Why Job Seekers Jump at the Wrong Opportunities

Why do some job seekers jump at *any* opportunity that flies by? Table 3.1 outlines several reasons. Check any of these reasons that might apply to you.

### Table 3.1: 10 Reasons Job Seekers Might Jump for the Wrong Opportunity

| ✓ If Cause Applies to You | Antidote |
|---|---|
| **1. Quick-fix mentality—the belief that a burst of work will produce permanent results.** This quick-fix mentality is equivalent to expecting one day of brushing your teeth to last you a year. | Don't fall into the trap of thinking that working on your career (growing skills, networking, building your brand) is something to be done only when you're in job search mode. Yes, this is the perfect time to start, and it is also the perfect time to commit to a long-range view of tending to your career. |
| **2. Lack of financial reserves— the reality of making ends meet leads to career compromises.** If you are unemployed and have limited financial reserves to sustain a job search, don't despair. | Strategically target one of the options noted in chapter 1 (see Secret #3), such as a stepping-stone or incubator position. Do your best to choose a position that offers "recycling" potential, where you can learn new skills or make new contacts that will be useful down the road. |
| **3. Fear—the known is more comfortable than the unknown.** For many, exploring career options means treading beyond your past comfort zones into unfamiliar territory. That territory may cause discomfort in a number of ways (for example, having to ask people for information and admit you don't have all the answers, being in a situation where you might face rejection because you don't yet have the right qualifications, or living with that unpleasant but necessary period of uncertainty that comes before all the answers fall into place). | Get comfortable with "not knowing." There are times throughout life when you have to look for and wait for answers. Think back to a time of uncertainty when you weren't sure yet what decision to make or you didn't know what the outcome of a situation would be. What strengths helped get you through, and what would you do differently this next time? |

| ✓ **If Cause Applies to You** | **Antidote** |
| --- | --- |
| **4. Desperation, discouragement, despair— a desire to end the pain of present circumstances.** If you're in career pain (your current boss is a bear, the commute is killing you, a special project is requiring 80-hour workweeks), it can be hard to think strategically. Or, you might have learned recently that the opening with your dream company is not going to come through. You think to yourself: "What's the use? I'll just take whatever comes along next." | These are symptoms of lost hope. Where do you find hope? Rekindle your hope, focus on what you want, and think strategically before you act! In cases where your current job is a killer, it might be entirely appropriate to move on to another position—even if it means a bridge job toward the ultimate goal. Just make sure that you're not jumping out of the frying pan and into the fire. |
| **5. Salary—the compensation for a new job is alluring.** It might, however, come at a heavy price once the realities of overtime and other stressors surface. Income is important but loses its luster if it robs us of energy that could be spent on other aspects of our lives. | In Beverly Kaye and Sharon Jordan-Evans' bestselling book on employee retention, *Love 'Em or Lose 'Em,* the authors surveyed why employees stay with a company. The top three reasons were exciting work and challenge; career growth, learning, and development; and working with great people. Fair pay, or salary, appeared fourth on the list. The exercises in this chapter will help you identify what constitutes exciting and fulfilling work. |
| **6. Convenience—the new position is an easy commute.** With the aggravation of congested freeways and long commutes, many job seekers jump at an opportunity that is close to home, only to find that there are other bigger frustrations associated with the job. | Some of the questions in chapter 11 will help you with your "due diligence" to get a realistic picture of your target company and its culture. |
| **7. Prestige—the company or position title is impressive.** One job seeker went to work for one of the world's hottest technology companies, headquartered in California's Silicon Valley. A few years down the road, she was happy to leave her impressive title, which had led to stress-related illnesses and difficulty conceiving (several years later, she is now the mother of two beautiful little girls). | Evaluate the opportunity in light of your priorities, looking carefully at the "Things That Matter" category in the Magic F.I.T.™ exercise later in this chapter. |

*(continued)*

*(continued)*

| ✓ If Cause Applies to You | Antidote |
|---|---|
| **8. Pressure—the job seeker conforms to someone else's goals or desires.** Is there a spouse, parent, family member, friend, or admired colleague who thinks, "you should be a _____ [fill in the blank]," when you know in your heart that this isn't the right direction? Or, perhaps there is someone who has put you in a box and says, "you'll only be a _____ , and how silly of you to think you could be more?" Or this one, "you'll never make any money doing that!" (Caveat: *Do* make sure that your dream goal is well-researched in terms of market demand.) | Often well-meant, these pressure-packed messages don't always have *your* best interest at heart. Sometimes there's a payoff for the other person to see you stay where you are—that other person might be scared to watch you grow, develop, and find joy or enthusiasm, especially if that person isn't him/herself growing, developing, and finding joy and enthusiasm. Breaking free of other people's expectations requires courage, but the rewards are huge. Ultimately, when you are healthy, happy, and whole, your energy and creative thinking can be unleashed and liberated to work in a way that you never dreamed. |
| **9. Lack of confidence—the job seeker sets sights too low and settles for a lesser position.** Two job seekers with equal qualifications might land very different jobs, depending on their confidence in themselves and belief that the "right" position is out there for them. | If you sense that lack of confidence is undermining your interview performance, you'll have a chance in chapter 4 to identify your success stories, which can boost your self-confidence by a notch or two. Chapter 6 will also help with mindset. |
| **10. Lack of focus—the job seeker has not thought about exploring options or committed to a focus.** Lack of focus is often at the root of other points described in this list. Some job seekers have "fallen" into careers because they've followed in a parent's footsteps or an opportunity serendipitously appeared. Sometimes these careers work out, and sometimes they don't. | Invest the time to confirm that the career direction you're heading in is, indeed, what you want. That's the whole point of this chapter! A small investment of time now can yield years of rewards. |

In this chapter, you can avoid "fish fever"—jumping indiscriminately at unpromising opportunities—by getting a clearer picture of what you want. You'll use the Magic F.I.T.™ model, with the acronym F.I.T. standing for ingredients that are critical to career success:

* F—**F**unction and **F**ulfillment
* I—**I**ndustry/**I**nterests and **I**dentity
* T—**T**hings that Matter and **T**ype

Invest the time now to zero in on these essentials. Skipping this process is like planning your dream vacation without having a destination in mind. When you have completed this chapter, you'll find that the information and insights gained will allow you to

* Make strategic choices to act offensively rather than defensively in your job search.
* Leverage your time by pursuing the "right" opportunities.
* Impress interviewers by knowing what you want.
* Gain confidence targeting positions you can be enthusiastic about.
* Increase your career satisfaction.

## The Solution to Job Stress

The National Institute for Occupational Safety and Health reported that 25 percent of employees see their jobs as the primary stressor in their lives, and 75 percent feel that workers today have more job stress than a generation ago. You can alleviate much of that stress by proactively choosing employment situations that give you that Magic F.I.T.™!

# Identify Your Magic F.I.T.™
Merriam-Webster defines the verb *fit* this way:

### To be suitable for or to harmonize with

When your work is not a good fit with who you are, it yields stress and frustration. The analogy of relationships illustrates the importance of finding a good fit. You've likely experienced a relationship where the other person needed something from you that you didn't have the capacity or desire to give; for example, an introspective friend who loves to engage in hours-long, one-on-one philosophical conversations when your idea of a good time is to participate in an action-packed motocross race with some of your closest friends.

You can see the parallel: If your job isn't a good fit, it can give you fits! Imagine working in a position that required you to write computer programs all day (a somewhat solitary and monotonous task that calls for precision and logic) when what really energizes you is to work with teams in a creative setting, conceptualizing and developing marketing ideas.

When your work is in alignment with things that are important to you, there is harmony and satisfaction. Instead of being a "square peg in a round hole," you can perform work that "fits like a glove."

*Success is getting what you want. Happiness is wanting what you get.*

—Anonymous

Figure 3.1 gives you a closer look at the elements within the Magic F.I.T.™ model. You'll note that there are two layers for each of the letters in F.I.T. The first layer—Function, Industry/Interests, and Type—focuses on external elements that are easily observable. The second layer—Fulfillment, Identity, and Things that Matter—hones in on internal elements that are less easily identifiable, but just as important.

**Figure 3.1: The Magic F.I.T.™ model.**

Later in this chapter, you'll have a chance to flesh out each Magic F.I.T.™ item as it relates to you. In the meantime, table 3.2 briefly describes each element.

If you're thinking that it will be a challenge to find a position that ideally suits all six elements—your functional skills, ideal industry/interests, personality type, fulfilling purpose, evolving identity, and things that matter—don't be discouraged. It *is* possible (I am living proof, along with many others I know!). However, recognize that it is a process of fine-tuning your career over time. Start by making sure you're clear about the first-level elements—Function, Industry/Interests, and Things That Matter—as you target new positions. Then, weave in your second-level elements—Fulfillment, Identity, and Type—to take your career to the next level.

## Table 3.2: Elements of the Magic F.I.T ™

| | **F** | **I** | **T** |
|---|---|---|---|
| **External Variables** | **F**unction<br>Function represents job titles and tasks; for example, titles such as accountant, copywriter, or customer service representative or tasks such as analyzing, planning, or writing. Although you're capable of doing a number of different functional jobs or tasks, you'll want to concentrate on your innate talents and skills, and favorite experiences. | **I**ndustry/Interests<br>Industry refers to *where* you will apply your functional skills. Frequently, your functional interests can be used within a number of industries. For example, a customer service representative (Function) with a passion for organic products might target call centers (Industry) or retailers (Industry) that specialize in natural products (Interests). | **T**hings That Matter<br>Wouldn't it be wonderful if you could open the medicine cabinet each morning and pop a pill that would motivate you to go to work? That pill *does* exist! It takes the shape of having your values and needs met. In the "Things That Matter" category, you'll identify what's most important to you in your next position. Understanding and aligning your work with these values and needs can take your job from humdrum to fun, and your career from good to great! |
| **Internal Variables** | **F**ulfillment<br>Fulfillment is synonymous with purpose. Remember in chapter 1 that I described your career purpose as being "radically rewarded and enthusiastically engaged in work that adds value to others." Your definition should capture the essence of how you will bring value to your employer, as well as how you will fulfill yourself. It's something you can intentionally look forward to on a Monday morning and say, "this is what I am committed to," as well as look back on Friday afternoon and say, "I have accomplished my purpose." | **I**dentity<br>Identity refers to how you see yourself—your internal self-image. It is the way in which you define yourself. What distinguishing characteristics do you want others to note in you? What do you *believe* you are capable of accomplishing? How do you want others to perceive you? Those who experience the greatest meaning and fulfillment in life and work periodically redefine themselves and move beyond their previously accepted limitations. | **T**ype<br>Type refers to your personality. You came wired-at-birth with four main personality preferences: where you focus your energy (your outer world or inner world); how you take in information (concretely or intuitively); how you make decisions (based on logic or feelings); and how you approach the world (in a planned or spontaneous manner). |

As you walk through this process, it's important that you commit to taking action toward your future. Oscar Hammerstein once said, "If you don't have a dream, how are you going to make a dream come true?" I'd like to make a request that will take you closer to seeing your career dreams come true. My request is that you do whatever it takes to discover and pursue career choices that best *fit* your individual needs. To solidify your intention, develop a commitment statement, similar to one of the examples shown here:

- *I am committed to being enthusiastically engaged in and radically rewarded by work that adds value to others.*

- *I am committed to pursuing my Magic F.I.T.™ so that my work will be uniquely fulfilling.*

- *I am committed to regularly reassessing my identity in a way that breaks through previously accepted limitations and allows me to engage in radically rewarding work.*

Choose one of the preceding statements or use your own words to capture the essence of your commitment, and then write it here:

I am committed to:

_____

_____

_____

Speak the commitment out loud. Make sure it rings true for you. Know that this little step can lead to big rewards as you live out that commitment on a daily basis.

## Loving Your Career Leads to Career Contentment

In *The Millionaire Mind*, Thomas J. Stanley, Ph.D. (Andrews McMeel Universal, 2001) catalogs the top 30 success factors of millionaires. Near the top of the list at number 6 is "Loving my career/business." Topping the list at number 1 is "Being honest with all people," followed by "Being well disciplined," "Getting along with people," "Having a supportive spouse," and "Working harder than most people." Whether or not your sights are set on millionaire status, it's clear that loving your career will lead to career contentment.

My hope for each of you is that you get a glimpse of a larger, grander, and more fulfilling career—one that causes you to look forward to jumping out of bed each morning. The Magic F.I.T.™ model is the vehicle to get to that goal. In the remainder of this chapter, you'll complete six steps using some simple checklists and easy exercises that will help you identify specifics for each of the Magic F.I.T.™ elements. If you'd prefer to use online assessments to unearth this information, see figure 3.2, "Online Assessments to Find Your Magic F.I.T.™," later in this chapter.

## Step 1: Find the Right Function

Step 1 in the Magic F.I.T.™ process begins with brainstorming functional areas (titles and tasks) that fit with your skills and talents. In the following Function Checklist, place a checkmark next to the functions that seem to make sense or feel right to you at this time. You'll have a chance to prioritize these functional areas later.

---

### Function Checklist

- ☐ Accounting
- ☐ Actuarial work
- ☐ Administration
- ☐ Advertising
- ☐ Affirmative action
- ☐ Architecture
- ☐ Assembly labor
- ☐ Auditing
- ☐ Automation
- ☐ Board leadership
- ☐ Budgeting
- ☐ Call center operations
- ☐ Cash management
- ☐ Category management
- ☐ Clerical
- ☐ Coaching
- ☐ Consulting
- ☐ Copyright law
- ☐ Corporate relations

- ☐ Counseling
- ☐ Credit and collections
- ☐ Customer service
- ☐ Design
- ☐ Development/fund raising
- ☐ Diversity
- ☐ Economics
- ☐ Education
- ☐ Engineering
- ☐ Environmental
- ☐ Financial
- ☐ General management
- ☐ Graphic arts/design
- ☐ Help desk
- ☐ Healthcare
- ☐ Human resources
- ☐ Industrial labor
- ☐ Information technology (IT)
- ☐ Intellectual property

---

*(continued)*

*(continued)*

- [ ] International relations
- [ ] Investor relations
- [ ] Laboratory work
- [ ] Law
- [ ] Light industrial
- [ ] Logistics
- [ ] Management consulting
- [ ] Manufacturing
- [ ] Market research
- [ ] Marketing
- [ ] Materials management
- [ ] Materials planning
- [ ] Medical
- [ ] Merchandising
- [ ] Mergers and acquisitions
- [ ] Minorities
- [ ] Networks/LAN/WAN
- [ ] Nonprofit
- [ ] Nursing
- [ ] Operations
- [ ] Packaging
- [ ] Paralegal
- [ ] Personnel
- [ ] Planning
- [ ] Plant management
- [ ] Process control
- [ ] Product development
- [ ] Product research
- [ ] Production
- [ ] Project management
- [ ] Public relations

- [ ] Purchasing
- [ ] Quality assurance
- [ ] Regulatory affairs
- [ ] Research and development
- [ ] Risk management
- [ ] Safety professional
- [ ] Sales
- [ ] Scientific
- [ ] Secretarial
- [ ] Security
- [ ] Senior executive management
- [ ] Senior financial management
- [ ] Senior IT management
- [ ] Senior operations management
- [ ] Systems analysis
- [ ] Systems development
- [ ] Systems implementation
- [ ] Tax planning/management
- [ ] Technical
- [ ] Technical support
- [ ] Telecommunications
- [ ] Therapy
- [ ] Trademark law
- [ ] Trading
- [ ] Training
- [ ] Venture capital
- [ ] Writing
- [ ] Other

Need more options? The most exhaustive list of position titles and functional areas is housed in the *Occupational Outlook Handbook* at the U.S. government's Bureau of Labor Statistics page online (the book is also available in print at libraries and booksellers). Go to www.bls.gov/search/ooh.asp?ct=OOH and click on one of the letters under the A–Z index.

After identifying your preferred functional areas, you will need to prioritize the items you checked. Choose the top two that have the most appeal to you and make the most sense at this point in your career. If you find that your top options are very similar to one another, you can target these options in your job search. Examples of similar options would be healthcare professional and nursing or budgeting and financial. If your top options are dissimilar, such as accounting and writing or law and marketing, it would be wise to spend time on "career reconnaissance," where you can explore and learn more about each area so that you can later target the one best functional area for you. Targeting two areas in your job search will likely slow your progress and send a mixed message to your networking contacts.

In the space below, write your top functional areas for your Magic F.I.T.™:

---

### Functional Preferences

_____

_____

_____

_____

---

## Step 2: Identify Your Ideal Industry and Interests

Step 2 helps you pinpoint industries where you can apply your functional talents. The following list of industries will serve as a starting point. The basis for the Industry Checklist in this section was contributed by ResumeMachine.com, a reputable Web-based résumé-distribution service. Place a checkmark next to the industries that appeal to you.

## Industry Checklist

| | |
|---|---|
| ☐ Accounting | ☐ Environmental |
| ☐ Advertising | ☐ Equipment |
| ☐ Aerospace | ☐ Executive search |
| ☐ Aggregates | ☐ Fashion |
| ☐ Agriculture/agribusiness | ☐ Film |
| ☐ Apparel | ☐ Financial services |
| ☐ Automotive | ☐ Food and beverages |
| ☐ Banking | ☐ Forest products/pulp/paper |
| ☐ Biotechnology/equipment | ☐ Franchising |
| ☐ Boats/marine | ☐ Furniture and fixtures |
| ☐ Broadcasting | ☐ Government |
| ☐ Brokerage | ☐ Hazardous waste |
| ☐ Building products/systems | ☐ Healthcare/hospitals |
| ☐ Chemicals | ☐ High-tech |
| ☐ Communications | ☐ Higher education |
| ☐ Computer services | ☐ Hospitality |
| ☐ Computers | ☐ Hotels/restaurants |
| ☐ Construction | ☐ Human resource services |
| ☐ Consulting | ☐ Import/export |
| ☐ Consumer packaged goods | ☐ Industrial |
| ☐ Cosmetics | ☐ Information technology (IT) |
| ☐ Credit/credit cards | ☐ Instruments |
| ☐ Data processing | ☐ Insurance |
| ☐ Defense | ☐ International |
| ☐ Direct marketing | ☐ Internet |
| ☐ E-commerce | ☐ Investment banks |
| ☐ Education | ☐ Laboratories |
| ☐ Electronics | ☐ Law firms |
| ☐ Energy | ☐ Leasing |
| ☐ Engineering | ☐ Leisure/recreation |
| ☐ Entertainment | ☐ Lighting |

- ☐ Lumber
- ☐ Machinery
- ☐ Managed care
- ☐ Management consulting
- ☐ Manufacturing
- ☐ Marketing
- ☐ Measuring equipment
- ☐ Media
- ☐ Medical
- ☐ Medical devices
- ☐ Metals
- ☐ Mining
- ☐ Motor vehicles
- ☐ Natural resources
- ☐ New media
- ☐ Non-profits
- ☐ Oil and gas
- ☐ Paper
- ☐ Perfume
- ☐ Pharmaceuticals
- ☐ Plastics
- ☐ Printing
- ☐ Public administration
- ☐ Public relations
- ☐ Publishing
- ☐ Real estate
- ☐ Recruiting
- ☐ Research and development
- ☐ Retail trade
- ☐ Rubber
- ☐ Security services/products
- ☐ Semiconductors
- ☐ Services
- ☐ Soap
- ☐ Software
- ☐ Specialty materials
- ☐ Sports
- ☐ Stone/gravel/silica
- ☐ Telecommunications
- ☐ Television
- ☐ Test equipment
- ☐ Textiles
- ☐ Transportation
- ☐ Travel
- ☐ Trucks
- ☐ TV/radio/cable
- ☐ Utilities
- ☐ Venture capital
- ☐ Waste
- ☐ Wholesale trade
- ☐ Wireless communications
- ☐ World Wide Web
- ☐ Other

You can find more industry options at the Bureau of Labor Statistics' Web site: www.bls.gov/oco/cg/home.htm. Once there, click the links on the right side of the page to explore exhaustive information on various industries. You can also search the North American Industry Classification System (NAICS) at the National Institutes of Health Small Business Office, http://epic.od.nih.gov/naics/ (click **New to the NAICS?**).

## Can't Decide on an Industry?

Healthcare/Pharmaceutical, Finance, and Professional Services look to be popular hiring industries in the near future. The aging baby boomer population and a rapid research and development rate in healthcare and pharmaceutics will fuel opportunities in these sectors. (Source: DBM.)

Rank your industry choices by order of preference. If your top choice is an industry where hiring is at a standstill due to transition conditions or economic factors, consider pursuing your second industry choice. In the following space, write the industry you've decided to target. (You can include more than one industry preference if they are closely related.)

## Industry Preference(s):

_____

_____

Now let's hone in further by looking at interests within your industry preference. Interests tap into subjects that naturally appeal to you or things about which you are enthusiastic and passionate. When you're engaged in an innate interest, time seems to pass more quickly. To unearth your interests, consider one of these exercises:

- **Do a documentary.** Interview friends and colleagues and ask them what they see as your primary interests. Sometimes an objective third party can identify something you've missed that was right under your nose. Chris found himself in job search mode after his pharmaceutical company announced a post-merger reduction in headcount. A conversation with his sales manager helped him recognize that he was the team's go-to person for Internet research and timesaving technology shortcuts. These technology skills (Interests) areas gave him added value when pursuing sales positions (Function) in the pharmaceutical industry (Industry).

- **Niche yourself with a specialty.** Many physicians specialize in a niche—cardiology, neurology, oncology, pediatric ophthalmology—giving them a clear target market for patients and, many times, greater financial rewards.

Examine your industry for specialty categories and identify where your interests lie. For instance, in the field of human resources, there are specialty areas of compensation and benefits, recruiting, employee relations, and organizational development, to name a few. What industry niche might be your specialty area?

**Inside-the-box thinking.** Walk around your home or office and carefully notice items that are important to you. Put those items into a large box. Analyze the items in the box. Is there a common thread or pattern that emerges? As an example, someone who loves making quilts with special Chinese silks might take an Industry focus of import/export to a more meaningful level by targeting companies that import hard-to-find silk fabrics.

**The time trap.** Keep a log for an extended period of time and note what you love to spend hours doing, both on and off the job. Even if it's watching soap operas, you might be able to incorporate this interest into your industry focus. For instance, one smart entrepreneur took her Industry focus on entertainment a step further by creating the *Soap Opera Digest* based on her love of daytime drama.

**Find a hole.** Look carefully at your industry for unmet needs and untapped opportunities. Perhaps there is a hole that needs to be filled. Every gadget and innovative service we enjoy today was born out of somebody's need and subsequent frustration. Cordless phones came about because people wanted mobility while they chatted. Personal chefs are in demand today because busy professionals don't have time to cook. Have you created a solution for something that frustrates you on the job? If so, perhaps you can transform it into a niche that will increase both your job satisfaction and your marketability.

Based on the results of the above exercises, note the special interests you would like to incorporate within your industry target:

| **Interests** |
| --- |
| _____ |
| _____ |
| _____ |

## Step 3: Think About the Things That Matter

Step 3 identifies your "career needs"—those things that really matter to you. Everyone has unique needs. Some of those needs are extremely basic and common to us all, such as feeding and watering ourselves on a daily basis. Our bodies have a clear system to signal hunger or thirst—our stomachs growl and our mouths get dry. We also have higher-level needs that are less readily apparent, such as the need to be imaginative on the job or the need to have appreciation expressed for our work. Unfortunately, the signaling mechanism for these career-related needs is not always so clear. Instead of a growling tummy to signal hunger, we might have a growling temper, a lack of energy, or a sick feeling in our stomachs on Monday mornings to signal that our career-related needs are not being met.

Needs are key to understanding motivation. Psychologist Abraham Maslow developed a Hierarchy of Needs model in the 1940s that is acknowledged today by both psychologists and business leaders as fundamental to understanding human motivation. The original hierarchy presents five basic levels of need:

1. Physiological: Food, water, shelter, sleep

2. Safety: Security, freedom from fear

3. Belonging and Love: Friends, family, spouse, affection, relationships

4. Self-Esteem: Achievement, mastery, recognition, respect

5. Self-Actualization: Pursuit of inner talents, creativity, fulfillment

The theory states that people are motivated by unsatisfied needs. The lower-level needs (physiological and safety) must be met before a person is motivated to satisfy a higher need (self-esteem and self-actualization). For example, someone who has not eaten for three days (level-1 needs) will not be motivated to pursue achievement and mastery (level-4 needs).

I have identified some career counterparts to Maslow's model, as table 3.3 illustrates.

### Table 3.3: Hierarchy of Career Needs

| Maslow's Hierarchy of Needs | Career Counterparts |
|---|---|
| Level 1: Physiological (food, water, shelter, sleep) | Basic paycheck, manageable work hours |
| Level 2: Safety (security, stability, freedom from fear) | Work environment free of violence, abuse, pollutants, danger, or continual threat of job loss |
| Level 3: Belonging and Love (friends, family, spouse, affection, relationships) | Organizational culture and camaraderie; relationships with supervisor, peers, coworkers, customers |

| Maslow's Hierarchy of Needs | Career Counterparts |
|---|---|
| Level 4: Self-Esteem (achievement, mastery, recognition, respect) | Impressive title; awards; a sense of appreciation received through praise/thanks, promotions, level of responsibility or authority, upper-range salary, perks; a belief that company policy is fair and respectful of the employee; career activity synergizes personal/life goals |
| Level 5: Self-Actualization (pursuit of inner talents, creativity, fulfillment) | Personal growth; full utilization of talents on the job; enthusiastic engagement in work; experiencing the "tingle factor"; using your talents, perhaps even sacrificially, for the greater good |

When the "Things That Matter" are present in your work, your attitude can soar and your satisfaction can skyrocket. A chain reaction then occurs that benefits employers, customers, and shareholders. The Gallup organization, in a survey on the impact of employee attitudes on business outcomes, noted that organizations where employees have above-average attitudes toward their work had 38% higher customer satisfaction scores, 22% higher productivity, and 27% higher profits.

In the following list, place a check next to the needs and values that are important to you. Check as many items as you like.

## The Things That Matter to Me

☐ Autonomy—you want freedom to act independently

☐ Achievement—you enjoy completing goals or projects

☐ Advancement—you want your career to allow upward mobility

☐ Adventure—you want excitement associated with your work

☐ Ambition—you enjoy pushing yourself to continually move forward

☐ Authority—you want to hold power and clout within your organization

☐ Beauty—you want surroundings that are aesthetically pleasing

☐ Casualness—you want a company environment that is low-key and easygoing

*(continued)*

*(continued)*

☐ Communication—you want to keep others informed and involved; you want to be kept in the loop

☐ Courage—you want to stand up for your beliefs

☐ Creativity—your work will require imagination and innovation

☐ Cultural diversity—your work will embrace and further matters of diversity

☐ Entrepreneurialism—you want to be able to create something new; you want to own your work

☐ Ethics—you want a work environment that supports a high level of ethics

☐ Excellence—you want to have mastery of existing and new skills in your work

☐ Honesty—you want to work where honesty is valued by leadership and others

☐ Independence—you want the ability to manage your time and work at your own pace

☐ Influence—your input will influence strategy and direction

☐ Intellectual stimulation—you want ongoing intellectual challenges

☐ Job security—you want a position that offers long-term career stability

☐ Leadership—you want to manage organizations or influence others

☐ Learning—you want the opportunity to continually add new layers of skills or knowledge

☐ Location—you want the geographic location of your work to be a good fit

☐ Logic—you want your work to require you to apply reasoning and judgment

☐ Loving—you want your work to allow you to show warmth, respect, and consideration to others

☐ Meaningful work—you want to find deep satisfaction in your work

☐ Monetary reward—you want your salary to be at the top end of the range for your industry

☐ Movement—you want physical activity to be an important part of your work

☐ Order—you want your work environment to be organized and efficient

☐ Personal development—work will afford you ongoing growth and understanding

☐ Recognition—you want to receive credit and appreciation for your work

☐ Relationships—you want strong working relationships on the job

☐ Respect—you want to earn respect from others

☐ Responsibility—you want decision-making responsibilities

☐ Risk—you enjoy work that involves a measure of risk

☐ Service—you want to help others in your work

☐ Size of company—whether boutique-ish, midsize, or corporate giant, company size is important to you

☐ Spirituality—you want spirituality to be expressed and honored in your workplace

☐ Teamwork—you want the ability to work regularly with others

☐ Time—your work will allow time for home-life and external interests

☐ Traditional—you want the company environment to be well-established or conservative

☐ Travel—you want your work to require travel

☐ Uniqueness—you want to be known for an exclusive or unique skill

☐ Variety—you want your work to involve a range of activity

In the following spaces, prioritize up to 10 of your choices. These "Things That Matter" will be important to uncover as you interview for a new position.

### The Things That Matter to Me

1. _____

2. _____

3. _____

4. _____

5. _____

6. _____

7. _____

8. _____

9. _____

10. _____

## Step 4: Define Fulfillment

Step 4 will transform your job from "paycheck" to "purpose" as you write a fulfillment statement for your career. Fulfillment, or purpose, is the reason *why* you work. If the primary reason behind your work is simply to earn a paycheck, I propose with confidence that there can be much, much more. If you're wondering whether I'm advocating that you trade in your paycheck for purpose, the answer is a resounding *no!* Purpose and poverty don't need to go hand in hand. I am very much in favor of your earning an attractive income, if that is important to you. The secret is to pair your purpose with market demand—there must be employers or customers who will need and pay for your services or products. When this is the case, you can find profound fulfillment because you have identified your passion, which drives perseverance, enthusiasm, creativity, productivity, and income to peak levels.

To find what profoundly fulfills you, look for the "tingle factor." The tingle factor is that goose-bumpy feeling that comes from doing something you absolutely love. The tingle factor causes you to think, "I can't believe they pay me to do this!" Recognize that it is unrealistic to experience the tingle factor on a continuous basis. We're not in search of nirvana! Instead, your ideal work should allow you to experience the tingle factor randomly but regularly. For me, it comes a few times each week. For instance, as a coach, I experience the tingle factor when a client sinks her teeth into a liberating new truth and comes away encouraged, inspired, and confident. As a writer, I experience it after I've wrestled with and won the words that perfectly capture the concept I want to express.

The positive impact you make on others, as well as your own life, is often a clue to uncovering fulfillment. The answers to these questions can provide insight into what is uniquely fulfilling to you:

- ✶ What is your personal purpose? What is your professional purpose? How do these complement each other?

- ✶ What difference do you want to make in the workplace?

- ✶ What do you want to be known for?

- ✶ What kind of living legacy do you want to have?

- ✶ What gifts, or core strengths, do you bring to your supervisor, colleagues, customers, or clients?

Based on the answers to these questions, you can begin drafting a fulfillment statement. It should be short, just one or two sentences, and resonate with you. Here are some examples that various professionals have penned:

- ✶ To encourage professionals to value their inborn talents and worth, and use their strengths to enrich the world (career coach).

- ✶ To cause students to think, examine their belief systems, and grow in their knowledge and understanding (teacher).

⚡ To connect consumers with products and services that enhance their lives (salesperson).

⚡ To provide technology solutions that serve, rather than restrict, business owners (IT sales liaison).

This recipe might help you in writing your own fulfillment statement:

**Action Verb + Who and What + Benefit to Others**

Using this format, table 3.4 illustrates how some of the preceding examples can be broken down.

### Table 3.4: Example Fulfillment Statement Recipes

| Action Verb | Who and What | Benefit to Others |
|---|---|---|
| To encourage | professionals to value their inborn talents and worth and use their strengths to | enrich the world |
| To cause | students to think, examine their belief systems, and | grow in their knowledge and understanding |
| To provide | technology solutions to business owners | that serve, rather than restrict, business owners |

Use the blank rows in the following box to write a few drafts of your own fulfillment statement. When you're comfortable with the wording, finalize your statement in the final row.

### Draft Your Fulfillment Statement

| Action Verb | Who and What | Benefit to Others |
|---|---|---|
| Draft 1: | | |
| | | |
| Draft 2: | | |
| | | |

*(continued)*

*(continued)*

| Action Verb | Who and What | Benefit to Others |
|---|---|---|
| Draft 3: | | |
| | | |
| | | |
| Fulfillment Statement: | | |
| | | |
| | | |
| | | |

## Step 5: Enhance Your Identity

Step 5 involves an assessment of how you want to see yourself and what you believe you are capable of accomplishing. You should do this identity assessment periodically because life and work experiences cause us to change and grow. It's obvious when children grow: They need a larger size of clothing. It's not so obvious when adults grow: It takes a very conscious examination of our thought patterns, level of self-reliance, and degree of confidence to recognize when it's time for us to try on a larger size of life—an enhanced identity.

In enhancing your identity, it's helpful to start with a simple list of adjectives that capture the essence of you. For instance, here's a 10-point list of how I view myself: encouraging, inspirational, knowledgeable, leading, conscientious, thorough, capable, intuitive, gracious, successful. Having these priorities in focus helps me to act in concert with them.

What characteristics describe your career identity? Check any of the words in the following checklist that are part of your career identity and will be important to prospective employers.

### Ingredients of My Career Identity That Are Important to Employers

☐ Accountable      ☐ Amenable

☐ Accurate      ☐ Articulate

☐ Adaptable      ☐ Assertive

☐ Aggressive      ☐ Authentic

☐ Ambitious      ☐ Awesome

- ☐ Bright
- ☐ Bottom-line–oriented
- ☐ Broad-minded
- ☐ Capable
- ☐ Calm
- ☐ Caring
- ☐ Cheerful
- ☐ Chic
- ☐ Clean
- ☐ Clever
- ☐ Collaborative
- ☐ Committed
- ☐ Compassionate
- ☐ Competitive
- ☐ Compliant
- ☐ Composed
- ☐ Communicative
- ☐ Confident
- ☐ Connected
- ☐ Conscientious
- ☐ Consistent
- ☐ Cosmopolitan
- ☐ Courageous
- ☐ Creative
- ☐ Credible
- ☐ Daring
- ☐ Deadline-oriented
- ☐ Delightful
- ☐ Detail-oriented
- ☐ Direct
- ☐ Driven
- ☐ Dutiful
- ☐ Dynamic
- ☐ Eager
- ☐ Efficient
- ☐ Elegant
- ☐ Encouraging
- ☐ Energetic
- ☐ Enthusiastic
- ☐ Entrepreneurial
- ☐ Ethical
- ☐ Exclusive
- ☐ Even-tempered
- ☐ Experienced
- ☐ Extroverted
- ☐ Fashionable
- ☐ Fast
- ☐ Flexible
- ☐ Forgiving
- ☐ Free-spirited
- ☐ Friendly
- ☐ Fun-loving
- ☐ Funny
- ☐ Future-oriented
- ☐ Generous
- ☐ Gracious
- ☐ Helpful
- ☐ Honest
- ☐ Imaginative
- ☐ Independent
- ☐ Influential
- ☐ Innovative
- ☐ Inspirational
- ☐ Intellectual

*(continued)*

*(continued)*

| | |
|---|---|
| ☐ Intelligent | ☐ Reliable |
| ☐ Introverted | ☐ Research-driven |
| ☐ Intuitive | ☐ Resilient |
| ☐ Just | ☐ Resourceful |
| ☐ Knowledgeable | ☐ Respected |
| ☐ Leading-edge | ☐ Respectful |
| ☐ Level-headed | ☐ Savvy |
| ☐ Logical | ☐ Self-starting |
| ☐ Loving | ☐ Sincere |
| ☐ Loyal | ☐ Smart |
| ☐ Mature | ☐ Sophisticated |
| ☐ Methodical | ☐ Spontaneous |
| ☐ Meticulous | ☐ Strategic |
| ☐ No-nonsense | ☐ Street-smart |
| ☐ Open-minded | ☐ Stylish |
| ☐ Optimistic | ☐ Successful |
| ☐ Organized | ☐ Supportive |
| ☐ Passionate | ☐ Tasteful |
| ☐ People-oriented | ☐ Team-oriented |
| ☐ Perseverant | ☐ Thorough |
| ☐ Persuasive | ☐ Thoughtful |
| ☐ Polite | ☐ Top-ranked |
| ☐ Positive | ☐ Tough |
| ☐ Precise | ☐ Trendy |
| ☐ Productive | ☐ Trustworthy |
| ☐ Professional | ☐ Upbeat |
| ☐ Problem-solving | ☐ Visionary |
| ☐ Quality-oriented | ☐ Well-trained |
| ☐ Quick | ☐ Wise |
| ☐ Quiet | ☐ Witty |
| ☐ Relational | ☐ Other |

From the words you checked off, write the top 10 terms that capture the essence of your work identity here.

---

### The Essence of My Work Identity

1. _____
2. _____
3. _____
4. _____
5. _____
6. _____
7. _____
8. _____
9. _____
10. _____

---

What do you believe you are capable of accomplishing? At 20 years of age, you will have a different answer to this question than you will at 30, 40, 50, and so on. The next job you target is directly linked to what you believe you are capable of accomplishing. The good news is that you are usually capable of much more than you believe. Let's raise the bar on your beliefs! When reflecting on any self-imposed limitations you've held in the past, you set the stage to adopt beliefs that serve you better and allow you to move forward in your career.

In the following space, write a few sentences that raise the bar on what you believe you are capable of accomplishing in your next position:

---

### What I Can Accomplish in My Next Position

_____

_____

_____

_____

_____

---

# Step 6: Know Your Personality Type

Step 6 allows you to better understand personality type and how it relates to your behavior, both on and off the job. Type theory stems from the work of influential psychiatrist Carl Jung who, more than 80 years ago, proposed that differences in peoples' behavior were the result of preferences related to basic functions of personality. These basic functions include how we take in information and how we make decisions.

Taking Jung's work to another level, the mother-daughter team of Katharine Briggs and Isabelle Myers developed an assessment to classify people's observable behavior. With this effort, the assessment known as the Myers-Briggs Type Indicator® (MBTI®) was born and is now administered to more than 2.5 million people each year. Briggs' and Myers' two-fold purpose for developing the MBTI® was noble: 1) to better match people and jobs; and 2) to contribute to world peace through a better understanding of people's type.

When you understand type, you can pursue positions that will complement, not clash with, your personality preferences.

## Using Personality Type to Have a Better Interview

A basic understanding of personality type can give you insights into your interviewers' personality and how to best communicate with him or her. For instance, an interviewer who asks for lots of details or says "wait a minute, I missed hearing a step in your response" might prefer information delivered in a sequential, concrete, and ordered fashion. Conversely, an interviewer who seems impatient with step-by-step details and wants the big-picture view might appreciate responses that use metaphors and weave together multiple concepts. For more on connecting with interviewers, see chapter 14.

The basic tenets of personality type measure four scales:

1. **Energy:** The direction in which your energies typically flow—outward, toward objects and people in the environment (*Extroversion,* or its abbreviation *E*) or inward, drawing attention from the outward environment toward inner experience and reflection (*Introversion,* or its abbreviation *I*).

2. **Perception:** Whether you prefer to take in information through your five senses in a concrete fashion, focusing on "what is" (*Sensing,* or *S*) or with a "sixth sense" in an abstract or conceptual manner, focusing on "what could be" (*iNtuiting,* or *N*).

3. **Judgment:** Whether you make decisions based on facts and logic (*Thinking,* or *T*) or based on personal or social values (*Feeling,* or *F*).

4. **Orientation:** Whether you orient your outer world in a methodical, deliberate manner, seeking closure (*Judging,* or *J*), or in a spontaneous, play-it-by-ear approach, remaining open to more information (*Perceiving,* or *P*).

The assessment yields a four-letter code, such as *INFJ* or *ESTP*, to indicate your personality preferences. These four preferences, according to Jung, become the core of our attractions and aversions to people, tasks, and events. The following examples shed light on Jung's and Myers-Briggs' theory as it relates to career choice:

- People with a clear preference for "Extroversion" (E) will likely be attracted to work where they can interact with people extensively or with large groups of people. People with a clear preference for "Introversion" (I) will be attracted to occupations where they can interact one-on-one or with small groups, or concentrate quietly on ideas, impressions, or information.

- Those with a combined preference for "iNtuiting" and "Feeling" (NF) will likely be attracted to work such as advocacy, facilitation, or counseling; conversely, these same people would likely have an aversion to work that requires repetitive tasks, such as a production line job.

- Those with a combined preference for "Sensing" and "Feeling" (SF) often choose occupations that require work with details in a way that allows them to help others. Accordingly, professions such as healthcare (physician, nurse, medical records technician, therapist), management or administration (often in social services or education programs), data management (bookkeeping, librarian, secretary), or law enforcement (police detective, guard, site administrator) might be appealing.

- Those with preferences for "Sensing" (S), "Thinking" (T), and "Judging" (J) will likely be drawn to task-oriented work that might involve measurement, logistics, monitoring, or management.

- People with a combined preference for "iNtuiting" and "Thinking" (NT) will likely be attracted to work that involves problem-solving, brainstorming, strategy, or leadership.

Personality type clearly impacts career choice. For instance, the *MBTI Manual* (Third Edition, Consulting Psychologist Press) indicates that, on a national basis, only a small percentage of the population have the NT preference (10.3%). Yet when comparing this percentage of the population with a sample of MBA students, the percentage of students reporting an NT preference was almost double that of any other type. Often, MBA graduate programs lead to an executive career track, something that's likely to be attractive for the NT group (although not a guarantee of excellence on the job).

Use table 3.5 as a starting point to identify your preferences for the four scales of energy, perception, judgment, and orientation. This is not a test—there are no right or wrong answers! This is about identifying your natural preferences, just as you have a natural preference for right-handedness or left-handedness. When responding, don't think about what is most socially acceptable or how you've trained yourself to be on the job. Instead, think about how you would naturally respond, with no one looking over your shoulder or judging you. Read the paired items from left to right, and then check the box that best describes your preference. Mark only one box for each of the pairs.

### Table 3.5: Identify Your Energy, Perception, Judgment, and Orientation Preferences

| Extroversion | Introversion |
|---|---|
| **Energy: How You Recharge and Focus Your Attention** | |
| ☐ Devote more energy toward outer world, focusing energy and attention to objects and people in the environment | ☐ Devote more energy toward the the inner world, focusing attention on clarity of thoughts, ideas, impressions |
| ☐ Prefer group settings | ☐ Prefer individual or small-group settings |
| ☐ Like expanding your social circle and sphere of friends | ☐ Carefully consider adding new friends due to the time and energy commitment of maintaining deep relationships |
| ☐ Energized by starting and engaging in conversation; mingle easily with strangers | ☐ Find it draining to keep the conversation going; small talk with strangers is taxing |
| ☐ Process thoughts by thinking out loud; often have a quick response or witty comeback | ☐ Process thoughts internally before speaking; often think of the perfect response hours later |
| ☐ Active, enthusiastic, energetic, animated | ☐ Reflective, calm demeanor, understated |
| ☐ Enjoy entertainment that involves action | ☐ Enjoy entertainment that sparks mental stimulation |
| ☐ Prefer variety in workday; dislike working on one thing for a long time, especially if on your own | ☐ Enjoy working on one thing for a long time |
| ☐ Enjoy the spotlight | ☐ Happy to work behind the scenes |
| ☐ Prefer to have a breadth of interests | ☐ Prefer to have a depth of understanding about a few interests |
| ____ Total checkmarks for Extroversion column | ____ Total checkmarks for Introversion column |

Circle the preference that received the most checkmarks (if there is a tie, select Introversion):

Extroversion (E) or Introversion (I)

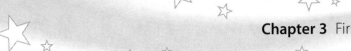

| Sensing | iNtuiting |
|---|---|

### Perception: How You Take In Information

| | |
|---|---|
| ☐ Trust information you can take in through your five senses | ☐ Trust information you can take in through inspiration, inference, impressions |
| ☐ Enjoy details and concrete, physical data | ☐ Enjoy abstract ideas and meanings |
| ☐ Use precise, literal language; give detailed explanations | ☐ Use general, figurative language; speak in metaphors and analogies |
| ☐ Present or take in information in a step-by-step, sequential fashion | ☐ Present or take in information tangentially |
| ☐ Are pragmatic and results-oriented | ☐ Are conceptual and idea-oriented |
| ☐ Hands-on; trust experience | ☐ Theoretical; trust ideas |
| ☐ Realist, "what-is" perspective | ☐ Visionary, "what-if" perspective |
| ☐ Past or present, "here-and-now" orientation | ☐ Future orientation |
| ☐ See facts and details before seeing underlying patterns or whole concepts | ☐ See behind-the-scenes before seeing individual facts and details |
| ____ Total checkmarks for Sensing column | ____ Total checkmarks for iNtuiting column |

Circle the preference that received the most checkmarks (if there is a tie, select iNtuiting):

Sensing (S) or iNtuiting (N)

| Thinking | Feeling |
|---|---|

### Judging: How You Make Decisions

| | |
|---|---|
| ☐ Base decisions on logic and reasoning | ☐ Base decisions on personal or social values |
| ☐ Focus on analysis and objectivity | ☐ Focus on people and harmony |
| ☐ Deem it more important to be truthful than tactful | ☐ Deem it important to be tactful as well as truthful |

*(continued)*

*(continued)*

| Thinking | Feeling |
|---|---|
| ☐ Prefer objective, analytical presentation of facts | ☐ May sense that your or others' feelings are not being valued when discussion centers on an objective, analytical presentation of facts |
| ☐ Value fair treatment for everyone, with a one-standard-for-all philosophy | ☐ Evaluate situations based on the individual, with an exception-to-the-rule viewpoint |
| ☐ Tend to be critical; point out flaws | ☐ Easily show appreciation to others; overlook others' flaws |
| ☐ Detached, aloof; process-oriented | ☐ Connected to people; people are integral to the process |
| ☐ Often oblivious to others' feelings | ☐ May be viewed as overly accommodating or overemotional |
| ☐ Facts drive decisions | ☐ Impact on others factors heavily into decisions |
| ☐ Make tough decisions despite any negative personal reactions | ☐ Tender; effect of a decision on others can be more important than logic |
| _____ Total checkmarks for Thinking column | _____ Total checkmarks for Feeling column |

Circle the preference that received the most checkmarks (if there is a tie, select Feeling):

Thinking (T) or Feeling (F)

| Judging | Perceiving |
|---|---|

### Orientation: How You Orient Your Outer World

| Judging | Perceiving |
|---|---|
| ☐ Prefer a planned, organized, systematic approach to life | ☐ Prefer a spontaneous, flexible approach to life |
| ☐ Prefer to have things settled | ☐ Prefer to leave things open |
| ☐ Formal and orderly; efficient | ☐ Informal and easygoing; casual |
| ☐ Like expectations to be clearly defined | ☐ Are comfortable with ambiguity |

| Judging | Perceiving |
|---|---|
| ☐ Make lists, enjoy completing a task on time or early | ☐ Starting the task is fun; finishing a task on time is optional |
| ☐ Prefer to take in only the amount of information necessary to make a decision | ☐ Remain open to new information as long as possible in order to miss nothing that might be important |
| ☐ Start early to reduce stress of deadline pressure | ☐ Do most creative work when under deadline pressure |
| ☐ Let's get this done | ☐ Let's wait and see |
| ☐ Enjoy organization; apply procedures to help structure task | ☐ Enjoy variety and diversity; procedures can impede creativity |
| ☐ Decide quickly on goals and stay the course in achieving them | ☐ Change goals when made aware of new information |
| _____ Total checkmarks for Judging column | _____ Total checkmarks for Perceiving column |

Circle the preference that received the most checkmarks (if there is a tie, select Perceiving):

Judging (J) or Perceiving (P)

Write your preferences for each of the four scales in the blanks that follow:

---

### My Preferences

Energy (Extroversion or Introversion):

_____

Perception (Sensing or iNtuiting):

_____

Judgment (Thinking or Feeling):

_____

Orientation (Judging or Perceiving):

_____

Identifying your individual preferences for energy, perception, judgment, and orientation is only the first step in understanding type. Together these four preferences mesh to create a richly complex personality type, which can best be understood by completing the MBTI® (or, for career purposes, the MBTI® Career Report). If you have not had the opportunity to take this assessment, I encourage you to do so. The results will enable you to target tasks that you find interesting and express your preferences on the job, which is like cycling with the wind at your back rather than in your face. You will need to work with an individual who is specially qualified to administer the MBTI® assessment (many career coaches and counselors possess this qualification). Alternatively, you can use an assessment similar to the MBTI called The Keirsey™ Temperament Sorter®-II. (See figure 3.2, "Online Assessments to Find Your Magic F.I.T.™," for more information on these assessments.) Two other great resources are the books *Do What You Are* (Little, Brown) by Paul D. Tieger and Barbara Barron-Tieger and *What's Your Type of Career?* (Davies Black) by Donna Dunning, which provides detailed information about how type relates to career choice.

## Step 7: Set Your Salary Range

In addition to steps 1–6, you'll need to add one more item to your Magic F.I.T.™ so that it truly FITS! That final item is *salary*. Identify the range that you're targeting for your next position. Of course, you won't be mentioning your salary requirements to many people at this early stage. However, it's important that you put pencil to paper to calculate what you would accept on the low end, what the industry average is, as well as what your ideal or dream salary would be. If you need help getting a handle on what these numbers should be, ask colleagues what they consider to be the range for your target position (the phrasing "what is the range?" will be better received than "what do you make?"). Also, visit www.salary.com for salary information adjusted for hundreds of metro areas throughout the U.S. The basic salary report from this site is free; a personalized salary report is available for approximately $30.

List your three salary figures in the following box.

---

### Salary Figures

Low-end salary I would be willing to accept:

$ _____

Industry average:

$ _____

Dream-job salary:

$ _____

---

# Using Online Assessments to Discover Your Magic F.I.T.™

You might want to dig more deeply to identify the right F.I.T., especially if you're a Career Explorer (see "Are You a Career Hunter or Career Explorer?" in chapter 2 for the difference between the two). In addition to the preceding exercises, a number of Web-based career assessments are available. Career and life coach Nancy Branton, a recognized expert in assessments (www.CareerLifePotential.com), has researched hundreds of instruments for this book and narrowed them down to a manageable list of highly validated and reliable assessments. Figure 3.2 outlines these assessments, which are categorized as Comprehensive or as identifying Interests, Personality/Work Styles, Skills/Strengths, Values/Motivators/Self-Beliefs, and Purpose. For each assessment, you'll find which F.I.T. element is addressed, along with cost, rating, where to access (all are available online unless otherwise noted), and general comments. Some assessments require special training to obtain, in which case you would need to work with a qualified coach or counselor.

| Name of Assessment | (F) | (I) | (T) | (f) | (i) | (t) | Cost[1] | Spec Qual[2] | Rating[3] | Where to Access | Comments |
|---|---|---|---|---|---|---|---|---|---|---|---|
| **COMPREHENSIVE** | | | | | | | | | | | |
| MAPP™ Career Motivational Appraisal | F | I | T | f | i | t | $$ | No ◊ | *** | www.assessment.com | This instrument measures your potential and motivation for various vocational areas. A comprehensive report details the following: interest in job content, temperament for job, aptitude for job, people, things, data, reasoning, mathematical capacity, language capacity, vocational analysis, top 10 vocational areas, and 19 major vocation areas. You can review 900 O*NET job descriptions that are ranked from highest match to lowest match. From there, you can access the *OOH (Occupational Outlook Handbook)* and educational opportunities. You'll also receive a Motivational Qualities Report that lists items to use in a résumé.<br><br>The assessment is based on constructs of worker traits defined by the Department of Labor and found in the O*NET and *Dictionary of Occupational Titles (DOT)*. It is based on more than 40 years of research that was initially done by Kenneth G. Neils and subsequently by Henry Neils, president of Assessment.com. |
| 16 PF® Personal Career Development Profile Plus Report | F | I | T | | i | t | $ | Yes | *** | www.ipat.com | This Web-based (or paper-and-pencil) instrument produces scores for 7 broad interest areas (influencing, organizing, creating, helping, analyzing, producing, and venturing) and 27 career fields with role patterns and occupational interests. Sections in the narrative report include problem-solving resources, patterns for coping with stressful conditions, inter-personal interaction styles, organizational role and work-setting preferences, career activity interests, career field and occupational interests, and personal career lifestyle effectiveness considerations. This well-researched assessment is based on Cattell's Personality Factors and the Big Five Personality Theory. |

**Figure 3.2: Online assessments to find your Magic F.I.T.™**

| Name of Assessment | (F) | (I) | (T) | (f) | (i) | (t) | Cost[1] | Spec Qual[2] | Rating[3] | Where to Access | Comments |
|---|---|---|---|---|---|---|---|---|---|---|---|
| **COMPREHENSIVE (continued)** | | | | | | | | | | | |
| Career Leader (Business Career Interest Inventory, Management and Professional Reward Profile, and Management and Professional Abilities Profile) | F | I | T | | i | t | $$$ | No | *** | www.careerleader.com | Career Leader is the most comprehensive career planning system available for business careers. It is comprised of three Web-based inventories: the Business Career Interest Inventory (BCII) defines career interests by measuring your strength of interest in eight business core functions; the Management and Professional Reward Profile (MPRP) assesses your values about work rewards; and the Management and Professional Abilities Profile (MPAP) gives you information about your business skill strengths and weaknesses. Your integrated profile is compared to more than 20 major business career paths and includes information on your preferred work environment. Any potential patterns of personal styles that might derail your career are discussed.<br><br>The BCII is based on Butler & Waldroop's Business Core Function Model and has been well researched. The MPRP is based on conjoint analysis technology; and the MPAP is a business skills self-rating instrument. |
| Strong and MBTI® Career Report | F | I | T | | | t | $ | Yes | *** | www.cpp.com | This Web-based (or pencil-and-paper) assessment produces a report that integrates the Strong with MBTI results, suggesting occupations and helping you identify work environments and tasks that might be satisfying. It also provides strategies for career development and hints for staying motivated in the career exploration process. The assessment is based on Holland's Vocational Personality Theory and Jung's Personality Theory. |

[1]★ = free
$ = less than $20    $$ = $20-$50    $$$ = $50-$100    $$$$ = $100+

[2]◊ = can be taken without a coach/counselor but recommend use of a coach/counselor

[3]* = good, ** = very good, *** = excellent)

| Name of Assessment | (F) | (I) | (T) | (f) | (i) | (t) | Cost[1] | Spec Qual[2] | Rating[3] | Where to Access | Comments |
|---|---|---|---|---|---|---|---|---|---|---|---|
| **COMPREHENSIVE (continued)** | | | | | | | | | | | |
| The Birkman Method® Preview Report | F | I | T | | i | t | $$$$ | Yes | *** | www.birkman.com | Based on a Web-based assessment, a multitude of reports are available that your consultant can help select based on your needs. One such report is the Preview Report, which is made up of 5 separate reports: Life Style Grid®, Areas of Interest, Strengths and Needs, Career Management Report, and Your Career Narrative. You will receive a specific listing of job families and occupations that fit you the best. The occupations link to the *OOH*.<br><br>This assessment was based loosely on Jungian theory and then developed through more than 50 years of research. |
| The Keirsey™ Temperament Sorter®-II and Campbell™ Interest and Skill Survey® Bundle<br><br>(These are also listed individually under Interests and Personality) | F | I | T | | i | t | $$ | No ◊ | *** | www.keirseycampbell .com | The CISS® instrument provides a report with results on 7 occupational orientations, 25 basic scales, 60 occupational scales (linked to O*NET occupations), extraversion scale, and academic focus scale. Based on interests and skill confidence, it recommends occupations to pursue, develop, explore, and avoid. The online version allows you to link to an extensive CISS® Career Planner, a step-by-step guide to career planning. CISS® is based on Dr. Campbell's model for occupational orientations and corresponds to Holland's Occupational Themes. The Keirsey™ Temperament Sorter®II—The Career Temperament Report™ is a Web-based instrument that focuses on how your temperament and personality type tend to be expressed in the work world. The report provides information on aptitudes, favorite activities, values, preferred workplace rewards, and characteristics of an ideal job. It also includes a list of occupations with a brief description and link to the O*NET™ system for further information. The assessment is based on Keirsey's Temperament Theory.<br><br>At the time this book went to press, for a special price of $29.95 (rather than $37.90), you can take both of these instruments. |

| Name of Assessment | (F) | (I) | (T) | (f) | (i) | (t) | Cost[1] | Spec Qual[2] | Rating[3] | Where to Access | Comments |
|---|---|---|---|---|---|---|---|---|---|---|---|
| **SKILLS/STRENGTHS** | | | | | | | | | | | |
| O*NET® OnLine Skills Search | F | I | | | | | ★ | No | ** | http://online.onetcenter.org/skills | In this Web-based activity, you select from a set of skills in six broad groups. The report provides occupations that correspond to your skills by degree of match. The report links to O*NET OnLine Summary Reports. |
| Clifton StrengthsFinder™ | F | | | | | | $$ | No | *** | http://gmj.gallup.com/book_center/strengths finder | This Web-based instrument indicates your top 5 out of 34 themes of talent in Gallup's taxonomy of strengths. The book *Now Discover Your Strengths* by Marcus Buckingham and Donald O. Clifton (Free Press, 2001) contains a unique identification number that allows you access to the Clifton StrengthsFinder Profile on the Internet. The assessment does not directly tie to jobs. It is based on a model of Positive Psychology. |
| America's Career InfoNet—Skills Profiler | F | I | | | | | ★ | No | ** | www.acinet.org/acinet/skills_about.asp | This assessment consists of three tools: Skills Identifier, Skills Explorer, and Skills Gap Analyzer. It is useful to identify skills, find occupations that match skills, and identify any gaps in skills for desired occupations. |
| Knowdell Motivated Skills Card Sort | F | | T | | | | $ | No | ** | www.careertrainer.com | Using this manual card sort, you can assess your proficiency and motivation in 48 transferable skills areas while identifying the motivated skills that are central to personal and career satisfaction and success. The card sort also highlights your burnout skills so that you can avoid jobs that require those skills. |
| **INTERESTS** | | | | | | | | | | | |
| Career Liftoff® Interest Inventory | F | I | | | | | $ | No ◊ | ** | www.careerliftoff.com | The Career Liftoff® generates information on 6 occupational themes and 30 career fields. For the top occupational interest areas, a description of specific interests and representative jobs is provided tied to O*NET occupations. Based on Holland's Vocational Theory, this assessment is very helpful for determining college major and for making a career transition. |

[1] ★ = free
$ = less than $20     $$ = $20-$50     $$$ = $50-$100     $$$$ = $100+

[2] ◊ = can be taken without a coach/counselor but recommend use of a coach/counselor

[3] * = good, ** = very good, *** = excellent)

| Name of Assessment | (F) | (I) | (T) | (f) | (i) | (t) | Cost[1] | Spec Qual[2] | Rating[3] | Where to Access | Comments |
|---|---|---|---|---|---|---|---|---|---|---|---|
| **VALUES, MOTIVATORS, SELF-BELIEFS (continued)** | | | | | | | | | | | |
| Campbell™ Interest & Skill Inventory (CISS®) and CISS Career Planner | F | I | T | | | | $ | No ◊ | *** | www.advisorteam.com/ciss | This instrument provides a report with results on 7 occupational orientations, 25 basic scales, 60 occupational scales, extraversion scale, and academic focus scale. Based on interests and skill confidence, it recommends occupations to pursue, develop, explore, and avoid. Results are linked to O*NET occupations. The online version allows you to link to CISS® Career Planner, an extensive, step-by-step guide to career planning. The assessment is based on Dr. Campbell's model for occupational orientations and generally corresponds to Holland's Occupational Themes. |
| Strong Interest Inventory® Profile with Skills Confidence Inventory Profile and Interpretive Report | F | I | T | | | t | $ | Yes | *** | www.cpp.com | This Web-based (or paper-and-pencil) instrument provides a report on the top 10 occupations that match your interests, top 5 basic interests, highest scoring occupational themes, and information on 5 personal styles. The full report provides scores on the 6 occupational themes, 30 Basic Interest Scales, 122 occupations, and 5 measures of personal style. It ties to O*NET occupations.<br><br>Occupational themes indicate interests, work activities, potential skills, values, and skills confidence. The assessment is based on Holland's Vocational Personality Theory. |
| **VALUES, MOTIVATORS, SELF-BELIEFS** | | | | | | | | | | | |
| O*NET® Work Importance Profiler™ | | | T | | | | ★ | No | *** | Download and use a computerized version: www.onetcenter.org/WIP.html<br><br>Download and print a paper/pencil version: www.onetcenter.org/WIL.html | This computerized (or paper-and-pencil) instrument provides you with information about your top 2 work values and your top 10 work needs, and then offers occupations that match your values. The assessment is based on Dawis' and Lofquist's Theory of Work Adjustment. |
| Self Worth Inventory© | | | | | i | | $ | No | *** | www.crgleader.com | This instrument identifies your current level of self-worth as it pertains to self, family, peers, work, and projected self. It also charts levels of self-concept and self-esteem and includes alternatives for increasing self-worth. The instrument is based on extensive qualitative research and field testing. It is based on a general concept of self-worth. |

| Name of Assessment | (F) | (I) | (T) | (f) | (i) | (t) | Cost¹ | Spec Qual² | Rating³ | Where to Access | Comments |
|---|---|---|---|---|---|---|---|---|---|---|---|
| **VALUES, MOTIVATORS, SELF-BELIEFS (continued)** | | | | | | | | | | | |
| Values Preference Indicator® | | | T | | i | | $ | No | *** | www.crgleader.com | This will identify your primary values, associated needs, and related fears. The report includes a Personal Action Plan. |
| Career Orientations Inventory (contained in the workbook *Career Anchors: Discovering Your Real Values* by Edgar H. Schein [Pfeiffer & Co.]) | F | I | T | | i | | $ | No | *** | Bookstore | This paper-and-pencil inventory and other activities contained in the workbook help you understand your career anchors and learn about your orientations toward work, motives, values, and talents. It also uncovers the one element that you will not give up, even in difficult circumstances. This instrument is based on Schein's Theory of Career Anchors. |
| Values Arrangement List (VAL™) | | I | T | | i | | $ | No ◊ | *** | www.harcourtassessment.com | This Web-based survey measures and defines your life and operational values (conscious and unconscious). It is based on Aristotle's Theory of Values. |
| **PERSONALITY/WORK STYLES** | | | | | | | | | | | |
| Myers-Briggs Type Indicator® Career Report Form | F | I | | | | t | $ | Yes | ** | www.cpp.com | This Web-based (or paper-and-pencil) instrument produces information about your 4-letter Myers-Briggs Type, including how your type affects your career choice, career exploration, and career development, as well as job families and occupations for your type and the most/least popular occupations for your type. The assessment is based on Jung's Personality Theory. |
| The Golden Personality Type Profiler® | F | | T | | i | t | $ | No ◊ | *** | www.harcourtassessment.com | This instrument provides a description of your personality style, organization style, teamwork style, leadership style, communication style, motivators, learning style, careers for your type, and career development suggestions. It contains 36 facet scales within four global scales (extroverting/introverting, sensing/intuiting, thinking/feeling, and organizing/adapting), along with an additional global scale of tense/calm with two facets. It is based on Allport's Trait Theory and Carl Jung's theory of personality. |

¹★ = free

$ = less than $20     $$ = $20-$50     $$$ = $50-$100     $$$$ = $100+

²◊ = can be taken without a coach/counselor but recommend use of a coach/counselor

³* = good, ** = very good, *** = excellent)

| Name of Assessment | (F) | (I) | (T) | (f) | (i) | (t) | Cost[1] | Spec Qual[2] | Rating[3] | Where to Access | Comments |
|---|---|---|---|---|---|---|---|---|---|---|---|
| **PERSONALITY/WORK STYLES (CONTINUED)** | | | | | | | | | | | |
| Work Behavior Inventory | | | | | i | t | $ | Yes | *** | www.hrconsultantsinc.com or info@hrconsultantsinc.com | The WBI identifies your preferred work styles. These work styles match those in the O*NET Online summary reports for occupations. It assesses your leadership style, influencing style, and emotional intelligence. Specific career development recommendations are also provided. The assessment is based on the Big Five Personality Theory. |
| The Keirsey™ Temperament Sorter®-II The Career Temperament Report™ | F | I | T | | i | t | $ | No | ** | www.advisorteam.com | This instrument produces a report that focuses on how your temperament and personality type tend to be expressed in the work world. It provides information on aptitudes, favorite activities, values, preferred workplace rewards, and characteristics of an ideal job. Included are a list of occupations with a brief description and a link to the O*NET™ system for further information. It is based on Keirsey's Temperament Theory. |
| **PURPOSE** (Although not assessments, these books can be helpful in identifying purpose.) | | | | | | | | | | | |
| *Putting Purpose to Work: A Guide to Writing Your Purpose Statement* (available online at www.inventuregroup.com) | | | | f | | | $ | No | ** | www.inventuregroup.com | This guide helps you to write a purpose statement. |
| *How to Find Your Mission in Life* by Richard Nelson Bolles (Ten Speed Press, 2001) | | | | f | | | $ | No | ** | Bookstore | In this pocket resource, author Richard N. Bolles (creator of the best-selling career book *What Color Is Your Parachute?* [Ten Speed Press]) brings a God-centered perspective to the task of writing a mission statement. |

[1]★ = *free*
$ = *less than $20*       $$ = *$20-$50*       $$$ = *$50-$100*       $$$$ = *$100+*

[2]◊ = *can be taken without a coach/counselor but recommend use of a coach/counselor*

[3]* = *good, ** = very good, *** = excellent)*

## 10 Quick Tips for Acing Online Assessments

As you approach online assessments, consider these tips:

1. **Work with a knowledgeable career coach or counselor to help pull together all the results.** Ask what his or her training and experience are with the various instruments. (A good place to look for a coach or counselor is among the Career Masters Institute members who contributed the Magic Tips in the appendix of this book. Warning: If you come across a career consultant who promises access to insider hiring contacts and a guaranteed job placement for a fee of $5,000, run for the hills!)

2. **Don't rely on just one assessment to cover all of the Magic F.I.T.™ areas.** If you are already clear about certain areas of the F.I.T., take only those assessments that will fill in the rest of the picture. Take assessments when you are fresh and rested, and allow plenty of time to finish without rushing.

3. **Don't take results too literally or look to assessments as an instant solution to career direction.**

4. **Pay attention to areas with low scores, as well as high scores.** It's good to also be clear on what you don't enjoy!

5. **Focus on key points and patterns in the results.** If you find a career track that looks promising, proceed with objectivity! Make sure it's consistent with other elements of the Magic F.I.T.™

6. **Develop a list of two or three strong possibilities for career direction.** Look for areas that pique your interest and excite you.

7. **Take time to thoroughly research those two or three possibilities.** Read up on the industry, talk to people experienced in the field, and "taste test" the profession if possible via volunteer work or job shadowing. Ask yourself: Does the career align with your motivated skills, interests, and values? Will additional education be required? If so, what are the pros and cons and the options for obtaining them? What are the salary ranges, including salaries for the top 5 percent of performers? What career paths are available beyond your entry point? Is the industry in an up or down trend? Does the organizational culture of most companies in the industry match your profile? How does it align with your purpose and values? What are the pros and cons and do the pros outweigh the cons? (See table 3.7, "Comparing Your Career Options," for ideas on how to capture and compare this data in a spreadsheet format.)

8. **Look for careers that hit the "sweet spot" in the F.I.T.**—it's the place where Functional skills, Industry/Interests, Things that matter, Fulfillment, Identity, and Type ALL overlap.

*(continued)*

*(continued)*

9. **Experiment with mixing and matching F.I.T. elements.** For instance, if you're clear that preserving natural ecosystems is your mission in life (Fulfillment) and you excel at investigation (Function), consider a biologist position with the federal government. If you are also passionate about birding (Industry/Interest), consider a research position with the Audubon Society.

10. **If after thorough research you're still not crystal clear on the right path for you, choose the career direction that most aligns with your purpose and values (Things that matter).** You can fine-tune your career down the road to make it a better fit.

## Table 3.7: Comparing Your Career Options

| Occupation | Skills Needed | Market Situation | Income Range | Values Fit | Pros | Cons |
|---|---|---|---|---|---|---|
| Occupational Therapist | New degree required | Good demand | $36–55,000 | Fits beautifully with my life-purpose statement. | Market situation; always wanted to help people in this way. | I'd be on-site, which wouldn't give me the flexibility I desire. Have to go back to school. |
| Grant Writer | Business writing, research skills—can do this now | Good demand | $50,000+ | I could do grant writing for organizations that would be in synch with my life-purpose statement. | Can be home-based; no commute; gives me more time with my kids. | Requires business development to bring in projects if I go self-employed route. |
| Filmmaker | Requires additional training | Jobs are rare as hen's teeth | $40K–$millions if you hit it big | Not sure I'd be comfortable with the culture. | Very creative environment. | Difficult to break into. Takes years to get career rolling. |

# Coaching Questions to Decide on the Best Career Direction

To evaluate the results of your research, answer some of these questions:

- What did you like most about what you learned? What triggered your interest?

- What did you like least about what you've learned? What left you yawning? What sent up a red flag?

- What new insights, choices, or decisions have you come to?

- What aspects of this career are in sync with your purpose and career values? How?

- If you visualize yourself in this position, how does it feel?

- Are you inspired to do this?

- What would it take to be able to say "yes" to this new direction? What steps can you take to make that happen?

- How does this compare to the status quo? What benefits would the new position bring you? Do the time, cost, and difficulty of training outweigh the benefit?

- Recognize there are always a gain and a loss with any transition. What conflicting feelings might you be having now (for example, self-doubt and trepidation mixed with excitement and anticipation)?

- What positives would you lose in leaving your old career (friends, benefits, and so on)? Can they be plugged in somehow to the new choice?

- What will the ramp-up time be? How long before you're productive?

- If this is a stepping-stone toward something bigger, what time period do you see yourself committing to this position (for example, "I'm willing to do tech support for one year because I need a job, but if there aren't opportunities for promotion at the end of that time, I will consider moving elsewhere")?

- On a scale of 1 to 10, how okay are you with this decision? What would it take to make it a 10 —Volunteering? Taking a class? Giving yourself a trial period? Giving yourself permission to go with it even though you don't have all the answers? Changing one aspect of the career to suit you better? Knowing that you can tweak the job as you go along?

- Based on what you now know, and if you had no restrictions holding you back, what would your ideal job be?

- Do you believe you can do this? (If not, ask yourself the following: What have you done in the past that was similar? What was in place in order to make that take place? How can you put similar supports in place to undergird you in this next move?)

✦ What works best NOW?

✦ What's at the root of not making a decision? What steps can you take to remove that root?

✦ How will you know when it is right for you to make a decision?

✦ If you're not thoroughly certain about this, can you give yourself permission to start "down the trail," recognizing that there might be some side roads that you'll come across that you wouldn't otherwise have known about had you never started down the path?

✦ What declaration can you make about pursuing this new opportunity?

Recall from chapter 2 that if you are a Career Explorer, this discovery process might take some time. Invest the time now; the payoffs can last a lifetime.

## Decisions, Decisions

One of these strategies might be helpful if you're having trouble making a decision about which career direction to follow:

- **Decision Tree:** Sketch a tree that shows large branches for each of the major career options; smaller branches coming off of the main branches are labeled with words that describe the potential opportunities associated with each major option. Which branch is the fullest or has the most appealing "fruit"? Perhaps the option you desire the most is high up in the tree, difficult to reach. What hindrances are in the way, and how will you remove them?

- **Guided by Goosebumps:** You probably know the feeling—those tingly goosebumps that appear on your arms or neck, telling you things are happening even though you can't see them. As you explore your options, pay attention to when the goosebumps appear. If you're torn between two options, goosebumps might just be what tip the scales.

- **The Beanie Ball Cap:** Remember the little ball caps with a rotor atop that twirls in a breeze? Pretend you're wearing one! The rotor whirls at full speed when your head and heart love a particular career direction, but it freezes at a standstill when the direction is totally unworkable. Which option buzzes your beanie the most?

- **Shock Therapy:** Heaven forbid, if you were given the news that you had six months to live, what kind of career would you choose?

- **The Great Debate:** Pretend you're arguing both the pros and cons of your career options. Which option wins?

- **Imaginary Roundtable:** Assemble an imaginary roundtable of wise, impartial advisors and ask their advice on which direction is best.

- **The Butler:** An English butler is at your disposal. He approaches you with two silver platters, one in each hand. Career option "A" is in his left hand, and "B" in his right. Which platter do you reach for?

- **Guided Imagery:** After bringing yourself to a state of deep and total relaxation, imagine yourself in a totally safe and calm environment. A benevolent being, perhaps an angel, clothed in white, approaches. You feel a sense of peace in his/her presence. The being gives you a present that is representative of your future career direction. You slowly unwrap it and discover a _____. You thank the gift giver and ask for wisdom in using your gift wisely.

# Finalize Your Magic F.I.T.™

After completing the seven steps in the Magic F.I.T.™ system, use table 3.8 to pull it all together. For easy future reference, transfer each of your responses from Steps 1 through 7 to the following table.

### Table 3.8: My Magic F.I.T.™ Elements

|  | F | I | T |
|---|---|---|---|
| External | Step 1:<br>**F**unction | Step 2:<br>**I**ndustry/<br>Interests | Step 3:<br>**T**hings That<br>Matter |
|  |  |  |  |
|  |  |  |  |
|  |  |  |  |
| Internal | Step 4:<br>**F**ulfillment | Step 5:<br>**I**dentity | Step 6:<br>**T**ype |
|  |  |  |  |
|  |  |  |  |
|  |  |  |  |
| Step 7:<br>Salary | Low-End Salary<br>$ _____ | Industry Average<br>$ _____ | Dream-Job Salary<br>$ _____ |

# Create Your Focus Statement

Based on the work you've completed in finding your Magic F.I.T.™, you're ready to write your focus statement for your next position. The benefits of doing so are threefold:

- **Motivation:** Your focus combines the unique ingredients that will energize and motivate you throughout your job search.

- **Meaning:** Your focus hones in on what *you* want, as opposed to striving after the dreams of someone else (be it parents, spouse, friends, or co-workers).

- **Map:** Your focus will keep you on course as you make decisions about what interview opportunities to pursue.

I've provided an example focus statement to help get you started.

*I am committed to targeting opportunities that will use my branch management skills in the field of financial services, specializing in mutual funds, where I can develop management and marketing strategies that will grow shareholder value and investors' net worth. This type of position is in sync with my personality preferences for "intuiting" and "thinking" (seeing the big picture, brainstorming, making decisions based on logical facts) and meets my core values and needs of intellectual stimulation, leadership, logic, and monetary reward (with salary in the range of $75,000–$90,000).*

Here's how the target statement relates to the Magic F.I.T.™:

---

I am committed to targeting opportunities that will use my

[step 1, Functional abilities]   branch management skills

[step 2, Industry] in the field of  financial services, specializing

in [step 2, Interests]   mutual funds, where I can

[step 4, Fulfillment]   develop management and marketing strategies that will grow shareholder value and investors' net worth.

This type of position is in sync with my personality preferences for

[step 6, personality Type]  "intuiting" and "thinking" (seeing the big picture, brainstorming, making decisions based on logical facts)

and is consistent with my self-image [step 5, Identity] and values [step 3, Things That Matter], such as

intellectual stimulation, leadership, logic, and monetary reward (with salary in the range of $_____ to $_____).

---

In the following template, write your own target statement using the information you filled in earlier in table 3.8.

I am committed to targeting opportunities that will use my
[Functional abilities]

_____

[Industry] in the field of _____,

specializing in [Interests] _____where I can

[Fulfillment]_____

_____.

This type of position is in synch with my personality preferences for
[personality Type]_____

_____

_____

_____

and is consistent with my self-image [Identity] and values [Things That
Matter], such as

_____, _____,

_____, _____, and

_____, as well as my salary needs of

$_____ to $_____.

When networking, you might want to use just the first sentence in your focus statement to help others know what you are looking for. Omit the second sentence and reserve salary for discussions with hiring managers. In chapter 5, we'll look more closely at developing sound bites for networking and interviewing. In the meantime, this focus statement will help keep you on course as you evaluate new job opportunities.

# Chapter Wrap-Up

Remember that achieving career contentment is a process. It doesn't happen overnight. It requires honing in on and weaving together all six of the Magic F.I.T.™ elements. Gaining a new awareness of each item puts you on the right path. And, if you've fleshed out answers to each of the seven steps, you'll be far ahead of the competition for your target job.

An intentional focus on these F.I.T. elements will allow you to be "radically rewarded and enthusiastically engaged in work that adds value to others." The final four words in that definition of career purpose—adds value to others—contain an important truth. Your work must bring value to others, specifically your company, colleagues, or customers, so that your career is in synch with marketplace demands. Chapter 5 outlines how to add value so that interviewers will view you as a competitive candidate.

## 10 Quick Tips for Focusing on Your Magic F.I.T.™

1. **Step 1—Find the right <u>F</u>unction.** Functions represent job titles and tasks, such as engineer and graphic artist or market research and product development.

2. **Step 2—Identify your ideal <u>I</u>ndustry and <u>I</u>nterests.** Industry refers to where you will apply your functional skills, whereas Interests tap a specialty area that you connect with or are especially enthusiastic about. For instance, a nurse might target oncology as an Industry and then focus on pediatric oncology as a special Interest within oncology.

3. **Step 3—Think about the <u>T</u>hings That Matter.** When what you do from 8 to 5 aligns with your values and needs, you will find greater energy, motivation, and career satisfaction. Employers value employees with energy and motivation. What motivates you? Autonomy? Authority? Influence? Monetary reward? Recognition? Teamwork? Variety? Know the top 10 things that matter most to you in your career.

4. **Step 4—Define <u>F</u>ulfillment.** Fulfillment transforms your job from paycheck to purpose. Fulfillment, or purpose, is the reason why you work. To define fulfillment, pay attention to the "tingle factor"—that goose-bumpy, addictive feeling that comes when you do something you absolutely love. Be sure to pair your purpose with market demands to ensure that you don't compromise your paycheck for purpose!

5. **Step 5—Enhance your <u>I</u>dentity.** Your identity, what you believe about yourself, is directly linked to the type of position you'll target. You are usually capable of accomplishing much more than you believe you can. Raise the bar on beliefs! Blast through self-imposed limitations. Adopt beliefs that serve you better and allow you to move forward in your career.

6. **Step 6—Know your personality <u>T</u>ype.** Understanding your type allows you to pursue positions that complement, rather than clash with, your personality preferences. The basic tenets of personality type measure four scales: Energy—the focus of your energy and attention flows to the outer world or is directed toward inner experiences and reflection (Extroversion or Introversion); Perception—your preference for taking in information via "what is" or "what could be" (Sensing or iNtuiting); Judgment—your preference for making decisions based on facts and logic or personal/social values (Thinking or Feeling); and Orientation—your preference for coming to closure or remaining open to more information (Judging or Perceiving).

7. **Step 7—Set your salary range.** In addition to the six F.I.T. steps, your last step adds a final "S," for salary, so that your target truly FITS! Identify a range for your target position, listing the industry average for your position, a low-end salary figure that you would be comfortable with (one that won't make you feel as though you're being taken advantage of), and a top-end, dream-job number.

8. **Avoid "fish fever"**—jumping indiscriminately at any opportunity that pops onto the radar screen.

9. **Commit to the long haul.** Finding the perfect Magic F.I.T.™ will take time. Keep an aerial perspective on your progress, proceed with small steps, and be patient with yourself. First, be clear about your functional strengths (step 1 in the process), and then systematically work through the remaining steps.

10. **Remember the benefits of the Magic F.I.T.™** An intentional focus on the F.I.T. elements will allow you to leverage your time by pursuing the right opportunities, to impress interviewers by knowing what you want, to gain confidence targeting positions you can be enthusiastic about, and, ultimately, to land a position that is radically rewarding.

## Magical Coaching Questions

What might tempt you to jump at the wrong opportunity?

_____

_____

_____

Which of the Magic F.I.T.™ elements had you already incorporated into your prior positions?

_____

_____

_____

Which Magic F.I.T.™ elements will you focus on incorporating into future positions?

_____

_____

_____

What system or reminder can you put in place to ensure that you weigh those new elements when considering new opportunities?

_____

_____

_____

# Chapter 4

# Capture Your Value with "Smart" Success Stories

*The basic building block of good communications is the feeling that every human being is unique and of value.*

—Author Unknown

E = MC² captures Einstein's brilliant theory of relativity. I've translated that memorable formula into job search terminology so that *you* can be brilliant in your quest for new employment! In the realm of job search, E = MC² reads like this:

**Employment = Mechanics × Commitment-Squared**

Let's explore what each of those terms means to you:

- **Employment:** Receiving, and accepting, a job offer that is in sync with your career goals

- **Mechanics:** Applying savvy strategies, systems, and tactics—the ins and outs—of job search

- **Commitment-Squared:** Holding optimum mindset, emotional energy, and intelligent attitude throughout the job search process.

If you've purchased this book, I'll assume that employment—a great career—is your goal. To get that, you'll need to put into practice the nuts and bolts of job search and interviewing, which I've referred to as "mechanics." Add to that a double portion of commitment. Together, these ingredients translate not just to employment, but to career success—radical rewards and enthusiastic engagement in work that adds value to others.

In chapter 3 you began to apply some of the mechanics of job search by targeting the right position via the Magic F.I.T.™ exercises. This was the first step on your job search journey. Some of the next steps that you're now ready to walk through include the following:

- Developing success stories and sound bites for your job search campaign
- Targeting companies and networking to identify opportunities and openings
- Communicating your value and return-on-investment to hiring managers as you network and interview

Chapters 4 and 5 are devoted to the mechanics of preparing the success stories and sound bites that will make you stand out with style. Chapter 6 will take a look at the "Commitment-Squared" element of the employment formula, giving you a mindset that is a critical piece of the puzzle *and* can magnetically attract more opportunities to you, as well as keep your attitude afloat should there be some unexpected twists and turns down the road. If you sense that you could use a shot of attitude adrenalin right now, feel free to jump ahead to chapter 6 and then come back to this chapter. I'd like you to feel fresh when tackling chapters 4 and 5 because they will be the *foundation* for preparing your networking scripts and interview responses. The work you do now will enable you to avoid the most common downfall of many candidates: talking to networking contacts and interviewers unprepared.

# Conveying Value to Employers

Secret #4 from chapter 1 holds the key to landing an offer. Offering profit, or value, should be at the heart of your job search message. Use it to describe how you'll work in a manner that will make your employer a better, stronger, more profitable company. Value can be woven into your interview responses at every turn. Three methods for conveying value include

- Linking your past successes and future solutions to employer buying motivators
- Demonstrating a return on investment (ROI)
- Emphasizing benefits instead of features of your qualifications

Let's look at each of these three methods more closely.

## The Employer's Motivation to "Buy"

"Walk a mile in my moccasins." This old Indian adage can help you adopt an employer-focused mindset. Consider the hiring manager's perspective in what will motivate him or her to engage your services as an employee. Yes, the hiring manager will be thinking about how you can benefit the company and the team. But she is also thinking about how you will help her individually, whether it is to lighten the load in her inbox or solve a pressing issue. Whatever the situation, recognize that she will want you to make her look good. You can approach the interview with confidence, knowing that you (unlike many candidates) understand her concerns about getting the job done and keeping costs down while keeping morale up.

Numerous "Employer Buying Motivators" drive business. These 10 buying motivators are key to why hiring decisions are made:

- Buying Motivator #1: Make Money
- Buying Motivator #2: Save Money
- Buying Motivator #3: Save Time
- Buying Motivator #4: Make Work Easier
- Buying Motivator #5: Solve a Specific Problem
- Buying Motivator #6: Be More Competitive
- Buying Motivator #7: Build Relationships, Brand, and Image with Internal/External Customers, Vendors, and the Public
- Buying Motivator #8: Expand Business
- Buying Motivator #9: Attract New Customers
- Buying Motivator #10: Retain Customers

In subsequent chapters, you'll have a chance to explore how you can link your résumé and networking/interviewing language to these 10 buying motivators.

## What's Your ROI?

ROI, short for *return on investment,* is a business term widely used by companies to determine how quickly their decision to invest in new equipment, advertising, or an expansion will pay for itself. In the case of a hiring decision, the employer is investing in salary, benefits, training, work space, and equipment.

In the corporate world, savvy career professionals concentrate on generating a return on investment for their employers. For instance, a top sales performer can show that a $125,000 salary will be justified by her ability to bring in $500,000 in new sales contracts. A materials manager might find methods to reduce waste or recycle scrap, which may add up to a six-figure savings. A production line worker might make a suggestion that, when implemented, leads to a spike in productivity, which can be tied to the bottom line. Whatever your role, challenge yourself to look for ways to boost your employer's success, and then document that success.

## Benefits vs. Features

As with most people, hiring managers are tuned to radio station WIFM, or "what's in it for me?" Benefits explain what's in it for them! High-paid advertising copywriters know that benefits sell, whereas features can put you to sleep. Let's compare features and benefits for a minute by using career coaching services as an example.

A few features that a career coach might have:

- Certified Career Management Coach
- Nationally Certified Résumé Writer
- Founder of Career Coach Academy
- Executive Director of Career Masters Institute

You'll note that the features are title-oriented. Yawn. Features might carry some weight, but they don't really describe the benefit of what a career coach can do.

On the other hand, these statements describe benefits:

- Helping people who feel stuck in their careers uncover options that can move them from drudgery to dream job.
- Equipping job seekers with insider strategies that shorten the time it takes to find a new job.
- Helping people eliminate the guesswork and frustration from career transition and job search.
- Helping job seekers who wish networking would just go away to find self-marketing methods that are both comfortable and compelling.
- Lighting a fire under the dream you've relegated to the back burner, helping you break through roadblocks and find meaningful life-work…purpose produces passion!

The preceding benefits use carefully chosen language to address needs that a prospective client might have. Part of your goal in writing success stories is to address the needs, or pain points, of a prospective employer. To do so, concentrate on knitting in benefit-oriented words such as these verbs and nouns:

| | | |
|---|---|---|
| Accelerate | Grow | Relief |
| Build | Guarantee | Relieve |
| Create | Help | Save |
| Decrease | Honor | Secret |
| Discover | How To | Steps |
| Eliminate | Improve | Strategies |
| Enhance | Increase | Strengthen |
| Equip | Less | Techniques |
| Find | More | Tips |
| Formula | Numbers | Uncover |
| Free | Proven | |
| Gain | Reduce | |

How many of the words from the list did you see in my benefit statements?

---

### S.O.S.

The familiar Morse code of S.O.S. stands for *Save Our Ship*. Although most companies that you will target aren't necessarily sinking, they will likely need some help bailing out from an overflow of work or plugging a hole caused by someone's absence.

When writing your success stories and sound bites, offer your own S.O.S. Response, in the form of *Solutions Or Services*. Positioning yourself as a provider of solutions or services will give your candidacy favored status.

---

In the remainder of this chapter, you'll see how each of these three techniques—linking to buying motivators, demonstrating a return on investment, and focusing on benefits—are woven into example success stories and sound bites.

# Inventorying Your Success Stories

In this section, you'll take stock of your success stories. When I give the upcoming exercise to my clients, I sometimes hear, "I don't have any success stories." They assume that if they didn't single-handedly initiate and execute a project of monumental proportions, they have no success stories. However, *any* information that helps support your candidacy qualifies as a success story. Although you'll want the majority of your success stories to have a positive outcome, it's also acceptable to include a few anecdotes that describe an unsuccessful attempt or lesson learned. Employers will be suspicious if you can't admit to having met with some failure or disappointment over the course of your career. Later, you'll identify and think through your response to potential negatives so that you're ready with a positive response in the interview. The key is to *leverage the lessons learned*. In doing so, the situation can be categorized as a success!

Everyone can uncover success stories, especially when this definition is adopted:

> **Success Story:** An anecdote or account providing evidence that you have the knowledge, hard and soft skills, and motivation to excel in the target job.

Let's expand on the elements in this definition. *Anecdotes*—short descriptions of a relevant incident—can be interesting, amusing, or biographical in nature. *Knowledge* can be gained through employment, education (class activities, group projects, case studies), and unpaid experience (internships, work study, job shadowing). Even community service, team or sports involvement, and parenting can contribute to your knowledge bank. *Hard skills* refer to your technical skills and talents, whereas *soft skills* are those less-tangible but often-important interpersonal and communication skills. Beyond knowledge and skills, employers today are also interested in whether you have the inner drive and ambition to do the job.

*Motivation* stems from being rewarded and engaged by work that aligns with your Magic F.I.T.™ (see chapter 3). The verb *excel*—the final part of the definition of a success story—implies that you are bottom-line oriented, with a commitment to delivering results that help add revenue, reduce costs, or boost productivity.

Each of these examples illustrates a success story that conveys value:

- **Materials Management Success Story (materials coordinator describing a reduction in order-cycle time):** In my last position as a materials coordinator at Lanco Foods, I participated on a team that cut our order cycle time by about 75 percent. We analyzed turnkey processes and identified two key areas for improvement: order placement and payment closure. I then took the lead on writing new procedures for order placement and taught our customer service team how to implement the procedures. Within six months, our order cycle was shortened from 45 days to 11 days.

- **Marketing Success Story (retail marketing specialist describing an increased return on trade spending):** I inherited a retail marketing specialist position where the return-on-investment on trade spending was below the target of 10:1—it was actually at 8:1, and we ended up delivering a 50 percent increase. After analyzing syndicated data and interviewing marketing specialists at other stores to learn what they were doing to get higher returns, I initiated a campaign to increase the displays in some of our top customers. I prepared proposals and accompanied sales reps as they made presentations to store managers. Within three months, my action plan allowed us to exceed the benchmark in trade spending with a return ratio of 12:1 versus the target of 10:1.

- **Secretarial Success Story (executive secretary to litigation attorney describing an initiative that increased her boss' billable hours):** I noticed that the attorney whom I supported was frustrated about keeping up her billable client hours. After observing her typical days and thinking about where I could help, I approached her about letting me handle some of her e-mail, which seemed to be stealing a lot of time from her day. She agreed, so I designed a series of boilerplate auto-responses that allowed me to respond to approximately 30 percent of her e-mail. This action allowed her to reclaim an hour or more a day in billable time. At $250 an hour, this translated to almost $6,000 per month in additional revenue. The attorney mentioned our system to the managing partner, and we're now in the process of databasing those auto-responses so that all of the legal secretaries can use them to lighten the administrative load of the rest of the attorneys.

- **Event Planning Success Story (stay-at-home mom transitioning back into the work force describing her lifelong skills in event planning):** I'd like to tell you about how I recently generated a 200 percent increase in revenue through my event planning—I'm certain I was born with these skills, so I'll first share a quick story about my earliest recollection of planning an event. When I was only five years old, I invited four of my neighbor friends for a dog party. I unknowingly covered all the event-planning bases: program, theme, publicity, food and beverage, etc. Everyone was to bring their dog, with the plan that we would train them to do a trick, have them wear party hats, and feed them doggie treats. I had a 101 Dalmatians theme, advertised the event with posters on my front-yard tree, and talked my mother into baking cookies and making punch. Several decades later, I'm the one that the principal of Johnson Middle School calls on to help with the Fall Festival, our chief fund-raising event of the year. I've expanded the event significantly to include in-kind and cash donations from local businesses, entertainment by television soap stars, and additional revenue centers, such as the silent auction. Before I became involved, our highest earnings were only $4,500; this past year, we raised $14,000.

**Teacher Success Story (kindergarten teacher describing her success with language arts):** I was challenged by teaching a kindergarten class at Washington Elementary, where 80 percent of the students were from non-English–speaking homes. I addressed the needs of emergent readers through phonemic awareness, phonics, concepts of print, decoding, guided reading, and shared reading. Writing skills were cultivated through modeled, shared, interactive, and journal writing, and I introduced spelling at the appropriate developmental level. By the end of the year, all of the students were at or above grade level in their reading scores, excited about "graduating," and confident about entering the first grade. My success with these students led to my principal asking me to share my strategies with the other kindergarten teachers.

## Questions to Elicit Success Stories

Answers come when you are asked the right questions. Here are 25 questions to ask yourself that will help percolate great ideas for your success stories (recent graduates and individuals returning to the work force can find additional questions in *Interview Magic*):

1. What are you most proud of in your career?

2. What are you most proud of in each of your past positions?

3. What challenge or crisis did you face on the job and what was your approach for solving each situation?

4. In what way did you help your employer generate more revenue?

5. In what way did you help your employer save money?

6. In what way did you help your employer increase productivity?

7. What was the most interesting suggestion or project you initiated?

8. When were you complimented by a supervisor, co-worker, or customer?

9. What positive comments (or ratings) were documented in your performance evaluations?

10. When do people say to you, "You are amazing…you make it look so easy!" or "How do you do that!?"

11. What skills or talents are you especially known for?

12. What kinds of work activities cause you to lose track of time?

13. What special projects or teams have you worked on?

14. How were goals and productivity measured on the job?

15. When did you go above and beyond the call of duty?

16. What do you do that your co-workers don't do? What would happen if you weren't on the job?

17. What would others point to as evidence of your success?

18. When did your actions motivate or influence others to do something that they initially did not want to do?

19. When did you have to make a tough decision under pressure?

20. Under what circumstances did you display character and integrity?

21. How did you overcome a challenging situation with a co-worker or team member?

22. When did you have to quickly learn new information or skills? How did you go about this?

23. When did you use your verbal communication skills to influence or improve a situation with a co-worker, team member, or customer?

24. When did you diplomatically address a politically delicate situation?

25. How did you go about making a presentation to internal or external stake-holders? What was the outcome?

# Using the SMART Format to Answer Behavioral Interview Questions

Many interviewers prefer that you deliver your responses to behavioral interview questions using a format that first outlines what was happening, then what you did about it, followed by what resulted from the actions. Common variations on this format include the following:

- **STAR:** **S**ituation/**T**ask, **A**ction, **R**esult

- **CAR:** **C**hallenge, **A**ction, **R**esult

- **PAR:** **P**roblem, **A**ction, **R**esolution

In coaching people for networking and interviewing, I've found that a variation on this format called the SMART Story™ works well. SMART stands for

- **S**ituation and **M**ore

- **A**ction

⚹ **R**esults

⚹ **T**ie-in or **T**heme

A SMART Story™ will allow you to craft your interview responses with a definitive beginning, a middle, and a dynamite ending and provide the many details that interviewers are hungry to hear about. It also is unique in that the final step positions you to neatly link the response back to the employer's competency question, inquire further into the employer's needs, and focus the conversation on how you can *do* the job instead of simply *auditioning* for the job. Here's how it breaks out:

⚹ **Situation and More:** Frame the story with contextual details, offering specific numbers about the situation. What was the specific situation you were faced with? Use numbers to describe who and what was involved? Where and when did it occur? What was the impact of the situation? What was the timeframe for the story?

⚹ **Action:** What specific action did you take to tackle the task, overcome the challenge, or resolve the issue? If others were closely involved, how did you interact with them? What were your thoughts or decision-making process? What was your specific role in relation to the team?

⚹ **Results:** Essential to your success story are numbers-oriented, bottom-line results. They will help you convey your return-on-investment (ROI) value and give you leverage in salary negotiations.

- What measurable outcome did you achieve? Think beyond your own work role to how others were impacted, including your boss, your team, your department, your company, your customers, your community, or your industry.

- If it was a group effort, what measurable outcome did the group achieve or contribute to? Did you contribute to a 5 percent increase in productivity; support a team that met or exceeded goal by 9 percent in a difficult economy; participate in an effort that improved customer satisfaction scores; collaborate with team members to accomplish work with 25 percent less staff; or provide ideas that halted a conflict or impasse that had held up progress?

- If the outcome wasn't rosy, what conclusions did you reach or what positives did you learn from the experience?

- Compare your performance. You can make comparisons to a variety of numbers, including your prior work performance, the company's past record, the industry standard, or your competitor's average.

⚹ **Tie-in and Theme:** Use a question or statement to link this story back to important issues or link it to a theme of key competencies sought by the employer. Statements might convey enthusiasm or knowledge gained:

- "I found that I thrive in these sorts of situations, as they give me a chance to use my problem-solving skills," or

- "I learned that it's important to regularly communicate progress status to every member of the team," or

- "My supervisors have commented that my problem-solving, customer relations, and innovation were key to being a good fit for the position," or

- "From the conversation I had with one of your vendors, it sounds like my strengths in vendor relations would be of help."

An occasional question can also be effective in tying the story back to the employer's needs. For instance,

- "Would you like additional detail or another example?" or

- "How will this experience relate to your current needs?" or

- "Is the department encountering similar opportunities [or challenges] to the one I just described?"

The SMART Story™ format will help you structure your writing. It will take an investment of time to develop these stories, so keep in mind the payoff:

Interviewers will be impressed because you offered tangible evidence of your success stories.

Interviewers will remember you over other candidates who provided vague, unspecific responses.

You will feel more comfortable and confident during interviews because you have tip-of-your-tongue evidence that documents your ability to do the job.

You will be fully prepared to answer behavioral interview questions, which require tangible, step-by-step details about your behavior in past situations.

Note the numerous facts and figures included in the following SMART Stories™:

## SMART Story™

**Situation and More:**                                      **My role:** *Production Worker*

**Where:** *Wamco Manufacturing, my current employer*

**When/Timeframe:** *January through March of this year*

**Who else was involved or impacted:** *Production shift team of 10 and maintenance mechanic*

**What was the task or challenge:** *I managed to work with outdated equipment that continually broke down and caused long down times. The company had been hit hard financially due to industry issues and didn't have the funds to invest in new equipment or even special maintenance.*

**Action:** **What was your thought process? What steps did you take? What decisions were made? Describe the sequence.**

*At first, we waited for the maintenance mechanic to come to fix things— sometimes that took awhile because this guy had to cover our facility and another facility across town, since they had laid off the mechanic for the plant across town. If he was working on a problem at the second facility, it would take him hours to get to us. Sometimes, the boss would let us go home for the day. I hate waiting around, so after about the third or fourth breakdown, I talked to the maintenance mechanic and asked him if I could help. At first he said no. Then I asked him if I could just watch what he did. He said yes. It wasn't too complicated. So the next breakdown, the mechanic let me work with him on the repairs. Later on, when things broke down on the vacuum-seal line, I was able to work on it.*

**Results:** **Use numbers to relate your results.**

*There were at least three times this past month that I had the problem fixed, and we were back up and running in less than an hour. In the past, it might have taken two or three hours to fix it. Our manager wants a goal of 300 units per day, so in a few cases, we kept our production numbers up even with the breakdown. This past month, we made our production goals, which is the first time in several months. Some other factors came into play as well, but part of it was the repair work I did.*

**Tie-in/ Theme:** *I know that productivity is key to a profitable operation. Are your productivity numbers where you'd like them to be?*

(Competency Theme: *Initiative, problem-solving, teamwork, mechanical ability*)

## SMART Story™

**Situation and More:**                    **My role:** *Office Manager*

**Where:** *Inco Insurance, my current employer*

**When/Timeframe:** *March through September of this year*

**Who else was involved or impacted:** *Employees (25 claims processors and 5 support staff)*

*(continued)*

*(continued)*

**What was the task or challenge:** *My challenge was to stop losses of more than $1,000 per month. I didn't realize that the systems I put in place would not only stop those losses but increase our productivity. Here's what happened…*

**Action:** **What was your thought process? What steps did you take? What decisions were made? Describe the sequence.**

*I was new to the position and familiarizing myself with expenses. I compared and analyzed office expense figures with several prior years and realized that, even though our headcount was down by 25 percent, our expenses were up by almost 30 percent. None of our vendors had implemented any price increases, so I began to look for other reasons. I noticed that CDs and boxes of file folders seemed to be "walking off by themselves." In one of our weekly group meetings—something new I implemented to improve teamwork—I explained that one of our goals included cost controls. To help meet that goal, a new check-out system would be implemented for items valued in excess of $20, but that incidentals would be on an "honor system." I posted a bar graph in the supply room reflecting volume in use of supplies over the past six months, along with reduction goals for each ensuing month. I asked staff members for suggestions on incentives and decided what would be feasible. When we reached our monthly goals, I rewarded staff with their choice of an early-dismissal day or a catered box-lunch party.*

**Results:** **Use numbers to relate your results.**

*Supply costs were not only reduced more than 35 percent, there was greater camaraderie among the team. It led to the claims processors openly sharing helpful resources and making suggestions, some of which were implemented and helped improve our productivity numbers by about 15 percent.*

**Tie-in/ Theme:** *It confirmed to me that communicating clear objectives to staff, along with soliciting their input, is a wise management policy.*

*(Competency Theme: Communications, problem solving, analytical, motivator)*

## SMART Story™

**Situation and More:**         **My role:** *Vice President, Business Development Manager*

**Where:** *State Bank & Trust*

**When:** *The current calendar year, June 200x–May 200x*

**Who else was involved or impacted:** *A 30-branch Northern State Community Banking District*

**What was the task or challenge:** *I enjoy telling my "how-I-went-bald" story! It started with being given the charge by my Senior VP to turn around a two-year history of double-digit declining revenues for the district. At the time, the district was ranked last among 17 for revenue performance and had been through four business development managers over the course of three years.*

**Action:** **What was your thought process? What steps did you take? What decisions were made? Describe the sequence.**

*Here's the storyboard. I piloted a new business-development program for the district, which included creating sales strategies for a full complement of products and services (commercial loans, trust and investment services, cash management services, retirement and depository accounts, government guarantee programs, computerized banking, and alliance banking). I scheduled a two-day meeting for the 30 branch managers in the district, and I used a very motivational "All-Star" theme. At the meeting, I created a vision for what could be accomplished, laid out the program, and then used interactive train-the-trainer systems so that they could teach the strategies to 150+ sales reps in the district. I laid down the challenge, telling them that if we reached our goal early, I would shave my head! I had already cleared this with the Senior VP.*

**Results:** **Use numbers to relate your results.**

*Bottom line, we secured 44 new customers with $16+ million in loan commitments approved, added nearly $4 million in deposits, and secured first-time fee revenue of $162,000 from establishing new international business. We broke all records for loan and deposit growth in the district's 30-year history and boosted the district's ranking from #17 among 17 to #2 in less than two years. And, yes, I was proud to be bald for a time!*

**Tie-in/ Theme:** *In visiting some of your branches, I had a few ideas about how fee-based revenue could be introduced.*

(Competency Theme: *Leadership, motivator, innovation, strategic, analytical, communication*)

## SMART Story™

**Situation and More:**　　　　　　　　　　　　　　**My role:** *Mother*

**Where:** *Home*

**When:** *The past six years*

**Who else was involved or impacted:** *Children, husband*

*(continued)*

*(continued)*

**What was the task or challenge:** *Adapting to my new role as mother after having had a record-setting career in sales.*

| | |
|---|---|
| **Action:** | **What was your thought process? What steps did you take? What decisions were made? Describe the sequence.** |
| | *I remember the mind shift I had to go through when I first had my daughter. It felt odd to be out of the business world, where I had been regularly recognized for my sales abilities. Being so goal-driven, I knew that I had to have goals in place for myself. The goals I started with may not sound too exciting, but they were appropriate goals for that time of my life—things like not losing my patience when the baby had a fussy night—no small feat when you're seriously sleep deprived. A few years later, I graduated to bigger, more lofty goals, like "selling" broccoli to my 4-year-old!* |
| **Results:** | **Use numbers to relate your results.** |
| | *Bottom line, I recognized that an innate value for me is performance— setting and achieving goals, for every aspect of my life, whether personal or professional. It's what allowed me to rank among the top 10 percent in a region of 46 while in my last position at Cosamar, Inc.* |
| **Tie-in/ Theme:** | *I know that my initiative and problem-solving skills will serve me well in the position you need to fill. Could you tell me a little more about your clients?* |

*(Competency Theme: Initiative, problem-solving, goal-oriented)*

# Writing Your Success Stories

Use the blank forms that follow to capture your stories. Be generous with the contextual details. In the form, you'll see a Competency & Keyword area. Leave it blank for now. You'll come back later to complete this section. Don't be concerned about finding the perfect wording or magic words at this stage. And, remember that you'll be delivering these stories in verbal rather than written format. That means you don't have to be concerned about perfect punctuation or syntax as you write. Spoken language is far more flexible and forgiving than written language.

Before you get started on your stories, I want to make a somewhat unusual request. I'd like the first SMART Story™ that you write to be about your current job search situation. Write about the Situation and More in past tense, such as: "I conducted a job search while still employed, working a 60-hour work week," or "I conducted a job search during a time when my industry had experienced a severe downturn." The Action, again in past tense, might include "I read *Job Search Magic*, developed a solid set of success stories, networked beyond my comfort zone, enlisted the support of a job search group, and said 'no' to certain activities so that I could devote as many as 15 hours a week to my job search while I was also working full time." The Result will be written in present tense. Make it a vision statement, such as "I am employed with one of the leading widget companies in the area, performing radically rewarding work that is in sync with my personality, talents, interests, and values." And, finally, tie it to a Theme: "The experience underscored my self-initiative and perseverance, gave me the ability to learn new research strategies, and sharpened my communication skills. In addition, I have an acute understanding that career success is all about tapping into purpose and passion while providing value to employers."

After you've written about your current situation, you can then dive into your other SMART Stories™.

## Some Points to Guide You

These points will guide you in the writing process.

- **Use the "it's about them, not me" perspective when describing your stories.** This means that, ultimately, your SMART Stories™ must be related to "them"—the employer—and *their needs*. Think in terms of what will motivate the employer to buy, the return-on-investment you offer, and your benefits vs. features.

- **Use the same standards of quality that a judge or jury would accept.** Choose vivid examples, weave in expert testimony (for instance, from customers, co-workers, vendors, or supervisors), and incorporate appropriate statistics.

- **Write SMART Stories™ about your work for each of your past employers.** The heaviest concentration of stories should be about your current or most recent experiences. Pen a SMART Story™ for each recent accomplishment on your résumé.

- **Assign themes to your SMART Stories™ that underscore competencies needed for the target position.** For instance, competencies for a customer service rep might include customer-focused orientation, interpersonal judgment, communication skills, teamwork, problem solving, listening skills/empathy, and initiative.

- **Write SMART Stories™ for non-work experiences.** It is fair game to draw on volunteer work, school experiences, and general life incidents. (If you sense you need additional experience, identify and quickly act on how you can best prepare yourself through reading, attending a course, job-shadowing, volunteering, or taking a relevant part-time job.) Regardless of what point your career life is at, *everyone* should recollect influential or life-altering events throughout youth and adulthood. Write SMART Stories™ about these times.

- **Numbers speak louder than words!** Load the stories with numbers, dollar amounts, productivity measurements, comparisons, and the like. (Be cautious about conveying proprietary or confidential company information.

In these cases, use year-to-date or quarterly comparisons and translate the numbers into percentages.) Be specific and offer proof. Instead of saying, "I learned the program quickly," make it crystal clear with language like, "I studied the manual at night and, in three days, I knew all the basic functions; in two weeks I had mastered several of the advanced features; and by the end of the month, I had experienced operators coming to me to ask how to embed tables into another program."

**Include emotions and feelings.** Yes, feelings. When describing the situation, don't be afraid to include details such as these: "the tension among the team was so serious that people were resigning"; "the morale was at an all-time low"; or "the customer was irate about receiving a mis-shipment that occurred because of our transportation vendor." When writing about emotions or feelings, be mindful *not* to whine or disparage anyone, even through a veiled reference.

**Avoid personal opinions.** You can, however, include the opinion of a supervisor or another objective party. Instead of saying, "I believe my positive outlook really helped keep the customer happy," rely on someone else's opinion: "My supervisor commented in a memo how my outlook helped us save a key account that was in jeopardy of being lost. I have a copy of that memo if you'd like to see it."

**Choose your words carefully.** There might be a tendency to say, "I was chosen to lead this project" when it would be more powerfully worded as, "The VP sought me out, from among 12 eligible specialists, to spearhead this critical project."

**Pace the stories so that each is approximately two to three minutes in length.** Set up the story briefly with facts, place the greatest weight on the action portion of the story, wrap it up with numbers-driven results, and tie it back to the interviewer's needs. Occasionally, vary the delivery by dropping in a result at the front end of the story.

**Make the stories relevant.** You have myriad experiences in your background. Sift through them and select the stories that best substantiate your competencies, knowledge, skills, and motivation to excel in the target job.

Remember to review the 25 questions listed earlier in case you encounter writer's block. Enjoy the process…and may you gain a clearer picture of your value and grow in confidence as the stories emerge!

## Two Heads Are Better Than One!

If you prefer to collaborate on your SMART Stories™, enlist the support of a colleague, mentor, or trusted friend. If you'd like to benefit from working with a professional coach, visit Career Coach Academy (www.CareerCoachAcademy.com) for a list of Certified Career Management Coaches around the country.

## Catalogue Your SMART Stories™

I'd like you to develop a *minimum* of 10 stories. Sound like a lot? I want you to feel fully confident and completely prepared! DBM, a leading global workplace consulting firm, revealed that job seekers participated in five to seven interviews per job opportunity. This is common in a tight economy where jobs are few, applicants are plentiful, and employers are willing to take their time and sort through top candidates to find just the perfect fit. Ten stories will get you started; however, if you anticipate an extended series of interviews, consider writing 20 or more stories so that you have enough "ammunition" to shine throughout the process.

Complete the Situation and More, indicating your role, where (what company), when (what time period and for how long), who was involved or impacted, and what was the specific situation. Describe the Action taken, as well as the Results. Leave the Keywords and Competencies and Potential Interview Questions sections blank for now. You'll fill them in later as link job postings or job descriptions to your various success stories. (You may make multiple photocopies of the SMART Story™ Worksheet.)

---

### SMART Story™ Worksheet

**Situation and More:**

Your role: _____

Where: _____

When: _____

Who else was involved or impacted: _____

_____

What was the task or challenge: _____

_____

_____

**Action:**

What was your thought process? What steps you take? What decisions were made? Describe the sequence.

_____

_____

_____

---

**Results:**
Use numbers to relate your results.

_____

_____

_____

**Tie-in / Theme:**
Keywords & Competencies:    _____

_____

Potential Interview Questions:   _____

_____

# Rate Your Stories

After you've completed writing your SMART Stories™, you can rate each one. For each story, give yourself a point for every item you can say "yes" to on this 10-point quiz.

**My SMART Story™…**

___ 1. Is connected to my target employer's needs, concerns, or issues… conveys the "it's all about them, not me" mindset.

___ 2. Is succinct, with a beginning (situation), middle (action), and end (result and tie-in), using the simplest and fewest words possible.

___ 3. Includes numbers to describe the situation, action, and results.

___ 4. Documents specific competencies relevant to the position.

___ 5. Uses keywords common to the target job or industry.

___ 6. Frames the situation/task with contextual clues, such as the who, what, when, and where, as well as emotions or feelings present (without disparaging or blaming anyone).

___ 7. Provides interviewers with insight into my decision-making process and details the sequential steps I took.

___ 8. Is devoid of my personal opinions or intentions that I did not act on.

___ 9. Is specific, avoids vague phrases, and uses the active rather than passive voice.

___ 10. Is relevant to my career field, giving evidence that I can excel at meeting the deliverables the employer needs.

How did you score? If most of your SMART Stories™ earned a 9 or perfect 10, reward yourself. If your stories scored in the 7–8 range, this is a great start. They will probably require the addition of a few details or numbers to become 9s or 10s. If most of your stories scored 6 or less, take a break and rest your brain a bit. (Chapter 6 offers some ideas for jump-starting yourself.) When you come back, look at the pattern of the stories to determine where they can be reinforced, and edit wherever appropriate.

# Chapter Wrap-Up

You *can* control your success, provided you are "always prepared." You should be feeling like the proverbial Eagle Scout by now! Know that the work you've completed in this chapter is key to "controlling the controllables"—the systems and steps that you can control in the job search process. Evidence-based success stories are at the heart of your interview message. When you're ready to move on, chapter 5 will help you convert your success stories into a cohesive career brand…one that can position you as a trusted expert, attract your ideal employer, and communicate the value of hiring you.

## 10 Quick Tips for Capturing Your Value

1. $E=MC^2$ in a job search context refers to Employment = Mechanics $\times$ Commitment-Squared, meaning that a job offer is gained through mechanics (strategies, systems, tactics) multiplied by a double dose of commitment (mindset, emotional energy, attitude). Focusing on providing value to the employer is an essential employment strategy.

2. Avoid the most common mistake of candidates—going unprepared to interviews. A critical step in preparation is to craft relevant success stories.

3. Use the SMART Story™ method to structure relevant success stories, remembering to include contextual situational clues, sequential actions, numbers-driven results, and a tie-in to the employer's needs.

4. Translate your value into ROI (return on investment).

5. Tap into the 10 reasons employers are motivated to buy (hire you).

6. Focus on benefits rather than features to inject value into your stories.

7. Load your stories with numbers, such as year-to-year comparisons, records, past highs, past lows, target goals, size of project, number of persons involved, and budget or project figures (when not confidential).

8. Add flavor to your stories using emotion, humor, and metaphors.

9. Write S.O.S. responses that provide solutions or services.

10. Remember the mindset mantra, "them, not me," when writing your stories. Employers will filter everything they hear through the screen of "will the candidate's skills help me?"

## Magical Coaching Questions

What's the greatest insight you've gained from your work in this chapter?

_____

_____

_____

How will you use what you've learned to move your search forward?

_____

_____

_____

_____

Chapter

5

# Communicate Your Value Via a Career Brand

*There are four ways, and only four ways, in which we have contact with the world. We are evaluated and classified by these four contacts: what we do, how we look, what we say, and how we say it.*

—Dale Carnegie

Ask yourself these two questions:

★ What do you want to be known for?

★ What kind of employer do you want to connect with?

These two questions capture the essence of what branding is all about: image and connection. Think of your brand as a uniquely individual image with a magnet attached to it. What unique combination of skills or competencies do people recognize in you? Why do people in the work world trust you? What do you want to contribute to your world of work? What kind of employer will be drawn to, connect with, and pay a premium for that?

## How Can a Career Brand Help?

Perhaps you're thinking, "I don't need a brand...I just need to land a job!" You might be surprised to learn that a brand *will* help you land a job because many of the same dynamics behind why a consumer chooses Crest over Colgate also apply in hiring.

The benefits of a brand are numerous. A compelling career brand can

- Make you more attractive to employers, even when there are no formal job openings (see chapter 11 on networking and "The Four Stages of a Job Opening")
- Control what interviewers remember most about you
- Lower the barriers to hiring by creating trust and conveying value
- Elevate you from the status of commonplace commodity to one-of-a-kind service
- Differentiate you from the competition
- Guide you in your decisions about which interviews to pursue
- Create employer desire to buy (hire)

What happens if you don't create a brand? Obviously, the opposite of everything in the preceding list. Worse yet, potential employers will determine your brand for you, and it might not be the brand you intended to project! It's a bit like looking at Rorschach ink blots. Two people, with no suggestions to sway them, often see two very different things in the ink blots. But, if one points out that there is a butterfly in one of the ink blots, the other will likely look hard to find and focus on that butterfly. The same is true with branding. Without prompting from you, the employer will see what he wants to see in you. With a few sound bites that bring your brand into focus, the employer is more likely to concentrate on the strengths or value you want him to see.

## The Elements of Your Brand

No longer reserved for corporate giants, brands are now applicable to career-minded individuals like you and me. For your brand to accomplish its purpose, it must knit together these three A's:

- Authentic Image
- Advantages
- Awareness

The good news is that you have already put in place the first two of the three A's. Your Authentic Image is the genuine you—not costumed to play the part of someone else, but cast in the right role...a role that allows you to be radically rewarded and enthusiastically engaged in work that adds value to others. Your Magic F.I.T.™ work in chapter 3 pointed you toward your Authentic Image. The second A, Advantages, is synonymous with benefits and value. You concentrated on identifying benefits and value in chapter 4, especially in writing numbers-oriented results for your SMART Stories™. The final A, Awareness, refers to communicating your brand in a manner that makes people attentive and responsive to it.

Authentic Image, Advantages, and Awareness add up to one word: *Marketing*. In a job search, you are the product and your employer-to-be is the consumer.

> ### Job Search = Marketing
>
> In chapters 3 and 4, the focus was on what you want and what you can offer to an employer—your product, so to speak. Now it's time to look at your product through the eyes of consumers (employers) and their awareness and perception of your product. In this and future chapters, the focal point will be what the employer needs and whether the employer perceives that you can meet those needs better than your competitors.

The focus of this chapter will be on how to make employers aware of, and how to communicate (or market), your career brand. We'll do that in two ways:

- Verbal branding
- Visual branding

# Verbal Branding—Creating Your Sound Bites

Sound bites, like success stories, will help you feel prepared to meet any networking or interview situation. Sound bites should be short, from 20 seconds to two minutes in length, and can be used for these types of situations:

- To convey your unique key strengths in an interview
- To articulate your goals and help networking contacts understand what you are looking for
- To offer a brief, value-packed introduction of yourself

To be prepared for these and other job search conversations, you'll equip yourself with three key sound bites:

- **Three-Point Marketing Message** (a succinct sound bite, less than 30 seconds, used to convey your unique key strengths and integrated throughout your résumés and cover letters, networking, informational interviews, and job interviews)
- **Verbal Business Card** (a succinct sound bite, less than 30 seconds, used in networking, informational interviewing, and job interviewing to articulate your goals and the benefits you offer)
- **Mini-Bio** (a short message, between one and two minutes, the elements of which can be mixed and matched to offer a relevant career capsule in networking, informational interviewing, or job interviewing)

Companies often communicate their brand in as few as three or four words with a pithy tagline (e.g., FedEx's "The World on Time" or Nike's "Just Do It"). Luckily, in job search, you'll be able to use more than a few words—written or spoken—to capture the essence of who you are. The theme and language used in your résumé and cover letter can support your brand from a written perspective. Moreover, the success stories and sound bites you choose when communicating with interviewers can support your brand from a verbal standpoint. (Note that for our purposes, I'll include written words as part of verbal branding because taglines and other written messages take on a verbal connotation when we say them—albeit sometimes silently in our minds—to make sense.)

## Your Three-Point Marketing Message

A Three-Point Marketing Message is the most recyclable sound bite you'll use when networking and interviewing. You can use it again and again. The three-point message should be part of your response to the age-old interview question, "tell me about yourself." It's also a great way to wrap up the interview and leave the interviewer with a clear message about your qualifications. You can weave the three points throughout your job search communications, including résumés, inquiry/approach letters, and follow-up letters. The following example is especially memorable because of its catchy alliteration:

| | |
|---|---|
| Sound Bite of Three-Point Marketing Message: | As a sales representative for the hotel industry, my strengths lie in the areas of Research, Relationships, and Revenue Enhancement. |

### Customize Your Message for Each Employer

Ideally, your Three-Point Marketing Message should be customized for each employer. Remember, it's not about you; it's about them. Always connect your strengths to what the employer needs most.

## Combining Your Three-Point Marketing Message with Other Job Search Tools

Figure 5.1 shows an example of how to integrate the three points into your résumé. The strengths are listed under the Strengths subheading near the top of the résumé.

You can also vary the wording on your Three-Point Marketing Message and combine it with a SMART Story™:

# CHRIS CABALLERO

555 East Serena
Los Angeles, CA 90000

Relocating to Chicago

(555) 555-5555
c_caballero@hotmail.com

## SALES / BUSINESS DEVELOPMENT
### Hospitality ◆ Convention ◆ Meeting ◆ Visitors Bureau

**Strengths:**

**Research**—Developed qualified business leads using traditional and online research methods.
**Relationships**—Quickly established loyal and trusting relationships with key accounts and networking contacts.
**Revenue Enhancement**—Set new records for group and convention business at major-brand and boutique hotels.

## PROFESSIONAL EXPERIENCE

**Assistant Director of Sales**—MAJOR HOTEL, Los Angeles, California          1/00–Present
(396-room property, with 42,000 sq. ft. of function space)

Manage more than $2 million in group business. Prospect and book national and state association accounts. Attend national and regional trade shows to increase market share. Travel 4–6 times per year for sales trips and trade shows. Coordinate familiarization trips with Bureau and hotel for lead generation. Exclusively sell and coordinate Rose Bowl group business. *Contributions:*

◆ Increased revenue 45% during tenure, with average sale up 17%.

◆ Delivered record group bookings first year in position, with 25,000 group room nights in 2000.

◆ Increased total bookings each subsequent year (despite challenge of post-9/11 market)…on track to close 32–34,000 group room nights this year.

◆ Maximized Rose Bowl business by working closely with Tournament of Roses Association and targeting Fortune 500 companies that sponsor floats and host VIPs. This year, sold out before July (in past years, sell-out occurred as late as December for this New Year's Day event), while also increasing minimum stay and rates.

◆ Expanded communications and working relationships with Convention & Visitors Bureau, gaining more business from special events such as the People's Choice Awards, Emmy Awards, and major Broadway shows.

**National Sales Manager**—GRAND HOTEL, Los Angeles, California          9/98–12/99
(800-room property, with 40,000 sq. ft. of function space)

Recruited to manage convention and group business within the Southeast Region. Prospected new business and expanded existing accounts. Traveled 6–8 times per year for sales trips and national trade shows. *Contributions:*

◆ Met and exceeded quota, earning maximum bonus for revenue increases.

**National Sales Manager**—EXCLUSIVE HOTEL, Los Angeles, California          11/96–9/98
(84-room boutique hotel located inside historic private club)

Developed and executed marketing plan to capture untapped group business. Established relationship with Bureau, offering niche-market services for convention-goers desiring full workout facilities in an upscale setting. *Contributions:*

◆ Grew group business from virtually nil to more than 2,500 room nights per year (record still unsurpassed).

**Prior Experience** with major brands—management trainee, convention service manager, sales manager.

## EDUCATION, PROFESSIONAL DEVELOPMENT & AFFILIATIONS

**BA, Sociology**—Northwestern University (1995)
**Seminars**—Dale Carnegie, Professional Selling Skills (PSS), Professional Sales Negotiation (PSN), Hilton Sales College
**CSAE** (California Society of Association Executives)

**Figure 5.1: A résumé with a Three-Point Marketing Message integrated into it.**

| | |
|---|---|
| Variation on Three-Point Marketing Message: | The reason I've exceeded quota in all my positions—and the reason I'm confident I could do the same for you—is that I've mastered the 3 R's of sales: Research, Relationships, and Revenue Enhancement. |
| SMART Story™: | In my last position, where we were faced with stagnant revenues, my research skills helped me unearth a prospect list that included Fortune 1000 companies, including ABC Company, DEF Company, and GHI Company. I turned that cold data into warm leads, and gained access to decision makers at 9 of the 10 target companies. Bottom line, our revenue increased 45 percent during my tenure and our average sale increased 17 percent. Based on what you've told me about your operation, it sounds like research might be an area that you'd like to concentrate on first. |

## What Your Three-Point Marketing Message Should Include

Your Three-Point Marketing Message should convey your three most marketable selling points. They are likely common themes in your SMART Stories™ or the focus of your résumé. These three points might be functional strengths, unique experiences, or even soft skills. This social work case manager identified two functional strengths (counseling and teaching) and one soft skill (client advocacy) as part of her Three-Point Marketing Message:

| | |
|---|---|
| Sound bite of Three-Point Marketing Message: | As a case manager with more than 15 years of experience, my greatest assets for this position are counseling, teaching, and client advocacy. |

It's likely that you have more than three key skills or strengths for your target position. However, it's unlikely that your networking contacts or interviewers will be able to remember much more than three things about you. One interviewer, who understandably requested anonymity as he related this story, admitted that after interviewing a string of candidates and taking indecipherable notes in the process, he and his fellow interviewers couldn't even remember the name of their star candidate. I'll give you some tricks for using physical "plops" and other memory-enhancing artifacts for your listeners in the chapters to come. Recognize, however, that when it comes to verbal delivery of your strengths, simple is better.

## Creating Your Message

What will your Three-Point Marketing Message be? Here's an easy two-step process to create your marketing message. First, select an introductory phrase. You can choose one of these or write your own:

- ☐ I've always been recognized for…

- ☐ My background is unique because…

- ☐ Throughout my career as a _____ [functional title], I've always been drawn to…

- ☐ As a _____ [functional title], I'm known for…

- ☐ The reason I've exceeded quota in all my positions—and the reason I'm confident I could do the same for you—is that I'm an expert in…

- ☐ My strengths as a _____ [functional title] lie in the area of…

- ☐ At the heart of my experience are these three strengths…

- ☐ I am passionate about…

- ☐ My former supervisors and co-workers concur that the key to my success is…

- ☐ Clients frequently compliment me for…

- ☐ I've developed a reputation for…

- ☐ I'm very good at…

Second, add your three key points to the introductory phrase. Use grammatically parallel language in describing the three terms or phrases so that the wording flows better. For instance, these three phrases are parallel, "researching prospects, building relationships, and driving revenue." These terms are also parallel: "research, relationships, revenue." You can see, then, that this wording is not parallel—"researching, relationships, and drove revenue"—making it sound awkward and stilted.

Identify and write your three key points here:

1. _____

2. _____

3. _____

Now, combine the introductory phrase you selected previously with your three key points and write it here:

_____

_____

_____

Speak the Three-Point Marketing Message aloud. Make any adjustments needed until it feels comfortable and sounds strong.

## Your Benefit-Driven Verbal Business Card, or "What's in It for Me (the Employer)?"

Similar to the focus statement you developed in chapter 3, a benefit-driven Verbal Business Card helps networking contacts or employers recognize both the type of opportunity you want and the benefits you bring to the table. As you saw in chapter 4, hiring managers are tuned to radio station WIFM, or "what's in it for me?" Now's your chance to tell them. In the preceding chapter, I listed 10 employer buying motivators (also known as benefits), each of which addresses the employer's profit need or pain point—a situation where the employer is hurting and needs help solving a problem. When you focus on benefits, you

- Appear business-savvy
- Connect with the employer
- Indicate your understanding of the need for profitability and productivity
- Demonstrate a track record for contributing to the bottom line

What benefits do you bring to a prospective employer? What are you better at than others who have similar credentials? What "invisible" factors might be behind your success? The answers to these questions will strategically reposition you from run-of-the-mill to out-of-the-ordinary.

I'd like you to brainstorm ideas on how you can benefit an employer in each of the 10 buying motivations. To illustrate that this exercise isn't just for people in executive or sales positions, table 5.1 shows examples for an administrative assistant who worked in a small real estate office.

### Table 5.1: Examples Tied to Employer Buying Motivators

| Employer Buying Motivator | Example Brainstorming on Solutions or Services That Benefit My Target Employers |
|---|---|
| Buying Motivator #1: Make Money | Worked overtime to help boss close a multimillion-dollar real estate transaction that generated $240,000 in commission. |
| | Developed administrative systems that supported a new fee-based consulting line of business for the company. Revenues on this grew from startup to $60,000 in one year. |
| Buying Motivator #2: Save Money | Shopped for better pricing on office supplies. Cut costs on key expenses by approximately 10 percent. |
| Buying Motivator #3: Save Time | Wrote and cataloged standardized word-processing clauses to speed document processing and project completion. System saved an average of 20 percent time. |

I wouldn't ask you to do anything that I wouldn't be willing to do myself! To make certain that any business-related professional can link their activity to employer buying motivators, I put myself to the test. Table 5.2 outlines benefits related to my services as a career coach:

### Table 5.2: Examples Tied to Employer (Client) Buying Motivators

| Employer (Client) Buying Motivator | Example Brainstorming on Solutions or Services That Benefit My Target Employers (Clients) |
|---|---|
| Buying Motivator #1: Make Money | Help career-minded professionals with strategy to campaign for a raise or promotion. Help job seekers with salary negotiations. |

*(continued)*

*(continued)*

| Employer Buying Motivator | Example Brainstorming on Solutions or Services That Benefit My Target Employers |
|---|---|
| Buying Motivator #2: Save Money | Help job seekers sort through the career marketing scams on the Internet. Help job seekers identify strategies to stretch their job search dollars. |
| Buying Motivator #3: Save Time | Offer insider job search strategies that short-cut the length of time to reemployment. Offer professionals time-management strategies so that they can concentrate on projects that will give their careers the greatest traction and leverage. |

Now it's your turn. In table 5.3, list as many benefits as come to mind for each of the Employer Buying Motivators. Remember to make it an S.O.S. (solutions or services) response whenever possible (see chapter 4).

### Table 5.3: My Benefits That Relate to Employer Buying Motivators

| Employer Buying Motivator | Brainstorming on Solutions or Services That Benefit My Target Employers |
|---|---|
| Buying Motivator #1: Make Money | |
| Buying Motivator #2: Save Money | |
| Buying Motivator #3: Save Time | |

Buying Motivator #4: Make Work Easier

_____

Buying Motivator #5: Solve a Specific
Problem

_____

Buying Motivator #6: Make the Company
More Competitive

_____

Buying Motivator #7: Build Teams or Individuals;
Enhance Relationships or Image with Customers

_____

Buying Motivator #8: Expand Business

_____

Buying Motivator #9: Attract New Customers

_____

Buying Motivator #10: Retain Customers

_____

To finalize your Verbal Business Card, combine your Magic F.I.T.™ Function and Industry targets from chapter 3 with the benefit ideas you listed in table 5.3. This example for a communications professional pairs function and industry (pinpointed in chapter 3) with benefits:

I'm a communications professional targeting director-level opportunities with industrial manufacturers where I can leverage my track record for developing award-winning creative teams and delivering record returns on marketing communications.

Table 5.4 shows how the preceding Verbal Business Card relates to each of the elements from chapter 3:

### Table 5.4: Elements and Wording of a Verbal Business Card

| Element | Sample Wording |
| --- | --- |
| Function | I'm a communications professional targeting director-level opportunities with… |
| Industry | industrial manufacturers… |
| Benefit (linked to Buying Motivators #1 and #7) | where I can leverage my track record for developing award-winning creative teams and delivering record returns on marketing communications. |

Use the following worksheet to create your Verbal Business Card.

### My Verbal Business Card

| Element | Draft Wording |
| --- | --- |
| Function | I'm a _____ targeting _____ opportunities |
| Industry | in the _____ industry |
| Benefits | that will allow me to _____ _____ _____ _____ . |

## Your Mini-Bio

The final sound bite to be crafted for your verbal branding is a short biography, which we'll call a Mini-Bio. Also known as an "elevator pitch," this is another sound bite you'll need to have down pat. Some (but not all) of these elements will appear in your bio:

- Three-Point Marketing Message
- Number of years of experience
- Prestigious employer(s)
- Title or functional area
- Scope of responsibility (budget, staff, special projects)
- Verbal business card
- Key selling points or strengths
- Key accomplishments
- Impressive educational degree or credentials
- Fulfillment/purpose/mission statement
- SMART Stories™
- Tagline
- Inquiry/call to action

Building on the communication professional's example cited previously, let's look at how these elements can come to life. In table 5.5, the left column notes the element, whereas the right column breaks down the Bio.

### Table 5.5: Elements and Wording for Mini-Bio

| Element | Sample Wording |
|---|---|
| Verbal Business Card | I'm a communication professional targeting director-level opportunities with industrial manufacturers where I can leverage my track record for developing award-winning creative teams and delivering record returns on marketing communications. |
| Number of years of experience | Over the past 10 years, |
| Prestigious employer(s) | I've worked with the region's leading lighting manufacturer |

*(continued)*

*(continued)*

| Element | Sample Wording |
| --- | --- |
| Title or functional area | in senior-level positions as an Advertising Manager and Director of Communications |
| Scope of responsibility | with charge of a staff of 25 and six-figure project budgets. |
| Sound bite of Three-Point Marketing Message | Throughout my career as a creative director, I've been recognized for my expertise in advertising strategy, project management, and creative development. |
| Key accomplishments (tied to Three-Point Marketing Message) | I can offer some examples if you'd like. As an advertising strategist, my skills delivered an ROI of 15:1 on marketing funds, which, as you know, is well above average.<br><br>As a project manager, I have numerous contacts with artists, copywriters, and printers and have a track record for bringing projects in on time and on a shoestring budget. It wasn't unusual for me to save $5,000 on printing costs when our total budget was $25,000.<br><br>And, because of my strong creative background, many of the campaigns I directed earned national advertising awards. |
| Tagline | I'm known for turning ideas into dollars. |
| Inquiry/call to action (use when speaking to a networking contact) | What companies come to mind that might benefit from someone with my background?<br>OR<br>What companies are you aware of that are doing interesting work with their marketing communications? |

You're allowed some wiggle room with the length of your Mini-Bio. It can be about a minute or two. Keep in mind that if it's too short, you won't be able to

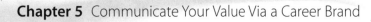

give people a good sense of who you are, what you're looking for, and what you can do for others. If it's too long, you'll confuse people and risk sounding long-winded.

### What's Your Tagline?

Some job seekers borrow (with appropriate credit) company taglines or corporate references to describe themselves. For instance, a project manager conveyed his track record in this way, "My boss likes to call me Mr. FedEx because I have a reputation for delivering projects on time."

Create your Mini-Bio using the outline in the following worksheet. At this point, fill in each box; however, you do *not* have to use every element when you introduce yourself. In fact, it will probably sound too wordy if you do. Instead, you can mix and match the different elements so that you have some variety when speaking to people. I've placed an asterisk (*) next to the ingredients that are most important and should be mentioned in most every introduction. This should be a fairly simple exercise because you have already developed much of the information needed. The example in table 5.6 will give you ideas for phrasing and connecting the different elements of your introduction.

### Table 5.6: Elements of My Mini-Bio

| Element | Wording |
|---|---|
| Sound Bite of Three-Point Marketing Message (you completed this earlier in the chapter) | |
| Number of years of experience | |
| Prestigious employer(s) | |
| *Title or functional area (you identified this in chapter 2) | |
| Scope of responsibility | |

*(continued)*

*(continued)*

| Element | Wording |
|---|---|
| *Verbal Business Card | |
| *Key selling points or strengths | |
| *Key accomplishments (tied to Three-Point Marketing Message) | |
| Impressive educational degree or credentials | |
| Fulfillment/purpose/ mission statement | |
| SMART Story™ (choose an impressive one from your work in chapter 3) | |
| *Tagline | |

*Inquiry/call to action
(use when speaking
to a networking contact)

It's important that you practice speaking your Bio. Start by practicing alone in front of a mirror. Then ask someone to critique you. Know the material inside and out, backwards and forwards. Make adjustments until you can comfortably deliver it without feeling like you're a telemarketer following a script!

Like Tinker Toys, you can combine your elements in ways that will bring your career brand to life. This section has given you the gist of verbal branding. There are certainly other tactics you can use to convey your brand, so be creative. For instance:

- Add your tagline to your e-mail signature.

- Include the themes from your Three-Point Marketing Message on your personal business card.

- Create a portfolio that is divided into sections for the three themes of your Three-Point Marketing Message.

- Use a relevant success story in an interview thank-you/follow-up letter.

- Have pens or stickies made with your name and tagline.

What else can you think of?

### Need Help with Branding?

Check out the Reach Certified Personal Brand Strategists at www.reachcc.com. Professionals committed to assisting you excel, these strategists are incredibly successful themselves, exude a passion for personal branding, and understand the power that branding has to transform careers and lives.

# Visual Branding—Look and Act the Part!

In chapter 2, when describing the Uncover Phase of Job Search, I forewarned that you would be judged on three dimensions: competency, chemistry, and compensation. The second dimension, chemistry, requires a reciprocal connection between you and the company. Yes, *your* opinion of the company does count in this matter! You must connect with the company, its people (especially the hiring manager), and its customers. The converse is also true. The company's people (again, especially the hiring manager) must connect with you. In visual branding, we'll concentrate on how your visuals—image and dress—can create some good chemistry.

## Your Image

Entering a room to meet a new employer can be like walking into a whole new chapter of your life. At that moment, you can influence the employer's perception of you based on your actions, attitudes, and attire. To illustrate this point, recall the movie *Catch Me If You Can,* an extraordinary true tale of a brilliant young master of deception. Eluding a dogged FBI agent (played by Tom Hanks), the story follows Frank W. Abagnale, Jr. (played by Leonardo DiCaprio) as he successfully passes himself off as a pilot, a lawyer, and a doctor, all before his 21st birthday.

Abagnale was able to hoodwink so many people because he *confidently acted* the part in every respect. The result? An image that people perceived as real. Of course, I am not in the least suggesting that you lie about yourself. I do suggest, however, that as part of your visual branding you *confidently act the part in every respect.*

### Role Models

To confidently act the part, you'll need a clear description of the image you want to project. One of the best ways to do this is to look for role models. Who in your industry do you admire? Who is successfully doing the type of work you want to do? Even better, who is a notch above the role you'd like to be in?

### Why Are Role Models Important?

I'll let you in on a secret. When employers are ready to interview, the first place they go to is the desk of their top performers. Hiring managers painstakingly analyze top performers to determine the behaviors and competencies that make them so successful. In turn, those behaviors and competencies will be the high-water mark you're measured against. Find and emulate a successful role model and you'll improve your chances for interview success.

Once you've identified a role model or two, study their image by asking yourself these 10 questions:

1. How would you describe this person?

2. What actions does he or she take that cause success?

3. What do you like about the way he or she treats others?

4. What is his or her mindset and attitude?

5. Who does he or she associate with?

6. How does he or she dress?

7. What is his or her posture like? How does he or she stand, walk, sit?

8. How does he or she communicate with others? What, and how much, does he or she say? Not say?

9. Is there something about the way he or she spends their lunch or free time that feeds success?

10. What does your role model *not* do (for example, avoid making excuses, blaming others, stretching the truth, and so on)?

It's sometimes difficult to see yourself as others perceive you. To give you a fresh perspective, compare yourself with a role model using the questions in table 5.7. In approaching this exercise, make sure that your self-talk is inspirational and encouraging, not critical and disapproving. Think to yourself, "This enhanced image that I want to project is something worthwhile and attainable."

### Table 5.7: Positive Traits of Role Models

| Questions | What I Admire About the Role Model | Success Traits I Already Possess | Choices I Can Make to Improve My Image |
|---|---|---|---|
| How would you describe this person? | | | |
| What action does he or she take that causes success? | | | |
| What do you like about the way your role model treats others? | | | |

*(continued)*

*(continued)*

| Questions | What I Admire About the Role Model | Success Traits I Already Possess | Choices I Can Make to Improve My Image |
|---|---|---|---|
| What is this person's mindset and attitude? | | | |
| Who does he or she associate with? | | | |
| How does your role model dress? (style, colors, and so on) | | | |
| What is this person's posture like? How does he or she stand, walk, sit? | | | |
| How does your role model communicate with others? What, and how much, does he or she say? Not say? | | | |
| Is there something about the way this person spends his or her lunch or free time that feeds success? | | | |

What does your role model *not* do (for example, avoid making excuses, blaming others, stretching the truth, and so on)?

If needed, enlist the support of a trusted colleague on this role model exercise. If you do solicit a support partner, make sure you choose someone who will be respectful and kind, yet direct and honest—someone with a heart for helping people become all that they can be. First, ask the person to tell you what you're doing right. Then, give the person permission to tell you things you might not want to hear. Further, give permission to point out where this person senses you're resisting change. We cannot change until we are aware of what we need to change!

Finally, let me make perfectly clear that I'm *not* asking you to become a clone. Instead, I'm suggesting that you adopt elements of what you like best from others to enhance your own individuality and marketability.

### Bugged by Being Compared to Others?

It is frustrating to think that people are judging you based on your image. However, the reality is that image does factor into the hiring process—even if it isn't supposed to. In the hiring game, when two candidates have equal skills and one has an image that fits better with the company, the candidate with the right chemistry will get the job. Candidates who don't examine this topic with fresh eyes put themselves at a disadvantage.

## How People Perceive You

How would you like others to describe you? When it comes time to hire, it's not unusual to hear an employer say something like this to employees: "We need to replace Lori in the bookkeeping department while she's on maternity leave—do you know anyone with a bookkeeping background who is very detail-oriented and trustworthy?" The employer is looking not only for competencies, but chemistry.

Image is part of chemistry. Image is about behaving in a manner consistent with how you want people to perceive you. Review the list of 10 adjectives you identified in chapter 3 ("Step 5, Enhance Your Identity") and answer the following questions.

## Image Worksheet

1. Are these terms you identified in chapter 2 in sync with top performers in your target field? If so, great. If not, what adjustments should you make to your list?

   _____

   _____

   _____

   _____

2. Write a few sentences about how you want networking contacts and potential employers to perceive you.

   _____

   _____

   _____

   _____

3. What behaviors or attitudes do you already exhibit that are consistent with this description? What do you need to do to ensure that these behaviors or attitudes are evident to an interviewer?

   _____

   _____

   _____

4. What image elements will you improve on or enhance? How will you do so?

   _____

   _____

   _____

## Your Wardrobe

Remember that corporate America uses colors and visual images as part of its branding. In career branding, your colors and visual images are communicated through your wardrobe. As we discuss wardrobe, consider that your attire for the interview shouldn't be an anomaly, like a one-night tuxedo rental for a special occasion. One candidate dressed beautifully for an interview and, once hired, didn't don a suit coat again, much to the chagrin of the executive team. Your interview attire should be part of who you are, as well as who you are committed to becoming.

---

### Always Look the Part

Attire for networking meetings should be similar to that for interviews. If you aren't dressed professionally or groomed meticulously when meeting with an influential networking contact, that contact might be hesitant to recommend you to an employer. Pay attention to every detail, including the type of pen you carry, the quality of your business card holder, and the style of notepad you use to take notes.

---

A picture is worth a thousand words. When it comes to meeting influential contacts and potential employers, *you* speak a thousand words—even before you open your mouth. Approach your business wardrobe as if you were mute and the wardrobe were going to do all the talking. That's how important dress is to your interview success.

With business attire across the board these days, a one-size-fits-all recommendation on this subject won't fit. Use good judgment. Assess the type of companies you'll be targeting and dress to their standards. Image experts offer varying advice regarding dressing for interviews. Some counsel you to dress a little nicer than the norm for the business; others advise you to dress the same as your interviewer, just cleaner! Either can work. I defer to the advice of my dear mother when it comes to dress: If you err, err on the side of formality…dress a little nicer than the norm.

## Dress for Women

The wardrobe recommendations that follow apply to traditional business environments. From head to toe, here are some guidelines:

 **Suits and shirts:** Two-piece matching suits (with the same fabric for the jacket and skirt or pants) give the best impression. For the most conservative companies, opt for solid colors or subtly patterned fabrics in deep blues, greys, or black; complement the suit with a solid or light-colored blouse or sweater. Pants with a matching or complementary jacket are acceptable. For less conservative atmospheres, follow and have fun with fashion trends! As this book goes to press, print blouses are in, along with a skirt and jacket that blend but don't necessarily match.

- **Dresses:** In formal environments, consider a smart-looking dress with a jacket that matches or complements the dress. For less formal environments, business dress *sans* jacket is fine, especially if you're applying for a non-managerial role.

- **Fabrics:** Pick tried-and-true fabrics that are tasteful, hang well, and don't wrinkle excessively. Linens are lovely, but you'll likely be wildly wrinkled before you get to your meeting. Reserve fabrics with a high sheen (such as satin) for the evening.

- **Hosiery:** Hose should be natural color, with no patterns.

- **Shoes:** Close-toed shoes, pumps, or flats should complement the suit or dress. Avoid extremes in heel height or style, such as stiletto heels that could double as a weapon. Avoid sandals or strappy shoes. Polish any scuffs and repair worn heels.

- **Jewelry:** Avoid anything that jingles, clanks, or makes noise. Limit jewelry to one ring per hand, one bracelet per wrist, and one earring per ear. Necklaces may be worn as long as they are not the focal point—you want interviewers concentrating on your face, not your necklace. Avoid any body piercing beyond earrings.

- **Hair:** Clean and neatly cut. Style long hair in a conservative manner, making sure it doesn't fall in your face or cause you to touch your face to push it away. Avoid an overly styled hairdo that involves excessive mousse or hairspray. If you color your hair, make sure that roots are hidden.

- **Makeup:** Conservative and natural-looking is safest; avoid bright colors. Stay away from excessive face powder that gives a pancake-makeup, aged appearance.

- **Nails:** Use neutral or clear polish; French manicures are acceptable. If you have to resort to a pencil or other device to dial the phone, shorten your nails.

- **Scents:** For those with a tendency toward perspiration or body odor, carry a fresh blouse or change into your interview suit in an inconspicuous area just prior to the interview. Perfumes, lotions, or creams should be very subtle—remember that many people have chemical allergies and are bothered by what you might consider pleasant. If you want a very light scent, spray cologne into the air and walk through it. This trick will leave a nice close-up scent without being overwhelming.

- **Special touches:** For some, visual branding includes a signature item that is a staple of the wardrobe, such as a tasteful lapel pin or silk scarf.

- **Modesty:** Modesty is becoming a lost art. The interview is not a date. Avoid clingy, see-through fabrics and low-cut blouses. When sitting, skirt lengths should not go more than an inch or two above the knee. Even if it's in fashion to show some tummy, don't do it in the workplace. Wear the right size! Squeezing into snug clothing will make you look heavier than you really are. Cover any visible tattoos with makeup and light powder.

**Not So Extreme Makeovers**

If you're in the market for an image update, enlist the support of an expert. One of my trusted authorities on the subject is Mary Ann Dietschler (www.CoachMaryAnn.com).

## Dress for Men

Men, if you have an inkling that you need guidance in putting together an impressive interview wardrobe, don't hesitate to enlist the support of someone who is known for his or her taste in clothing. Better to be embarrassed before just one friend (your wardrobe advisor) than in front of several strangers (your potential boss).

- **Suits and shirts:** A navy blue or gray suit is your surest bet. Choose a white, long-sleeved dress shirt to accompany it, even in summer. Make sure it is crisp, clean, and not fraying or balling from wear. Opt for conservative fabrics. If you need guidance in purchasing (or borrowing) a suit, ask a friend who has a sense of style to come along as your haberdashery consultant. Many companies promote business-casual dress. Even so, men should wear a suit and tie; or if the atmosphere is very casual, opt for a sharp navy blazer and dress slacks when interviewing.

- **Belts:** The belt should fit your suit pants—typically one inch wide—with no unusual or distracting buckle. The belt should be appropriate for the suit color (black belts for black, gray, or navy suits; brown belts for brown suits).

- **Socks:** Dark dress socks are required with suit pants or dress slacks. Avoid socks that do not match your shoe color.

- **Shoes:** Leave the athletic shoes at home. Leather lace-up shoes, freshly polished, are best. Pay attention to the health of the heels and the shine of the shoes; if needed, get your interview shoes to the shoe repair shop for new soles or a general rejuvenation.

- **Jewelry:** A watch and one ring are fine, along with conservative cufflinks. Avoid gold chains and earrings, even a small diamond in one ear.

- **Hair:** Make sure your hair is clean and freshly cut, with your neck neatly shaved. Facial hair might be a part of your normal look, but if it isn't a part of the company's normal look, it could cost you some points in the chemistry and connection department.

- **Nails and facial care:** Gentlemen, spa services are no longer just for metrosexuals (urban males who spend a great deal of time and money on appearance and lifestyle)! For most men who frequent spas, it's not about pampering or looking good; it's about not looking bad. This might be the time to go the extra grooming mile to tidy the fingernails and cuticles (no polish), exfoliate the face, and remove excessive hair from the nose, ears, or upper back.

✸ **Scents:** You might be tempted to add an extra splash of aftershave or cologne for good measure. Don't do it! Interviewers don't want to smell you before they see you. Again, be considerate of the thousands of individuals who endure life with allergies to fragrances.

# Chapter Wrap-Up

You covered a lot of important ground in this chapter. Applause, applause! With the work accomplished thus far, I can guarantee you've gained an edge over your competition. Why? Because many job seekers have tunnel vision when it comes to job search—they see it as an isolated career event, the focus of which is writing a résumé and then hoping that the résumé will generate some interviews.

In reality, job search is a holistic, big-picture process marked by a series of business meetings between you and networking contacts, and ultimately you and the hiring decision maker. The focus of these meetings is achieving an outcome where both parties get their needs met. The employer wants value or return on investment, and you want a good *fit* where you can be radically rewarded and enthusiastically engaged in your work. This win-win perspective gives you equal footing with employers and adds to your confidence and bargaining power.

So, congratulate yourself on having an edge. Over the past few chapters, you have

✸ Created an attainable goal backed by a comprehensive, cohesive plan

✸ Intelligently targeted a position that takes into account your Magic F.I.T.™ (functional strengths and fulfillment, industry and interests, things that matter, and personality type)

✸ Developed success stories and sound bites that focus on benefits (solutions or services) and value (return on investment and employer buying motivators)

Taken steps to look and act the part with a cohesive image and compelling career brand

You've completed Phase I, the Analyze Phase, of job search, as well as much of Phase II, the Express Phase (see chapter 2 for "Five Phases of a Job Transition"). The Express Phase also includes writing your résumé. You can jump to chapter 7 if you'd like to start that process now, or you can review chapter 6, "Manage the "Buoy Factor"—How Mindset Can Sink or Support You." Chapter 6 is a must-read at some point during your transition because it will equip you with the mental tenacity required when you're searching for a job.

# 10 Quick Tips for Communicating Your Career Brand

1. Job search is marketing. You are the product and the employer is the consumer. A clear and compelling career brand helps employers perceive the benefits of your product, giving you an advantage in the job market.

2. Successful career brands weave together three A's: Authentic image, Advantages, and Awareness. Project an image of your authentic self, focus on the advantages the employer receives from your getting the job done, and make employers aware of those advantages.

3. Branding can be accomplished through verbal and visual means. Verbal branding includes your sound bites and success stories, whereas visual branding is accomplished through your actions, attitude, and attire.

4. Hone your product benefits into a Three-Point Marketing Message that conveys your unique strengths. This is a critical sound bite.

5. Create a Verbal Business Card to keep you focused, help networking contacts know how to help you, and explain your value to interviewers. Align your statement with employer buying motivators.

6. Mix and match your success stories and sound bites to create a comfortable yet compelling Mini-Bio. Consider using a tagline that helps people remember you in a unique and favorable light.

7. Practice. You must be able to deliver your sound bites naturally, without appearing as though you've memorized a script.

8. Visual branding means you must look the part. Ask for wardrobe advice from someone who is successful and has a good sense of style. If uncertain about how to dress for interviews or networking, err on the side of formality.

9. Visual branding also means you must act the part. Candidly evaluate your mindset, beliefs, behaviors, and attitudes. Are these consistent with others in your field who have attained notable success?

10. Find a person or two who will respectfully and selflessly support you in your commitment to shaping and enhancing your ideal image.

## Magical Coaching Questions

Envision life a year or two down the road. As you grow personally and develop your ideal image, what will the rewards be? Be specific with respect to the positive impacts on your career, work relationships, personal relationships, self-esteem, finances, and so on.

_____

_____

_____

Thinking back to the image description you wrote earlier in this chapter, who can support you in achieving this goal?

_____

_____

_____

In the next seven days, what small step can you take to get started toward your ideal image?

_____

_____

_____

What system or structure will you put in place to build momentum and periodically track your progress?

_____

_____

_____

_____

# Manage the "Buoy Factor"—How Mindset Can Sink or Support You

*"It is your attitude and not your aptitude that determines your altitude."*

—Zig Zigler

Buoys—those brightly colored objects that aid in nautical navigation—remain afloat, day in and day out, whether calm seas or rough waters. Beaconage buoys, seen by seagoing vessels, are equipped with radio-beacon technology to mark channels and guide mariners to safe passage. Closer to shore, buoys denote boundaries or caution you of submerged danger, such as a reef or shoal. Certain shapes of buoys, horseshoe and crown, also serve as life preservers.

Regardless of their shape or function, buoys have two things in common. They float, and they are anchored in some fashion.

**What allows you to stay afloat?**

**What are you anchored to?**

As a verb, *buoy* refers to raising one's spirits. In the process of accessing and acing interviews, you will likely encounter days that feel like smooth sailing, whereas others might be reminiscent of stormy seas. To be successful, you must address both the mechanics and mindset of job search and interviewing. Previous and future chapters cover the mechanics in detail. This chapter is devoted to the mindset piece of the equation, specifically the mental, physical, and emotional factors that will keep your attitude afloat. We'll call it the Buoy Factor.

# The Buoy Factor

The Buoy Factor is a measurement of how quickly you regain your self-confidence and recover from discouragement. The operative word here is *recover*—not that you won't encounter days of discouragement (you will), but how fast you'll make a comeback (you can).

People with a high degree of buoyancy display several common characteristics. They are

- Purposeful
- Confident of their value
- Persevering
- Proactive
- Optimistic
- Empowered, with inner strength
- Anxiety-free
- Balanced
- Diligent about self-care
- An inspiration to others

The Buoy Factor doesn't require perfect and unwavering self-confidence, just the skills to regain it in an appropriate amount of time. Henry Ford said, "Whether you believe you can do a thing or not, you're right."

# The "I CAN" Mindset

When operating in full force, your Buoy Factor will enable you to say, "I *CAN* do this." You *can* do it, when you apply this meaning to the I CAN acronym:

- I—Inspire Daily
- C—Control the Controllables
- A—Act Now
- N—Never Give Up!

This chapter is an *a la carte* chapter—choose the sections that best relate to your circumstances. Not everyone will be coming from the same place. As you read this, you might be in a "good" place—with minimal pressure to find a new position, you're certain about your course and have the energy and optimism to proceed with confidence. Others of you might be in a "not-so-good" place—perhaps there is pain from an unexpected layoff, discouragement about an extended period of unemployment, fear regarding low financial reserves, or frustration stemming from other pressing issues.

If you're in need of inspiration, focus on the "Inspire Daily" segment of the chapter; if you feel like things are out of control, concentrate on the "Control the Controllables" segment; and so on.

# Gauge Your Buoyancy

To help gauge your buoyancy, use the quick quiz in table 6.1. Circle the score that best represents your response to each item, with 1 meaning true, 2 mostly true, 3 occasionally true, 4 mostly false, and 5 false. I suggest using a pencil and dating the exercise, as you might want to reassess yourself down the road to measure your progress.

The point of the exercise in table 6.1 is to become aware of your mindset. The good news is that once awareness is present, you are in a position to do something about it. If your scores are lower than you would like, do not be discouraged and do not disparage yourself. Instead, view them as a signal that it's time to act.

Very low scores might indicate that there has been a significant loss, health issue, or other difficult episode in your life. If this is the case, treat yourself with the same devotion, concern, and tenderness you might use in caring for a loved one with a serious illness. In some cases, speaking to a counselor or therapist might be beneficial—if so, give yourself permission to take the time necessary to regroup and make a comeback.

Review where your scores are low. Then, as you read through the following chapter sections, concentrate on the strategies that will allow you to bump up your Buoy Factor. Remember, this is an a la carte chapter, so munch on the material that your mind, body, or spirit is most hungry for.

## Table 6.1: Gauge Your Buoyancy

| Lately, I find that I am... | 1 = True | 2 = Mostly True |
|---|---|---|
| 1. Feeling overwhelmed about what needs to be done | 1 | 2 |
| 2. Lacking energy to do the important things or procrastinating about the important things | 1 | 2 |
| 3. Dealing with stress in ways that aren't healthy for me | 1 | 2 |
| 4. Forgetting what really matters in life; losing the ability to laugh at myself | 1 | 2 |
| 5. Impatient with people; yelling at my kids or the dog | 1 | 2 |
| 6. Over-reacting to things that aren't that important | 1 | 2 |
| 7. Doubting my abilities or value | 1 | 2 |
| 8. Fearful or anxious about the future; discouraged or lacking hope | 1 | 2 |
| 9. Focusing more on the negatives than I do the positives in my life | 1 | 2 |
| 10. Unable to give myself fully to roles as spouse, partner, parent, or close friend | 1 | 2 |
| 11. So focused on one compartment of life that other areas have suffered | 1 | 2 |

| 3 = Occasionally True | 4 = Mostly False | 5 = False |
|---|---|---|
| 3 | 4 | 5 |
| 3 | 4 | 5 |
| 3 | 4 | 5 |
| 3 | 4 | 5 |
| 3 | 4 | 5 |
| 3 | 4 | 5 |
| 3 | 4 | 5 |
| 3 | 4 | 5 |
| 3 | 4 | 5 |
| 3 | 4 | 5 |
| 3 | 4 | 5 |

*(continued)*

*(continued)*

| Lately, I find that I am... | 1 = True | 2 = Mostly True |
|---|---|---|
| 12. Not making the time or finding the energy to care for my physical needs (exercise, nutrition, regular medical checkups, and so on) | 1 | 2 |
| 13. Lacking enthusiasm or inspiration; not involved in anything that excites, stimulates, or challenges me | 1 | 2 |
| 14. Feeling isolated or lonely; withdrawing from people and situations | 1 | 2 |
| 15. Lacking the support I need to accomplish my goals | 1 | 2 |
| 16. Lacking calmness and peace of mind | 1 | 2 |
| 17. Distracted by issues that I have no control over | 1 | 2 |
| 18. Complaining about circumstances but not taking action | 1 | 2 |
| 19. Blaming others for my circumstances | 1 | 2 |
| 20. Having trouble being grateful for much | 1 | 2 |
| Subtotal your scores for each column | = | = |
| Add each column subtotal for a grand total | My total score: | |

Steps to Scoring:

1. After circling a number for each item, add up each column.
2. Then, add the column totals across and enter your total score on the last line.
3. Identify your score in the scoring key below.

## Scoring Key

| 91–100 | Your focus, energy, peace, and optimism are at a peak and you bounce back instantaneously; you're a beacon of hope and optimism for others. |
|---|---|
| 80–90 | You have the mental, physical, and emotional strength to bounce back quickly from most discouraging circumstances. |

| | 3 = Occasionally True | 4 = Mostly False | 5 = False |
|---|---|---|---|
| | 3 | 4 | 5 |
| | 3 | 4 | 5 |
| | 3 | 4 | 5 |
| | 3 | 4 | 5 |
| | 3 | 4 | 5 |
| | 3 | 4 | 5 |
| | 3 | 4 | 5 |
| | 3 | 4 | 5 |
| | 3 | 4 | 5 |
| | = | = | = |

| | |
|---|---|
| 70–79 | Your self-confidence is intact, but there are periods when you don't bounce back as quickly as possible. |
| 60–69 | There is some leakage in your mental, physical, or emotional reservoir, causing you to lose time, focus, energy, or peace of mind; your buoyancy could be bumped up a notch or two. |
| 46–59 | Your mental, physical, or emotional reserves are low. |
| 31–45 | Your mental, physical, or emotional reserves are nearly bankrupt. |
| 20–30 | Your situation might benefit from the intervention of a therapist or medical professional. |

# Inspire Daily

Recall a time when you felt utterly inspired, ready to take on the world, confident that everything would work out for the best. What would your career be like if you could have that feeling on a daily basis? Tasks would get tackled immediately, people would want to have you on their team, ideas would flow, and energy would be focused on what really matters. Successful people have mastered the art of recharging themselves with daily inspiration. You can, too! Here's how.

## Master the Law of Inner Action

In the physical life, the action of sowing a sunflower seed will yield a sunflower plant, given the right growing conditions. In the inner life, the seeds you sow will spread as swiftly as narcissus plants. Sowing seeds of pessimism only yields more gloom-and-doom thoughts. Conversely, sowing seeds of optimism yields hope, giving your mind the right growing conditions to plan and be open to how things can work out. Formally stated, the Law of Inner Action is simply a variation on the biblical adage, "you reap what you sow."

Gottfried de Purucker's esoterical writings yielded a number of insights, including this memorable quote: "Sow an act, and you will reap a habit. Sow a habit, and you will reap a destiny, because habits build character. This is the sequence: an act, a habit, a character, and a destiny." I would add two items to lead off de Purucker's sequence: *a thought, and a choice.*

Thoughts and choices, or inner action, precede outer action. To get to action that will bolster your Buoy Factor, bolster your thought life. Thoughts and choices either *empower* or *impale* us.

From your work in table 6.1, identify items where you scored a 1, 2, or 3. For your convenience, the 20 items from table 6.1 are presented again in table 6.2, along with a column to identify any self-defeating thoughts associated with the item and a column to rewrite those thoughts into self-supporting thoughts. If you scored a 2 for the first item, "Feeling overwhelmed about what needs to be done," list the self-defeating thoughts that are associated with that statement, followed by new self-supporting thoughts. I've provided an example near the beginning of the table.

### Table 6.2: Rewriting Thoughts

| Lately, I find that I am... | Self-Defeating Thoughts | Self-Supporting Thoughts |
|---|---|---|
| EXAMPLE: Feeling overwhelmed about what needs to be done | My to-do list is overwhelming. I'll never get this all done. I'm | I am committed to tackling these tasks in priority order. I am learning to give myself permission |

|  | feeling crushed. I should have said "no" to serving on that committee. | to let go of the low-priority items. I will ask Joe for help on a couple of these tasks. |
|---|---|---|
| 1. Feeling overwhelmed about what needs to be done | | |
| 2. Lacking energy to do the important things or procrastinating about the important things | | |
| 3. Dealing with stress in ways that aren't healthy for me | | |
| 4. Forgetting what really matters in life; losing the ability to laugh at myself | | |
| 5. Impatient with people; yelling at my kids or the dog | | |
| 6. Over-reacting to things that aren't that important | | |
| 7. Doubting my abilities or value | | |
| 8. Fearful or anxious about the future; discouraged or lacking hope | | |
| 9. Focusing more on the negatives than I do the positives in my life | | |
| 10. Unable to give myself fully to roles as spouse, partner, parent, or close friend | | |
| 11. So focused on one compartment of life that other areas have suffered | | |

*(continued)*

*(continued)*

| Lately, I find that I am... | Self-Defeating Thoughts | Self-Supporting Thoughts |
|---|---|---|
| 12. Not making the time or finding the energy to care for my physical needs (exercise, nutrition, regular medical checkups, and so on) | | |
| 13. Lacking enthusiasm or inspiration; not involved in anything that excites, stimulates, or challenges me | | |
| 14. Feeling isolated or lonely; withdrawing from people and situations | | |
| 15. Lacking the support I need to accomplish my goals | | |
| 16. Lacking calmness and peace of mind | | |
| 17. Distracted by an issue that I have no control over | | |
| 18. Complaining about circumstances but not taking action | | |
| 19. Blaming others for my circumstances | | |
| 20. Having trouble being grateful for much | | |

## Be in Charge of Your Own Inspiration

Inspiration starts with the letter *i*, reminding us that *I* alone am in charge of inspiring myself. No one else can do this for you. Take the first two letters of the word—*in*—and realize that you must also *internalize* the inspirational message for it to shift from head to heart. Do any of these activities inspire you?

- Attending workshops (industry conferences, meetings with motivational speakers)
- Talking with others who have persevered and succeeded
- Recalling your past successes
- Journaling about what you'd like to accomplish in the future
- Setting specific goals
- Meeting small or big goals
- Learning something new
- Exercising
- Taking action
- Reading inspirational material
- Attending religious services
- Praying or meditating
- Getting away to refresh and reinvigorate

## Need a Dose of Daily Inspiration?

Browse the archives at www.dailymotivator.com or pay a small fee and receive daily e-mails with inspirational quotes and stories.

## Inspirational Triggers Worksheet

As a career professional in the 21st century, it is a prerequisite of success to know what inspires you. Don't wait for someone else to do this for you! Use the following lines to catalog your inspirational triggers:

_____

_____

_____

_____

_____

*(continued)*

*(continued)*

How will you weave these inspirational activities into your daily or weekly habits?

_____

_____

_____

## Keep a Future Focus

Viktor Frankl, a psychiatrist and survivor of a Nazi concentration camp, chronicles his Auschwitz experience in *Man's Search for Meaning.* Beyond the despicable deeds done, the dehumanization, and the loss of touch with loved ones, Frankl describes the psychological severity of not knowing when, or if, the imprisonment would end. In order to bear the terrible *how* of his existence, Frankl looked for a *why*—an aim—that brought meaning. He personally applied this philosophy to endure the torture of the concentration camp. Later in his life, he applied this philosophy in working with patients, asking them to focus on the future and create assignments that were to be fulfilled. As part of Frankl's future focus while imprisoned, he pictured how he would someday stand in front of audiences and lecture on his experiences—a vision that became reality.

Job seekers who are between jobs can hold a twofold focus that incorporates rewards in both their career and personal lives. The career focus might be tied to your Fulfillment statement, which you wrote in chapter 3. For instance,

> **When I am in my new position, I will enjoy developing history lessons that cause students to think critically, examine their belief systems, and grow in their knowledge and understanding...I will start outlining a unit now and explore what new resources might be available.**

Note how the resultant action step keeps this job seeker involved in and current about his profession.

The personal focus might be something like, "this time next year, my credit cards will be paid off." Or, "this time next year, I will have put away enough money to take that trip I've been thinking about."

Use the lines that follow to write out your future focus. You might want to preface your statement(s) with one of these phrases:

- Next year this time I will...
- I look forward to the day when I will...
- What I'll do when I've landed this next job is...

---

**Future Focus Worksheet**

**My Career Future Focus**

_____

_____

_____

**My Personal Future Focus**

_____

_____

_____

---

## Symbols Help Create a Future Focus

Consider one of these symbols to help keep your future focus:

- A collage of pictures and words representing you in your new, successful role

- A job description written by you that includes the ideal responsibilities and challenges you'd like in your next position

- A diagram that shows the people you'll network with to generate leads, the names of interviewers you'll speak with, the company you'll be working at, the money you'll be making, and the new opportunities that will be open to you

- A photo of yourself at a time in your life that you felt very successful or were demonstrating who you are in a positive way

- The wrong side of a tapestry or stitchery project that, from the underside view, looks scrambled and gives no clue to the beauty on the upside

- A picture of a road that reminds you that life is a journey

- A rosebud that will open shortly

*(continued)*

*(continued)*

- A desk plate that contains your name and professional title (these can be custom-made for a reasonable price at many sign shops or copy shops)

## Remind Yourself of Your Value

Value is at the heart of your self-esteem. At least once a day, recall your value. The benefit-oriented ideas generated in table 5.3 and the Verbal Business Card Worksheet in chapter 5 can serve as the basis for your affirmations—positive statements that something is *already* so. These affirmations describe a marketing professional's value:

**I am of value to employers because of my ability to connect with customers and establish strong relationships. Employers love to have me on their team because of my ability to quickly unravel complicated problems and come up with creative solutions that a lot of my colleagues are amazed by. Certain companies are clamoring for someone with my background because my marketing skills contributed to gaining #1 market share for two of the last three products I worked on.**

---

### Affirmations Worksheet

If you find the process of writing out affirmations helpful, do so below. I've provided a few suggested phrases to get you started:

- I bring value to employers because I am good at…

- I bring value to employers because I help impact the bottom line by…

- I bring value to employers because I help solve problems associated with…

- I bring value to employers because I help save time and money through my ability to…

Use present tense when writing and make sure the statements ring true for you; if you overstate or stretch the truth, your mind won't believe them and you'll undermine the purpose of the affirmations—reminding you that something is *already* so.

_____

_____

_____

_____

---

———————————————————————————————————

———————————————————————————————————

———————————————————————————————————

---

Make your affirmation sentences a part of your self-talk—that conversation with yourself that goes on inside your head throughout the day. In addition, post them on index cards and say them aloud at least daily.

## Reframe the Situation with a New Perspective

Reframing is a technique described in *Co-Active Coaching* (Davies-Black Publishing), a coaching how-to textbook authored by veteran coaches Laura Whitworth, Henry Kimsey-House, and Phil Sandahl. Reframing involves looking at a seemingly negative situation with a fresh perspective and a sense of renewed possibility.

The ancient Daoist parable about a ruler and his son helps illustrate the concept of reframing. One day, the son's horse runs away. The ruler responds, "Surely, this is a bad thing." The next day, the horse returns with three more wild stallions by his side. The ruler responds, "Surely, this is a good thing." The following day, the son sets about taming one of the new horses, only to fall off and break his arm. The ruler responds, "Surely, this is a bad thing." The next day, the military comes to recruit all able-bodied young men for war and passes over the son because of his infirmity. The ruler responds, "Surely, this is a good thing."

When you are faced with a problem, deficiency, or obstacle, ask yourself these questions:

- How might this be a good thing?
- What's the silver lining here?
- What's the flip side to this?
- What opportunities are present in this challenge?
- What can I learn from this situation?
- If I had to convince someone that this seemingly negative situation is a good thing, what would I point to?
- If you feel like you're saying goodbye or losing something in your particular career transition, what might you be gaining or saying hello to?

In addition, consider adding a theme to your situation, such as "this will be a time of allowing more awareness into my way of being."

## Deal with the Do-Be's

Are you a do-be? Do-be's are people who find their value in doing, rather than being. (I myself lean toward do-beism but have made great strides toward recovery!) There is a tendency to think that doing (working) is the sole avenue for fulfillment and self-worth. When that avenue is taken away (unemployment), there can be an identity crisis. Unemployment can be hard on do-be's. The secret lies in recognizing that your value is intrinsically in you and being who you were meant to be, both on the job and off the job.

Try one of these strategies for curbing the do-be's:

- Remind yourself that compensation is not the only measure of your value. Whether you're employed or between opportunities, remind yourself that you are still the same talent-filled being.

- Do not rely on someone else to define your value—not your boss, co-worker, friend, spouse, parent, or anyone else. On your own, or through the eyes of the God who loves you, you must find the *immeasurable* worth that you have as a human being. Recognize that worth in others, as well.

- Acknowledge that life work, which encompasses everything outside of your work life (relationships, recreation, self-care, home environment, spiritual growth, personal growth, and so on) is as significant as career work. And, without tending to these elements, you will not be able to function optimally at work.

- Identify job search–related outlets for your skills. For instance, if you're a project manager, project manage your interview preparation. If you're a customer service rep, provide excellent customer service to your potential employers in all your interviews and follow-up communications. If you're a teacher, educate your interviewers about how you can improve learning.

- Live in the moment, be aware of your surroundings, and focus on the small miracles.

- Make a list of things that you like about yourself apart from work. *(I like the way my intuition serves me in figuring out problems. I like that I'm a good friend to others. And so on.)*

## Control the Controllables

One of the secrets of buoyant people is that they concentrate on what they can control. You *can't* control how interviewers will respond to you, nor the competition you face for a particular job. You *can* control how you respond to interviewers, and the manner in which you convey your advantages as a candidate. You *can't* control whether networking contacts will pass along leads or ideas to you.

You *can* control how frequently you will network, to some degree *who* you will network with, and how easy you will make it for people to help you.

This concept—controlling the controllables—is foundational to all the other strategies in this chapter. Let's look at what you can control.

## Control the Basics

A few of the job search items that are in your range of control include

- Number of networking calls you will make each week
- Number of hours per day you will spend on your search
- Types of activities you will focus on in your search
- Amount of time you will devote to your job search (if you're unemployed, put in a full work week of 30 to 40 hours; if employed, put in 10 to 15 hours each week to generate momentum)
- Amount of time you will devote to developing SMART Stories™ and preparing for interviews (5 to 10 hours per interview; this can be part of your allotted job search time)
- Developing a "plan B" should "plan A" not come to fruition
- Developing a dynamite résumé and support marketing materials
- Sending a follow-up note to interviewers or networking contacts
- Showing up prepared, on time, well-groomed, and with an upbeat attitude to every networking meeting or interview
- Participating in professional associations that will increase your visibility and reputation among hiring managers
- Practice interviewing in front of a video camera
- Studying press releases about your target company
- Reading professional journals and checking news/media sources to stay current on your industry
- Taking a course to keep your skills and knowledge fresh and ahead of the curve
- Making a name for yourself by writing articles or through public speaking

Personal things that are in your range of control include the following:

- Amount of exercise, rest, sleep, and nutrition you give yourself
- Attitude and self-talk—what you believe and tell yourself quietly in your head

- Acting "as if" you are already successful (see "Act Successful" later in this chapter)

- Accountability vs. entitlement mentality—echoing John F. Kennedy's sentiments in "ask not what your country can do for you, but what you can do for your country," ask not what the company can give you, but what you can give the company

- News and media you'll allow yourself to consume (is it inspirational or depressing?)

- Time each day for activity that will boost your spirits (stopping to smell the roses, reading to your child, exercising, reading an inspirational autobiography, and so on)

## Are You Feeding on Garbage?

GIGO, an acronym for *Garbage In, Garbage Out,* is a famous computer axiom meaning that if invalid data (garbage) is entered into a system, the resulting output will be trash. Although originally applied to computing, the axiom holds true for other systems, such as production, manufacturing, or decision making. As it relates to the Buoy Factor and your mental wellbeing, "garbage in" might be overdosing on depressing news coverage, consuming television programs that have no redeeming quality, eating up time at Internet sites that offer no value, or even spending too much time with people who are not supportive and uplifting. Is there something you're mentally digesting that might qualify as "garbage?"

## Controlling the Controllables Worksheet

To make progress in controlling the controllables, first make a list of those things you'd like to let go of. For instance, worries about money, discouragement about a setback, or concerns about how to gain access to an important networking contact or employer.

Things I will let go of:

_____

_____

_____

_____

_____

Now, itemize the things you can control (draw from the earlier list of bulleted items for ideas or create your own).

My controllables are

_____

_____

_____

_____

_____

What actions can you take to help shift your list of controllables from a conceptual phase to a firm commitment?

_____

_____

_____

## Find Bone-Marrow People

*Every one of us gets through the tough times because somebody is there, standing in the gap to close it for us.*

—Oprah Winfrey

At some point, we all need someone who can stand in the gap for us—someone who selflessly comes by our side in good times and bad. I call them bone-marrow people.

Bone marrow is where new blood cells are formed. Dean Eller, CEO of the Central California Blood Center, describes marrow this way: "It's where life is produced." He knows first-hand the importance of bone marrow and blood. Dean stood by his daughter Jennifer as she battled acute myelogenous leukemia—one-third of those diagnosed die within 30 days. Jenny was blessed with an additional four years of life, in large part because of blood donations and a marrow transfusion. During her illness, virtually every ounce of blood in her body was there because people had donated hundreds and hundreds of pints of blood. A marrow transfusion requires a perfect match—about one in 20,000 are compatible. Diseased marrow is a death sentence. With a successful marrow transfusion, the body has a chance to regenerate with new, healthy blood cells. Some transplant recipients even celebrate a "re-birthday" because new marrow means renewed life, hope, and possibilities.

Just as bone marrow creates life for your body, Bone-Marrow People create life for your mind and spirit. When you've been in the presence of Bone-Marrow People, you become more, not less—closer to, not farther from, your ideal self. My business coach and life coach—Judy Santos and Heather Scheferman—fit this description. My best friend Jean Gatewood also fills the bill, as do several other friends and career-coaching colleagues. I am rich in the support department, which helps me find the "I CAN" energy to be <u>I</u>nspired daily, <u>C</u>ontrol what I can control, <u>A</u>ct now, and <u>N</u>ever give up.

---

### Bone-Marrow Worksheet

Who are the bone-marrow people in your life?

_____

_____

How frequently do you need a transfusion of their wisdom and support?

_____

What specifically do you need them to be or do?

_____

_____

If you don't have those special people in your life, how can you tell those closest to you what you need from them?

_____

_____

To whom are you a bone-marrow person? In what way?

_____

_____

How can you be a bone-marrow person to yourself?

_____

_____

_____

---

If you have bone-marrow people in your life, consider yourself blessed. If not, hire a coach. That's what we do best!

## Do's and Don'ts for Friends and Family Supporting You in a Job Search

Consider suggesting a few of these do's and don'ts to people supporting you in your job search. Authored by Robbie Cranch, who recently endured the slings and arrows of an extended job search, the advice is especially helpful when you're faced with a prolonged search:

### DO'S for Support Partners

- Ask your friend to describe the ideal position and industry she or he is targeting.

- Ask for a copy of your friend's résumé, and read it.

- Offer sincere acknowledgement of your friend's strengths.

- Ask how you can specifically support him or her.

- Be careful that your kindness or generosity does not translate to charity.

- Keep your eyes peeled and pass along *any* potential opportunity.

- Offer leads, not advice.

- Be sensitive to your friend's changed financial picture.

- Unless your friend needs to talk things through, keep the conversation light and upbeat. At the same time, let your perspective be transparent—while you understand this is a serious bump in the road, you believe in him or her.

### DONT'S for Support Partners

- Never ask "how are you," if you're not willing to hear a truthful answer.

- Avoid saying, "I know how you feel" unless you, too, have been on an extended job search.

- Don't assume your friend is just dabbling in a search if she or he has a two-income household.

*(continued)*

*(continued)*

- Never ask, "What do you do all day?" or wonder aloud why it is taking so long to find a job (the number of ads seen in the classifieds usually has *no* relation to your friend's real job picture).

- Be careful about saying, "I know you'll find something terrific." It might sound like encouragement, but to a person dealing with prolonged unemployment, it might come across as patronizing and superficial. Instead, try something like, "I know this is a really hard time, and I'm wishing you all the best."

## Choose Positive Thoughts

*The greatest discovery of our generation is that human beings can alter their lives by altering their attitudes of mind. As you think, so shall you be.*

—William James

Think positive! It sounds hackneyed, but it's true. Master your thought life, and you'll master your world. We are capable of thinking only one thought at a time—we alone choose whether we'll put a positive or negative spin on it. Ever notice how people who choose the positive spin typically have positive outcomes? Likewise, those who hold a doom-and-gloom perspective often attract a negative outcome. If you have a tendency to assume the worst before knowing all the facts, pick up an interesting book by Martin Seligman, *Learned Optimism: How to Change Your Mind and Your Life* (Free Press). In it, Seligman details how to shift from negative to positive thinking—a skill that will boost anyone's Buoy Factor.

Consider these exercises to increase hope-filled thinking:

- **Flipping:** When you hear yourself thinking negatively, ask yourself, what's the opposite of that thought?

- **Affirmations:** Review the section on "Remind Yourself of Your Value" for how to write affirmations. If you're not comfortable making an absolute statement ("I am successful"), alter the affirmation slightly to indicate you're growing toward the goal ("I am equipping myself with the knowledge and action plans to make this project a success").

- **Joy Journal:** I'm an advocate of journaling. Here's a new twist on the idea. Keep a Joy Journal—a diary devoted exclusively to things you're grateful for. Reread the pages when negative thoughts creep up.

- **A Great Day:** Set aside a day or evening where every syllable you utter reflects only optimism, gratitude, and hope.

- **The Pedometer:** Similar to wearing a pedometer that clocks the number of steps you take on a walk or run, consider clocking the accomplishments you've made this hour, day, week, or month. Review those accomplishments frequently to help remind yourself of the miles covered and progress made.

## An Attitude of Gratitude

Instead of focusing on the things that have gone wrong (the roadblocks with research, the hot lead that ended in a dead-end, the interviewer who offered the job to someone else), be grateful for what has gone right (the chance to master an important new skill, the knowledge you gained in the midst of following the lead, the chance to practice interviewing so that you're all the more prepared for the next one, and so on). Attitude is a controllable. What are *you* thankful for?

## Be Agile

Expect the unexpected. How can you control the unexpected? By being alert, nimble, and responsive to the need to change. There will always be something that pops up to either derail our plans or, in some cases, shift our plans so that we get on an even better track. It is a powerful thing to be able to adjust—to our surroundings, our circumstances, the people we encounter, and the curves that come our way in life. If we expect all these things to adjust to us, our rigidity invites disappointment and frustration. There is power and freedom in expecting the unexpected.

## Bolster Reserves of Time, Energy, and Finances

Reserves are extras of important things—extra time, extra energy, extra finances, extra space, and so on. Reserves give you a cushion and a safety net from which to operate. Having extras of good things lowers stress and gives you the freedom to take calculated risks. For instance, an abundance of energy makes you feel invincible, as though you can tackle a big project; an abundance of finances gives you the freedom to wait for the right career opportunity; an abundance of interview opportunities allows you to operate from a position of power and choice. Even if you're currently operating from a position of low reserves, there are some steps you can take to rev up your resources.

### Time Management for Job Search

How much time should you spend on your search? These guidelines will help:

- **Part-time search:** If you're conducting a part-time search (you're still employed), time will be your most precious commodity. A campaign with momentum requires 10 to 15 hours a week.

- **Full-time search:** If you're conducting a full-time search (between opportunities), time is on your side, but it needs to be managed well. For a strong search, clock 30 to 40 hours a week, just as if it were a full-time job. Interview preparation will range between 5 to 10 hours per interview. This is what it takes to thoroughly research a company, talk to insiders, understand critical needs, and practice your SMART Stories™ and sound bites.

These questions will help you to create reserves of time in your schedule:

- What are the priority projects or people you will say "yes" to?

- What projects or people should you say "no" to in order to free up more time?

- If you have trouble saying no to people, what system can you put in place to make it easier to say no? For instance, start by memorizing the line, "I'd love to help with that, but my prior commitments won't allow it."

- What typically interrupts or distracts you and causes you to lose time?

## Chunk Your Time

Try this tip from Tim Wright of www.wrightresults.com for creating time. "Chunk" your time by evaluating your energy level and allotting, say, the next 30 minutes to one particular task. Do absolutely nothing other than the designated task for the next 30 minutes. When 30 minutes is up, reevaluate whether you'll spend the next chunk of time on the same task or a different task, and what amount of time you will devote to the task. If you're at home practicing your SMART Stories™ for an interview, for example, assess how much energy you have to focus on the task—is it 20 minutes, 30 minutes, an hour? Set a timer if need be. Then, do nothing other than rehearse your SMART Stories™ during that chunk of time. Do not distract yourself by getting a cup of coffee, checking e-mail, or even using the restroom (you can allot the next five-minute chunk of time for that!). This is a great method for staying focused and getting the most out of your time.

## Energy

How can you build reserves of energy? The answer rests in self-care—making decisions and taking action that will support and sustain you. Those decisions and actions might include any of the following:

- **Structure:** Orchestrate your day so that priorities are taken care of *first*.

- **Habits/rituals:** Practice daily or weekly routines that make you feel strong and empowered.

- **Exercise:** This is your secret weapon in fighting stress and fighting feelings of being overwhelmed.

- **Rest:** Pushing yourself will only further deplete your energy.

- **Nutrition:** *You* know what foods nourish you and what foods drag you down.

- **Water:** Eight glasses a day keep the ailments away; also limit alcohol intake during your job search.

✧ **People:** Stay away from "toxic" people and stick to bone-marrow people.

✧ **Projects:** Say "no" to projects that are draining or pull you from your focus.

If you don't take care of your body, mind, and spirit, who will?

## Finances

If finances are tight during your search, look into an emergency loan, consider what material items you might sell, explore temporarily downsizing your living accommodations if possible, and simplify wherever possible. Look into part-time, temp, contract, or consulting positions that might ease cash flow. Be frank with immediate family about the situation and make cost-cutting a group effort. There are some great free money-stretching resources on the Web—type *"frugal," "cheap-skate,"* and *"bargain"* at www.google.com and you'll have dozens of ideas. Shop at consignment boutiques for interview attire—these shops are often loaded with gently worn, but low-cost, designer garments. With respect to job search, never pay money to an employment agency to place you in a position, and be wary of career marketing firms that guarantee they will help you find a job for a high-priced investment.

If it's been a while since you've had a paycheck and debt is a concern, there are free or low-cost sources that can help. The National Foundation for Credit Counseling provides credit counseling, debt-reduction services, and education for financial wellness. Member locations can be found by calling 800-388-2227 for 24-hour automated office listings, or visit their Web site at www.nfcc.org or their affiliate Web site www.debtadvice.org. Many churches also offer financial counsel through Crown Financial Ministries (www.crown.org), or call 800-722-1976 to obtain the name of one of their local financial counselors.

## Manage Any Negative Emotions

If you are a casualty of a corporate layoff or left your job for reasons other than your own volition, you might be experiencing some negative emotions. If so, it's important that you deal with them before they derail you. Interviewers can sense it when interviewees are worried, scared, sad, angry, and so on. They can also spot candidates who harbor resentment against past employers. Those candidates have a slim chance of being hired, as employers are suspicious that they'll speak negatively about others down the road. Jettison a negative emotion by

✧ Acknowledging it—objectively note that the emotion is there

✧ Expressing it—in a socially acceptable manner

✧ Releasing it—let go and move forward

# Act Now

If we were as relentless in our commitment and action as life is in its daily demands, success would be certain. Act. Persist. Success will be certain!

## The 80/20 Principle

Choose your actions wisely. Devote the greatest part of your energy to that which yields the greatest results. The 80/20 principle recognizes that it is the minority (20 percent) of the effort that yields the majority (80 percent) of results. For instance, 80 percent of a company's profits come from 20 percent of its customers. It might be a slightly different proportion, but it is virtually always heavily unbalanced.

These activities might be "20-percenters," yielding the greatest results for your investment of time:

- Meeting with your career coach
- Attending a networking meeting that will put you in front of hiring decision makers
- Rehearsing your two-minute profile and SMART Stories™
- Getting insider information on one of your target companies
- Meeting with people in your target companies
- Attending an event that pumps up your spirits (job clubs, motivational speaker, and so on)

These activities might be "80-percenters," not yielding the momentum and leverage you need:

- Looking for job postings on career sites
- Attending job fairs
- Networking with people who don't have access to decision makers

---

### 80/20 Worksheet

What is the 20 percent activity that will yield the 80 percent result for you?

_____

_____

_____

---

What do you need to do more or? Less of?

_____

_____

_____

## Join a Job Search Support Network

"I wish I had found my job club sooner," notes a neighbor of mine who admirably weathered an 18-month job search. The job search resources and synergy that come from these networks is undeniably powerful. Frequently, they include access to insider leads and guest speakers who are experts in résumé writing, interviewing, and networking. National organizations such as the Five O'Clock Club (www.fiveoclockclub.com) have an excellent reputation. Many areas have locally operated groups that are free to members, with the requirement that they give back in volunteer time. To find these local organizations, inquire with local temporary agencies, the unemployment office, employment development department, or Chamber of Commerce. If there are no job search groups in your area, start your own. Make up a flyer with telephone tear-off slips and post it in a public place. Churches, upscale grocery stores such as Whole Foods Market, and neighborhood shopping malls often have a bulletin area to help people connect.

Another benefit of a job search club is the camaraderie and comfort of being with people who have walked a mile in your moccasins. The format and dynamics of a support group are proven, as demonstrated in formal organizations such as Alcoholics Anonymous and Weight Watchers, as well as in informal grief-support groups. Fortunately, job search groups are more upbeat than the latter. When newcomers to the group see someone land a job, it rekindles hope. It also provides an outlet for helping others. Tossing around strategies that might help another job seeker will make you feel good, and might give rise to ideas that will also apply to your own search.

## Get on the Radar Screen

If it seems as though things have stalled (the interviewer hasn't called back, you can't get in to see networking contacts, and so on), consider a radar screen activity—action that gets you in front of decision makers. It might be sending a follow-up letter, making a call, or e-mailing an informative article to a networking contact or interviewer. Another smart radar screen activity involves attending a seminar or meeting. During the event, be sure to ask an intelligent question or make a comment that makes your presence known!

## Act Successful

*We are what we pretend to be, so we must be careful what we pretend to be.*

—Kurt Vonnegut, Jr.

Act "as if." Act as if you already have that dream job you're after. Attitudes, actions, vocabulary, dress, posture, knowledge, habits, self-talk, and mindset all play a part. How do you need to act to be successful in your job search and interviewing? Even if you're conducting a full-time search and don't have an office to go to, put on nice clothes *every* day. Attend to your grooming each morning as if you were headed to work, even if you plan to spend the day at home sending out follow-up letters and making phone calls. Plan to have lunch with a friend occasionally before going back to "work."

## Consider Volunteering

If you're conducting a full-time search, consider allotting some time to volunteering. Donating your talents has a twofold reward. It gives you an avenue to use your skills and feel of value. When performed in an organization where potential hiring decision makers can see your work product, it can produce job leads and potential offers.

Be discriminating about your investment of time. And, approach your volunteerism with a service-oriented attitude. If on day one of your volunteer project, you start asking for job leads or introductions to potential networking contacts, you might appear too self-serving.

## Pump Up Another Part of Your Life

Feel like all you do is live and breathe job search? If so, it might be helpful to take a short break and pump up some other part of your life. Now might be the perfect time to do the following:

- Refresh relationships with friends or family members.
- Read a little something other than industry trends and interviewing books.
- Catch up on some much-needed fun and recreation.
- Spend time doing something you really enjoy.
- Choose to be with people who have a knack for making you laugh and feel good.
- Reconnect with the spiritual side of yourself.
- Do things that are good for your physical health.
- Pick up an old or new hobby.
- Tackle a home improvement project that can be done in a short period of time.

The latter can be as simple as tidying the pantry or cleaning out closets. For me, there's something therapeutic about clearing clutter from closets. I love the feeling of spaciousness and order that comes, and it gives the sense that there is room for something new to move into my life.

# Never Give Up!

*When things go wrong as they sometimes will;*
*When the road you're trudging seems all uphill;*
*When the funds are low, and the debts are high*
*And you want to smile, but have to sigh;*
*When care is pressing you down a bit—*
*Rest if you must, but do not quit.*
*Success is failure turned inside out;*
*The silver tint of the clouds of doubt;*
*And you can never tell how close you are*
*It may be near when it seems so far;*
*So stick to the fight when you're hardest hit—*
*It's when things go wrong that you must not quit.*

—Author Unknown

Perseverance is one of the characteristics of someone with a strong Buoy Factor. Job search and interviewing requires perseverance extraordinaire. You learned some good techniques in the three preceding "I CAN" sections. Here are some final strategies that will ensure that you never give up.

## Persevere

Thomas Edison noted that "genius is 1% inspiration and 99% perspiration," while Woody Allen quipped that "80% of success is showing up." There aren't too many short cuts when it comes to job search and interviews, and nothing substitutes for hard (and smart) work. Enough said!

### "Nadia" Doesn't Know the Word "No"

Age and health challenges didn't stop Nadia from persevering. She endured a life-threatening back injury that confined her to bed for nearly two years. After what seemed an eternity of doctors' visits, surgery, and therapy, she was able to walk again. With a new lease on life and her children now grown, she decided to enter the work force at age 44, initially as a teacher. Shortly thereafter, she landed a position with the Department of Energy where, for the next seven years, she launched and managed some of the most successful consumer educational programs in the history of the department. She then

*(continued)*

*(continued)*

set her sights on a position with the United Nations. It took two years of planning, writing, and calling on people before the UN opportunity opened up. After her time at the UN came to a close, she found herself in job search mode during the worst job market in decades. With the additional challenge of being a "mature" worker, Nadia, at age 66, spent one year of constant networking and interviewing. Her hard work and buoyant spirit paid off, eventually landing her a position with a leading telecom manufacturer at a six-figure salary. Nadia never gave up!

## Don't Take Things Personally

"We found a candidate who was a better fit." If you hear this response in your interview travels, do not take it personally. If you do, it can send you into a downward spiral of discouraging self-doubt. Eleanor Roosevelt once said that "No one can make you feel inferior without your consent." You must not give your consent! And, if your mix of experiences and personality aren't right for the company, the *we-found-a-candidate-who-was-a-better-fit* response might have saved you from a frustrating career situation. Remember that every "no" brings you one step closer to a "yes!"

Adopt the "happy puppy syndrome" when job searching and interviewing. Puppies are notorious for *expecting* that you're happy to see them and want their company. Their Buoy Factor is usually quite high! When it seems that an interviewer might be avoiding follow-up with you, examine your belief system. Is that a certainty? Or is it that the interviewer might have gotten busy and had to put the hiring process on the back burner? If you've ever been in a position to interview others, you know that this can easily happen.

One client of mine, Paula, seemed to be getting the brush-off from a recruiter who, at one point, had told her she was a top candidate in the running for a management position. Paula could have immediately assumed she was at fault with thoughts of, *he must have found a better candidate* or *he doesn't want me,* but she didn't. Instead, she continued to leave polite voice-mail messages and send proactive follow-up notes every Friday for at least six consecutive weeks. It turned out that Paula *was* still in the running, but a confidential internal problem that involved shifting Paula's would-be boss into a different position had to take place before the search could be resumed. Paula never gave up, didn't take things personally, and ended up impressing the recruiter even more because of her perseverance.

When following up, avoid communicating your frustration or anger. This is a great opportunity to demonstrate your professionalism.

**Interviewing Is Like Dating**

Interviewing is a little like looking for a good dating partner—you can't expect every date to be Mr. or Ms. Right. At the same time, you should do all you can to ensure that your qualifications are highly competitive. When an interview doesn't result in an offer, follow up with something like this, "I'd like to bring value to your organization and be considered for future opportunities. What would you suggest I do to enhance my qualifications when a similar position opens up?"

## Listen for the Leading

*Coincidence—God Winks—are little messages to you on your journey through life, nudging you along the grand path that has been designed especially for you.*

—SQuire Rushnell, When God Winks

Coincidence, intuition, synchronicity, serendipity, the hand of God? SQuire Rushnell, in his short book *When God Winks: How the Power of Coincidence Guides Your Life* (Atria Books), chronicles dozens of stories that defy an explanation of random chance—stories that encouraged people to persevere and move ahead.

Rushnell writes of Beth, whose sobbing in the airport over her father's unexpected death caught the attention of fellow traveler Kevin Costner. Costner expressed sincere condolences, also mentioning "good things always come from sad times." He then extended an open invitation to Beth to stop by and watch the filming of a movie he was shooting in her home town. Two months later, Beth had opportunity to do so. The film's public relations executive was called over to sit with her—it was love at first sight. That night she called her mother to say, "Today, I met the man I'm going to marry." Within eight months, they were husband and wife.

Rushnell also tells of his own God Wink that helped confirm the direction his career would take. At the youthful age of 15, his dream was to be a radio announcer. A job interview 10 miles away with the general manager of a local television station required that he hitchhike, a relatively safe undertaking in those days. The traffic on his rural road was sparse. Every car passed him by. Fearful he hadn't left enough time to get to his appointment, he began to lose faith. Eventually, the car that did stop to scoop him up was driven by none other than his favorite disc jockey, his pop hero at the time. The DJ knew the GM and told Rushnell to pass along a hello. Rushnell made it on time, *and* he got the job. That first position eventually led the wannabe radio announcer to an award-winning 20-year career as an executive with the ABC Television Network.

---

### Winks Worksheet

What *winks* have you seen that hint of good things to come?

_____

_____

_____

What events, places, or persons have been encouraging signs along your way?

_____

_____

_____

---

# Enjoy the Adventure of Not Knowing

Job search can seem fraught with not knowing. How long will it take? Will I find work before my unemployment checks or savings runs out? Will it be work that I enjoy? Will they call me back for a second interview?

Dealing with uncertainty is one of *my* least favorite tasks! My tendency is to want to know what the future holds, to have details pinned down. Many of us do. Recall from chapter 3 where we discussed Type and the four preference scales of Introversion-Extraversion, Sensing-Intuiting, Thinking-Feeling, and Judging-Perceiving. That fourth dimension, Judging-Perceiving, can lend insight into how you manage the *not knowing*. Those with a preference for Perceiving (P) enjoy leaving their options open and often take a wait-and-see attitude. If this describes you, the *not knowing* might actually be fun and adventurous. Those with a preference for Judging (J) enjoy closure and are less comfortable with ambiguity, making the *not knowing* doubly frustrating. If you are a J (like me), adopt some of the mindset of a P: Let your search be more of an adventure!

## An Attorney Manages the Not Knowing

Valerie was leaving her law firm and exploring whether she would continue working as an attorney or pursue a different career direction. To help manage the current uncertainty, she was able to look back to a time several years ago when she had another period of unemployment. During that time, she was able to help care for her terminally ill grandmother. The day her grandmother passed away, she received a call about a new position. In retrospect, she describes the time with her grandmother as "a precious gift" that she would not have otherwise had. The entire experience helped her trust that things would again unfold in her current circumstances.

---

## Not Knowing Worksheet

What can you point to that will help you enjoy the adventure of not knowing? The answers to these questions might help:

Be an historian. Look back into your history for an event where you had to wait to learn the outcome. What were the positive things associated with this time?

_____

_____

_____

Where did you receive emotional or material provision for your needs?

_____

_____

In cases where the outcome wasn't positive, what did you learn from that situation that will make this one easier?

_____

_____

What's the worst that might happen in your current situation?

_____

_____

What actions will you take to minimize that risk?

_____

_____

---

Finally, give yourself permission to *not* have all the details figured out. Like going on a first date with someone, you rarely know whether this will be "the one." Instead, trust that as you walk it out—with steadfast commitment, focused energy, and intelligent action—your story will unfold and answers will come.

## Leverage What Works

Similar to the 80/20 principle, leverage means to focus on the self-care activities that work best for you. If you know that getting to church or temple is crucial to your mental well-being, get yourself there (find an accountability partner if necessary). If you know that exercise is the linchpin in your emotional well-being, get out and move (write it into your calendar if necessary). If you know that being around bone-marrow people is the difference between delight and depression, see those people (schedule several appointments each week if necessary). If you know that time alone is the best way for you to recharge, steal away during a lunch hour or schedule an entire weekend of solitude.

As Nike advises, *just do it!*

# Chapter Wrap-Up

Employers prefer to hire people with energy and enthusiasm—people who conduct themselves with purpose, confidence, and perseverance—people with buoyancy! Buoyant workers have an optimistic outlook when problems arise on the job. They bounce back quickly from setbacks. They are an inspiration to others, affecting morale and productivity. They get hired and promoted faster. *You* can be that person. Just say *I CAN!*

## 10 Quick Tips for Managing Mindset

1. **Mindset can either sink or support you in your job search and interviewing.** To keep your attitude afloat and boost your Buoy Factor—that measurement of how quickly you regain your self-confidence and recover from discouragement—adopt the I CAN mentality: Inspire Daily; Control the Controllables; Act Now; and Never Give Up.

2. **Inspire yourself by mastering the Law of Inner Action.** Success starts on the inside, with the inner action of thought and choice. Sow positive inner actions, and you'll reap positive outer actions—behaviors that lead to more leads, interviews, and offers. Consciously be aware of your thought life and convert any self-defeating thoughts into self-supporting thoughts. Always hold a positive picture of the future, remind yourself of the value you offer employers, and frame situations from a possibility perspective.

3. **Inspire begins with the letter *i*, reminding us that I alone am in charge of inspiring myself.** Identify your inspirational triggers (being with other people, reading inspirational stories, exercising, and so on) and weave them into your daily or weekly habits.

4. **Control the controllables.** Controllables include "soft" items like your attitude, self-talk, and self-image, as well as "hard" items, such as devoting a certain number of hours each week to networking and preparing for interviews, putting contingency plans in place, managing your time, and taking care of yourself.

5. **Surround yourself with bone-marrow people**—individuals who selflessly stand beside you with encouragement, ideas, and inspiration.

6. **Act now!** Apply the 80/20 principle, focusing on the minority (20 percent) of effort that yields the majority (80 percent) of results. Twenty-percent activities might include meeting with your coach, attending meetings that put you in front of hiring decision makers, rehearsing (with a video camera!) for interviews, getting insider information on a target company, meeting with people in target companies, or attending an event that pumps up your spirits.

7. **Act successful.** Act like you already have the job. Act like you have value (you do). Adopt the attitudes, actions, vocabulary, dress, posture, knowledge, habits, self-talk, and mindset that personify people who are successful in your target position.

8. **Never give up.** Be as relentless in your action as life is in its daily demands. Success will be certain.

9. **Leverage what works.** When the stress piles on, focus on the self-care activities that give you the most momentum, whether it be exercising, going to church/temple, meeting with friends, or finding time for introspection.

10. **Success in job search goes well beyond the mechanics of what to say to an interviewer.** It requires a buoyant spirit that embodies purpose, confidence, and perseverance. Tending to your mental, physical, and emotional health is a sure way to boost your Buoy Factor.

---

### ⭐ Magical Coaching Questions

A buoyant mindset stems from a combination of mental, physical, and emotional health. What individual daily habits need to be in place for each of these elements to thrive?

_____

_____

_____

*(continued)*

*(continued)*

When a significant setback comes, what do you need to do that hour, or that day, to care for your mental, physical, and emotional needs?

_____

_____

_____

What do you need to do to empower yourself today?

_____

_____

_____

*Part*

# 2

# Resumes and Career Marketing Documents

Chapter 7:    The Blueprint for a Magic Résumé

Chapter 8:    How to Write Great Keyworded Copy

Chapter 9:    Accomplishments: The Linchpin of a Great Résumé

Chapter 10:    E-Résumés, Cover Letters, and Other Career Marketing Documents

Chapter

# 7

# The Blueprint for a Magic Résumé

*"Planning must be a deliberate prelude to writing.*

—E. B. White, Author

E. B. White is the coauthor of *The Elements of Style,* a "bible" for anyone who writes for a living or, for that matter, anyone who writes at all. White proposes that the first principle of composition is to "determine the shape of what is to come and pursue that shape." Just as an architect prepares blueprints before a contractor can build, you need an outline before you can write. A lack of planning at this stage will cost you time, energy, and momentum, so resist the temptation to jump in and start composing (you'll get to that in chapters 8 and 9).

In this chapter, you'll decide on the format, or structure, of your résumé, and then select the categories, or building blocks, that make up a magic résumé.

---

 *Note:* Résumé Magic, the original book in the *Magic* series, provides a comprehensive look at résumé writing. At nearly 600 pages, you'll find in it answers to virtually any résumé question or quandary. Highlights from the book are included in the next few chapters.

---

## Two Tried-and-True Winning Formats: Chronological and Functional

Ninety-nine percent of business résumés fall into one of two distinct genres: chronological or functional. (The other one percent can be lumped into a "creative" category, reserved for those artistic gurus who have been blessed with extra right-brain gray matter!) This section details the main characteristics of each type and helps you choose which is best for your situation.

# The Chronological Format

Just as its name implies, the chronological format offers a chronology—a historical timeline—of your work experience. The distinguishing characteristic is that descriptions of what you did and how well you did it are grouped together with the employer information.

The bulk of the résumé is devoted to the Experience section, also known as your Employment History. In most cases, your most recent employer is listed first, and your least recent employer is listed last. Other sections, such as Education and Affiliations, generally follow the Experience section.

The chronological format wins "The People's Choice Award." Why? Plain and simple. Employers prefer it! In economic parlance, the buyer (your prospective employer)—who usually holds the upper hand in the supply-demand model—can better evaluate what the seller (you, the candidate) has to offer. Most hiring managers have an innate curiosity about what you've done and where you've done it. A logical, straightforward chronological format answers their questions.

## A Chronological Format Worked for David

*Magic*

Because the chronological is the most common format, you're probably familiar with its look. Nonetheless, check out David Dillingham's résumé for a *Before* (7.1) and *After* (7.2) of a standard chronological format. Compare how bullets are used in the *Before* and *After* résumés. This sales tool worked for David, landing him a job with a leading textbook publisher.

## Points

Many! The chronological format is easily digested and won't raise suspicions that you are attempting to hide vocational skeletons, such as a former conviction as a serial job hopper. A chronological format's most obvious advantages are these:

- Showcases a progression of increasingly responsible positions, especially preferred by executive recruiters and decision-making boards for management and top-tier executive slots.

- Demonstrates that you are qualified to take the next step in your career.

- Highlights impressive employers who will add weight to your credentials because of their name recognition, comprehensive training programs, or strong market position.

- Answers the employer's question of whether your work history has been stable.

## Pitfall

The chronological format really puts you under the microscope and can make you feel a bit naked. It's like wearing skimpy spandex to the gym: If you're not in great shape, it will show every roll and dimple.

**David D. Dillingham**
**4321 South Johnstone Boulevard**
**Laguna Niguel, CA.  92321**
**(714) 455–4431**

**PUBLISHING WORK EXPERIENCE:**

**International Publishing - Los Angeles, CA**
**Careers Division, Marketing Manager 10/00 to Present**
**Children's Division, Field Sales Representative 8/99 to 9/00**

◆ Responsible for Marketing Twenty-five Million Dollar Careers List
◆ Maintain Correspondence between Authors, Editors and Sales Force
◆ Hire, Train and Manage Marketing Assistants
◆ Developed Marketing Materials, Sales Tools and Advertisements for Sales Force and Consumers
◆ Service Universities, State Colleges, Community Colleges, Proprietary Schools, Post Secondary Vocational Technical Schools and Bookstores
◆ Demonstrate Product through Personal Visits, Book Fairs and Trade Shows
◆ Plan Travel Itineraries, Yearly Budgets and Forecasting of Sales Goals
◆ Develop, Maintain, and Service Accounts
◆ Annually Obtained and Increased Sales Goals

**Eastern Publishing Company- New York, NY**
**Field Sales Representative 6/96 to 7/99**

◆ Represented Mathematics List to Universities, State Colleges and Retail Bookstores
◆ Set Appointments, Processed Orders, and Provided Customer Service
◆ Responsible for Administrative Tasks, Filing, and Documentation of all Data
◆ Prepared Mailings, Handled all Correspondence

**Harcourt Publishing Company- San Francisco, CA**
**Inside Sales Representative 1/91 to 5/96**

◆ Sold Computer Science, Physics, Mathematics, Science and Nursing Textbooks
◆ Contacted Accounts via Telemarketing
◆ Uncovered Potential Reviewers and Authors
◆ Increased Territory 30%

**EDUCATION:**

B.S. Degree in Political Science, University of California- Berkeley, 1991
A.A. Degree, The Community College, El Cajon, California

**APPLICABLE SKILLS:**

PowerPoint, Word, Access, Excel, WordPerfect, Lotus Notes, Internet Explorer, Employee Appraiser, Professional Selling Skills Training (PSS), Los Angeles County Aids Project Volunteer

**Figure 7.1: Before.**

# DAVID D. DILLINGHAM

4321 Johnstone Boulevard                                                                            (714) 555-5555
Laguna Niguel, CA 92321                                                                        ddd234@excite.com

## SALES & MARKETING

### Publishing Industry

## SALES & MARKETING EXPERIENCE

**MARKETING MANAGER**—International Publishing, Los Angeles, CA                    2000–Present

Manage marketing for $25 million careers list. Develop product strategies, marketing materials, sales tools, and advertisements for international sales force of 500. Hire, train, and manage marketing assistants. Forecast and manage operating budgets and sales goals. Personally sell to and service universities and retail booksellers. Promote product at trade shows and book fairs.

♦ Delivered 27% sales growth through development of innovative international marketing strategies.

♦ Doubled individual sales volume from $149,000 to $312,000, an unprecedented increase for territory.

♦ Led region of 10 reps in sales volume, achieving 22% above goal (well above company average of 8%).

♦ Initially challenged with turnaround of product line that had not been serviced in over a year; successfully converted key clients from primary competitor and captured new nationwide sales.

**FIELD SALES REPRESENTATIVE**—Eastern Publishing Company, New York, NY                    1996–2000

Generated sales for Mathematics Division in seven western states and three Canadian provinces.

♦ Gained access to prestigious clients, such as Stanford University and UC Berkeley (previously "no see" accounts).

♦ Increased sales in territory that had a several-year history of stagnant sales.

**INSIDE SALES REPRESENTATIVE**—Harcourt Publishing Company, San Francisco, CA                    1991–1996

Promoted 100+ item catalogue of computer science, physics, mathematics, science, and nursing textbooks to college bookstore market in California, Nevada, and Oregon.

♦ Increased territory sales 30% to rank #1 in division (with no prior industry knowledge).

♦ Researched and uncovered potential reviewers and new authors.

## EDUCATION & TRAINING

**Bachelor of Science, Political Science**—University of California, Berkeley                    1991
Professional Selling Skills Training (PSS)

## COMPUTER SKILLS

MS Office (PowerPoint, Word, Excel, Access), WordPerfect, Lotus Notes, MSIE, Employee Appraiser

♦ ♦ ♦

**Figure 7.2: After.**

## The Functional Format

A functional résumé relies on categorical, skills-based sections to demonstrate your qualifications for a particular job. Company names, employment dates, and position titles are either deemphasized or intentionally omitted.

I'm convinced that the functional format was invented for my husband. In the course of a decade or so, he had lived and worked in seven different states, with as many different jobs, including cross-country ski instructor, heating and air-conditioning mechanic, interdenominational minister in two national parks, grocery bagger, camp manager, and environmental impact analyst. His tangential career path (prior to settling down with the girl of his dreams!) definitely didn't lend itself to a chronological presentation. (He has since parlayed all those experiences into an academic career track and now uses a chronological format to catalog high school and university teaching experience.)

If your professional pilgrimage hasn't been "politically correct" either, give serious consideration to a functional format.

*Magic*

## A Functional Format Helped Grace Get a New Life

Grace needed a change. The survivor of a messy divorce, she opted to explore other career options to give her a change of pace. After nine years as a classroom teacher, she wanted to pursue customer-service work in the private sector. Her new résumé is a strong example of a functional format and landed her a "fun and upbeat" job in the tourism industry. Here are Grace's *Before* (7.3) and *After* (7.4) résumés.

# GRACE COLTERMAN

One Riverplace Parkway
Selton, Alabama 42315
(423) 413-9887

---

**OBJECTIVE**      Teacher:  Elementary Education (K–8)

**EDUCATION**      UNIVERSITY OF ALABAMA
                   Degree:    Bachelor of Arts, Public Relations / Journalism – 1987
                   Honors:    Dean's List; Greek Leadership Award;
                              Outstanding College Students of America

**CREDENTIAL**     Multiple Subject Clear Credential – 1989

**EXPERIENCE**

  **Teaching**      Alton Unified School District, Alton, Alabama          9/92–Pres.
  **Experience**    <u>**1st Grade Teacher**</u>
Plan and implement integrated curriculum in all subject areas.  Utilize Project READ, a multisensory approach to reading with emphasis on phonology strategies.  Applied Rebecca Sitton's Integrated Spelling & Writing program, focusing on daily writing across the curriculum.  Taught core literature books using whole language approach and incorporating McCracken Reading ideas.

Mifflin Union High School, Mifflin, Alabama
<u>**3rd Grade Teacher**</u>                                                9/91–6/92
Applied current teaching techniques, including AIMS projects, manipulatives, writing process, and cooperative learning.  Implemented the Total Reading Program, a multi-sensory phonetic reading program that emphasizes development of reading, language, and spelling skills.  Developed and taught units on reptiles, Indians, and Mifflin County; integrated all curricula areas and culminated in group experiences with the entire 3rd grade.  Taught segments of a Physical Education course in a pilot cooperative teaching program.

<u>**Kindergarten Teacher**</u>                                            9/89–6/91
Utilizing a thematic approach, created and taught lessons incorporating programs such as Math Their Way, Project AIMS, Come With Me Science, and Sunshine/Story Box with big book illustrations emphasizing whole language.  Administered the Brigance testing format; gathered parent input to determine children's classroom readiness prior to new school year.

  **Student**       Atherton School District, Atherton, Alabama
  **Teaching**      <u>**2nd Grade Teacher**</u> — Sterling Elementary School          3/89–5/89
                   <u>**4th Grade Teacher**</u> — McKinley Elementary School          1/89–3/89

**RELATED**        Alton Unified School District, Alton, Alabama
**ACTIVITIES**     • Served on School Site Council.
                   • Coordinated school-wide Speech Festival and Peach Blossom Oral Interpretation and
                     Speech Festival.
                   • Participated in Learning Club, a monthly group for 1st graders and their parents; program
                     focuses on introducing math and reading activities to parents that can then be reinforced
                     with students at home.

**INTERESTS**      Coaching (Cross-Country) • Public Speaking • Yearbook Publications

---

**Figure 7.3: Before.**

# GRACE COLTERMAN

One Riverplace Parkway                                          gracec@juno.com
Selton, Alabama 42315                                           (423) 413-9887

## GOAL

Customer support position where my strengths in communications, sales, and administration will be of value.

## PROFESSIONAL EXPERIENCE

**COMMUNICATIONS:** *Public Relations, Advertising, Training, Staff Development*

♦ *Degree in Public Relations/Journalism:* Completed comprehensive training in public relations, including advanced course work in mass communications, newswriting, editing, advertising, media, and graphic arts.

♦ *Writing/Verbal Skills:* Excellent communication skills for effective customer communications, proposals, correspondence, flyers, newsletters, internal communications, and public speaking.

♦ *Staff Development:* Successfully coordinated and implemented monthly training programs—assessed learning needs, created curriculum, presented instruction, and secured nationally recognized guest speakers.

♦ *Background as Educator:* Able to provide client-centered interactive training sessions, emphasizing practical applications for customer education and/or staff development.

**SALES:** *Presentations, Negotiations, Customer Relations, Event Planning, Fund-Raising*

♦ *Persuasive Communicator:* Made formal presentations to boards and decision makers; sold new program ideas and secured approval for funding. Demonstrated ability to sell varied products as "floater" for upscale retailer; generated daily sales equal to that of experienced sales associates.

♦ *Customer Relations:* Selected by management as liaison and troubleshooter to resolve concerns with coworkers, external customers, and vendors.

♦ *Event Planning:* Organized well-received special events in work and community volunteer capacities. Planned events for up to 400. Initiated fund-raising projects to offset a $250,000 reduction in state funding.

**ADMINISTRATION:** *Program Management, Planning, Development, Budgeting, Supervision*

♦ *Management:* Held direct accountability for planning, staffing, facilities management, and coordination of educational program with 250 enrollees and 15 instructors. Hired, placed, and evaluated certificated instructors.

♦ *Program Development:* Created successful programs (business-school partnerships, volunteerism, community outreach), from concept development through implementation at multiple sites.

♦ *Planning:* Served on cross-functional team that conducted strategic planning, developed budgets in excess of $345,000, determined programming, and ensured compliance for school site serving 650+ students.

## EMPLOYMENT HISTORY

Prior experience in education as a teacher and site administrator.  Excellent record with former employers, Alton Unified School District (1992–Present) and Mifflin Union School District (1989–1992).

## EDUCATION

**DEGREE:** *Bachelor of Arts in Public Relations/Journalism—University of Alabama (1987)*

**References on Request**

**Figure 7.4: After.**

## Choosing Your Résumé Format

Take the quick quiz that follows to give you an idea of which of the two main formats (chronological or functional) to use. *If the indicator in the first column is true for you, place a check mark in the shaded box. If it is not true for you, place a check mark in the unshaded box.* Although your situation might not be clear-cut, limit your responses to one check mark per row.

| One-Minute Quick Quiz | | |
|---|---|---|
| **Indicator** | **Chronological** | **Functional** |
| Strong career progression over past five-plus years, seeking position similar to current or most recent position | ■ | ☐ |
| Impressive employers (large, strong name recognition; favorable reputation; Fortune 500 companies) | ■ | ☐ |
| Executive or management candidate | ■ | ☐ |
| Working through executive recruiter for your job search | ■ | ☐ |
| International job search | ■ | ☐ |
| Conservative field or industry (law, accounting, government) | ■ | ☐ |
| Reentering the workforce (same career) after a several-year hiatus | ■ | ☐ |
| Reentering the workforce (different career) after a several-year hiatus | ☐ | ■ |
| Changing careers (new function, say, from secretarial to sales) | ☐ | ■ |
| Changing fields (same function, new industry) | ■ | ☐ |
| Leaving the military, performing similar job function | ■ | ☐ |
| Leaving the military, pursuing different job function | ☐ | ■ |
| Lots of volunteer experience related to your chosen field | ☐ | ■ |
| New graduate with experience related to chosen field | ■ | ☐ |
| New graduate with experience *unrelated* to chosen field | ☐ | ■ |

| Indicator | Chronological | Functional |
|-----------|:---:|:---:|
| Performed very similar responsibilities repeatedly for past employers and looking for similar position | ☐ | ◼ |
| Unstable work history (changed jobs too often, lots of gaps in employment timeline, spouse relocated frequently, and so on) | ☐ | ◼ |
| "Overqualified" and looking for less responsibility | ☐ | ◼ |
| "Seasoned citizen" with extensive work history looking for less responsibility | ☐ | ◼ |
| **Totals** | | |

Add the check marks for both the Chronological and Functional columns and place the total for each column in the Totals row. If the number of "chronologicals" outweighs the "functionals," you should probably use a chronological format. If the reverse is true, and you have more "functional" responses, consider presenting your skills in a functional format.

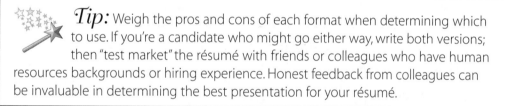

*Tip:* Weigh the pros and cons of each format when determining which to use. If you're a candidate who might go either way, write both versions; then "test market" the résumé with friends or colleagues who have human resources backgrounds or hiring experience. Honest feedback from colleagues can be invaluable in determining the best presentation for your résumé.

Now that you've selected a format, let's move on to the categories for your résumé.

# Selecting Category Headings

Your résumé will begin to take shape as you decide on a heading style and choose categories that will best showcase your experience. Many people base their résumés on the three most common categories—Objective, Experience, and Education—while overlooking other categories that can help catapult their résumés to the top of the "must interview" list. You'll take a look at each of these categories and check mark which are most appropriate for your situation. You'll also receive a refresher course on what not to include—such as information that is illegal, passé, superfluous, or grounds for potential discrimination. At the end of this chapter, you'll have an opportunity to fine-tune your outline for structural integrity and visual appeal.

In creating your résumé outline, you will look at the following categories:

- Data bits, or contact info
- Objective or Focus statement
- Key Features, or Qualifications Summary
- Professional Experience
- Skills
- Education, Credentials, and Licenses
- Affiliations
- Supporting material (such as publications, presentations, patents, awards and honors, bio bites, and endorsements)

## Dashboard Data, or Contact Info

Make yourself readily accessible to potential employers. The following list includes 10 pieces of contact data, or "dashboard data," that you might use on your résumé to make sure employers can reach you easily. Put a check mark in the box next to each of the items you will use in your résumé header. (Your name is a given!) Keep in mind that your name, phone number, and e-mail address are the most important elements.

---

### Data Bits Worksheet

- ☐ Name
- ☐ Street address
- ☐ City, state, ZIP code
- ☐ Residence telephone number
- ☐ Business telephone number
- ☐ Mobile telephone number
- ☐ Pager number
- ☐ Fax number
- ☐ E-mail address (your personal e-mail, not your company's)
- ☐ Web page URL or blog with an online résumé (your own, not your company's)
- ☐ Availability for relocation
- ☐ In this box, indicate the number of data bits you'll include in your résumé heading.

Review the headers of résumé samples throughout this book for ideas on how to combine your information. Pay special attention to those that include the same amount of dashboard data as you plan for your heading. Using your computer, create the header for your résumé now. When you're finished, move on to the next step in your résumé outline.

## Objective, or Focus Statement

You're probably familiar with the term *Objective* as it relates to résumé writing. For 50 or more years, objectives enjoyed preeminent positioning in résumés as a one-sentence statement encapsulating the age-old question of "what do you want to be when you grow up?" More often than not, objectives tended to be *de rigueur* statements that were vague, trite, canned, and self-focused.

Today, your focus should be on the employer's needs. Answering those needs will create desire and interest in you. Yes, you can still define what sort of position you want. Yes, you can still convey your qualifications. And, yes, you can still use the term *Objective* if you prefer. The difference is in the perspective—don't write about what *you* want out of the employment relationship. Instead, direct your writing toward what *your employer* wants and how you can give it to them. This can't be emphasized enough:

Focus on the employer's needs!

This explains the use of the word *Focus* in place of *Objective*. *Focus* conveys more energy and concentration. Arguably, it's a matter of semantics. You can use a number of terms, as long as you weave the employer's needs into your statement. Here's an alphabetical list of some alternative headings you can use for this section:

| | | |
|---|---|---|
| Aim | Mission | Specialist |
| Competency | Objective | Specialization |
| Concentration | Proficiency | Strengths |
| Expertise | Proposal | Talents |
| Focus | Purpose | Target |
| Forte | Qualifications | |
| Goal | Skills | |

Many of these terms can be mixed and matched to make different headings, such as *Focus & Qualifications* or *Specialization & Qualifications*. Or you can add terms such as *Career, Professional,* or *Vocational* in front of several words in the list. For instance, *Career Target, Professional Competencies,* and *Vocational Skills* can each work as a heading. You'll also note some nontraditional words, such as *forte,* which I've included to expand your thinking. These words are best used when woven into a cover letter to describe your strengths or vocational goals. Use such words only if they fit your style of speech.

Your Focus statement will be brief—one or two sentences at most. It can stand alone or be used in combination with a Qualifications Summary (which is covered in the next section). You are a good candidate for a standalone Focus statement if your situation is aligned with any of these four scenarios:

- You specialize in a particular position and want to have that same position in your next job. Note that *Expertise* implies a number of years of experience at your craft. Don't use this term if you're just starting out. Study this example:

### EXPERTISE

Licensed Clinical Social Worker with 12-year record of creating award-winning social service programs, accessing "hidden" funding and grant money, and delivering services to medically underserved populations.

- You're a recent graduate with limited paid experience:

### FOCUS

Management Training Program—BBA graduate with 4.0 GPA from one of the nation's top business schools. Well grounded in simulated corporate scenarios that required solutions to complex manufacturing, distribution, and marketing issues.

- You're applying for entry-level, line, or support positions:

### INTENT

To support management in a secretarial role where my technical skills, initiative, and understanding of client-driven organizations will be of value.

- You're transitioning from one career to another:

### GOAL

To parlay 15 years of legal experience as a top-notch business litigator into a career as a consultant, motivational speaker, and business coach.

- ☐ Check this box if you'll use some form of a Focus statement in your résumé. Select a word from the list on page 197 that best suits your needs and write it on the following line: _____

## Key Features, or Qualifications Summary

In recent years, a Qualifications Summary has emerged as a tool to both define the type of job you want *and* to summarize why you're qualified for the job. Because the Qualifications Summary serves both purposes, it is understandably longer than an Objective or Focus statement. If you use a Qualifications Summary, you won't need a Focus statement. The following ingredients typically make up a Qualifications Summary:

- Functional specialty or title (for example, accountant, regional manager, materials manager, or production planner)

- Number of years of industry experience (for example, insurance, finance, manufacturing, or agriculture)

* Expertise, strengths, or specialization (for example, delivered more than $10 million in cost reductions through introduction of just-in-time, stockless, and future-state inventory programs)

* Certification, graduate degree, or licensure (for example, APICS-certified or MBA with strong finance and marketing skills)

* Language skills or international business skills (fluent in Spanish, with conversational French and Italian; familiar with Asian business protocol)

You'll find that this introductory summary section can also be called any of the following:

| | | |
|---|---|---|
| Accomplishments | Keyword Summary | Skills Summary |
| Background | Professional Profile | Strengths |
| Career Summary | Professional Qualifications | Summary of Qualifications |
| Features and Benefits | Qualifications | Title [your job title used as the heading] |
| Highlights | Representative Experiences | |
| Key Features | | |

Who should use a Qualifications Summary? Consider using one if any of the following is true:

* You have at least five, and preferably more, years of experience in your craft.

* You're qualified for the management or executive echelon. The sheer breadth of your experience demands a summary, just as a 200-page thesis calls for an introductory abstract.

* You're a professional or have broad experiences in your field. A Qualifications Summary will pull broad-based generalist skills into one easy-to-digest paragraph.

* Your most impressive accomplishments won't be seen until the latter part of the résumé. In this case, a Qualifications Summary will position the heart of your experience at the heart of the résumé.

* You are targeting a position that calls on experience found only in the early stages of your career. Mentioning earlier experiences in a Qualifications Summary will breathe new life into dated employment.

* Your résumé will have to pass the rigors of Internet search engines.

☐ Check this box if you'll use some form of a Qualifications Summary in your résumé. Select a term from the list on this page that best suits your needs; then write your selection on the following line: _____

# Professional Experience

Professional Experience, or any of its synonyms, is the mainstay of a chronological format. If you will use a professional experience category, you can choose a title from this menu:

| | | |
|---|---|---|
| Career Experience | Employment History | Professional Record |
| Career Highlights | Employment Record | Record of Experience |
| Career History | Experience | Relevant Experience |
| Career Record | Experience Highlights | Work Experience |
| Contract Assignments | Professional Experience | Work History |
| Employment | Professional Highlights | Work Record |
| Employment Background | Professional History | |
| Employment Experience | | |
| Employment Highlights | | |

Although Professional Experience implies remuneration for your services, this category can also include nonpaid internships or significant, full-time volunteer positions related to your career goal. If this is the case, title the section something like "Experience" or "Career Highlights" rather than any of the terms in the list that begin with the word *Employment*.

If you've chosen to write a functional, or skills-based, résumé, you can still include a skeleton of your professional experience to lend credibility to your work history. This condensed listing needs to include only your position title, the employer, and dates of employment. You can omit the dates if they reflect employment gaps or instability, but be prepared to explain them in an interview. Here is an example:

**Customer Service Associate**—Titan Truss Co., Veoria, CA (2005–Present)

**Reservations Assistant**—Sequoia Tours, Tourtown, CA (2003–2005)

**Customer Care Representative**—Travel World, Tustin, CA (2000–2003)

**Data Entry Processor**—Crayton Industries, Marysville, CA (1998–2000)

☐ Check this box if you'll include in your résumé a traditional timeline of your work experience. Select a term from the preceding list that best suits your needs; then write your selection on the following line:

_____

# Skills

This category offers employers a skills-based menu of your talents, rather than a chronological list of employment. Don't confuse the Skills section with an

introductory qualifications paragraph or a bulleted summary of your talents. In this case, the skills section is for candidates who can best benefit from a functional résumé format.

Some alternative headings for a Skills section appear in the following list. Keep in mind that such a heading is only a categorical section heading; you can use sub-headings under this category heading to outline up to a half dozen skill areas that reflect your talents and strengths.

| | | |
|---|---|---|
| Abilities | Key Qualifications | Strengths |
| Core Competencies | Knowledge, Skills, and Abilities | Summary of Qualifications |
| Expertise | Proficiency | Talents |

☐ Check this box if you will use a skills-based presentation of your qualifications. Fill in the following blank with the heading you have selected:

_____

## Education, Credentials, and Licenses

These sections are self-explanatory. If you have trade school or college training, say so—that is, most of the time. The exceptions to this rule pertain to a degree that was "almost" completed, the "wrong" degree, or a degree in progress. If you have only a high school diploma, do not list it or the name of the high school. The exception is if you are a recent high school graduate looking for work. Include credentials, certificates, and licenses that required course work, internships, or a testing process, provided that the credential or license is still relevant to your field.

Recent grads can go heavy on this section. In other words, if education is your biggest selling point, don't be afraid to let it take up "prime shelf space"—that visual center of the page. In figure 7.5, Stephen leveraged his lack of paid experience by positioning an impressive Education category at the center of the page. He then stretched it to more than three inches of vertical space by using a variety of subheadings (Dual Major, Coursework Highlights, and so on).

Consider any of the following alternative headings for your Education section. You can combine several terms, such as Degrees and Licenses, to save space on the résumé.

| | | |
|---|---|---|
| Academic Credentials | Continuing Education | Industry Training |
| Academic Preparation | Credentials | Licenses |
| Certificates | Degrees | Professional Certification |
| | Education | Professional Training |

---

**EDUCATION**

UNIVERSITY OF THE PACIFIC

| | |
|---|---|
| **Dual Major:** | Bachelor of Science, Business Administration—Option in Finance<br>Bachelor of Arts, French |
| **Coursework Highlights:** | Entrepreneurial Finance; Portfolio Management and Theory; International Finance; Business and Real Estate Economics; Monetary Policy and the Banking System |
| **Honors:** | Melvin Peters Scholarship Recipient (based on academic performance)<br>Dean's List (seven consecutive semesters)<br>President's Honors (among top graduating seniors in School of Business) |
| **GPA:** | 3.9 GPA (4.0 scale) |
| **Cocurricular Activities:** | Financial Management Association (President, VP Fundraising—set record for fundraising); Alpha Kappa Psi, Professional Business Fraternity (VP Fundraising); Le Cercle Français French Club (President, Treasurer);  International Business Association (various committees) |
| **Language Studies:** | French (fluent in language and business protocol)<br>Burmese (fully fluent)<br>Japanese (conversational skills) |

---

**Figure 7.5: An example where education takes center stage.**

☐ Check this box if you have education, credentials, and licenses that will help sell your experience. Select a term or terms from the preceding list that best suit your needs; then write your selection on the following line:

_____

# Affiliations

Affiliations can be boiled down to two basic flavors: career and civic. The first has to do with organizations dedicated to a profession, industry, or functional specialty. The second category covers community, nonprofit, and for-fun groups. Volunteerism can fall under either category, depending on whether you are a mentor to business professionals or a role model for youth.

If numerous affiliations elevate you to "overachiever" status, consider splitting them into a career-related category and a community-related category for greater readability and impact. If you have only one organization to include, make sure it carries weight, or don't include it. (See the upcoming tip on single-item lists.)

Choose one of following terms if you'll be using an Affiliations category:

| | | |
|---|---|---|
| Activities | Community Organizations | Professional Affiliations |
| Affiliations | Community Service | Professional Associations |
| Associations | Industry Affiliations | Professional Memberships |
| Charitable Commitments | Leadership | Public Service |
| Civic Involvement | Memberships | Trade Organizations |
| Community Activities | Mentorship | Volunteerism |
| Community Involvement | Organizations | |

## Single-Item Lists

If you have a category with just one item in it (such as an affiliation, award, or interest), avoid listing it under a separate category. A single item can look "lonely" on its own, diminishing its impact. It also wastes two additional lines of space on the résumé (the heading line and the line space between the heading and the item). Extra space, called white space, also draws the reader's eye to the item. If the single item is fabulously impressive, fine—list it by itself. If it isn't, you have probably succeeded in drawing attention *away* from some other feature on your résumé that should have earned more recognition. This doesn't mean you need to exclude one-liner items from your résumé. If the item will support your candidacy, look for another category to weave it into, such as a Qualifications Summary or Accomplishments section.

☐ Check this box if you're involved in industry organizations that will add to your marketability. Select a term from the preceding list that best fits your needs; then write your selection on the following line:

_____

## Supporting Material

Supporting material can include publications, presentations, patents, awards and honors, bio bites, endorsements, and the like.

Publications include books you've written or contributed to and articles published in newsletters, newspapers, trade journals, magazines, or the Internet. You can list a master's or doctoral thesis here; however, if this is the sum of your publications, combine it with your Education category. Self-published booklets, pamphlets, and guides can be included. You can also weave other writings into this section, such as a script for training videos, copy for advertisements or brochures, or ghost writing for speeches. When this is the case, title your heading "Professional Writing" rather than "Publications."

Presentations should include events where you were the primary presenter or co-presenter. Include presentations made at professional conferences, business symposia, college classes, and company meetings of a district, regional, national, or international scale. Do not include presentations on par with proposing or pitching your services to a customer for a sale. If making presentations is critical to your skill set and you want to emphasize this to the reader, group this experience with other experience in a Qualifications Summary, Professional Experience section, or Special Skills section.

Patents, pending or otherwise, should be included if research, product development, or design skills are required in your field.

If you have a generous amount of material for the Publications and Presentations section, you might find that using separate headings for each category provides a cleaner presentation of your information.

Awards and honors can include awards relating to your career accomplishments, community volunteerism, contributions to service organizations, or academic accolades. The following is an example:

### COMMUNITY & ACADEMIC HONORS

Big Brothers/Big Sisters, Volunteer of the Year

Business & Professional Woman of the Year, Central California Nominee

Tri-County Regional Occupation Program, Outstanding Service Award

State University, Outstanding Senior Graduate, Social Science Department

State University, voted by professors as Commencement Speaker

Sound bites—snippets of videotape or conversation that capture the essence of a situation—are popular in news and entertainment reporting. "Bio bites"—bits of information that reveal interesting layers of your life—add impact to your résumé and are especially effective when used as a closing tool.

Bio (as in autobiography) bites can include details on where you grew up, travel experiences, language skills, athletic abilities, and other interests. Use caution in divulging telltale information that reveals your age, religion, ethnicity, political persuasion, or a stance on controversial issues that might be used to discriminate against you. If you know your audience's preferences, however, you might want to include some of this information. *The rule of thumb is that the information should support your candidacy;* otherwise, don't include it.

The following are other possible names for the Bio section:

| | | |
|---|---|---|
| Interests | Bio Highlights | Personal Portrait |
| Other | Miscellaneous | Characteristics |
| Of Interest | Background | Personal Data |
| Bio Data | Profile | |

You can use bio bites to fill in "missing" elements from your background. Beau, an experienced sales representative, was targeting a sales position with Upjohn's Animal Health Division where he would be selling veterinary medical supplies to cattle feedlot operators, veterinarians, and animal-feed stores. He had the sales background but lacked a degree and the formal animal-science training required for the position. We wrote this Bio data to strengthen his candidacy:

### BIO DATA

Raised on fifth-generation cattle ranch (stocker operation), with involvement in all aspects of livestock management. Frequently called on to doctor cattle in remote areas, using knowledge gleaned from self-study of veterinary-medicine textbooks. Competed five years on the amateur rodeo circuit.

Mike, a district manager in his 50s, drew a picture of his health and stamina by including this information at the close of his résumé:

### INTERESTS

Runner—Participate in Bay to Breakers Race

Golfer

Downhill Skier

Reader

Mike reported that the Bay to Breakers Race (a famous, fun, but rather grueling runner's event held annually in San Francisco) was one of the first things interviewers commented on when meeting him. Although he was in his 50s, he competed in a "youthful" industry (wireless communications). This information helped to set him apart and underscore his energy, stamina, and physical fitness. He landed a district manager position with a preeminent communications provider and was given the coveted task of launching the first wireless PCS market in the nation.

Endorsements are a new spin on an old process: letters of reference (or recommendation). Letters of reference have long been part of the hiring system; in most if not all cases, you will be asked to provide them. This request usually comes after you have submitted your résumé (typically during or after the interview) and signals that an employer is interested in you as a viable candidate. A letter of reference gives hiring managers another person's opinion of you so that they don't have to rely solely on the claims you make in the résumé or interview. These third-party recommendations add weight and credibility to your candidacy.

Endorsements are snippets, or sound bites, of letters of recommendation; performance evaluations; letters of appreciation from customers or vendors; or verbal comments from clients, co-workers, or supervisors. If you want to use verbal comments, get your source to put them in writing for maximum credibility.

This technique works especially well for people who want to transition from one field or profession to another. For instance, Jane, a stay-at-home mother who is reentering the workforce and targeting a position in sales, could use these endorsements to emphasize her selling skills:

> "Jane solicited more than $10,000 in donations from business owners, making our fund-raising event the most successful in the school's history." (Sean Lemming, Chief Administrator, Loma Linda High School)

> "She is an articulate and persuasive public speaker, delivering arguments at City Council Meetings that persuaded us to vote in favor of her position on a controversial issue." (Jacob Schmidt, City Councilperson)

> "A born leader, Jane joined our 200-member service club five years ago and has chaired four key committees in that time. Most recently, she was unanimously elected to the office of President-Elect." (June Wong, President, Junior League of Loma Linda)

Choose any of these names for a header for an endorsements section:

| | | |
|---|---|---|
| Character References | Customer Testimonials | Recommendations |
| Complimentary Quotes | Endorsements | Testimonials |
| Customer Comments | Excerpts from Letters of Support | Vouchers |
| | Industry Endorsements | What People Are Saying About [Your Name] |

You might want to use endorsements without placing them in a separate category. Jean, a client who had some of the most glowing, sincerely written recommendation letters ever, could easily have been hired based solely on these letters. Yet she didn't want to provide prospective employers with six pages of reference information on the first contact (a smart move on her part). In Jean's case, we included each endorsement as a bulleted item under each of her employers (see figure 7.6).

☐ Check this box if you have supporting material that you will use in your résumé. Select a heading (or headings) from the preceding list that best fits your needs; then write your selection(s) on the following line:

_____

# What Not to Include

There are a few sound bites that will put you at risk for discreet discrimination. Resist the temptation to include these items:

- **Date of birth.** Some companies automatically return résumés to candidates who have referenced their date of birth or age.

- **Marital status/children.**

- **Personal data.** Height, weight, health status, ethnicity, and so on.

---

**Advertising Sales Manager**—Computer Trends, Houston, TX, 1997–Present

♦ Recruited to boost flat advertising sales for computer publication serving the Houston area. Delivered a 64% increase in sales without additions to the sales force. Personally doubled ad sales in peripherals category.

♦ *"Jean's performance has been extraordinary . . . leads by example . . . energetic support for individuals she supervises . . . consistently made contributions outside the purview of her department . . . very visible ambassador of goodwill."* (Editor/General Manager)

**Account Executive**—Info Business Systems, Houston, TX, 1995–1997

♦ Ranked #1 in sales of records management systems, despite no prior industry knowledge. Promoted to key account sales (multisite government and education customers, traditionally managed by owner/general manager).

♦ *"Jean brought high energy, infectious enthusiasm and professional integrity . . . had a keen understanding of the organization's goals . . . was dependable and reliable to the $n^{th}$ degree."* (V.P., Sales)

**Sales Manager/Sales Associate**—The Finance Group, Dallas, TX, 1989–1995

♦ Within 3 months of hire, ranked in top 5% of producers among 2,000 sales associates. Promoted to manage 40-member sales team—reversed stagnant sales performance from #59 to #7 among 75 offices.

♦ *"Clear analytical skills . . . scrupulously honest . . . manifests drive and enthusiasm that is contagious."* (C.E.O.)

---

**Figure 7.6: An example of featuring endorsements.**

✸ **Photograph.** Don't do it, even if your physiognomy is suitable for the cover of *GQ* or *Cosmopolitan*—which brings me to the exception to this rule. Actors and models do use a photo, typically an 8 by 10 head shot, on the back of which is the résumé—a listing of performances or shoots/products featured.

✸ **Letters of recommendation.** Save them for a timely follow-up contact.

✸ **Salary history/requirements.** If at all possible, save this hot potato for the interview process. You might want to mention a salary range in the cover letter if the employer has specifically asked for it. Check out chapter 10 for tips on dealing with this important issue in cover letters.

✸ **"Date-stamping" the résumé.** Don't place the date you prepared the résumé in the lower-right corner (or anywhere else); also avoid listing when you are available to begin work unless you're applying, for instance, to a school district that has a school-year calendar or year-round track to staff.

✸ **Reference list.** Save this one, too, for the interview or a follow-up contact. You might, however, conclude your résumé by centering the words,

"References on request." Don't sacrifice additional line spaces by using a separate category heading. No, you don't need to include these words. However, it is still a common practice to do so. Here are two reasons why:

- It informs readers that the end of the résumé has come—this is especially helpful if the last category they've read is about your experience rather than a more typical closing category, such as Education or Activities.

- It brings balance and visual closure to the page. Centering the reference line at the bottom of the page helps to balance your name and contact information, which might be centered at the top of the page.

## Putting It All Together

Congratulations! Phase I of construction is almost complete. Skim back over this chapter and note which format (chronological or functional) you've chosen, as well as the category boxes you've checked and the headings you've chosen for them. Fill this information into the following form. If you're more comfortable at a computer, input your outline on a blank screen or use a résumé template in your word-processing program.

---

**Your Résumé Outline**

**Contact Information Header Style:**

_____

_____

_____

_____

_____

_____


**Chosen Category Headings:**

_____    _____

_____    _____

_____    _____

_____    _____

_____    _____

---

If you filled in more than five category blanks and plan to write a one-page résumé, you'll need to combine some of the categories; otherwise, your résumé will be too busy-looking.

For a clean, concise presentation, three to five categories per page works best. With the "as few rooms as possible" principle, consider combining an Objective and Qualifications sections or combining short categories (headings that will have only a few items under them) with the Qualifications section or Professional Experience section.

# Chapter Wrap-Up

Now that the skeletal outline of your résumé is finished, it's time to add some heart and soul by learning to write great copy! Chapter 8 shows you how.

## 10 Quick Tips for Structuring Your Résumé

1. Decide on the format, or structure, of your résumé. The most common formats are chronological and functional. A summary section is often included in the chronological format. Review samples in this book or other books for ideas on the "look and feel" you want for your résumé. Make sure the format you choose complements your career circumstances.

2. Use a chronological format if you have a strong career progression over the past five-plus years and are seeking a position similar to your current or most recent position.

3. Understand why employers prefer the chronological format: Its sequential layout is easy to follow and doesn't raise suspicions about job-hopping or other skeletons in the vocational closet.

4. Recognize the downside to a chronological format: It makes it easy for hiring managers to spot gaps between jobs, a lack of career advancement, demotions, and so on.

5. Although not a cure-all for every career inadequacy, the functional format can camouflage the appearance of an unstable, unorthodox, or interrupted career caused by gaps between jobs, job-hopping, spouse relocation, typecasting, limited paid experience, and returning to a career after time off for family or personal issues.

6. Use a functional format if you are changing careers or reentering the workforce after a several-year hiatus and pursuing a different career. The functional format also works well if you have performed the same responsibilities for multiple employers and are looking for a similar position because it avoids repeating information for each employer.

7. If using a functional format, remember to create categorical, relevant, skills-based sections to document your qualifications for a particular job. Company names, employment dates, and position titles should either be deemphasized or intentionally omitted.

8. When considering the summary or objective statement for your résumé, avoid the temptation to be all things to all people. Likewise, avoid the tendency to write about what you want out of the employment relationship. Instead, focus on what the employer needs. It's about them!

9. Aim for five or fewer category headings on a one-page résumé to create a document that's clean-looking and inviting to read. Typical headings will be Summary or Skills, Experience, Education, and Affiliations or Community Involvement. In many cases, a section for supporting information, such as interests or biographical highlights, is appropriate.

10. Avoid categories or information that could put you at risk for discreet discrimination, such as date of birth, marital status, height or weight, ethnicity, a photograph, and salary history.

---

### ★ Magical Coaching Questions

When will you complete your résumé outline?

_____

_____

What might prevent you from meeting this deadline?

_____

_____

What action can you take to take overcome those potential distractions?

_____

_____

_____

## Chapter
# 8

# How to Write Great Keyworded Copy

*Writing is easy. All you do is sit staring at a blank sheet of paper until the drops of blood form on your forehead.*

—Gene Fowler, American Writer

Don't let this humorous analysis cause you dismay. Even experienced writers can feel some fear and trepidation when facing the start of a new project. You already developed a good outline from which to work (in chapter 7), which puts you beyond the "blank sheet of paper" stage. Using your outline, you'll learn how to flesh out details that will add weight to your candidacy. First, we'll review keywords and how important they are to the copywriting equation. After that, you'll begin to draft text for the various categories of your résumé. By the end of the chapter, you will have a strong rough draft of your résumé.

## Keywords

Every résumé, regardless of whether it is in electronic or paper format, should contain keywords that signal employers that you have the skills, talents, and experience to match their job requirements.

Keywords refer to those words that describe your title, knowledge base, skill set, impressive "name-brand" or Fortune 500 employers, prestigious universities attended, degrees, licensure, software experience, or affiliations, to name a few. Keywords are typically nouns or noun phrases—their substantive nature has caused them to supersede many of the "action verbs" of the 1980s and 1990s. The next *Before* and *After* résumé excerpts illustrate the conversion from action verbs to noun-based keywords.

### *Before*

Troubleshot, repaired, maintained, and monitored computers to component level.

Administered networks, wrote scripts, and conducted diagnostic tests.

### *After*

Extensive component-level troubleshooting, repair, maintenance, and monitoring of advanced supercomputers, massively parallel computer systems, mainframes, PCs, Macs, Sun workstations, and UNIX-based workstations for National Energy Research Supercomputer Center (NERSC).

Advanced skills in UNIX and network system administration support, scriptwriting, electronic testing equipment, diagnostic testing, videoconference services, SMTP-based e-mail, TCP/IP protocol, LAN/WAN, and Internet usage.

Compare the first *Before* sentence with the first *After* sentence and note the additional details with respect to the types of computers worked on and where the work was done. The emphasis on keywords necessitates elaboration. Don't be afraid to go into more detail. The constraints of copyfitting your résumé to exactly one page don't apply in plain-text résumés because page breaks will vary depending on the receiver's software and default settings. This allows you to fudge a bit on length. At the same time, do not turn it into a full-length, unedited autobiography. Remember, even though a plain-text résumé lacks the luster of pretty fonts and fancy formatting, it is still a marketing piece.

> *Tip* The most common type of keyword that employers search for is a position title. To improve your "hit" ratio, use your industry or discipline's keywords along with logical synonyms. For instance, the keywords "materials manager" might be referred to as "supply chain manager," "logistics manager," or "purchasing manager" in another company. To cover your bases, consider leading off your résumé summary (or objective) with a list of synonyms.

## Where to Find Keywords

There are a number of resources, both offline and online, for locating keywords.

### Offline Resources for Keywords

- Your professional association—read its newsletter (there may also be an online version), attend meetings and conferences regularly, and network outside those meetings with colleagues and mentors.

- Informational interviews with other industry contacts.

- Your company's formal job description of your position.

- Job descriptions from your targeted companies (gaining access to them can be tricky).

- Classified advertisements (a.k.a. "help wanted" ads) in newspapers, periodicals, and Web sites.

* Recruiter job orders.

* Current "how to" résumé books with sample résumés from your profession.

* The most current edition of the *O\*NET Dictionary of Occupational Titles* (JIST Works).

Without question, involvement in your industry's professional association is the number-one method to stay up-to-date on keywords. There is just no substitute. In the words of Gerry Crispin (coauthor of *CareerXroads*), workers who refrain from involvement in professional associations "are *obsolete* from the day they don't connect." (*Obsolete*—now there's a word that would never find its way into a keyword search.)

## Online Resources for Keywords

With access to the Internet, you can find an exhaustive collection of keywords to help your résumé surface from the sea of résumés. Here's where to look:

* Visit one of the career or niche Web sites listed in chapter 12.

* Tour your target company's Web site and click its link to jobs (it will most likely say *careers, jobs, employment,* or *opportunities*). Note the keywords used in postings relevant to your search. Also skim through pages such as About Us or Press Releases for keywords and terms that can help you master the company's unique "corporate-speak."

* Don't confine your sleuthing to targeted companies. You can access a list of 40,000+ small and large companies in 190+ categories at sites such as BizWeb (www.bizweb.com).

* Bring up one of the following *search engines* (an electronic directory that searches for documents, pages, or sites). Most of them have a "careers" section that you can explore. Or, at the search engine's home page, you can search for "career Web sites" or other keywords pertaining to your discipline, such as **"civil engineering" + jobs.** If you get an avalanche of sites (they sometimes number in the hundreds of thousands), be prepared to refine your search by city or a subdiscipline. Following are a few of the more popular search engines:

  * **Google:** www.google.com

  * **Yahoo!:** www.yahoo.com

  * **Netscape Search:** http://channels.netscape.com/ns/search/default.jsp

  * **Lycos:** www.lycos.com

  * **AltaVista:** www.altavista.com

  * **Ask Jeeves:** www.ask.com

## How to Position Keywords

Software and search engines will quickly find keywords regardless of where you place them on your résumé. Even if you were to bury keywords at the bottom of a résumé, the computer would still find them. Of the recruiters and HR professionals interviewed, all indicate that the placement of keywords does not matter in the data-mining process. Nonetheless, it stands to reason that if keywords are the golden lure to gain employer interest, they should be displayed prominently. Eventually, human eyes will be sifting through your material, and they—unlike a computer—will appreciate the positioning and presentation of key material. For maximum readability, place keywords within the first 20 to 24 lines that appear on a computer screen (before it is necessary to scroll down to view additional information).

Keywords that appear under the first employment entry will also spark employer interest. Several Internet researchers commented that this is an indicator of a "fast match," meaning that the candidate has recent, relevant experience and can be placed quickly. If this is the case, you may want to forgo a summary section or use a light hand on it. The result is that your first employment entry will rise into that all-important first screen.

Now that you have a clearer picture of keywords, let's look further at the categories of your résumé that will contain these keywords. As you continue to work through this chapter, keep your outline from the preceding chapter in front of you because you will write copy for *only* the categories in your outline. Just skip over any categories you won't be using—with one possible exception. Please write an Objective, or Focus statement, even if you don't plan to use the term Objective as part of your résumé format!

The effort won't go unrewarded: Your Focus statement will be tied to the Magic F.I.T.™ identified in chapter 3 and will help you convey your goals in informal networking and formal interviewing situations. The more articulate your communication, the more impressive your presentation.

# The Objective or Focus Statement

"I don't care what I do, I just want a job." You might not care, but chances are that the employer does. Part of your task is to make the hiring manager's job easier. Don't give that person the investigative assignment of determining your strengths and where you'd best fit into the company. When surveying employers' résumé preferences, a number of pet peeves turned up, two of which apply to the Objective:

- "Not defining the type of position you want."
- "Not researching the company to know what jobs are available."

So if you don't know what positions are available, find out—call on your networking sources or contact someone within the organization, whether a human resources manager or department representative.

Following are two alternatives for presenting your Focus statement.

## Title Statement

You can quickly convey your job focus with a short noun phrase, known as a title statement, centered below the header of your résumé. This technique is clean, gets across your point, and saves you one or two lines of space by eliminating the Objective category heading (see figure 8.1).

---

**ROBERT ORLANE**

1442 W. Netherly
Fontana, CA 93745                    rorlane@yahoo.com                    Mobile: (213) 222-7777
                                                                         Home: (213) 222-6666

**CUSTOMER SERVICE / SALES SUPPORT PROFESSIONAL**

**PROFESSIONAL EXPERIENCE**

   **Customer Service Coordinator**—PC Manufacturers, Inc., Fontana, CA

   [etc.]

---

**Figure 8.1: An example of a title statement.**

## Traditional Objective

Recall that you selected a title for your objective category in the preceding chapter. To write the copy for this brief category, break it down into three key pieces of information:

1. The position you want

2. The key skills that qualify you

3. The benefit(s) or value to an employer

Table 8.1 gives examples of these three points. The majority of the examples in table 8.1 begin with a noun (typically the title of the position desired), shown in Column 1. Reading across the table, Column 1A illustrates wording that will connect your target position with your key skills. Many of the examples in this column are interchangeable and might work well for your particular situation. Columns 2 and 3, key skills and benefit(s)/value to the employer, can be combined, as in the examples for the retail buyer and social services position.

## Table 8.1: Components of the Objective Statement

| Column 1<br><br><br>Target Position | Column 1A<br><br>Connective Tissue to Pull the Sentence Together | Column 2<br>Key Skills That Qualify You for the Position | Column 3<br>Benefit(s) or Value to the Employer |
|---|---|---|---|
| Marketing research position ➔ | that will use my strengths in ➔ | demographic research and analysis ➔ | to target, develop, and maintain a dominant market share for your company. |
| Opportunity | in which my | sales support, customer service, problem-solving, and human relations skills | will grow and retain your customer base. |
| Retail buyer | with impressive record of | | contributing to gross margin improvement, comparable store sales, and product development. |
| Computer programmer of adventure/ arcade games | with proficiency in | C/C++ and assembly language. | Noted for producing clean, readable, and imaginative code to speed the release of products. |
| Plant management position | in which | production planning and materials-management skills can be used to | capture cost savings and maximize plant productivity. |

| Column 1 | Column 1A | Column 2 | Column 3 |
| --- | --- | --- | --- |
| Target Position | Connective Tissue to Pull the Sentence Together | Key Skills That Qualify You for the Position | Benefit(s) or Value to the Employer |
| Elementary teacher | with commitment to | | creating a rich, multimedia learning environment through student-centered activities and integrated lessons with meaning-ful "real-world" applications. |
| Social services position | that will benefit from my | | 12-year record of creating award-winning social service programs, accessing grant money and "hidden" funding, and delivering essential services to medically underserved populations. |

Now it's your turn. The following exercise defines the elements that make up an easy-to-assemble Focus statement.

# Exercise for Assembling a Focus Statement

1. **Position you are targeting.** (If you are targeting two types of positions in your search, write Focus statements for both.)

   a. _____

   b. _____

2. **Key skills that qualify you.** Develop three key skills, even though you might not use all of them in the Focus statement.

   a. _____

   b. _____

   c. _____

3. **Benefit(s) or value to the employer.** Again, develop three, even though you might not use all of them. In the next chapter on writing accomplishments, you'll find a complete list of employer "buying motivators" on pages 232–234; you might find it helpful to sneak a peek at that list before answering this question.

   a. _____

   b. _____

   c. _____

Now, transfer your answers into the following résumé text:

### FOCUS

Career opportunity as (1.a.) _____ that will benefit from my (2.a.)_____, (2.b.)_____, and (2.c.)_____.

or

### OBJECTIVE

(1.a.) _____ that will use my strengths in (2.a./b./c.—use one or more of your answers) _____ to (3.a./b./c.— use one or more of your answers) _____.

You can also write an Objective/Focus statement by starting with an infinitive. However, avoid cliché, "me-focused" wordings such as the following.

### OBJECTIVE

To obtain a position as a _____ with opportunity for growth and career advancement.

It's understood that you want to expand your skills or advance your career (the alternative is to be stagnant and bored), so drop this idea. Further, the infinitive "to obtain" is candidate-focused; instead, when beginning an Objective with an infinitive verb, use one that is employer-focused, such as the examples in table 8.2.

### Table 8.2: Employer-Focused Infinitives to Start an Objective Statement

| Sample Profession | Infinitive at Beginning | Qualifying Skills/ Benefit to Employer |
|---|---|---|
| Secretary | to support | management in a secretarial role where my technical skills, initiative, and understanding of client-driven organizations will be of value. |
| Engineer | to provide | professional engineering skills in the design of large-scale public-works projects. |
| Motivational Trainer | to parlay | legal experience as a top-notch litigator into a career as a business coach and motivational speaker. |
| Caseworker | to link | individuals in need of financial, medical, and mental-health services as a social-service caseworker. |
| Marketer | to assist | your marketing team in identifying, reaching, and persuading customers toward brand loyalty. |
| Sales Rep | to grow | your customer base through aggressive cold calling, telemarketing, and networking. |
| Teacher | to develop | inquisitive, lifelong learners as an educator of young children. |
| Counselor | to influence | at-risk youth through guidance as a reality-based counselor and tutor. |
| Draftsman | to combine | award-winning CAD skills and business focus with an architectural firm specializing in hospital design. |

When in doubt, "to contribute" and "to provide" work for a number of professions. In the following space, write your job title under the heading "position"; then fill in the center column with the infinitive you selected. The third column—Qualifying Skills/Benefit to Employer—will be your answer to either question #2 or question #3 (or a combination of both) from the exercise.

| Position | Infinitive at Beginning | Qualifying Skills/ Benefit to Employer |
|---|---|---|
| _____ | to _____ | _____ |

This might take some tweaking to smooth out. Review the examples from sample professions in table 8.2 for different ideas on how to connect the infinitive and skills/benefits.

# The Qualifications Summary

The Qualifications section can be a synopsis of your résumé—everything you write below the Qualifications will support what you've said in the summary. This order mandates that you stay focused and not meander. In crafting your Qualifications Summary, consider these ingredients:

1. Title/functional area
2. Subcategories of functional area or core competencies
3. Industry
4. Number of years of experience
5. Expertise, strengths, specialization
6. "Combination" accomplishment or highlights of accomplishments
7. Advanced degree, certification, licenses
8. Language skills, international business skills
9. Technical/computer skills
10. Personal profile/management style
11. Affiliations
12. Employers or colleges with name recognition

Figure 8.2 is an example summary. The superscript numbers in the summary correspond to the 12 items in the preceding list and demonstrate how you can arrange these ingredients.

> [1]**SALES MANAGER**
>
> **Emphasis in [3]Business Publishing / [2]Advertising / [2]Marketing**
>
> ♦ Fast-track [4]17-year sales and management career in competitive industries and markets ([3]publishing, computers, commercial real estate--California, Florida).
>
> ♦ [6]Earned distinction as #1 sales producer with each of my three career employers.
>
> ♦ [5]Especially adept at assembling, coaching, and motivating market-dominant sales teams.
>
> ♦ [8]International orientation: lived and worked five years in Tokyo; multilingual skills include fluent Spanish and conversational Japanese.

**Figure 8.2: An example of a summary.**

Ingredients and order used: 1) title/functional area; 3) industry; 2) subcategories of functional area or core competencies; 4) number of years of experience; 3) industry; 6) "combination" accomplishment or highlights of accomplishments; 5) expertise, strengths, specialization; and 8) language skills, international business skills.

To help develop your Qualifications Summary, I'm repeating the 12-item ingredient list in table 8.3, this time with room for you to fill in information applicable to your background. Don't be concerned if you can't come up with information for each category. And even if you do have material for each element, you might not use it all—remember that the title of this category ends with the word *summary*.

### Table 8.3: Ingredients of the Qualifications Summary with Room for Your Information

| Ingredients for Qualifications Summary | Example (Dana) | Your Information |
|---|---|---|
| 1. Title/functional area | International sales support | |
| 2. Subcategories of functional area or core competencies | Export documentation, government relations | |
| 3. Industry | Manufacturer of surveillance technology | |
| 4. Number of years of experience | Seven | |

*(continued)*

*(continued)*

| Ingredients for Qualifications Summary | Example (Dana) | Your Information |
|---|---|---|
| 5. Expertise, strengths, specialization | Internal communications with credit, production, engineering, manufacturing, and shipping to improve on-time shipment of orders | |
| 6. "Combination" accomplishment or highlights of accomplishments | Led preliminary market research and coordinated opening of international sales office in Mexico City. Supported sales growth of 35%. | |
| 7. Advanced degree, certification, licenses | N/A | |
| 8. Language skills, international business skills | Fluent in Spanish; serviced Central and South American customer base. | |
| 9. Technical/computer skills | MS Office 97; WordPerfect; Access | |
| 10. Personal profile/ management style | Dedicated and loyal; five-year record of perfect attendance. | |
| 11. Affiliations | N/A | |
| 12. Impressive employers and schools with name recognition | N/A | |

The sample information from Dana in table 8.3 yielded this Qualifications Summary.

> **Customer service professional** with seven years of experience servicing international accounts in the United States and Latin America. Worked in tandem with marketing team to support a 35% increase in sales. Improved on-time shipment of orders through collaboration with credit, production, engineering, manufacturing, and shipping matrix. Well-versed in export documentation, international transport, and government export regulations. Fluent in Spanish language, culture, and business protocol.

After completing the preceding table, take a clean sheet of paper or sit down at your computer and begin trying different combinations of your information. The length of the summary will be determined by your material.

If you find the task of formulating a Qualifications Summary more difficult than you anticipated, take heart:

*What is written without effort is in general read without pleasure.*

—Samuel Johnson, English lexicographer,
1709–1784

The Qualifications Summary is the hardest part of the writing process. In fact, I'll admit that, when writing for clients, developing the summary (and I've written thousands) always taxes my gray cells. It's much like developing an abstract for a 200-page dissertation, which is not an easy task. However, once you have completed it, your concise synopsis tells employers who you are and what you have to offer. Memorize your summary because it will come in handy in networking and interviewing situations. (You'll want to adapt it from the telegraphic style of résumé writing into complete sentences with personal pronouns to make it sound smooth and natural.) You can also print your summary on cards for use in informal networking situations.

# Professional Experience

To catalog your employment history, use the résumé worksheet guides in appendix B. Your word-processing program might have a résumé template that you prefer; if so, outline your employment history at your computer. This is the basic information you'll use:

- Company name
- City and state (without ZIP code) where you were employed (not the company's corporate headquarters)
- Month and year you began employment
- Month and year you left the company (use the word "Present" if you are still employed)
- Position title

The next step is deciding how to distribute the weight among the positions, or how much copy you will write for each position. This step will save you time and help you avoid writing full descriptions for every position. Don't give each of your positions equal treatment in terms of length—your résumé is not a socialist project! Instead, determine where your most relevant experience is and leverage the greatest weight on that position.

## How Far Back?

The jury isn't unanimous on this question. In the résumé preference survey I conducted when I wrote *Résumé Magic,* more human resource managers (63 percent) indicated that a candidate with 15 to 30 years of experience should *not* limit the experience listed on a résumé to the past 10 to 15 years. Several who voted for "full-term" résumés, however, commented that a short statement to summarize dated experience would suffice. On the other hand, you are still left with 37 percent of human resource managers who feel a listing of 10 to 15 years is sufficient. To satisfy both camps, detail the most recent 10 to 15 years in a traditional presentation (company name, dates of employment, title, position description, and accomplishments). The further back in the most recent 15 years, the less you need to say. Even if early information is eminently impressive, it will not carry as much weight, simply because it happened more than a decade ago. For experience that is more than 15 years ago, use one of these summary techniques:

> Eight years of prior background in production environments, gaining hands-on experience as Expediter, Cardex Clerk, Production Scheduler, and Manufacturing Analyst.

or

> Prior background in production environments, gaining hands-on experience as Expediter, Cardex Clerk, Production Scheduler, and Manufacturing Analyst.

Enumerate dates only when the dates don't go back too far, with too far being defined as approximately 25 years of total experience. Dates that take you back more than three decades might just as well be emergency flares—they'll attract as much attention.

## Where to Find Material for Your Job Descriptions

Consider one or more of these sources to help develop copy for your job descriptions:

★ Your company's formal job description of your position (use this as a starting point only—most company job descriptions are lengthier than you'll need for your résumé and many are outdated).

★ Job descriptions of positions similar to your own from your targeted companies (gaining access to them can be tricky).

★ Internet postings or detailed classified ads in newspapers, periodicals, and Web sites (comb ads for positions similar to your position and note the key qualifications required).

★ Recruiter job orders (if you are working with a recruiting firm or personnel agency).

★ Informational interviews with industry contacts (find out from managers with hiring authority what they believe the most important functions and keywords are for jobs similar to yours).

★ Your professional association's newsletter (almost every association has a newsletter, from which you can glean the latest in industry trends, technology, processes, and keywords).

* "How-to" résumé books with sample résumés from your profession (make sure that the books have been published recently—technological advances can cause keywords to change rapidly).

* The Department of Labor's *Occupational Outlook Handbook* online at www.bls.gov/oco/home.htm.

* JIST Works' www.CareerOINK.com, which combines the *Occupational Outlook Handbook* and other data into one huge but easy-to-navigate database. You can find information on 14,000+ job titles, each with cross-references to related job titles ($9.95 subscription fee).

In table 8.4, you'll see an example of how information from a classified ad was spun into text for a résumé job description.

### Table 8.4: Using an Ad to Write a Qualifications Summary

| Classified Ad | Résumé/Cover Letter Copy |
| --- | --- |
| SALES REPRESENTATIVE—Immediate opening for Sales Rep. Qualified to sell roofing and building materials in northern-state territory. Prefer college degree w/ 5+ yrs. proven sales exp. to suppliers, contractors, distributors, applicators, and architects. Position offers salary, comm., bonus, expenses, co. car, liberal benefits, and career growth. Send résumé. | QUALIFICATIONS SUMMARY SALES / TERRITORY MANAGEMENT **Building Materials/Construction Industries** More than 10 years of experience in building materials supply in positions as sales representative, branch manager, and principal/manager for local and regional companies. Delivered sales growth of $8 million over a 7-year period. Strong network of contacts with northern-state suppliers, contractors, distributors, and architects. Thorough knowledge of the trades. Excerpt from cover letter: Beyond the experience found on my résumé, I'd like to add that I virtually grew up in the roofing business. My father owned [name of well-known roofing and building materials supply company], so I had an early exposure to the industry and the people associated with it. I continue to maintain a number of those relationships—many of whom would be potential clients for your company. |

## How Long Is Too Long?

Think like an advertising copywriter: Be concise but give enough data to create interest and a desire to meet you. Try to keep your job descriptions to around five lines. More will begin to look too dense and you should either prune it or break it into two paragraphs.

### One Page or Two?

Résumé length should be determined by several factors, including the number of years of experience you posses, your position level, and your industry (for instance, résumés for educators are typically longer than résumés for sales professionals). Use this general rule of thumb for deciding on length:

- One page for new graduates or people with 5 to 10 years of experience.

- Two pages for management-level candidates and those with more than 10 years of experience.

- Two to three pages for "C"-level executives (such as chief executive officer, chief operating officer, or chief financial officer).

# Skills

If you have chosen a functional format to present your experience, present the bulk of your talents and experience in this section. If you're using a chronological format or one of its cousins, skip this section. The development of a skills-based résumé could warrant an entire chapter, if not an entire book. The basics are presented in a three-step plan:

1. **Focus on three to five skill areas—these will become your subheadings under the Skills category.** Choose disciplines or occupational areas for your subheadings rather than personal skills. Note the difference between occupational skills and personal skills in the following table. Occupational headings carry more weight with employers—remember that most employers dislike functional résumés to begin with; to pull this format off, you'll need to make sure it's meaty.

| Occupational Skills | Personal Skills |
| --- | --- |
| Event planning, fund-raising, customer service, marketing, sales, engineering, case management, project coordination, training, office management, inventory management, and so on. | Analytical skills, communication skills, problem-solving skills, organizational talents, attentiveness to detail, and so on. |

2. **The selection of your subheadings will be driven by the types of positions you are targeting.** Choose for your subheadings words that can be broadly interpreted, compared to specific job titles. For instance, "Customer Service" as a subheading would be more widely understood by the general public and preferred over a company-specific title such as "Client Account Specialist."

3. **After you have selected your subheadings, develop two to five sentences that encapsulate your experience for each subheading.** To develop copy for your experience, refer back to the ideas under "Where to Find Material for Your Job Descriptions." You will add specific accomplishments later (see chapter 9). Whenever possible, pair experience statements with evidence of where you gained the experience.

It's very, very important to include clues that will help the reader understand when and where you've done things, sort of like a trail of breadcrumbs! There will be a natural curiosity among employers to know the "whens" and "wheres"; not saying so is one of the major irritants of a functional format. If you claim to have sales experience, employers will want to know whether it was recent experience with a reputable employer compared to running a lemonade stand in your youth. Answering these unvoiced questions will lessen suspicions about an unstable work history.

For instance, compare these *Before* and *After* versions:

### Before

> **Sales:** Demonstrated an aptitude for sales; regularly met sales quotas.

### After

> **Sales:** Readily transferable sales skills. Demonstrated ability to sell any number of products as "floater" for upscale retailer (Macy's); as a "rookie," generated average daily sales volume equal to or above that of experienced sales associates.

The *After* version tells the reader where you worked, that you can sell a variety of products, and how well you measure up to other salespeople.

# Education, Credentials, Licensure

Place the Education section near the top of the résumé if it is one of your strongest selling points. This applies to recent high school or college graduates. If you've graduated within the past five or so years and have a degree related to your profession, place it near the top of the résumé as well. CVs (Curricula Vitae), regardless of how long ago your degrees were received, also lead off with education.

## Recent High School Graduate

If you're in the age bracket of 17 to 19 and fresh out of high school, you'll want to mention your graduation. Include a section on coursework relevant to your job goal.

## Recent College Graduate

If you recently obtained your degree as a traditional college student (you went directly from high school to college as opposed to experienced professionals who returned for a degree), play up your education. Position it at the top of the page and list relevant courses, an impressive grade point average, interesting special projects, and leadership positions in college groups.

## Degree Obtained a Number of Years Ago

There is a three-year rule of thumb (although not a rule set in stone) for determining where to position your education. Place education near the top of the résumé if you received a degree within the past three years and the degree is related to your profession. If you graduated more than three years ago and gained relevant experience in the meantime, consider placing your education toward the bottom of the résumé, below your experience. When decades have passed since you walked the halls of ivy, definitely place education at the bottom of the résumé and eliminate dates of graduation.

## No Degree

No Education section is often better than a weak Education section. If you attended college a short time or took courses of no professional significance, you'll draw more attention to the lack of a degree by including an Education section than if you were to omit it entirely. To further camouflage any lack of education, make sure you use more than two major category headings in the rest of your résumé (such as Focus and Professional Experience categories). Three categories look more balanced on a one-page résumé, so consider adding a third category, such as a Skills, Affiliations, or Endorsements section.

## Including Credentials, Licenses, and Certificates

When you have several elements to list under Education, such as credentials, licenses, and certificates, try giving each listing a subheading. This looks especially clean if each series of items that follows the subheadings fits on one line.

# Affiliations and Other Supporting Material

In most cases, a simple inventory of your affiliations, presented in order of importance, will suffice. When your involvement included election to an office or other leadership position, mention the title either before or after the organization (be consistent with the placement of the titles). When you held an office but are no longer in that office, preface the title with "past." It is not necessary to include the date you joined each organization.

As a space saver, you can present the information in paragraph form with each organization separated by a semicolon. This presentation will buy you an extra two lines, three if you eliminate the subcommittees and leadership positions and abbreviate the word "association" throughout. Be cautious of abbreviations, however, because they might not be properly interpreted in keyword searches.

Publications, presentations, patents, awards and honors, biographical bits, and endorsements are often impressive and should be included in your résumé.

# Chapter Wrap-Up

You've made it through the bulk of the composition process. Congratulations! Your text is "raw" at this point, but that's okay—you'll take care of tweaking later.

## 10 Quick Tips for Résumé Keywords

1. Find at least three online postings that contain a full-blown description of your target position. Analyze these postings and highlight common keywords.

2. Weave the highlighted keywords into your résumé—add common synonyms to augment the keywords.

3. Consider hard skills (such as areas of expertise), soft skills (such as communication, interpersonal skills, and attitude), general information (such as affiliations and telephone area codes), and academic qualifications (such as degrees and certifications) as keywords.

4. Fortify keywords by following them with an accomplishment. For instance, you can reinforce the keywords "customer service" in this way: customer service—boosted customer satisfaction scores from 82% to 94%.

5. In your résumé objective or summary, include your position target as well as variations of the keywords. For instance, augment "Customer Service" with terms such as "Client Services," "Account Management," "Customer Relationship Management," or "Sales Support."

6. Don't overlook geographic keywords. If a recruiter is searching for someone in California's Silicon Valley and your home is in "Campbell" rather than "San Jose," add the appropriate terms. For instance, "Campbell, CA 95432—Silicon Valley/San Jose area."

7. If space allows at the bottom of a printed résumé, include a Morse Code-type keyword section (keywords punctuated by commas).

8. For résumés pasted into e-mail messages or e-forms where space is not an issue, include a separate keyword section.

9. Avoid the temptation of "planting" keywords that are not part of your experience just so that your résumé will be found in an electronic search. Some sneaky job seekers have tried coloring keywords with white text so that the terms are found in computer searches but are not visible to the human eye.

10. If you're submitting an MS Word document to employers, include keywords in the File, Properties, Summary, Keywords area to reinforce your keywords.

---

### Magical Coaching Questions

You've no doubt gained some new industry insights or additional market intelligence from researching keywords. How will you use this information in your networking and interviewing?

_____

_____

_____

If you are getting stalled in the task of writing your résumé, who or what resources can help?

_____

_____

_____

_____

# Chapter 9

# Accomplishments: The Linchpin of a Great Résumé

*It is most expedient for the wise…to be the trumpet of his own virtues.*

—Shakespeare
*Much Ado About Nothing*

Put 25 hiring managers, résumé writers, or job seekers in a room and ask them what information should be included in a résumé, and you'll get 25 different answers. Why such diversity of opinions, and zealously argued ones at that? Here are a couple of theories. First, résumés involve the subjective disciplines of writing and design. Both are subject to personal preferences, interpretation, and experience. What makes one person love the fluid, polysyllabic prose of William F. Buckley, while another prefers the choppy, nickel-word style of Ernest Hemingway? Why do some swoon over the etherealism of Monet and react nonchalantly to the abstract spatters of Jackson Pollock? It's a matter of individual interest and taste.

The second and more visceral reason for disagreement on résumé development is that résumés—or, more appropriately, the impetus for preparing a résumé—can threaten one's sense of security and significance. For many, the mere mention of a résumé conjures up fearful images of unemployment and the financial insecurities that accompany it.

Job search is a task replete with opportunities for roadblocks, rejection, and self-doubt. Because many feel their job hopes hinge on the perfect résumé, they are concerned about it—with good reason. The uncertainty of change is uncomfortable, so people want to lessen that discomfort by taking control: "If I follow the right résumé-writing rules or prescribed formulas, I'll get a job, and everything will be okay." Unfortunately, the rules of résumé writing are a bit like mercury:

They're slippery, they're hard to get a handle on, and they quickly change the minute you try to pass them along to another.

Validating the mercury theory is the wide range of responses I got when I asked employers a number of comprehensive questions about résumé preferences. Not one received a unanimous response—disappointing news for fellow left-brain types who like to "find the rules and follow them." Take heart, however, because there was *one* survey item that generated nearly universal agreement among human resources executives surveyed:

**Verifiable accomplishments should always be included.**

Assembling your accomplishments will be a relatively easy task based on the work you've already completed in chapter 4. There, you learned about the 10 Employer Buying Motivators and wrote SMART Stories™ that included bottom-line results. This chapter offers examples of résumé language that relate to those buying motivators, as well as strategies for presenting your accomplishments. By the end of this chapter, your résumé should be near final.

# Words to Woo Employers

Words that woo employers are words that address the employer's question of "Why buy?" The following examples illustrate how accomplishments, or impact statements, tie in to the 10 Employer Buying Motivators.

## Buying Motivator #1: Make Money

- Captured a 12% gain in net profit, a record for the company's 60-year history.
- Reengineered operations enterprise-wide to net more than $1 million in additional profits.
- Built sales for start-up company from zero to $6.5 million over a four-year period.

## Buying Motivator #2: Save Money

- Cut purchasing costs 24% through vendor partnership program.
- Sourced new overseas vendors, providing equivalent quality in raw materials at half the cost.
- Reduced expenses from 150% of target to goal attainment in all major expense categories.

## Buying Motivator #3: Save Time

✴ Retooled job descriptions to eliminate monthly overtime costs of $6,000.

✴ Performed the work previously required of two full-time employees.

✴ Reduced time requirements for month-end close of books from seven to two days.

## Buying Motivator #4: Make Work Easier

✴ Consolidated business forms to reduce paperwork and eliminate duplication of information.

✴ Merged four fragmented service centers into centralized unit to improve order-processing time 40%.

✴ Anticipated HR issues associated with company's growing pains and put "expandable" systems in place that accommodated a 25% annual growth in staffing.

## Buying Motivator #5: Solve a Specific Problem

✴ Troubleshot recurring computer crashes for key customer; traced problem to vendor software, facilitated corrections, and maintained account valued at $70,000 in annual income.

✴ Appointed to lead team that replaced antiquated computer system for telecommunications leader; produced application that satisfied regulatory and internal requirements, while providing added commercialization potential worth millions.

✴ Suggested tie-line communication system that enabled employees to call Xerox locations nationwide from customer sites without long-distance charges; idea generated $8,000 savings in branch for first year alone.

## Buying Motivator #6: Be More Competitive

✴ Led strategy task force that captured across-the-board, 10-point increase in national regulatory audit (scores indicate quality performance above national average, highest in organization's history).

✴ Initiated company-sponsored training and certification programs for technical team; investment positioned XYZ as local market leader and enabled company to earn first-time contracts with Fortune 500 clients.

✴ Managed post-acquisition strategy for divestiture of nonperforming assets and reinvestment in high-performance assets, in some cases generating as much as an eightfold increase in annual returns.

## Buying Motivator #7: Build Relationships/Image with Internal/External Customers, Vendors, and the Public

- Negotiated exclusive referral relationship with prestigious industry resource; alliance created image of a full-service organization for sole-proprietor firm, without the need for additional capital infusion.

- Debuted quarterly newsletter and expanded it to a 20-page publication packed with valuable communiqués on legal concerns, legislative issues, educational updates, and technology advancements.

- Spearheaded concept for educational/public relations video and brochures that document the mining industry's success in reclamation of mined areas into viable wetlands, agricultural lands, and commercial uses.

## Buying Motivator #8: Expand Business

- Introduced "service bundling," a concept new to the industry that captured an average 18% increase in 22 branches.

- Supported R&D in achieving 50% increase in new products brought to market.

- Launched first market in the nation for major Internet service provider; exceeded goals for all key performance indicators.

- Collaborated on new product development, pricing, and roll-out—all new products met or exceeded first-year distribution goals.

## Buying Motivator #9: Attract New Customers

- Cultivated relationships with influential Stanford physicians (previously inaccessible), gaining support for antiarthritic products to drive up regional sales 19%.

- Sourced new customers through electronic research, generating a 12% increase in active accounts.

- Attracted top sales performers from competitors with established client lists, expanding active customer database by more than 200%.

## Buying Motivator #10: Retain Existing Customers

- Increased customer-retention figures from 70 to 96%.

- Implemented direct-mail follow-up program for new customers; data reflects a 55% increase in repeat customers.

- Boosted policy renewals from below average to top 5% in the country.

These sample impact statements should trigger the salivary glands of any profit-conscious manager. Important to note is that the examples cut across professional boundaries. Buying motivators are "seamless" when it comes to your profession—virtually all employers want someone who can help make money, save money, save time, solve problems, and so on.

# Strategies for Presenting Accomplishments

Following are several résumé-writing trade secrets for presenting accomplishments. Each will strengthen your résumé communication and confirm your commitment to the bottom line.

## Numbers: The Universal Language

The sci-fi film *Contact,* based on Carl Sagan's novel, features an astrophysicist (Jodie Foster) who obsessively devotes her life to radio telescopes, hoping to make contact with other life forms in the universe. The solar system Vega comes through for her, and she, along with a cadre of the most brilliant scientists on the planet, are subsequently challenged with decrypting the mathematical code sent from an advanced source of life some 26 light-years away. At one point, a CIA agent steps in and wisecracks, "If this source is so sophisticated, why don't they just speak English?" Foster replies, "Seventy percent of the planet speaks other languages. Mathematics is the only truly universal language." Moral of the story: Numbers can clarify where words can confuse.

Numbers, unlike words, are universal, no matter what the reader's business idiom or corporate culture is. Note how the lack of numbers in this maintenance director's impact statement creates confusion about whether the statement is even an accomplishment.

### Before

> Implemented preventative maintenance program that improved downtime.

Thought-provoking! Did the maintenance program increase the amount of downtime? It's unlikely this is what the candidate intended to convey, but it could be interpreted in this manner. Specifying the production increase and the before-and-after numbers on downtime clears up any questions about "improving downtime."

### After

> Improved production 19% and reduced assembly-line downtime from 7 to .5 hours per week through implementation of preventive-maintenance program.

Here's another impact statement that, although it contains numbers, doesn't convey the full impact of the accomplishment:

### Before

Cut production lead time to 4–7 days, depending on model.

Compare this with the *After* version, which contains specific percentages for each model:

### After

Cut lead time by more than 50% on model "A" and 40% on model "B"—improvements enabled company to boast fastest order-fulfillment schedule among all major competitors.

In addition to the insertion of specific percentage reductions for each model, there is a comparison to help clarify the impact of the reductions in lead time. Comparison is another technique that talented résumé writers use to convey an individual's value to prospective employers.

## Comparison—A Powerful Form of Communication

You've heard the phrase, "it's apples to oranges—you just can't compare the two." In communicating, we often use comparisons to help make our point. Careful use of comparisons can help convey that you can run faster, jump higher, and "leap tall buildings in a single bound" better than the next candidate. For instance, this impact statement tells only half the story:

### Before

Improved branch ranking for sales volume to #1.

A comparison with some elaboration tells much more:

### After

As branch's sole account executive, improved sales production 42% and increased branch ranking from #12 to #1 in a 15-branch region.

In this case, the addition of the words "As branch's sole account executive" gives the reader a much clearer picture of your role in this accomplishment. And, by telling your reader there are 15 branches total, the increase from #12 becomes much more impressive because it shows that you turned around sales in a branch that was ranking near the bottom of the barrel.

Other comparisons you might make include the following:

**Comparisons between competitors**

Improved sales production 42% and increased company's market share from #2 to #1.

**Comparisons with the industry average**

Improved sales production 42%, well above national average of 8%.

**Comparisons with the company average**

> Improved sales production 42%, the largest annual sales increase in the company's 12-year history.

**Comparisons with your predecessor in the position**

> Improved sales production 42% in a territory that had experienced declining sales and negligent account service.

Proceed with caution when you compare yourself with a team member or predecessor, respected or otherwise. Such comparisons can be offensive, so it is best in these cases to stick with a comparison to industry averages, other branches, or competitors.

You'll also want to avoid sounding like the Lone Ranger in a business climate that venerates the consummate team player. At the same time, don't be afraid to list contributions that were accomplished as a team. When it comes to developing impact statements, candidates, especially female candidates, commonly make the mistake of entirely omitting an accomplishment if they weren't 100 percent responsible for it. If you are concerned about taking credit for something that was a team effort, there's a simple answer to your dilemma. Simply begin your impact statement with phrasing such as the following:

> Contributed to…
>
> Aided in…
>
> Helped to…
>
> Member of 7-person task force that…
>
> Collaborated with department managers to…
>
> Participated on ABC Committee that…
>
> Supported a…
>
> Company-wide efforts led to…
>
> Departmental efforts led to…
>
> Selected for national team that…

Douglas, a vice president for a manufacturer, used the following statement as part of his Qualifications Summary to share the applause for his team's collective accomplishments:

> Core management team member who contributed to organization-wide successes in unprecedented revenue growth, profit enhancement, and market positioning.

The noun phrase "core management team member" gives credit where credit is due, and the adjective "unprecedented" provides a comparison with the company average without going into details (specific accomplishments were covered later in the résumé under each of the past employers).

When you get right down to it, an argument can be made that any accomplishment is really a team accomplishment. Sales professionals don't achieve increases in orders without products developed by R&D, literature from marketing, orders processed by customer service, and parcels correctly assembled and delivered by warehousing and shipping. The rule of thumb is to give credit to the team if it was a joint effort, but don't hesitate to claim ownership if you were the one to envision, initiate, or take the leadership role in the effort. If it's the latter and it would be politically savvy of you to give credit to the team you headed up (especially when applying for in-house promotions), try one of these suggestions:

Led task force in…

Assembled 7-person task force that…

Chaired ABC Committee that…

Co-led sales campaign that…

Department team leader who…

Orchestrated cross-functional teams in accomplishing…

Directed collaborative efforts that realized…

Headed up national team that…

In résumé writing, there's a fine line to walk between self-adulation and self-effacement. Too much of the former, and you'll look like a narcissist. Too much of the latter, and you'll look like a Milquetoast. If you're unsure, err on the side of self-effacement, because reference checks that reveal your résumé to be inflated will be grounds for discontinuing your candidacy. You can always elaborate on your contributions in an interview, and you will probably score even more points when your explanations reveal that you did more than the marquee information contained in the résumé. Err too far in understating your contributions, however, and you won't get to the interview. If you're unsure, have a business-savvy friend review your impact statements and get his or her read on whether you're giving yourself enough credit.

## ROI—How Quickly Can You Deliver?

ROI is another effective tool to quantify your value to employers. The acronym stands for *return on investment* and is a term companies use to determine how quickly their investment in new equipment or advertising or an expansion will pay for itself. Concentrate on generating a return on your employer's investment in salary, benefits, training, office space, business cards, and all of the other hidden costs associated with hiring you. Some professions can more easily show a return than others, specifically those that directly affect revenue generation or expense controls. For instance, a top sales performer can show that a $125,000 salary will be justified by her ability to bring in half a million dollars in sales. Here are more examples that demonstrate ROI on a résumé:

- New Business Growth: Brought in more than $300,000 in new business during first six months in territory.

- Existing Account Growth: Added more than $200,000 in sales volume among existing accounts.

A purchasing manager can imply that his past record of negotiating impressive vendor concessions will validate his salary requirements, which happen to be 20 percent more than what the company paid its last purchasing manager! The following impact statements might guarantee his standing as the number-one candidate, despite his higher salary demands:

- Negotiated more than $300,000 in vendor concessions.

- Reduced transportation costs 20%, or $95,000 per year.

ROIs aren't limited to sales representatives or department managers. Support-staff members can also help to offset their salaries by paying attention to bottom-line contributions. Here's how one executive assistant to a management consultant showed her ROI:

- Initiated action on numerous matters, freeing consultant to maximize client time and increase monthly billable hours 27%.

Because the consulting firm was privately held (and thus the financial information was confidential), only the percentage increase in billable hours was listed, rather than the dollar amount it represented, which happens to be nearly $8,000 in new revenue each month. By tracking this information, the executive secretary provides herself with excellent leverage in negotiating future raises with her existing employer or salary increases with a new employer.

You can see how keeping track of contributions can pay off for you. Delivering a healthy ROI is not requisite to substantiating your job, but it is very helpful in promoting job security.

## The CAR Technique—Challenge, Action, and Result

CAR is a vehicle (pardon the pun) you use to highlight a specific **C**hallenge you encountered, the **A**ction you took, and measurable **R**esult from your action. This technique works especially well if you are transitioning from one industry to another because it focuses the reader's attention on your skills rather than on the industry in which you used the skills. Alex had a varied background in nonprofit association management and restaurant management and wanted to take those skills into the corporate sector. A separate Accomplishments section was allotted for his sales and management CARs, helping impress the reader first with his record of contributions rather than where he made the contributions (see figure 9.1).

You can also use the CAR technique in place of the job description and accomplishments under your professional experience. When doing so, make sure you are consistent in using the identical CAR format for each of your past employers. This creates a consistent, balanced visual impact and gives the appearance of a strong, long-term history for taking on challenges and delivering results.

---

### REPRESENTATIVE ACCOMPLISHMENTS

#### SALES/BUSINESS DEVELOPMENT

Challenge: Build sales in service-driven business catering to corporate clientele.
Action: Created and implemented targeted marketing, advertising, and promotional strategies.
Result: Delivered $78,000 increase in higher-profit segment of operation. Achieved 91% rating (above average) from independent review service.

Challenge: Recruited to turn around operation with stagnant sales ($750K) and declining patronage.
Action: Brought business-driven initiatives to non-profit setting for operation typically viewed as a "loss leader."
Result: Increased sales by 46% and 24% in major revenue categories.

#### MANAGEMENT/OPERATIONS/BUSINESS ADMINISTRATION

Challenge: Maintain uninterrupted member services during 5-month, $3.2 million construction project.
Action: Set up temporary business office, maintained access to key materials, designed alternative operating procedures.
Result: Accommodated all events without inconvenience, including 3-day tournament culminating in dinner for 400.

Challenge: Inherited operation performing below par for service and quality.
Action: Recruited new talent, retrained service staff, designed new quality/cost controls.
Result: Lowered operating costs, increased facility usage by an overall 23%, and earned favorable scores on recent member-survey.

---

**Figure 9.1: An Accomplishments section that uses the CAR format.**

Keep in mind that the CAR presentation technique is not a space-saver. If you're trying to keep your résumé to one page, try a more traditional presentation of your job descriptions and accomplishments.

Note how the word "solution" was substituted for "action" in the résumé example in figure 9.2. You can also substitute synonyms for "results," such as accomplishments, outcomes, contributions, or impacts. Brad's example in figure 9.2 is the Experience portion of his two-page résumé.

A note about the format: Hanging indents were applied to each paragraph to help the headings stand out. Also different in this example is the use of present-tense verbs rather than past tense in the solution paragraphs. This helps Brad connect with the hiring manager and gives the sense that Brad is shoulder-to-shoulder with the reader, advising on solutions to possible challenges the company might be facing. More important, the results paragraphs are strong with baseline and subsequent data that position Brad as *the solution* to the company's present challenges.

**PROFESSIONAL EXPERIENCE**

Zelner Unlimited, Salt Lake City, Utah                                                    2002-Present

**Sales Manager**

*Challenge:*  Recruited to revitalize stagnant sales and reverse declining profit performance in Rocky
Mountain states.

*Solution:* Design an intensive staff training campaign linking marketing, sales, customer service, and
operations; capitalize on use of team leaders to empower and motivate sales team of 27; negotiate
partnerships with add-on service providers to counter company's major disadvantage as a
standalone facility.

*Results:* Drove gross sales up from 60% of quota to 121% of quota; quadrupled several sales members'
production to in excess of $5 million; contributed 8% to bottom-line profits.

Parkland Properties, Inc., Denver, Colorado                                               1998-2002

**Sales Manager**

*Challenge:* Tasked with rebuilding field sales team with 3-year history of declining sales.

*Solution:* Utilize industry contacts to recruit experienced sales performers; groom existing sales team
through exposure to top performers, product incentives, and individual coaching in presentation
and closing techniques.

*Results:* In just four weeks, improved sales production 250% beyond prior year figures; rebuilt sales
team from 3 to 10 who generated collective revenues of $4.6 million, a record for the company.

Hall Enterprises, Denver, Colorado                                                        1989-1998

**Territory Manager**

*Challenge:* Rectify account relations in territory suffering from history of poor service.

*Solution:* Implement company-sponsored speaker series for accounts featuring topics of interest,
improve visibility in territory through consistent call schedule and direct mail campaign, target
and convert key accounts to exclusive contracts.

*Results:* Built sales from $440,000 to $1.2 million in two years; ultimately grew territory to $4.1 million
in sales despite an 80% reduction in geographic area.

Virtual Memories, Denver, Colorado                                                        1985-1989

**General Manager**

*Challenge:*  Tasked with start-up operations including site selection, capital equipment purchases, and
corporate office development.

*Solution:* Recruit and train sales and management team of 12; design integrated marketing, sales, and
operations strategies.

*Results:* Built company from zero sales to more than $2 million in first year; grew sales to high of $10
million during tenure.

**Figure 9.2: An example Experience section using the CAR format.**

# Where to Find Material for Your Accomplishments

For many people, developing impact statements is the hardest part of writing a résumé. Developing the responsibility portion of the résumé is generally easier because there are more sources from which to choose (refer to chapter 8 for source ideas, such as company job descriptions, job announcements, and so on). On the other hand, sources for accomplishments or impact statements are sometimes more difficult to come by.

## Performance Appraisals

One of the better places for unearthing accomplishments is from the files of your company's human resource department. Performance appraisals can provide a wealth of material; however, many job seekers haven't kept copies of performance appraisals and many more haven't even received written evaluations. If you do have access to your past performance appraisals, look for instances where you met or exceeded specific goals your supervisor set. Table 9.1 shows just a portion of a performance appraisal for a job seeker who is a loan officer at a regional bank.

### Table 9.1: Sample Performance Appraisal

| Key Objectives and Measurement Criteria | Results |
| --- | --- |
| Meet established funding goals of $750,000 per month. | Elizabeth funded 132 loans for $15,924,820 ($1,327,068 monthly average) on originations of 174 loans for $22,756,636 ($1,896,386 monthly average). |
| By December 31, pipeline to consist of 75% purchase transactions. | Purchase transactions amounted to 82% of all loans funded. |

Appraiser comments:

Elizabeth's ability to follow an aggressive and consistent marketing plan has been consistent. Her selling techniques are consistently used to achieve sales and marketing goals. She is a strong supporter of management in helping to carry out bank policies. Moreover, she is a very professional representative of the bank.

We used this year-end appraisal information to write the following impact statements. Note how we used excerpts from the appraiser's comments section of the performance evaluation.

Impacts:

- Generated $15.9 million in annual loan activity, exceeding annual goal by 76%.

- Ranked #1 in "purchase transaction" loans, which yield higher returns to the bank—year-end totals reflect 82% of all loans funded (above goal of 75%).

- Comments from manager include the "ability to follow an aggressive and consistent marketing plan…a strong supporter of management [and] a very professional representative of the bank."

## Your Career Management File

By far the best place to find information for impact statements is your own *career management file* (CMF). Every professional should have a growing CMF, so if you can't lay claim to one now, grab the nearest manila file folder or 9 by 12 envelope and label it "How I've Made a Difference." (You can also create a folder in your My Documents folder on your computer.) Your mission is to solve problems and help affect the bottom line. Just as a CEO needs meaningful data to measure progress, you, too, must gather data to document your contributions. Whether you're beginning a new position or remaining with your present employer, begin today to assemble data and track your progress on performance standards. Consider tossing the following items into your CMF:

- Notes from meetings with supervisors that state what is expected of you or how your performance will be measured.

- Notes (handwritten is okay) which substantiate that you met or exceeded what was expected of you.

- Notes (with detailed names, facts, figures, and so on) of what you consider to be your greatest contributions.

- Company printouts of information relevant to your profession (quarterly sales, productivity, expense controls, and so on). Remember to keep proprietary information extremely confidential.

- Job descriptions.

- Performance evaluations.

- Examples of work you've produced (such as a company brochure or new business form).

- Attaboys (or "attagirls") from the boss.

- Memos documenting your contribution to a team effort.

- Nice notes from customers.

From this raw material, you will compose powerful, substantiated, and impressive impact statements that will give you entrée to better jobs, outfit you with ammunition to win at the salary-negotiation table, and document the fact that you *are*

making a difference in the health of the company and in other peoples' lives. Next time you have a bad day at the office, take out your career management file and take note of what you have accomplished!

When your CMF begins to overflow, make separate file folders for each employer. To reconstruct data for past employers, you might need to call on former supervisors or contacts within the company. You might ask questions such as these:

- What were sales (or profits, production, cost issues, and so on) when I began with the company and what were they when I left the company?

- Did I (or teams on which I worked) make specific contributions that affected sales (profits, production, cost issues, and so on)?

- What do you think is my greatest contribution to the company?"

- What kinds of problems did I inherit?

- What were the challenges I was hired to meet?

- What numbers were in place when I started the job?

Obviously, the longer you've been away from a company, the harder it will be to find measurable data. That's why it's so important to maintain your CMF as you go. Much like preparing your tax return every April 15, the job is much easier if you've kept detailed records along the way.

As you add to your CMF, you'll begin to see how critical this file is to the all-important task of developing accomplishments for your résumé. It is difficult, if not impossible, to write powerful impact statements without a key ingredient that your CMF will now put at your fingertips: *baseline data*.

With baseline data, you can provide the impressive comparisons outlined earlier in this chapter. Comparison of baseline and subsequent data, or before-and-after facts, will help you draw a much clearer picture of your success, because it will provide the reader a frame of reference. Without a frame of reference or starting point, your results might not sound as impressive. For instance, these impact statements sound fairly strong:

## *Before*

- Built sales to $270,000 per annum.
- Increased account list to 200.

However, a skeptical reader (most résumé screeners are!) might wonder whether sales were already $250,000 when you started or you inherited an account list of 175. Note the addition of baseline data in these *After* impact statements:

## *After*

- Built sales from zero-base to $270,000 per annum (typical sales order for fastener products averages $75).
- From "no account list," formed relationships with 200 active accounts.

Giving a comparative frame of reference adds considerable weight to the sentences. Your reader now knows that

* Sales began at $0.
* You sell inexpensive fasteners where the average sales order is just $75 (it takes thousands of orders to get to the $250,000 mark).
* Your 200 accounts sprang from a nonexistent account list.

Very impressive!

# Impact-Mining: Probing Questions to Unearth Hidden Treasures

*Impact-mining* is a term for the interrogative process used to draw out a job seeker's accomplishments. At this time, review your SMART Stories™ from chapter 4 and transfer the results from those stories to the appropriate employment entry on your résumé. In addition, ask yourself this question, with respect to each of the following buying motivators: "How have I helped my employers to…"

* Make Money
* Save Money
* Save Time
* Make Work Easier
* Solve a Specific Problem
* Be More Competitive
* Build Relationships, Brand, and Image with Internal/External Customers, Vendors, and the Public
* Expand Business
* Attract New Customers
* Retain Customers

(Note: For more help in the area of impact-mining, see *Résumé Magic,* which contains 250 questions and sample responses specific to numerous industries and professions.)

When you're finished, you will have amassed a treasure chest of impact statements to choose from, the highlights of which you'll want to include in your résumé. You can weave others into your cover letter, follow-up letters, networking situations, and interview scenarios.

# Sifting Through the Accomplishments You've Gathered

Now that you've completed your impact-mining, you should have several potential impact statements for each employer. Next, take your impact statements and rank them separately for every employer, indicating the most impressive as number one. The number of statements you will use for each employer depends on the length of your résumé, the length of your career history, and the length of employment with each employer. The following guidelines might be of help in determining how many impact statements to use and where to position them:

- **The bulk of your experience is with your most recent employer:** If you've worked for your present or most recent employer for a number of years or for the bulk of your career (and this experience is relevant to what you want to do next), you'll want to give the most weight, and the most impact statements, to this employer. Seven to 10 impact statements might well be in order if this is the case.

- **Your employment history is evenly distributed among employers:** If your employment history has been fairly consistent in length of time spent with employers, use a similar number of impact statements for each employer, perhaps two or three for each. Give slightly more weight to the most recent employer, perhaps three or four impact statements total or one or two more than you allot to the remainder of your employers.

- **You have been employed with your most recent company for a short period of time:** If it's been too soon to have made a measurable difference at your current employer, refrain from an impact statement because a weak statement is less impressive than no statement at all. Likewise, be brief with your job description for this employer and begin with wording which implies that you are currently tackling some new challenge. Use, for instance, "Currently charged with…" or "Challenged with…" or "Recruited to…." For the remainder of your work history, follow the preceding guidelines for the scenario most closely aligned to your needs.

# Use Impact Statements to Portray Yourself as the Right Fit

You have a great deal of flexibility in forming and fashioning your résumé. In all likelihood, you could make a difference in a variety of positions and companies. To portray yourself as the right fit, carefully select and strategically position information that is relevant to the position or company. Remember that this is *your* marketing piece, unique to *your* situation, *your* strengths, and *your* singularity. Just as your gene pool is unique to humankind, your work history and accomplishments are unique to you. Although your background may be similar to other candidates, your résumé shouldn't cause readers to wonder whether you have an identical twin.

By far the best way to distinguish yourself from the crowd of candidates is through the use of definitive impact statements (accomplishments). As you finish developing your impact statements using the tools and tips in this chapter, the construction of your career story is nearing completion.

Take pleasure in your progress thus far: The framework is up (format selected), the space planning is done (categories selected), the interior is constructed (job descriptions written), and furnishings are decided on (accomplishments identified).

# Finalizing Your Résumé with Formatting, Editing, and Proofing

Next, it's time for the "punch list" (a construction term for the final touches). In résumé writing, that means tweaking the format for visual appeal, editing, and proofing!

## Formatting to Impress

How do you impress employers *before* they ever read your résumé? Just like the marketing wizards and advertising gurus do—with visual appeal. This next sidebar will help you with the task of tweaking the format of your résumé for maximum visual appeal.

### 10 Quick Tips for Résumé Formatting

1. Create a visual pattern—be consistent in your use of tab sets, fonts, and line spacing from section to section.

2. Apply white space liberally—learn how to add line space between paragraphs using the Format, Paragraph, Spacing command in MS Word.

3. Limit the number of tab stops on the page—more than three will cause the résumé to look too busy.

4. Use no more than two fonts on the page—one for your name and perhaps the category headings, and another for body text.

5. Use the same font and point size for every heading; use the same font and point size for all body text.

6. Use bullets that complement the body-text font—make sure the size of the bullet doesn't overpower or detract from the text.

*(continued)*

*(continued)*

7. Divide long paragraphs (more than six or seven lines) into two. Lead off each of the smaller paragraphs with a logical category title.

8. Avoid the "Leaning Tower of Pisa" effect of placing employment dates in the left margin surrounded by too much white space. Dates placed on the right margin allow you to shift body text toward the left and gain room for important content and keywords.

9. Balance the text between top and bottom margins so that there isn't excessive white space at the bottom of the page.

10. Print the résumé, tack it on a wall, and step back five or six feet. Make sure it has some semblance of form and design.

## Editing for Impact

Next comes editing. If you don't consider yourself to have above-average editing skills, enlist the services of an experienced résumé writer or editor. This will be a worthwhile investment.

### 10 Quick Tips for Résumé Editing

1. Address your audience. Every sentence should pass this relevancy test question: "Is my reader interested in this?"

2. Be accurate. Check and double-check all details, especially numbers.

3. Be brief. Carve out information that is repetitive or irrelevant.

4. Be clear. Ask two or three people to read your résumé. Is anything confusing?

5. Avoid jargon that is too specific to your current company (specific names of reports, company-specific acronyms, and so on).

6. Deliver the goods up front. Start accomplishment statements with the results and then describe the method for achieving the results.

7. Start sentences with action verbs (directed, led, performed, collaborated with) or sometimes noun phrases (operations executive, team member, team leader, sales professional) instead of passive statements such as "Responsible for" or "Duties included."

8. Sidestep any potential negatives. It's easier to address these issues in person.

9. Avoid baseless personality attributes. Use personality pairing to combine your soft skills with tangible documentation of the skills.

10. Use "résumé speak," which converts a quiet, conversational writing style into a punchy, quasi-advertising writing style.

# Proofreading for Perfection

When it comes to proofreading, follow the 10 tips in this next sidebar.

## 10 Quick Tips for Résumé Proofreading

1. Print the résumé. (It's easier to spot typos on a piece of paper than it is on a computer screen.)

2. Read it slowly, one word at a time. Give special attention to these items:
   - Dates of employment
   - Phone numbers and e-mail addresses (pick up the phone and call the numbers you have listed; send an e-mail to the e-mail addresses listed)
   - Spelling of proper nouns (your name, employers, cities)
   - Headings (if one category heading is boldfaced and underlined, are all of them boldfaced and underlined?; have you duplicated a category heading?).
   - Consistency of formatting (if one employer entry is indented half an inch, are all indented half an inch?)

3. Mark any changes on the proof with a pen (use ink colors such as green or red to help changes stand out).

4. Read it backwards, one word at a time. This process forces you to look at each word, rather than each sentence, where your brain can "fill in" information because it knows what the sentence is supposed to mean. Starting at the bottom of the résumé, take a business card or similar size piece of paper and cover up all but the last word. Read that word. Is it spelled correctly? Uncover the next to last word. Is it spelled correctly? Repeat this process for every word on the page. Mark any changes on the proof with a pen.

5. Make the changes to the document on your computer.

6. Print it again.

7. Read it again.

8. Compare the proof version with pen marks to the new proof. Check off that each correction was made.

*(continued)*

*(continued)*

9. Let it sit overnight. Looking at it with fresh eyes can make all the difference.

10. Ask two other capable proofreaders to read it with a critical eye.

# Chapter Wrap-Up

Congratulations! By following the recommendations in this and preceding chapters, you should have a killer résumé that is employer-focused, relevant, chock-full of accomplishments, visually appealing, and supportive of your personal brand! This will certainly help position you above your competition. Keep in mind, however, that the résumé is a critical job search tool, but not the magic potion for job offers. You'll get the most mileage out of your résumé when you combine it with smart networking activities, which you'll learn about in Part 3, "Job Search Strategies."

## 10 Quick Tips for Writing Accomplishments and Finalizing Your Résumé

1. Always include relevant accomplishments that link to employer buying motivators, such as helping the company make more money, save money, save time, make work easier, solve a specific problem, be more competitive, build relationships/image, expand business, attract new customers, or retain existing customers.

2. Work smart! Review the SMART Stories™ you developed in chapter 4 and recycle the Results as the basis for your accomplishments (pare down the wording for résumé accomplishments into succinct statements). You can also use the Tie-in or Theme from the SMART Story™ to introduce the accomplishment with keywords. For instance, "Technology Innovation: Cut R&D time-to-market 20% using live meeting technology to improve communications among offices in Asia, Europe, and the U.S."

3. Include numbers, such as dollar amounts, percentages, and totals, to convey the full impact of the accomplishment.

4. Use comparisons to demonstrate how you stand out from others, such as comparisons between competing companies, comparisons with the industry average, comparisons with the company average, and comparisons with your predecessor in the position. (Use discretion with your descriptions, so as not to disparage individuals.)

5. If your accomplishment was the result of a team effort, avoid sounding egotistical. Use phrases such as "Contributed to…" or "Member of 7-person task force that…" to give credit where credit is due.

6. When formatting your résumé, create visual appeal by applying white space liberally. Be consistent in using tab sets, fonts, and line spacing. Divide long paragraphs into two.

7. Balance the text of your résumé between top and bottom margins and left and right margins. Too much white space on the left side of the page can waste precious room; place dates on the right to avoid this.

8. Put your critical-thinking skills to use as you edit your résumé. Every sentence should be relevant, concise, accurate, and clear.

9. Write in a manner that creates momentum and excitement. When writing job descriptions, start with action verbs. When writing accomplishments, position numbers near the beginning of the sentence.

10. Proofread without rushing! Print the résumé, read it slowly, mark any changes, and then make the changes at your computer. Print it again and check that all the changes you intended to make were made. Then read it completely through again. Let it sit overnight and read it again. Enlist the support of others in proofing the résumé.

---

### ⭐ Magical Coaching Questions

Reality check! Some job seekers have tunnel vision when it comes to the résumé. They view it as the silver bullet that will magically result in job offers and therefore spend untold hours tweaking and perfecting wording when they should be out networking and uncovering employer needs. On a scale of 1 to 10 (1 is low, 10 is high), how would you rate yourself on this tendency?

_____

_____

_____

Based on your above score, what, if any, new action do you need to take so that you don't get caught in the résumé "tweaking" tunnel?

_____

_____

_____

---

*(continued)*

*(continued)*

If you have completed your résumé, how does it feel to have finished this important task?

_____

_____

If you have not completed your résumé, how can you break the task down into smaller steps?

_____

_____

How will you reward yourself when you finish?

_____

_____

_____

_____

# E-Résumés, Cover Letters, and Other Career Marketing Documents

*"Learning is not compulsory, but neither is survival."*

—*W. Edwards Deming*

A few years ago, job seekers had to ask themselves, "will I need an electronic résumé in my search?" Today, the question is not "will I…?," but "which kind…?" Ignoring the trends in technology is a bit like turning your back on the ocean—eventually you'll get blindsided by a wave that can leave you sputtering. Take the time to learn the basics.

Electronic résumés (e-résumés) come in assorted flavors—each with a specific form and function—including these two key types:

- **ASCII text résumés:** Used when pasting a résumé into an e-mail message or a Web site e-form/résumé-builder.

- **ePortfolios and blogs:** Web-based career marketing documents, which provide you with a 24/7 marketing presence on the Internet.

You'll find the essentials of electronic résumés in this chapter, as well as a brief look at eportfolios and blogs. Cover letter strategy and cover letter samples are also included, along with a review of miscellaneous career marketing documents.

## Creating ASCII Plain-Text Résumés

Your goal in creating an ASCII résumé is to strip your original résumé document of all formatting so that it is readable by any computer. There are several ways to convert a file to ASCII and several opinions on which type of conversion (with line breaks or without line breaks) is best. It depends on whether you'll need the résumé to be pasted into an e-mail or pasted into an e-form at a Web site. We'll cover two different sets of steps: one for converting a résumé to ASCII for e-mailing and one for converting to ASCII for posting at Web sites. We'll look at each process separately.

## Converting to ASCII for E-Mailing Using MS Word or Corel WordPerfect

1. **Change the margins.** With your word-processing software open and the résumé on screen, highlight the entire document (Ctrl+A). Click File, Page Setup. Enter 1.0 (for one inch) in the box labeled Left. Enter 2.0 (two inches) in the box labeled Right. This step shortens the length of the lines, which is important for controlling line breaks.

2. **Change the font.** Use a fixed-width font, such as Courier or Courier New. With the document still highlighted, change the font by clicking Format, Font. Scroll through the font selections in the drop-down box labeled Font or Font Face. Click on Courier. In the drop-down box for Font Size, choose 12 pt. Click OK. Use the Esc (escape) key to unhighlight the document. The 12-pt font places fewer characters on a line and helps prevent unattractive line wraps—aim for no more than 60 characters per line (a space counts as a character).

3. **Use Save As, choosing Text Only with Line Breaks.** Click File, Save As. In the Save As Type box, scroll down and select Text Only with Line Breaks if you're using MS Word. For Corel WordPerfect users, scroll up in the File Type box and select ANSI (Windows) Text.

4. **Rename and save the file.** In the File Name box, type a new name for the file; for example, *resume4emailing*. This will help you differentiate this résumé from other versions of the résumé you might create.

5. **Accept the warning.** You might see a popup box that says, "[Filename] may contain features that are not compatible with Text Only format. Do you want to save the document in this format?" Choose "Yes."

6. **Close the file.** Click File, Close to remove the file from the screen. After doing so, follow the steps on the next page for cleaning up the conversion.

## Converting to ASCII for Pasting into E-Forms

1. **Use the Save As function.** With your word-processing software open and the résumé on screen, click File, Save As.

2. **Choose Text Only.** Click the drop-down arrow in the Save As Type box; scroll down and select Text Only if you're using MS Word. For Corel WordPerfect users, scroll up in the File Type box and select ANSI (Windows) Generic Word Processor.

3. **Rename and save the file.** In the File Name box, type a new name for the file; for instance, *resume4eforms*. This will help you differentiate this résumé from other versions of the résumé.

4. **Accept the warning.** You might see a popup box that says, "[Filename] may contain features that are not compatible with Text Only format. Do you want to save the document in this format?" Choose "Yes."

5. **Close the file.** Click File, Close to remove the file from the screen. After doing so, follow the steps for quick cleanup of an ASCII conversion in the next section.

 *Tip* White space is your best ally in creating a visually appealing ASCII-text résumé. Use the Enter key on your keyboard to add a line space between paragraphs. This will "open up" the look of the résumé. Add a line space above and below important words or subheadings, such as job titles or "Accomplishments." Add line spaces between a bulleted list of sentences. Break long paragraphs into a series of shorter paragraphs. White space won't matter a bit to a search engine, but a real reader will eventually appreciate the readability.

## Quick Cleanup of an ASCII Conversion

1. **Use a text editor for cleanup.** Use a text-editor program to tidy up your résumé for e-mail transmission. Windows operating systems contain a built-in text editor called Notepad. To start the program, click the Windows Start button; then click Programs, Accessories, Notepad. Open the file (for instance, *resume4emailing.txt*) that you saved earlier (click File, Open).

2. **Format the contact information.** If your header (name, address, telephone, e-mail) was originally formatted with anything other than centered text, you'll find that the header information is all jumbled. Reformat this data, placing everything on the left margin. Use a separate line for your name; street address; city, state, ZIP; each telephone number; e-mail address; and Web résumé URL or blog (if applicable).

3. **Fix any glitches.** Review the document, repairing any bullets that went astray. All bullets should have converted to an asterisk (*), although sometimes they morph into a question mark. Other characters that might have converted incorrectly include ellipses, em dashes (—), or any letters with diacritical markings (for instance, the accented e's in résumé).

4. **Add white space.** To improve readability, separate each paragraph with two line spaces. Always place two line spaces before category sections to set them off clearly.

5. **Set off category headings.** Format résumé category headings (Qualifications, Education, Experience, and so on) in ALL CAPS. Consider accenting category headings by adding a series of tildes (~~~) or equal signs (===).

Use the same treatment for each résumé category. When choosing the character you'll use to set off category headings, select only from the characters you see on your keyboard (as opposed to any special symbols you can insert from your word-processing program).

Note how the following category headings were set off with different keyboard characters, each of which is readable by all types of computer systems.

PROFESSIONAL EXPERIENCE
~~~~~~~~~~~~~~~~~~~~~~~~~~~~~~~~~~

PROFESSIONAL EXPERIENCE
|-|-|-|-|-|-|-|-|-|-|-|

PROFESSIONAL EXPERIENCE
......................................

---

*Caution* You can add visual accents to an ASCII-text version by using standard keyboard characters, such as an asterisk (*), a plus (+), a hyphen (-), a tilde (~), or the lowercase letter *o*. Any of these characters will convert without distortion. Avoid special characters such as "smart quotes" ("curly quotes" as opposed to "straight quotes") or mathematical symbols such as the plus-or-minus sign. Although it's a standard keyboard character, the greater-than sign (>) can cause conversion confusion in an e-mail message, so avoid this character as a replacement for bullets.

---

6. **Delete unnecessary information.** If your original presentation résumé is two pages, it should contain your name and possibly a page number or contact number at the top of page two. Remove this header information from page two of your ASCII version because it is unlikely that it will appear at the top of a page when printed from an e-mail message. Leaving the header for page 2 tattles to the reader that you originally had a two-page or longer résumé, which can be a psychological weight that you don't want to add.

---

*Caution* When sending e-mail communications to prospective employers, don't let the informal nature of e-mail be your undoing. Despite the casualness associated with e-mail, you must still pay close attention to spell-checking and correctly punctuating messages. If you forego what you know to be good grammar, syntax, capitalization, or punctuation in an e-mail message, your reader might assume that you really don't know any better.

---

7. **Save your changes.** After cleaning up your ASCII résumé, you will need to resave it to keep the changes. With the document still in the Notepad text editor, click File, Save. The file will remain on your Notepad screen.

> *Caution* Are you sending more than you intended? When saving your résumé as an ASCII file, make sure it is only the résumé that you are saving. If you have included correspondence to other target companies or miscellaneous notes on your job search within the same file as your résumé, "cut" this information from the document and save it under a separate file name. You don't want to accidentally e-mail your résumé along with cover letters written to other companies!

8. **Do a test run.** To see what your ASCII version might look like to an e-mail recipient, test it by sending an e-mail message to yourself and to a friend who has a different e-mail program than yours. With the file named *resume4emailing.txt* open in the Notepad text editor, click Edit, Select All; then click Edit, Copy (or click the right button on your mouse, touch *a* on your keyboard; right-click the mouse again, then touch *c* for copy). Open your e-mail program (such as MS Outlook or Eudora) or establish your Internet connection (using an ISP such as America Online or CompuServe) to prepare an e-mail. Address the e-mail to your own e-mail address. In the Subject or Regarding box, type *ASCII résumé test* or some other title you prefer. (When applying to employers, you will reference the position title or a brief summary of your skills, such as "Award-winning Web designer, 6 years' exp"). In the message area, type yourself a brief cover letter (just as you would with a real employer); then one or two lines below your cover letter message, press Ctrl+V (or Shift+Insert) to paste the ASCII-text version of your résumé into the body of the message. Send the e-mail and within seconds you'll have a message waiting for you. Once you open it, you can print the message and get a feel for what your readers will receive when you e-mail your résumé to them. It's also wise to find a friend with a different e-mail program and run the same test.

After following the preceding conversion and cleanup formulas, you should have an e-ready résumé that you can use over and over again for e-mailing and posting to e-forms.

## Creating an ePortfolio

A comprehensive career-marketing tool, an ePortfolio is a Web site designed to showcase your talents, experience, and accomplishments. The advantages of an ePortfolio are that you are not limited to a one- or two-page résumé, and the documents provide you additional marketing exposure because they reside 24/7 on the Internet. Some people use the terms *Web résumé* and *ePortfolio* interchangeably. Others reserve *Web résumé* for a Web-based presentation of a traditional print résumé and *ePortfolio* for a Web-based presentation of a traditional print portfolio. We'll focus on the latter in this chapter.

## What to Include in an ePortfolio

Pages in your ePortfolio might include a project history, leadership profile, biography, executive summary, branding statement, philosophy statement, press clippings, technical skills, course work or professional-development workshops and seminars, research work, volunteer or pro bono work, publications, patents, awards, charts and tables, work-related pictures, testimonials, and success stories. Each category is typically given a separate page and identified with tabs that are indexed and linked to the home page of your ePortfolio.

ePortfolios can also include a streaming audio and video clip. For example, an audio file might contain your networking introduction and a few of your main career highlights. Video might include clips of presentations that you have given. If you need help with developing streaming audio and video, www.audiogenerator.com or www.audioblog.com can manage the process for you.

Within your ePortfolio, include your résumé in several downloadable file formats, such as Word document, RTF, PDF, and ASCII plain-text formats. And, if you publish a blog, you will want to add a link to your blog as well (as long as the content is professional and not personal).

## Resources for Custom-Designed ePortfolios

The following providers can create an impressive online presence for you:

- **www.brandego.com:** Founded by Kirsten Dixson, Brandego provides a comprehensive career-management solution that combines the best of personal branding, career ePortfolios, Web design, and direct marketing.

- **www.blueskyportfolios.com:** The creation of Phil and Louise Fletcher, BlueSkyPortfolios allows job seekers to take control of their online image and personal branding. The team designs, writes, and hosts online portfolios for job seekers across a wide range of industries.

- **www.powertalent.net:** Career expert Laura DeCarlo offers a complete set of enabling technology solutions and will help you design, build, and market an ePortfolio.

- **www.careerfolios.com:** Created by Pat Kendall, author of *Jumpstart Your Online Job Search* (Prima Publishing), CareerFolios offers several templates to choose from to create a straightforward online résumé within minutes. You simply copy and paste your résumé text into eforms.

- You can also use a blog platform to build an ePortfolio yourself (check the resources in the following section on blogs).

# Getting on the Blog Bandwagon

With 40,000 new blogs launched every day, blogs are rapidly becoming mainstream online publishing tools. Just what is a blog? Short for Web log, a blog is a

Web page of thoughts, ideas, and commentary reflecting the personality of the writer. Typically updated daily or at least weekly, a blog also allows for public interaction and comment on the blog author's postings. Blogger.com (owned by Google), which helps people create blogs, describes a blog as "a personal diary. A daily pulpit. A collaborative space. A political soapbox. A breaking-news outlet. A collection of links. Your own private thoughts. Memos to the world."

Corporate recruiters and executive search firms are now using blogs as a pre-screening tool. To stay on the radar screen and build a personal online brand, create a blog focused on your area of expertise. (At the very least, you can post to blogs of recruiters or high-profile contacts in your industry.)

## What to Include in a Blog

A blog gives you a chance to demonstrate your skills and expertise in your field, build a community, and create an interactive forum. You can write about projects you are working on, industry events, ongoing research, current trends, new products, and evaluations. You can also include articles or papers you have written, a bio, project histories, a downloadable résumé, an audio presentation, links to your Web site, your Web résumé, or links to other relevant Web sites. The content can also include a blogroll, which is a list of links to your favorite blogs. This allows you and your readers to connect with others who share similar interests.

## Creating a Blog

Creating a blog is fairly easy and does not require knowledge of complex coding. There are several services that will host your blog—some are free, whereas some charge a small licensing fee. Two free sites include the following:

- www.blogger.com/start
- http://spaces.msn.com

For a small fee, you can create a blog hosted by either of these sites:

- www.typepad.com
- www.blogharbor.com

Each site has a wizard to step you through the setup process. If you would like to host your blog on your own server, you can purchase Web log publishing software from www.movabletype.org.

You will need to publish regular posts and respond to questions from people posting to your blog. The goal is to create an ongoing dialogue with your visitors. Posts require a journalistic writing style. Remember, this is being published on the Internet and anyone can access your blog, so think carefully before posting any personal information. Your online content may be available for many years to come!

## Using RSS (Really Simple Syndication) Technology

If you create a blog or post to others' blogs, you'll need to proactively add information and review recent posts. However, if you prefer that blog posts be sent directly to your e-mail inbox, you can use RSS technology—this will help you track your favorite blogs and alert you when new posts are published. An RSS news aggregator can download information into your blog and is an easy way to produce content-rich information for your blog while reducing the amount of research and writing involved. You can find examples of RSS news aggregators at the following sites:

- **Feed Reader:** www.feedreader.com
- **Feedburner:** www.feedburner.com/fb/a/home
- **FeedDemon:** www.feeddemon.com
- **Bloglines:** www.bloglines.com
- **Pluck:** www.pluck.com
- **Newsgator:** www.newsgator.com/home.aspx

You can also use Google's alerts (described in the sidebar in chapter 11) as a source of information for content.

Advanced bloggers syndicate their blog content using RSS, giving them an especially high profile.

## Marketing Your Blog

To market your blog on the Internet, list it with these blog search engines:

- **Technorati:** www.technorati.com
- **Daypop:** www.daypop.com
- **Blogarama:** www.blogarama.com
- **BlogTree:** www.blogtree.com

Another way to market your blog is to post to other blogs and embed a link to your source/blog. In addition, cross-linking on your blogroll to other blogs will increase your blog's presence and ranking in the search engines.

### Monitor Recruiter Blogs

The Electronic Recruiter Exchange blog at www.erexchange.com/blogs will keep you up on trends used by recruiters and executive search firms.

# Cover Letters and Other Correspondence

Cover letters are critical to your search success. They are a measure of your intelligence, business savvy, and confidence, as well as your professional experience and skills. Approach writing them with respect and reverence.

In the old days, there were three straightforward parts to a cover letter:

- **The introduction:** Typically a perfunctory statement that mentioned the position you were applying for and how you learned of it.

- **The body:** One or two paragraphs that summarized your experience and career goals.

- **A final paragraph:** Often an invitation to review your résumé and request that the screener call if interested.

Today, those three parts have taken on new functions:

- **The carrot:** An introduction that is fresh, interesting, and relevant.

- **The corroboration:** Content that shows an intelligent understanding of the employer's needs and confirms your ability to fill those needs.

- **The close:** A confident finish that might suggest a meeting or invite the reader to take further action.

These elements are illustrated in the following sample cover letters (figures 10.1 to 10.3) and interview follow-up letter (figure 10.4).

# NENG YANG

333 North Vassar
Los Angeles, CA 90240
(213) 222-3333
nyang@excite.com

[date]

Li Kun Xie, Placement Specialist
Inner-City School District
1234 S.W. 42nd Avenue
Los Angeles, CA 90242

Re: School Counselor, Southeast Asian At-Risk Populations

Dear Ms. Xie:

A school counselor made the difference in my life.

Although limited in my ability to read or write English when I graduated from high school, my minority counselor encouraged me to go to college. A native of Laos, I had been in the United States for only a few short years. The prospect of college was appealing but daunting—no one in my family had ever gone beyond high school. Since that time, I have sharpened my literacy skills and gone on to earn a Master of Arts in Educational Counseling and Student Services. Working with special needs and underrepresented populations, such as those your district serves, is my primary goal.

From the enclosed résumé, you will note experiences in both academic/student services and psychological counseling roles. I am also active in the Hmong community—my reputation as a workshop presenter has earned invitations to speak at community groups and school districts throughout California. Literacy, family systems, and higher education for the Southeast Asian community are typically my themes.

Your School Counselor position would make use of these rich academic, cultural, and personal experiences. Moreover, your students have the promise of both a trained academic counselor and successful role model who understands the culture and the challenges facing youth.

In advance, thank you for your consideration. I look forward to meeting with your interview panel.

Sincerely,


Neng Yang

Enclosure

**Figure 10.1: Traditional cover letter.**

**GERRY COLDWELL**
4876 Yosemite Lane
Oakhurst, CA 93621
gerry@attbi.com
**(559) 222-7474**

[date]


[contact name, title]
[name of law firm]
[street address]
[city, state zip]

Dear _____:

Having obtained my J.D. from Boalt School of Law in May, I am presently seeking
interviews with firms that are recruiting recent graduates who demonstrate strong
potential to become valued members of your legal staff.  Although acquiring broad
experience is my immediate goal, I am especially interested in firms that devote a
portion of their practice to international law and/or "white collar" criminal law, areas in
which I would like to specialize in the years to come.

Among the experiences and qualities I bring to your firm are these: practical experience
developed while a Legal Intern with a criminal/civil litigation practice; leadership skills
demonstrated while founding the Legal History Club at Boalt and serving in a number of
community and fraternal organizations; and international experience gained while living
in Germany and traveling extensively throughout Western Europe.

Given the combination of these experiences, I am confident I have developed a
professional resourcefulness and personal diversity that will enable me to significantly
contribute to your firm.  I would appreciate the opportunity to personally convey what I
might contribute as an associate attorney.

Thank you for your time and consideration.

Sincerely,


Gerry Coldwell

Enclosure

**Figure 10.2: Direct-mail, or broadcast, letter.**

Jason Senong
EXECUTIVE RECRUITERS INTERNATIONAL
12122 W. 49th Street, Suite 123
Los Angeles, CA 90012

Dear Mr. Senong:

Conversations with John Bradford and Douglas Sterling indicate that your firm is a key player in the ag chemical industry when it comes to executive placement.

As you may have heard, Interchem International was recently acquired by Major Conglomerate, Inc. My division appears to not fit with MCI's long-term vision for growth. Accordingly, the timing is right to explore new opportunities. Could one of your clients benefit from my track record in domestic and international sales?

- As VP, Sales & Marketing for Interchem International, I was challenged with strategy plans and program execution to build domestic sales for the company's bio-tech subsidiary, one of the world's largest producers of synthetic technical pheromones. Over my six-year tenure, we were successful in growing business from start-up to near $40 million in annual sales.

- For the past two years, I have been charged with opening new markets in Europe, Asia, the Eastern Bloc, and Latin America as VP, International Sales. Our team's successes are significant, with more than $12 million in new business credited to the revenue line.

Given the right opportunity, I can duplicate these accomplishments. I would imagine medium-to-large ag chemical manufacturers would be most interested in my skills. There are tremendous market opportunities for specialty ag biopesticides in the Far East. From my perspective, these opportunities lie dormant for lack of proper distribution channels--something my contacts could quickly remedy.

May we talk?

Sincerely,


James Bradford

Enclosure

**Figure 10.3: Executive recruiter letter.**

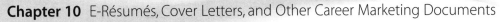

# CHARLES CANDIDATE

**555 N. 14th Street**                                                    **Work: (415) 555-5555**
**San Francisco, CA 94111**          charlescandidate@msn.com          **Mobile: (415) 555-5556**

[date]


Javier Gomez, V.P. Marketing
HI-TECH PARTNERS
55 Market Street
San Francisco, CA 94111

Subject: Promotional Market Manager

Dear Javier:

Thank you for the opportunity to interview for the Market Manager position. I appreciated your time and enjoyed talking with you about the position. The interview confirmed my initial positive thoughts of Hi-Tech Partners and the strategic course you have charted for the company.

As I understand it, your goal is to match the position with someone who can deliver these three key priorities:

- **Offer a strong track record**—With 10 years of experience at two respected Fortune companies, I have demonstrated a solid trajectory of advancement. Highlights with Sony include a #1 ranking among 150 sales managers nationwide, with 45% sales growth; for HP, again a #1 ranking among 24 market managers, based on nearly doubling sales volume over the prior year.

- **Be a visionary leader and change agent**—I am currently sharing a new and aggressive vision with my national account to triple sales. This is being accomplished by tapping the right people for the right position, leveraging team members' strengths, and restructuring elements of the sales team to focus on key deliverables.

- **Deliver results**—Generating record-setting results has been the hallmark of my career. My commitment to you in the first few months would be to understand fully the needs of the business, identify underdeveloped and untapped opportunities, and then create a strategic plan that addresses growth in both core business and new business development. This would be the blueprint for executing initiatives to align the sales team with their inherent strengths, implement sales training, develop licensed and branded promotional premiums, and emphasize conceptual selling to generate more business for your accounts.

Given these experiences and competencies, I'm confident the 50% growth you are targeting for the division is attainable. As my track record shows, I have always exceeded growth expectations and am certain I would do the same for Hi-Tech Partners.

I look forward to speaking with you again soon.

Sincerely,


Charles Candidate

**Figure 10.4: Performance-based interview follow-up letter.**

## 10 Quick Cover Letter Tips

1. Mention a referral source whenever possible. For example, "John Doe mentioned you were looking for new talent for your new procurement project."

2. After mentioning your referral source, mention a benefit: "My 10-year background as a procurement supervisor has enabled me to cut costs at least 20% without sacrificing quality."

3. Briefly summarize the breadth of your experience, whether number of years of experience, relevant titles you have held, or range of qualifications in a certain area.

4. Include accomplishments—always!

5. Set off accomplishments with bullets.

6. Don't restate verbatim information from the résumé.

7. Avoid obligatory language, such as "Enclosed please find a copy of my résumé." Instead, you might say, "You'll note on the enclosed résumé a track record for…"

8. Avoid lofty language. Read the letter out loud—if you stumble over polysyllabic words that are unnatural to your way of speaking, rewrite with simpler language.

9. When pasting a letter into an e-mail, make the letter as short as possible and use bullets to set off accomplishments. Recruiters get tired of scrolling through lengthy e-mails.

10. If you're sending your résumé as an e-mail attachment, combine the letter with the résumé into the same document attachment. This saves the recruiter from opening and saving two attachments. In the text of the e-mail, mention, "For convenience, I have included a duplicate copy of this letter as part of my attached résumé file."

# References

How many references do you need and who should you use? These guidelines will be of help:

- **Recent graduates** should include a minimum of three references consisting of college instructors, as well as former and present employers who can attest to your ability to juggle a full course schedule and manage that part-time job with maturity and professionalism.

- **Professionals** typically supply five or more individuals who fall within the "former bosses, subordinates, peers, clients, and vendors" category.

# ELAINE WELLER

elaineweller@msn.com
222 East Fruitlands ◆ Concord, MA 01642
(978) 444-2222

## REFERENCES

| Individual | Relationship and Range of Knowledge |
| --- | --- |
| Preston Whitehead, District Manager<br>ASTRA MERCK PHARMACEUTICALS<br>432 North Wilson Avenue<br>Lexington, MA 01565<br>(978) 444-3333<br>email@msn.com | Immediate supervisor at Astra Merck. Will verify three-fold sales increases in new hypertensive, respiratory, and migraine products. Can speak to my tenacity in courting "no see" physicians and turning them into loyal, major accounts. |
| Purvis Ellingham, Product Manager<br>ASTRA MERCK PHARMACEUTICALS<br>432 Route 2A<br>New Brunswick, NJ 02345<br>(888) 212-2121<br>email@msn.com | While I was employed with Astra Merck, Mr. Ellingham selected me and two other key sales professionals to collaborate on launch strategies for a new antiherpetic product. Northeast region met target goals ahead of schedule and gained top market share by close of first-year sales. |
| Marlene Sterling, District Manager<br>ABBOTT, DIAGNOSTICS DIVISION<br>432 North Wilson Avenue<br>Lexington, MA 01565<br>(978) 444-3333<br>email@msn.com | Immediate supervisor at Abbott Diagnostics. Can confirm consistent #1 ranking in a district with eight sales representatives, in addition to record incremental increases over goal, market share, and prescriptions sold. Will also elaborate on my ability to orient and train new sales representatives. |
| W. D. Steinberg, M.D., Chief of Pediatrics<br>CHILDREN'S HOSPITAL<br>2121 North Minarettes<br>Waltham, MA 01442<br>(503) 222-1122<br>email@msn.com | Dr. Steinberg served on the committee that granted hospital formulary status for new IV antibiotic. Can document my presentation skills, understanding of systems/disease processes, and ability to interface with medical team and hospital administrators. Children's Hospital was key to phenomenal territory sales growth. |
| William Metters, Ph.D., Executive Director<br>NORTHEASTERN MEDICAL SOCIETY<br>925 East Welton<br>Boston, MA 01223<br>(503) 222-1111<br>email@msn.com | Chief executive of a 2,000-member physicians group.  Dr. Metters can speak to my planning and public relations skills as he has observed me plan and publicize major educational events for NMS physicians that featured nationally recognized leaders in healthcare. |
| Candace Fourche, Executive Director<br>AMERICAN HEART ASSOCIATION<br>1234 E. Bountiful<br>Concord, MA 01452<br>(978) 444-3333<br>email@msn.com | Community leader. Solicited my assistance with several fund-raising events, the most significant of which was Heart's annual gala, a formal dinner-dance and auction that netted more than 35% over prior year. Ms. Fourche will confirm my event planning and media relations skills, as well as my ability to motivate a tireless volunteer corps. |

◆ ◆ ◆

**Figure 10.5: Sample reference list.**

⚡ **Senior executives** usually use the "my life is an open book" approach and provide broad access to former bosses, subordinates, peers, clients, and vendors.

Note how the earlier example of a reference list (figure 10.5) adds a sentence or two after (or to the side of) each contact, describing the relationship to the reference and what was accomplished while working with the person.

## Other Career Marketing Documents

You may find need for additional career marketing documents in your search, including these variations:

⚡ **Networking résumé:** A slimmed-down version of a multipage résumé for outreach to network contacts. It doesn't tell the whole story—just enough of the highlights to give contacts an idea of who you are.

⚡ **PowerPoint résumé:** Used during interviews to address an interview assignment or to share expanded details about key projects, initiatives, or accomplishments that relate to the specific needs of the hiring company.

⚡ **Executive profile:** A one-page narrative for executives, this profile gives an overview of your career and distinguishing highlights.

⚡ **Accomplishment summary:** Typically a one-page document, a summary sheet details a list of projects or accomplishments in a particular area.

⚡ **Special report:** The special report is a short document that details research on an industry issue along with proposed solutions for the issue. This is a powerful way for you to position yourself as a solution rather than just a job seeker!

For a comprehensive look at how to create these documents, check out *Executive Job Search for $100,000 to $1 Million+ Jobs* (Impact Publications) by Wendy S. Enelow and Louise M. Kursmark.

# Chapter Wrap-Up

Phase II, Express, of the Five Phases of a Job Transition (see chapter 2) is all about packaging your strengths and bottom-line value in both verbal and written form. This chapter has armed you with the information to create a complete suite of written marketing documents. As you tap the hidden job market and cover your bases with a traditional search (covered in chapters 11 and 12), you will likely gain additional insider information about your target companies and industry. Don't hesitate to revise your résumé to incorporate these new ideas. Doing so will ensure that your documents reflect the latest in industry trends and keywords.

# 10 Quick Tips for Creating E-Résumés, Cover Letters, and Other Career Marketing Documents

1. Resist any temptation to simply copy and paste your formatted résumé into eforms or e-mail messages. Instead, take the time to convert your formatted résumé into an ASCII plain-text résumé for online submissions and e-mail delivery.

2. Choose "Text Only with Line Breaks" when creating an ASCII résumé for e-mailing and "Text Only" when creating an ASCII résumé that will be pasted into eforms. Give each file a distinct name, such as resume4emailing.txt and resume4eforms.txt.

3. As the final step in the conversion process, tidy up your ASCII text résumé using a text editor (such as Notepad). Things to watch for include jumbled contact information, glitches caused by bullets or non-ASCII characters from the original document (such as em dashes, ellipses, and diacritical markings), and any unnecessary information (such as header information from a second page). Add white space between categories and set off category headings with a series of tildes (~~~) or equal signs (===). Save the changes after cleaning up the résumé.

4. Always do a test run to see what your ASCII version might look like when received by others. Send an e-mail message to yourself and to a friend who has a different e-mail program than yours.

5. Consider an ePortfolio to give employers a multidimensional picture of you. With this expandable online document, you can include items such as a project history, leadership profile, biography, executive summary, branding statement, philosophy statement, press clippings, technical skills, course work or professional-development workshops and seminars, research work, volunteer or pro bono work, publications, patents, awards, charts and tables, work-related pictures, testimonials, and success stories.

6. Get on the blog bandwagon. Consider creating your own blog with easy-to-use services such as blogger.com, or, at the very least, post to appropriate blogs to build your online presence.

7. Create a template for your cover letters to save time, but customize every letter to the needs of the particular company you are applying to. Review the 10 Quick Cover Letter Tips earlier in this chapter.

8. Leverage your reference list! Instead of a straightforward list of names with contact information, add a sentence or two after (or to the side of) each contact, describing the relationship to the reference and what was accomplished while working with the person.

9. Consider other career marketing documents that might be helpful, such as a networking résumé, PowerPoint résumé, executive profile, accomplishment summary, or special report.

10. Remember that all your career marketing materials are fluid documents that you should update frequently to reflect current trends in your industry.

---

### Magical Coaching Questions

Stretch request: Choose one of the career marketing documents described in this chapter that you have not used in the past and implement it within the next seven days. What benefit resulted from expanding your comfort zone?

_____

_____

_____

_____

# Job Search Strategies

Chapter 11:   Tap the Hidden Job Market with a Targeted Search

Chapter 12:   Cover Your Bases with Traditional Search Strategies

Chapter

# 11

# Tap the Hidden Job Market with a Targeted Search

*"There is a way to do it better...find it."*

—Thomas Edison

How many interviews do you want to have in your pipeline? More interviews mean more options. Too often, candidates pin all their hopes on just *one* interview, thinking their ship has come in, only to see it turn into a sunken dream. If you've experienced this scenario, you know it can really take the wind out of your sails. On the other hand, there is nothing more empowering than having options.

## The Difference Between Openings and Opportunities

To increase your options, you must increase your *opportunities*. Notice the emphasis on *opportunities* instead of *openings*. There's a world of difference between the two, as table 11.1 explains. Understanding this will give you an edge in your networking and interviewing.

### Table 11.1: Differences Between Job Openings and Job Opportunities

|  | Openings | Opportunities |
| --- | --- | --- |
| **Definition** | An advertised position soliciting a predefined skill set to perform specific tasks | An *un*advertised position or situation where your skill set can contribute to company/shareholder value |

*(continued)*

*(continued)*

| | Openings | Opportunities |
| --- | --- | --- |
| **Job seeker positioning** | In openings, the job seeker has a tendency to come as a "supplicant" on bended knee, positioned in a role to sell and convince others of his or her worth | With opportunities, the job seeker has the ability to come as a "value proposition," positioned as a business solution or service |
| **How accessed** | Comb through online postings and print want-ads to apply; human resources then winnows applicants to make the volume of résumés manageable, eventually conducting a formal, structured interrogative interview process | Target companies then read, research, and conduct "focused networking" with people who will lead you to conversations with decision makers; needs are uncovered and solutions offered through an informal, fluid inquiry/discovery process |
| **Materials needed** | Traditional résumé, cover letter | Knowledge of company/hiring manager needs and how your strengths can deliver a return-on-investment; targeted résumé or "solution or service" letter (discussed later in this chapter); project proposal |
| **Quantity** | Limited and restricted to those companies in hiring mode | Potentially limitless and unrestricted, as the focus is about building long-term relationships while exploring opportunities and innovations that will benefit the company's bottom line |
| **Your competition** | Typically stiff when advertised broadly | Minimal; you're often competing with only yourself |
| **Who controls the process** | Controlled by human resources; usually a predictable two- to eight-week process | Controlled by hiring manager and decision makers; less predictable process |
| **Human resources** | Actively soliciting and screening applicants | The human resources department is often unaware that you are even on the premises |
| **Connections** | You are typically anonymous and an unknown commodity | You build relationships that lead to your being trusted and gaining insider status because of recommendations by colleagues, employees, and/or friends |
| **What the employer looks for** | Features (an ideal "wish list," such as number of years of experience, degree, skill set, and so on) | Benefits (solutions or services offered) that will make the company money or save the company money, making you a valuable asset that boosts the bottom line |

| | | | |
|---|---|---|---|
| **Employer's preferred method of contact** | Anonymous submission of electronic or paper résumé | | Often e-mail or telephone to start, and eventually face-to-face exploration of issues that ultimately may lead to an employment proposal |
| **Effectiveness** | Leads to jobs 5 to 8% of the time (Source: DBM, a global human resources consulting firm) | | Leads to jobs 58 to 62% of the time (Source: DBM, a global human resources consulting firm) |

Here's more data to help you understand the difference between opportunities and openings. Mike Farr, in his book *The Very Quick Job Search,* another JIST Works publication, diagramed an insightful lifecycle of a job opening, shown in figure 11.1.

Juxtaposing this diagram with table 11.1, you can see that *opportunities* are available in the first, second, and third stages. On the other hand, *openings* are available only in the fourth stage. As a job seeker, you have 300 percent more chance to access opportunities than you do openings. *This is where the elusive "hidden job market" is hiding!*

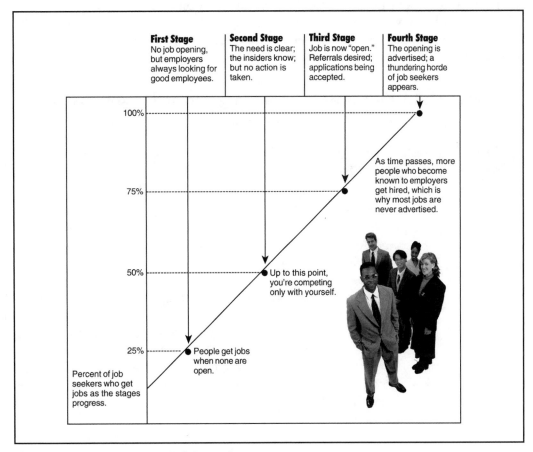

**Figure 11.1: The four stages of a job opening.**

Worse, should you spend your time only on jobs in the fourth stage, you'll significantly increase your competition and place yourself in an adversarial role with human resources, the gatekeeper to your potential dream job!

If you have already mastered the art of uncovering opportunities, congratulations. You might want to focus your attention in this chapter on how to research a company, which is covered in steps 2, 3, and 4. Along with communicating your value or return-on-investment to employers, *research is the most important step you can take toward acing an interview.*

If you need to pump up your pipeline—get more interviews lined up—the seven steps to a targeted/active search explained in this chapter will help you do just that!

# Determine Your Search Strategy—Targeted or Traditional

Will you conduct a targeted/active search or a traditional/passive search? Although both can work, experience has led me to favor a targeted/active search over a traditional/passive search. The strategy, pros, and cons for each are outlined in table 11.2.

### Table 11.2: Differences Between Targeted and Traditional Job Searches

| Type of Search | Strategy | Pros | Cons |
|---|---|---|---|
| Targeted/active or "New Economy" job search | In a targeted search, the starting point is companies—you identify specific companies you'd like to work for and target both *opportunities* and *openings* that align with your Magic F.I.T.™ (see chapter 3).<br><br>Access to these opportunities is made by connecting with | The upside to a targeted search is that it gives you more options (opportunities and openings).<br><br>In addition, it gives you a jump on your competition, giving you access to opportunities in the first, second, and third stages of a job opening (see figure 11.1). | The downside is that a targeted search is labor-intensive and may take you beyond your comfort zone when it comes to research and talking with people. And, although relationships created in a targeted search can be invaluable, sometimes the opportunity may not |

| | | | |
|---|---|---|---|
| | hiring decision makers and positioning yourself as a solution or service to needs that you have researched. | | materialize for months or years down the road. |
| Traditional/ passive or broad job search | In a broad, traditional search, the starting point is positions—you rely on advertised *openings* that align with your functional skills. These openings may be available with any number of companies.<br><br>Access to these openings is made via résumé submission. | One of the best pros to a broad search is that you *know* the company is hiring.<br><br>The other upside to a broad search strategy is that it is easy to click a few buttons and apply to online job postings (or fax or snail-mail résumés). | The downside is that *you* become the broad needle in the haystack, waiting and hoping that employers will find you. Further, you are limited to the fourth stage job openings (see figure 11.1). Finally, almost everyone knows how to conduct a traditional job search, which increases your competition immensely. |

In a world where jobs are disappearing due to automation and globalization, it's especially important that you understand active, "new economy" job search skills. To do so, master the seven steps of a targeted search:

1. Identify companies.

2. Read.

3. Research.

4. Talk to people "in the know" through focused networking.

5. Network online.

6. Stay on the radar screen.

7. Augment with traditional job search methods.

Even if you decide to conduct a broad search, you'll find that many of the preceding steps can rev up a traditional search, so don't skip the steps in this chapter.

In a broad, or traditional, search, openings are accessed through these methods:

1. Online searches

2. Résumé posting

3. Résumé distribution

4. Classified ads

5. Recruiters and agencies

6. Direct inquiry

7. Career events

Chapter 12 highlights how to access openings in a traditional/passive, or broad, job search. In this chapter, we'll cover the seven steps for uncovering opportunities in a targeted search.

# Seven Steps to a Targeted Search

In a targeted search, the starting point is identifying companies you'd like to work for. You'll then read, research, and talk to people in order to learn about TOP (**T**rends, **O**pportunities, and **P**roblems/**P**rojects) issues in these organizations. All the while, you need to stay on decision makers' radar screens and position yourself as a solution or service (we'll cover how to do that later in this chapter).

## Step 1: Identify Companies

A targeted search requires a list of companies in a specific geographic area (or areas). Career "experts" disagree on how extensive a list to start with. Some say it's a numbers game (lots = improved chances); others recommend that you focus on quality rather than quantity (less = more). Both strategies can work—the latter (less is more) is usually more manageable, less costly, and most expedient.

The number of opportunities within a company is a factor in deciding how many companies to target. Because larger companies have more positions, you might need fewer on your initial list. Ultimately, it comes down to connecting with and displaying an ability to meet the needs of a handful of potential employers.

To generate a list of, say, 30 to 50 companies, start by specifying the industry, interest/specialization, and geography/location. In chapter 3, you already defined your industry and interests (step 2 of the Magic F.I.T.™ system), along with your functional/position target (step 1 of the Magic F.I.T.™ system). Write your responses from step 2 in the following box, along with your preference for geographic area/location.

Industry sector (from chapter 3): _____

Interest/specialization within industry (from chapter 3): _____

Geography/location: _____

When considering companies, look at those that are

- Both within, and on the fringe of, your target industry
- Competitors of your current or former employer (if you're looking in a similar industry)
- Vendors/suppliers to your target industry
- Business customers/clients of your target industry
- Associations that support your target industry

For example, if you are targeting the agricultural industry with an interest in export marketing, your list of companies might include agricultural companies involved in exporting, along with suppliers of packaging materials, those that specialize in marketing strategies for exporters, or associations that support commodity marketing.

To create a solid list of companies, tap into these resources:

- People
- Print resources
- The Internet

## Finding Target Companies Through People

Start your sleuthing by asking work associates, recruiters, or friends what they consider to be leading organizations. Use queries such as these:

- "What resources would you suggest for finding a list of some of the best companies to work for?" or "Who do you know who might point me in the right direction?"
- "I'm looking at making a career move. In your circles, what companies have a reputation for being a great place to work?"
- "Who is the 'cream of the crop' when it comes to widget-makers in [fill in your industry]?"
- "Do you know people who don't complain about their work?" or "Do you know people who absolutely love their job? What company do they work for?"
- "Do you know where that successful guy Joe Blow works?" (If you admire someone for their professionalism, skill set, or character, chances are good that the person works for a great company. It's the principle of attraction—great companies attract great employees.)

Beyond your networking contacts and friends, inquire within local employment-related organizations. They often have resources that will point you to target companies:

- **State employment offices:** There are several thousand of these offices located around the country. To find the local and regional programs in your area, go to the Department of Labor's Find It! By Location Web site, www.dol.gov/dol/location.htm. When the map of the U.S. appears, click on your state, and then click the link to your State Gateway. If you're looking in California, you'll note that the state has more than 250 Comprehensive One-Stop and Affiliate One-Stop centers.

- **Community agencies for special groups:** If you are a veteran, minority, senior citizen, or ex-offender, or if you have a disability, contact your city government, job service office, church, synagogue, or public library for information on agencies that provide specific opportunities and specialized services.

## Finding Target Companies Through Print Resources

Reference librarians can be a career hunter's best ally. As a general rule, they are some of the brightest behind-the-scenes people you'd hope to meet! Request that he or she point you to business resources, such as

- Regional, state, or local business directories

- Directories of specialized business—inquire about directories for manufacturers, service companies, and so on

- Chamber of Commerce lists and directories—many Chamber of Commerce organizations publish a book of lists that identifies top local companies in a variety of categories

- Trade journals—the trade journal(s) for your occupation or industry should be *must* reading, whether or not you're on the lookout for a new job

These specific resources might be helpful:

- *D & B Business Rankings* (Dun & Bradstreet, annual): This publication ranks more than 25,000 of the nation's leading private and public businesses by sales volume and number of employees. These indicators are also used to rank businesses within each state and within industry categories. For example, if you are interested in knowing how Outback Steakhouse compares with its competitors, look up *Outback* in the alphabetic index. The index tells you that it is in Standard Industry Code (SIC) 58 for eating and drinking establishments. Refer to the SIC section. There you will find that Outback is ranked 30th in the nation in terms of annual sales volume. Also listed will be all the major competing restaurant chains, such as Lone Star.

- *Standard and Poor's Register of Corporations, Directors and Executives* (Standard & Poor's Corp, Annual): Here you'll find corporate officers, products, SIC numbers, sales range, and number of employees with a geographic and SIC index.

- *Thomas Register of American Manufacturers* (Thomas Publishing Company): Long considered the definitive source for manufacturers, Thomas Register annually updates its list of North American companies that specialize in industrial products and services. (The listings are also available online at www.thomasregister.com.)

⁂ ***The JobBank Series*** (Adams Media Corporation): This series of employment directories details local employers by category and company size, with 19 books devoted to the largest metropolitan areas in the country. Each book contains profiles of local companies in all industries, with up-to-date information including company descriptions, mailing and Web site addresses, phone, fax, e-mail, hiring managers, common professional positions, educational backgrounds sought, and more.

⁂ ***Guide to America's Federal Jobs: A Complete Directory of Federal Career Opportunities*** (JIST Works, Inc.): If your job target falls within the federal government, this resource is a must. The directory includes where to find vacancy announcements and application requirements for virtually any occupation, employment requirements and procedures for each agency or department, contact information, current salaries and benefits, and more.

Although you won't need a librarian's help to find the Yellow Pages, remember that this ubiquitous tool can also give you easy access to company names in certain company categories.

## Finding Target Companies Through Internet Resources

If you have access to the Internet, consider some of the resources in this section to assemble your list of target companies. As a caveat, be forewarned that data found on the Internet may not be centrally located or as neat and tidy as you'd prefer. If you can't find what you want online within an hour or two, resort to other resources. In the long run, it might be faster to go to the library or a bookstore!

### Association Web Sites

Professional associations sometimes list member companies at their Web sites. The following sites can help you find associations related to your profession and then locate these associations online.

⁂ http://info.asaenet.org—**The American Society of Association Executives'** site provides search capability to more than 6,500 associations. Once you find the association for your industry, click through to search for member companies.

⁂ www.weddles.com/associations/index.cfm—**Peter Weddle,** author of several employment-related and Internet resources (www.weddles.com), lists a directory of associations at his content-rich site.

### Search Engines

Use your favorite search engine and "drill down" for directories and company listings. Google and Yahoo! offer helpful business listings:

* **Google**'s http://directory.google.com/Top/Business/—Search more than 50 industry categories.

* **Yahoo!**'s http://dir.yahoo.com/Business_and_Economy/Directories/ Companies/—Search more than 60 industry categories.

## Best Lists

Best lists are a convenient way to assemble a list of target companies. Access a few of these lists at the following sites:

* www.fortune.com/fortune/—The cost of a six-month subscription to *Fortune* gives you access to Fortune's series of best-company lists, including a full list of the Fortune 100 companies, companies best for minorities, fastest-growing companies, the top 50 employers for MBA graduates, and the companies with the most-admired leaders. The latter catalogs nearly 500+ companies in 64 industries rated by long-term investment value, social responsibility, and other factors.

* www.forbes.com—A subscription to *Forbes* gives you access to *Forbes'* numerous lists of companies, people, and places. Company lists include best small companies, best big companies, largest private companies, world's largest companies, and fastest-growing technology companies.

* www.inc.com/resources/inc500/index.html—Each year, *Inc.* magazine publishes the "Inc. 500," a list of the nation's fastest-growing privately held companies. View the Top 25 Companies of the Year on their Web site or subscribe for a full list.

* www.greatplacetowork.com/best/list-bestusa.htm—**The Great Place to Work® Institute** offers a free listing of the 100 Best Companies to Work for in America. An annual book with the same title coauthored by Robert Levering and Milton Moskowitz for *Fortune* magazine provides details on why these companies made the list.

* http://jobsmart.org/hidden/bestcos.cfm—**JobSmart.org** lists more than a dozen "best" lists, including 100 Best Companies for Working Mothers, Top Entry-Level Employers for College Grads, 100 Best Places to Work in IT, 50 Best Companies for Latinas to Work for in the U.S., and more.

* www.craigslist.com—Originating in the San Francisco/Bay Area as one of the best regional sites on the Internet for jobs and lists of companies in hiring mode, **craigslist.com** has expanded its reach to cover several major metro areas throughout the U.S.

If you have the benefit of outplacement or transition assistance from a company such as DBM, Right Management Associates, or Lee Hecht Harrison, you might find best lists, or companies in growth mode, available within their resource libraries.

## Search by Location

There are some handy sites for honing in on companies within a certain radius of your home (or any address). One of the easiest to use is the SuperPages:

 **www.SuperPages.com**—At the home page, click on the Browse link to the right of the word *Keyword,* and select the industry appropriate to your search. After clicking on an industry, fill in the city and state in which you're searching. Check the box for *Search within 20 miles of the city,* and then click *Find It.* A new page will appear displaying the listings of businesses within 20 miles of your city. If you want something closer or farther than 20 miles of your city, click the drop-down arrow to the right of the word *Within* and you'll see distance options from one-half mile to 100 miles.

## Search Public Records

If you're targeting companies that require licensure (accounting, architecture, banking, engineering, healthcare, pharmacy, and so on), you can find these companies easily using a free public records directory, such as the following:

 **Search Systems**—www.searchsystems.net. On the home page, type into the Public Record Locator the name of your state, followed by the word *license,* followed by your industry. For instance, the keywords *California License Accounting* returns a page with a link that says *Licenses—Accounting Firms.* Click this link, and then type the County you are interested in. Click *Find,* and you'll have a list of all the accounting firms in the county, complete with mailing addresses.

## Purchase Mailing Lists

List brokers can provide you with mailing lists sorted by industry code, employee number, sales volume, geographic area, title of executive, type of business, professional specialty, franchise and brand, headquarters and branches, and more. The following online services provide such lists:

 **AccuData America**—www.accudata.com

 **D&B's ZapData**—www.zapdata.com (powered by Dun & Bradstreet)

 **InfoUSA**—www.infousa.com (this company authored *Direct Mail For Dummies* published by John Wiley & Sons)

 **GoLeads**—www.goleads.com (requires a minimum contract after a free trial)

 **Pro/File Research**—www.profileresearch.com

 **JobBait**—www.jobbait.com

 **American City Business Journals** www.bizjournals.com/—(You can purchase a *Book of Lists* containing key contact information and facts for thousands of top local businesses, industries, professions, governmental units, and non-profit organizations in 62 metropolitan areas.)

## Prioritize Your List of Companies

After accessing people, print resources, and Internet resources, you should have a healthy list of target companies to pursue. If the initial list is large and unwieldy, pare it down by focusing on any of these parameters that are important to you:

- Size of organization (employees)
- Size of organization (revenue)
- Company in growth mode
- Reputation of company
- Company well known for your functional (position) area
- Commute time
- Number or variety of opportunities within company
- Advancement potential or other résumé-building opportunities
- Passion for company's mission, products, or services
- Relationships already established with individuals in the company
- Opportunity to work under a certain individual or with high-caliber co-workers
- Company's culture
- Potential for flex-time
- Benefits or perks

The first item noted on the list (size of organization) might be a critical consideration. According to the U.S. Bureau of the Census, roughly 55 percent of the U.S. workforce is employed by small businesses with fewer than 100 employees—meaning that there are potentially twice as many companies available to you should you target small businesses. Figure 11.2 shows the specific breakout (excluding government employees and self-employed persons).

Choose a manageable number of companies on your list to start off your campaign.

## Build Data on the Companies

As you identify and prioritize target companies, begin assembling data on them (one handful at a time so as not to overwhelm yourself). We'll cover how to gather this data in steps 2 through 5. Use the worksheet on pages 286–287 for your profiling. Make copies for each company. As you gather additional data on your target companies, create a file folder for each company or create folders in MS Windows where you can keep information organized.

Candidates who walk into an interview armed with a complete Company Profile impress interviewers and outperform their competition. It's been said that

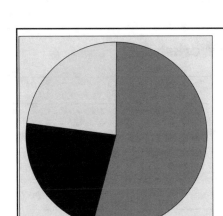

- Small businesses, firms with fewer than 100 people, employ 55% of the U.S. workforce.

- Businesses with 100–499 people employ 24% of the U.S. workforce.

- Businesses with 500 or more people employ 21% of the U.S. workforce.

**Figure 11.2: Where the U.S. workforce is employed (Source: U.S. Bureau of the Census).**

interviewing is a sport where you never get to see your competition. But here is a picture of your top competitors: They are insiders who already have relationships with the hiring manager and other company contacts. They are armed with Company Profile information. And, they have a track record for solving and serving. You'll be a top candidate when you assemble thorough Company Profiles. To gather this level of information, you'll need to read, research, and talk to people, which are the next three steps in the process.

## Step 2: Read

"A" Candidates read voraciously. If you're already in the habit of taking in daily news and industry news, congratulations. During a job search, consider doubling your regular reading activity. If you're one who pays scant attention to the headlines, quadruple your normal reading material while job searching and preparing for interviews.

Here's what you should be reading:

- Your target company's Web site, starting with

  - Any relevant opportunities on its Careers or Employment page.

  - The "about us" page and products/services page.

  - Press releases, especially those containing announcements of recent hiring or staff changes, as well as plans that indicate expansion or the launch of a new initiative.

  - Your target company's blog(s). Many companies have a blog, and the larger ones like Microsoft, Lockheed, Macromedia, Oracle, and General Motors will have several blogs written by different employees. You can find Microsoft's directory of blogs at www.microsoft.com/communities/ blogs/ PortalHome.mspx. There are 21 separate blogs in the Careers

# Company Profile Worksheet

Company: _____

Address, telephone, Web site: _____

Basic info (length of time in business, major milestones, key
products/services, strengths of company, number of employees,
annual sales/profit): _____

_____

Company's competitors: _____

Company executives, HR contact, hiring manager, and his or her bio highlights:

_____

_____

TOP issues (**T**rends, **O**pportunities, **P**roblems/**P**rojects): _____

_____

Internal key contact #1                          Contact info…important issues/keywords…
(name, title, telephone ext., e-mail address):    strategy for approach…my relevant S.O.S.
                                                  (Solution  Or Service) response

_____        _____

_____        _____

_____        _____

_____        _____

Internal key contact #2                          Contact info…important issues/keywords…
(name, title, telephone ext., e-mail address):    strategy for approach…my relevant S.O.S.
                                                  (Solution  Or Service) response

_____        _____

_____        _____

_____        _____

Internal key contact #3                          Contact info…important issues/keywords…
(name, title, telephone ext., e-mail address)     strategy for approach…my relevant S.O.S.
                                                  (Solution  Or Service) response

_____        _____

_____        _____

_____        _____

External key contact #1
(name, title, telephone., e-mail address):

Contact info…important issues/keywords…
strategy for approach

_____

_____

_____

_____

_____

_____

External key contact #2
(name, title, telephone, e-mail address):

Contact info…important issues/keywords…
strategy for approach

_____

_____

_____

_____

_____

_____

_____

_____

External key contact #3
(name, title, telephone, e-mail address)

Contact info…important issues/keywords…
strategy for approach

_____

_____

_____

_____

_____

_____

Notes and questions you'd like answered about ɘ company:

_____

_____

How I can add value to the company:

_____

_____

_____

_____

community alone. You can determine whether the company you're researching has a blog by using a blog search engine (for a list of blog search engines and information on setting up a blog, see chapter 10).

✦ Corporate career newsletters. Corporations are beginning to offer "career newsletters" to communicate information about the company, industry news and trends, employee views, and updates on recruitment events and campaigns. Three examples include the following:

- Siemens: Go to www.siemens.com, click on Jobs & Careers, and subscribe to the newsletter (located in the sidebar on the right side of the page).

- Microsoft: Go to www.microsoft.com, click on Careers (at the bottom of the page), and click on Careers Newsletter (on the left navigation bar).

- Royal Dutch Shell: Go to www.shell.com, click on Jobs & Careers, click on Shell Careers Newsletter (in the right-side bar).

✦ Regional and local newspapers, especially the business section. Watch for names that could turn into contacts. Evaluate every business-related article with an eye for a potential opportunity.

✦ National business news.

✦ Business journals covering news of your target geographic area.

✦ Online and print industry trade journals.

✦ Analyst reports.

✦ Industry white papers or special reports.

✦ Popular business books.

## Online News Alerts: Create Your Own News Channel

At http://news.google.com, you can scan daily headlines or search for specific keywords among 4,500 news sources updated continuously. For instance, if offshoring is an important issue to your profession, type *offshoring* in the search box at the top of the page and click Search News. In less than a second, hundreds of articles will be returned. Each article will include information about how recently the article was published. For search terms, consider names of companies you are targeting, names of key contacts or hiring managers (individuals who would be mentioned in the news articles), products, technology, and the like.

Receive relevant articles automatically by signing up for News Alerts. The alerts arrive daily, clustered as links in an e-mail. To sign up, go to www.google.com/alerts and enter your industry and target companies as alerts. Set up as many alerts as you'd like. You'll be aware of breaking news for networking and interview preparation. And, when you want to show appreciation to networking contacts who have helped you, e-mailing or mailing an especially relevant article can be a thoughtful yet inexpensive way to do so.

Similarly at www.cnn.com and findarticles.com, you can accomplish the same thing.

If you're not sure which journals or business books to read, ask successful networking contacts what they find most helpful. Or, ask a member representative in your trade organization(s) for reading recommendations.

Respond to what you read by keeping a log of

- Any news that will give you a clue about which companies are growing, including the following:

  - Information about commercial real estate leased for the prior week (leasing activity is often published in business news)

  - News of hiring, especially in sales, marketing, or R&D (the business section of your local paper sometimes publishes announcements of new people joining organizations)

  - News of major executive changes (these executives are often looking to bring fresh talent onboard)

- Names of people within the company (and, if applicable, what you liked about their contribution to the material you read)

- Names of people connected to the company (vendors, customers, analysts)

- Issues related to problems or growth

- Interesting projects or innovations

- Trends and how they might benefit your target companies

- Connections your external contacts might have to the company

- Ideas about how you can help with an S.O.S. (solutions or services) response

- Clues to the corporate culture of companies mentioned in the article

# Step 3: Research

Research—knowing the insider scoop—is essential. Most job seekers wait to do research until they have an interview lined up. In a targeted search, research comes prior to contacting the company—it's what helps you land the interview in the first place! If you want an advantage in your job search, this is the step to concentrate on.

"Research is a reflection of a candidate's work ethic and how well he or she will perform when in the job," notes Valerie Kennerson, Director of Global Staffing for Corning, Incorporated, a diversified technology company with 70 manufacturing locations and 20,000 employees worldwide. She goes on to explain that, "When deciding between two well-qualified candidates, the scales typically tip in favor of the candidate who is a little more prepared, interested, and engaged."

To look prepared, interested, and engaged, outline the following seven points:

1. Company data

2. Company's key products/services

3. Company's current TOP issues, or **T**rends, **O**pportunities, **P**roblems/**P**rojects

4. How your skills can be integrated with, and bring value to, the company's TOP issues

5. Key decision makers at the company

6. Strategic stakeholders

7. Competitive companies

When approaching a company, the more information you have, the better. Table 11.3 suggests the level of research you should conduct *prior* to approaching the company, as well as the additional knowledge you should obtain *in preparation for* a formal interview.

### Table 11.3: Two Levels of Research Recommended Before Approaching a Company or Conducting a Formal Interview

| Level I Research Prior to Approaching Company | Level II Research for Face-to-Face Networking Conversation or Formal Interview with Company |
|---|---|
| 1. Company data, including length of time in business, major milestones, strengths of company | 1. Company data, including length of time in business, major milestones, strengths of company |
| 2. Company's key products/services— B2B (business to business) or consumer | 2. Company's key products/services— B2B (business to business) or consumer |
| 3. Company's current TOP issues, or Trends, Opportunities, Problems/Projects: | 3. Company's current TOP issues, or Trends, Opportunities, Problems/Projects: |
| **T**rends—the company's five-year financial trends, strategic direction, and industry trends | **T**rends—the company's five-year financial trends, strategic direction, and industry trends |

| | |
|---|---|
| **O**pportunities—new projects on the drawing board and company priorities | **O**pportunities—new projects on the drawing board and company priorities |
| **P**roblems/**P**rojects—competition or challenges that are keeping the organization from being as productive or profitable as possible…projects that are on the drawing table | **P**roblems/**P**rojects—competition or challenges that are keeping the organization from being as productive or profitable as possible. What has been done to date to address these problems? What are the needs of the project with respect to planning and implementation? |
| 4. How your skills can be integrated with, and bring value to, the company's TOP issues | 4. How your skills can be integrated with, and bring value to, the company's TOP issues |
| 5. Names of key decision makers at the company | 5. Names and bios of key decision makers at the company—are they all homegrown and promoted from within, or have they been brought in from other companies? |
| 6. Strategic stakeholders—who are the customers, corporate alliances, vendors, suppliers, and consultants of the company? | 6. Strategic stakeholders—who are the customers, corporate alliances, vendors, suppliers, and consultants of the company? What is their relationship? What are they known for? |
| 7. Names of competitive companies | 7. Analysis of competitive companies—who are the key players in the industry? |

Here are a dozen resources to help you access the information in table 11.3:

- **People in the know** (discussed in step 4 of this chapter).

- **Business information sites:** Some sites provide basic business capsules at no charge, with extended news and market analytics for a fee:

  - Hoovers: www.hoovers.com is the first place to go when you're researching companies

  - Bizjournals: www.bizjournals.com/search.html (use your target company or industry to conduct a keyword search)

  - Dunn and Bradstreet: www.dnb.com

  - CEO Express: www.ceoexpress.com

  - Corporate Information: www.corporateinformation.com

  - Bloomberg: www.bloomberg.com (this site caters to institutional investors, with a price tag out of reach for most individuals; as an alternative, explore access to this data via any of your network contacts in the brokerage/financial services business)

* **Company Web site:** Read, of course, the careers section, which might give you an idea of the company's culture, affinity groups, succession planning, and advancement opportunities. In addition, review the site's press releases, about us, history, and investor relations pages, as well as its products/services pages. (Prior to a formal interview, you'll want to thoroughly exhaust the company's Web site.)

* **Company blog:** Read the company's blog to gain an understanding of the corporate culture, projects employees are working on, upcoming job openings not yet posted, and the challenges employees face.

* **Company marketing material:** Call and ask for marketing or sales literature if none is available at the Web site.

* **News sources:** Google.com searches can turn up interesting support information about the company or its industry (note the sidebar under step 2, titled "Online News Alerts: Create Your Own News Channel"). Journals for your industry can also provide leads.

* **Libraries:** Ask your new friend the resource librarian to run a periodical search using the company name and your functional area (marketing, sales, engineering, and so on) as keywords.

* **Associations:** Review your professional association(s) to search for any references to your target company. It might be that an employee from the target company will be presenting at an upcoming conference, or you might find an article that is of relevance to your target company's TOP issues.

* **Career Web sites:** Several career Web sites offer access to company research, such as vault.com, wetfeet.com, and craigslist.com.

* **Company annual report:** This is often available at the company's Web site or through the investor relations department. If you're questioned by investor relations when you request an annual report, mention that you are interested in investing in the company.

* **Publicly traded companies' 10-K (annual report) or 10-Q (quarterly report) filed with the Securities and Exchange Commission (SEC):** These reports are available free at www.freeedgar.com (EDGAR stands for Electronic Data Gathering, Analysis, and Retrieval system). Similar to an annual report, the 10-K contains more detailed information about the company's business, finances, and management, and is loaded with contact names.

* **Analyst reports intended for the investment community:** Read warily; analysts (who are employed by banks and won't want to offend potential client companies—the very companies they are analyzing) might be tempted to issue a rosier outlook for the company than what it really deserves. Use Google to find analyst reports on your company, or check sites such as Zacks (www.zacks.com) or Thomson Financial (www.thomson.com/financial/fi_investmgr.jsp).

**How to Navigate an Annual Report**

For an excellent guide on reading an annual report (or reading between the lines of an annual report), visit www.investorguide.com/igustockreport.html.

As you gather research data, keep track of it using the Company Profile worksheet from step 1. The added benefit to this preparatory work, of course, is that you will be more confident and centered before walking into networking and interview situations. And, in the eyes of most interviewers, a candidate who suffers from a few interview jitters but has done his research thoroughly will carry more weight than a candidate who has polished presentation skills but hasn't demonstrated a good understanding of the employer's top issues.

## Step 4: Talk to People in the Know Through Focused Networking

Often, career networking guides recommend that you network with everyone from your barber to your Aunt Sally's sister's husband's cousin when looking for job leads. It's true that employment referrals can come to you through these venues, but it might be the exception to the rule.

In this economy, the greatest payoff will come from fundamental business relationships—focused networking—with people inside your target companies, colleagues, customers/clients, distribution/retail partners, vendors, industry thought leaders/writers, outsourced service providers, peers or support staff in other companies, association members, experts in subject matter relevant to your profession, professional consultants (accountants, attorneys, industry recruiters, and so on), and the like…*people who are closely linked to decision makers at your target employers.*

These lifetime relationships are an *essential* part of any professional's toolkit—just as important as your degree or technical skills. Corporate mentality has shifted toward individuals bearing personal accountability for career management. As such, it is incumbent on the individual to build, maintain, and, when needed, be able to engage his or her networks. These networks serve as both an incubator for knowledge acquisition and a safety net during periods of career transition.

Networking continues to rank high on the list as an efficient job search strategy, verified by these statistics:

- Regardless of age, networking was rated the most productive search strategy. Specifically, candidates aged 21 to 37 attributed their new positions to networking 58 percent of the time, ages 38 to 56 attributed their new positions to networking 62 percent of the time, and ages 57+ attributed their new positions to networking 59 percent of the time. Other strategies, such as responding to ads or working with search firms, did not come close (source: DBM's Career Transition Study).

When a service-based business attempts to sell you something, the least effective to most effective methods for closing a sale are cold calling, Yellow Page ads, recognizing someone as an expert in the field, having an existing relationship with the service provider, being referred by a trusted source, and being a current satisfied customer (source: www.un-marketing.com). Clearly, referrals are more effective than cold calling. In job search, *you* are the service, so the case can be made that posting your résumé on a site where no one knows you from Adam is the equivalent of cold calling, which is proven to be an ineffective marketing method.

A warm referral, one provided by another person, receives 70 percent greater attention than a cold call (source: *Power Networking*, by Vilas and Vilas).

For some, networking comes easily. Others look upon it as a necessary evil. For those who sit in the latter camp, the 10 tips in this next sidebar might help reframe your thinking.

## 10 Quick Tips for Talking to New People

1. **Leverage your strengths:** If you are an excellent researcher, make this the centerpiece of your networking effort. If you are an excellent organizer, lay out a seven-step plan for approaching each contact. If you are an excellent writer, craft well-conceived letters to your contacts as the first step. If you are more introverted than extroverted, start with online networking or by approaching contacts that are of a like mind. If you love people, but it takes you a while to get to know them, volunteer regularly in places where your target contacts congregate.

2. **Look at networking as a learning (professional development) experience:** This is a chance to increase your industry knowledge, not through classroom training but in real-world, face-to-face research. Count your hours in networking as continuing education units (CEUs).

3. **Focus on what you can bring to the other person:** For people who shy away from networking, this mindset often brings an "a-ha!" moment. You have value—concentrate more on giving value to your networking contact than on what you'll receive.

4. **Listen:** Don't make this harder on yourself than it really is! Good networkers listen more than they talk—all you need is a comfortable opening question or statement to get the process started. Often people who think they aren't great networkers are good at networking because they listen so carefully.

5.  **Recognize that the recipient of your call might be happy to talk:** If you discovered that you have a strong preference for introversion (see chapter 3, step 6), you might not have a natural affinity for networking. On the other hand, the person you're about to contact might be extroverted, in which case he or she might thrive on talking and welcome your call.

6.  **Act as though this were a business meeting:** Think back to a time when you had to meet a new business associate, which blossomed into a fond business relationship. Consider that the person you are about to contact might become a long-term and respected colleague.

7.  **Commit to building long-term relationships:** A relationship nurtured over months and years will be stronger than one that is just a few days or weeks old. A contact you meet today might not lead you to your next job, but it might lead to your dream job in a year or two. Once you have made new contacts, stay in touch periodically, even after you've landed a new job.

8.  **Don't be afraid to ask:** After doing networking the right way—building rapport, and approaching the relationship as a giver and not just a taker—don't forget to ask for what you need. The worst someone can say is "no" or "I can't help you." Get beyond any fears of embarrassment or rejection—these worries are debilitating and serve no purpose.

9.  **Maximize short-term relationships:** Be completely credible and authentic, never overstating your achievements.

10. **Write instead:** If you're having trouble mustering the courage to call someone, write a brief letter or send an e-mail. (See *Cover Letter Magic*, also from JIST, for ideas.)

Focused networking is fundamental to uncovering opportunities. Neglect this step and you'll be extending your job search.

## Who Are Focused Networking Contacts?

Focused networking is a career management technique wherein you connect with people who have both a *relationship* with decision makers and *knowledge* of the target company, as figure 11.3 shows.

Contacts in Quadrant 1 will be most fruitful. These are often people inside the company (colleagues of hiring managers, potential co-workers, suppliers of the company, advisors to the company, and so on). Contacts in Quadrant 2 (for instance, professional association contacts, industry writers, and so on) and

| | | |
|---|---|---|
| **K**<br>**N**<br>**O**<br>**W**<br>**L**<br>**E**<br>**D**<br>**G**<br>**E** | **Quadrant 1**<br><br>Contacts who have relationships with decision-makers and knowledge of the target company. | **Quadrant 3**<br><br>Contacts who have relationships with decision-makers but little to no knowledge of the target company. |
| | **Quadrant 2**<br><br>Contacts who have knowledge of the target company but no relationships with insiders. | **Quadrant 4**<br><br>Contacts who have neither relationships nor knowledge of the target company. |

**Figure 11.3: Networking quadrants for a focused networking relationship.**

Quadrant 3 (friends or professional associates of the decision-maker) might lead you to contacts in Quadrant 1, whereas contacts in Quadrant 4 (your barber, your Aunt Sally's sister's husband's cousin, your friends at the gardening club) might yield little or no benefit. Spend your time in quadrants that will get you to Quadrant 1 contacts.

Potential contacts, along with tips for approaching them, are shown in table 11.4. In general, when asking for help, remember the acronym REAP, which stands for

- **R**esources—what should you be reading?
- **E**vents—what should you be attending?
- **A**ctivities—what should you be doing?
- **P**eople—who should you be talking to?

As contrary to your purposes as it might seem, do *not* ask your networking contacts for information about job openings. This often puts people in a position of having to say "no" to you, making them feel uncomfortable and less willing to help you in the future. On the other hand, contacts are often able to respond to requests for help with resources you should access, events you should attend, activities you should do, and people you should know. When you do these things, you will *reap* the benefit of uncovering new opportunities that will fill your interview pipeline!

## Find E-Mail Addresses

Yahoo's Advanced People Search is an amazing tool for finding people, especially at larger organizations. Go to http://email.people.yahoo.com/py/psAdvSearch.py and fill out as much or as little information as you want (fewer data entries may yield better results). Enhance your search by choosing an organization name (your target company) and organization type.

## Dealing with Voice Mail

Avoid leaving voice-mail messages. To improve your chances of accessing your contact, make calls during times when it's likely the person will be in: shortly after lunch (1:15 p.m.), around 5:30 p.m. when the gatekeeper might have gone home, or 7:30 a.m. as they're coming in to work. If you must leave voice mail, mention the name of someone whom the contact knows. For instance, "This is Susan Whitcomb. My number is 555-555-1212. We've not spoken before, but Jane at J&J Engineering mentioned you as someone who might be able to help me with some industry information. If your schedule doesn't allow you to call back soon, I'll try you again on Friday afternoon." This last sentence might work for you or against you. If the contact definitely doesn't want to speak with you, he might avoid your call on Friday. On the other hand, it gives you a reason to call back without looking like a pest.

In addition to the tips outlined in table 11.4, these general strategies for approaching contacts will be helpful:

- **Pave the way:** When contacting a decision maker at your target company, ask a peer to pave the way for you with a warm-up call. For instance, if John is your peer and Chris is someone you'd like to speak with, you approach John in this way: "John, I'm wondering if you could help connect me with Chris at XYZ Company. I think we'd both benefit from knowing one another…."

- **Relaxed settings:** Meet your new contact at an industry meeting, trade show, or social gathering. Face-to-face time at a conference, meeting, or event can be more relaxed than trying to eek out an appointment in a busy professional's daily schedule. You can either "accidentally" bump into them at the event, or e-mail or call ahead of time. If you contact them ahead of time, mention that you learned from Joe Blow (your mutual connection) that he or she will be at the event. Offer a sincere and customized compliment about the person or the company, and then state that you hope to have a chance to speak briefly and put a face with the name.

## Employee Referral Incentives

Think insiders might not want to speak to you, a stranger? Think again. Michael Foster, in his book *Recruiting on the Web* (McGraw-Hill), notes that many companies offer rewards to employees for referring a new hire, with a common starting point of 2 to 4 percent of the projected base salary of the new hire. The Employment Management Association estimates that the average award for an employee referral is approximately $1,300. Measured against search fees that can range up to $20,000 for a mid-level contributor, that number can grow significantly and still be a great recruiting bargain.

## Table 11.4: Tips for Approaching Focused Networking Contacts

| Contact | Tips on Approaching |
|---|---|
| People inside target companies who are at your level | Speaking with people who might be future co-workers can be more effective than asking to speak to the CEO (if you're not going to report directly to the CEO). A conversation with the top sales rep for the company, an engineer who headed up a recent project, a project manager who knows people in different departments, and so on can reveal insider information. And, at some point, the hiring manager might ask this person what he or she thinks of you. Meeting with him or her before you meet with the hiring manager can serve you well.<br><br>Personally e-mail or call with a warm referral, such as, *John, this is Susan. Jane Reddy suggested I connect with you. Is this a good time?* If not, ask when would be a good time to speak. If it is a good time, continue with: *I wonder if you could help me with some information. Jane mentioned you're in the production department at XYZ Co. I am a customer service rep and have some good skills, and am looking for opportunities in a company like yours. Jane thought you might be able to offer a good perspective on what it's really like to work at XYZ.*<br><br>After listening and establishing rapport, ask more questions: *What would you say is the strength of the department?* Save this next question for later, as some people won't readily admit to problems. *Where could they use the greatest help?* Then test the waters with *Who would you suggest I contact over in Customer Service? Joe Ramirez, you say? Great. What's the best way to approach him?* Remember to wrap up with *You've been a great help. Is there something I might be able to do for you?* |
| People inside target companies who are in leadership or a position to hire | See the solution/services letter later in this chapter. Alternatively, you can try this script that shows *chutzpah* (it's a little too nervy for my taste, but it can be pulled off by some): *This is John Doe. Garrett Bench at the Quarterback Club told me to call and, by the way, said he'd give you 5-1 odds on the upcoming Broncos game. Do you have time for a quick call? Here's the reason I'm calling: I'm a sales executive who's looking for a bigger challenge. I've got a 12-year record of beating quota by as much as 45%—even in down markets I came in with double-digit numbers over forecast. If my skill set were clearly able to add revenue to your company, would you be open to an exploratory conversation?* |

| Contact | Tips on Approaching |
|---|---|
| | If you don't have awesome statistics to number-drop, this script might work: *This is Jane Doe. Garrett Bench at the Heart Association told me to give you a call. Have I caught you at a good time? … I'm an administrative professional with excellent technology skills and have seven years of experience providing admin support to marketing managers. Garrett mentioned the new marketing project you're working on and it happens that that's just the type of work I'm looking to do more of. He also said you might be a bit short-handed in the admin department. If my skill set were clearly able to make your operation run more smoothly, would you be open to an exploratory conversation?* |
| Salespeople within target companies | Salespeople are typically gregarious and happy to talk. Start off with something like this: *I'm really impressed with what I know of your products, and I'd love to be associated with a team that helps bring them to market. Who would be the person to talk to about the [insert your profession here] end of things?* |
| Association contacts for your industry | Speak to the association president, a regional representative, membership chairperson, or program chairperson. Meet these people face to face at events and conferences. Call or e-mail if an event is not accessible. Mention, *I'm looking for a position in distribution center operations and have a strong background with companies on the East Coast, where I've recently relocated from. I've certainly acclimated rapidly to your mild winters, and now I'm acquainting myself with some of the local manufacturing companies. Could you recommend any resources, upcoming events, or people in the area that I might contact who could share useful information?* |
| Former employees of target companies | Some of the most truthful information you uncover may come from an employee who is no longer with the company. With no vested interest in politicking, former employees might be brutally honest about company culture, policy, key contacts, and the like. In addition to asking questions about TOP issues, ask, *What do you miss about working there?* and *What do you NOT miss about working there?* or *Would you recommend the company to a family member as a good place to work?* Finally, *Have you stayed in contact with any colleagues since you left the company? If so, Who would you suggest I contact?* |

*(continued)*

*(continued)*

| Contact | Tips on Approaching |
|---|---|
| Vendors or suppliers of your target companies | Call and ask, *Could I have the name of the individual who handles the XYZ account?* Once you have the name, you can either speak directly to him or her or e-mail with this type of message: *I understand you work with the XYZ account and wondered if you could help me. I'm especially interested in their purchasing operations because of the innovative Web sourcing they're doing. Who would be the appropriate person to speak with about that?* After learning a bit more about the issue, you may want to ask to meet face to face with the person. Ultimately, ask, *Who would you recommend I contact at XYZ to learn more? Ask permission to reference this person: May I say that I spoke with you?* |
| Competitors of your target companies | Although you might not gain access to names within your target company via its competitors, you *can* pick up tidbits that will likely be of interest to your target company. Start by speaking with someone who can help you better understand the product or service, such as someone in sales or customer service. |
| Clients or customers of your target companies | Ask about their experience with the company's products or services, such as what they liked or disliked about their purchasing experience, quality, delivery, warranties, ease of use, what improvements they'd suggest, etc. Become a customer yourself, purchasing the product or service (if affordable) and analyzing it for strengths, weaknesses, and opportunities.<br><br>A trusted relationship with a client can be worth its weight in gold, as target companies will value and respect this relationship. |
| Retailers or distributors of your target companies (if applicable) | Visit stores and talk to personnel. Ask why they like the product, ask their ideas for how the product could sell better, ask how the product could be serviced better, and ask what new trends or opportunities they see. |
| Advisors to the company (commercial bankers, accountants, attorneys, advertising agencies, commercial real estate brokers, and so on) | From these contacts, seek names of key players within target companies and advice on how to approach them. Inquire of changes that might impact the company. Ask the ad agency's account executive where the target companies are advertising; ask commercial real estate brokers whether the company has plans for leasing new space. (*Tip:* Network with a broker or a commercial sign company to learn who is coming to town and who is expanding their offices.) |

| Contact | Tips on Approaching |
|---|---|
| Your present or past colleagues/co-workers | This sort of dialogue should help: *Joe, this is Susan. We worked together on the Billings project at Macmillan Company. I hope all is well in your world. Listen, I don't want to take up too much of your time—do you have just a few minutes?* Joe says yes. *Part of the reason for my call is to ask your advice. I'm researching some potential opportunities at Target Company A and Target Company B—they both have great reputations for their graphic design capabilities—and I'm wondering who you might suggest I speak with in their marketing or sales departments.*

If Joe says no one comes to mind, follow with, *You don't know of anyone? Okay. How would you suggest I learn more about their graphic design department?* Joe mentions that Print-Co supplies some of their paper, and that Jane is the salesperson for the account. *Great. Anyone else come to mind that services them?... That's terrific. This will give me a good start. Any tips on how I should approach Jane?* Take notes. *Joe, you've been a great help. Let me make sure I've got the right e-mail address for you so I can keep you in the loop about my conversation with Jane.* This sentence gives you permission to follow up, should you need further advice.

If Joe has no suggestions on how to learn more, ask: *May I ask you to keep an ear to the ground for me? I can e-mail you my résumé if you'd like—feel free to forward it when appropriate. And, if I'm still looking a month from now, I'll touch base with you if that's okay.* Again, you've asked permission to follow up.

Finally, end with a networking "give" so that the conversation is not all "take." *And, while I've got that, let me shoot you a copy of an article I read recently that was really interesting—it's about new features in Photoshop...if we'd had this available back on that Billings project, we would have saved ourselves some outsourcing dollars. By the way, if there's some way that I can be of help to you, please let me know.* [Sometimes saving chit-chat for the end of the call is wise, taking less of the caller's time and not giving the appearance that you're buttering up someone.] *If you've got another minute, I'd love to hear what's new with you...any interesting projects you're working on now?*

*(continued)* |

*(continued)*

| Contact | Tips on Approaching |
|---|---|
| Employment professionals (recruiting, permanent/temp agency, alumni organizations) | Call the target company and ask the name of the recruiter or agency they use for sourcing positions at your level. The human resources department might be helpful, or the accounts payable department might provide you with a list of vendors that includes the recruiter/agency. Then, call the recruiter and develop a relationship. |
| Writers of industry/business articles, white papers, books; or the media | E-mail the writer and thank him or her for the insightful work, which you just couldn't put down! Mention something specific so it's clear you really did read the work and aren't being a sycophant. Be honest about your mission. Share who you are *(I'm a director of communications who managed creative teams that won Clarion awards and delivered record returns on marketing communications)*; what you want *(I'm looking for who headed up the project you referenced in your article/book)*; and how you might help in the future *(I'm wondering if I might have some contacts you'd want to interview for your next article)*. |
| Job search networks | Contact the leader of the job search network and inquire about the makeup of the group, what kind of commitment is expected, and how you might become a valuable member of the group (leaders like to hear that you're not just interested in what the group can do for you). Once you start participating in and contributing to the group, make inquiries about your target companies and other opportunities. |
| Contacts *outside* your immediate industry or normal sphere of influence | Do something *new*! Join a new e-list, visit a new group, attend a conference that relates to your industry that you haven't been to before. Sometimes "outsiders" can give you a fresh perspective or open up a whole new world. When meeting people, ask, *I'm new here. What do you like best about this group?... What resources should I make myself familiar with?... Who would you recommend I introduce myself to?* |

| Contact | Tips on Approaching |
|---|---|
| University/academic *thought leaders* | Approach academic contacts with something like, *I understand you teach Logistics at University of California–Davis. I'm looking for a position in that field and have good skills to offer. What companies are you aware of that are doing interesting things in this area? And then, Where could I learn more about them?* |
| Community leaders and local elected officials | Incumbents often want to be re-elected and are therefore responsive to constituent needs—they or staffers might be able to pass along a contact name or helpful resource. |
| Your family, friends, neighbors, ex-neighbors, healthcare professionals, members of groups (gym, political, sports, religious, hobbies), volunteer-mates, Christmas card list, and so on | Be specific. Don't say, *I'm looking for a job.* Instead, customize a specific request based on what you know about the contact (do they golf, belong to an environmental club, jog with someone, or attend a certain group where insiders congregate?). For instance, *Joan, do you still work with the Habitat for Humanity group? If so, Well, at your next meeting, would you mind asking the other members if they know of anyone at these construction firms that I'm researching? Since my company downsized, I'm exploring some new opportunities and am interested in talking with someone who could tell me what it's really like to work there—it'd be especially great if I could get in touch with some-one who handles the purchasing for their raw materials.* |

Note that a few of the suggested scripts in table 11.4 might be interchangeable with your different networking contacts.

✦ **The buddy system:** Attend an event *with* your warm contact and have this person introduce you to new key contacts. If your warm contact has a telephone system with two incoming lines and a "confer" button, that person can be speaking to you on one line and put you on hold, dial the target contact and get permission to have you join the call, and then press the "confer" button on the phone and have all three people connected. In a similar vein, author Diane Darling in *The Networking Survival Guide* (McGraw-Hill) noted that although only 5 percent of cold calls end in a sale, a sale is made as much as 80 percent of the time if the person making the referral sits in on the sales call.

✦ **Request for a random act of kindness:** When contacting people for the first time, in addition to mentioning the person who referred you to them, mention that you are looking for help, resources, or advice. Choose your language carefully. Do not say, "I just wanted to pick your brain a little." Instead, try something like, "I was hoping you'd have a few minutes to point me in the right direction" or "I understand you're knowledgeable in the area of _____ and I was hoping you could shed some light on something I'm exploring" or "I'm hoping you have time for a quick random act of kindness. I'm looking for the name of the person who heads up the _____ (this might be a department or a project)."

✦ **Gatekeepers:** When encountering a gatekeeper or secretary to an executive, befriend this person and be honest about your intentions. State that you would like to speak with Ms. Jones (the executive) at the recommendation of a couple of colleagues (these warm contacts should be well known to the executive). Convey an understanding that the executive's schedule is quite busy and ask advice about the best way to approach him or her. The gatekeeper might direct you to e-mail, send a letter, or call at another time. Follow his or her advice, and then send her a short e-mail back with a thank you for her assistance. He or she, too, should be a part of your network!

✦ **The S.O.S. response letter:** Write a letter that includes the name of your warm contact, conveys that you have done some research on the target company, and offers an S.O.S. (solutions or services) message, as this next example illustrates.

## The Give and Take of Networking

Your goal in focused networking is to connect with others in a give-and-take relationship where there is reciprocal benefit. Let's look at what you can give, as well as what you'll want to take away from your encounters.

### The Give

Before approaching anyone, consider what your "give" will be. Here are some ideas:

✦ An online or print article you found that would be of interest to your contact

Lionel Lillifax, Chief Financial Officer
Nano-spec
123 E. 54th
Philadelphia, PA 17555

Dear Mr. Lillifax:

Your company's success with nanotechnology is impressive. I have invested in your stock and spent time understanding why you are successful. I first learned of the company after purchasing a Babolat tennis racket last August and was intrigued by the use of the carbon nanotubes in the yoke of the racket. During my research, I studied your 10-K and had conversations with Marion Davenport and Michael Miller in your research and distribution departments. Both of them urged me to contact you (and may already have mentioned our conversations to you). Based on my research, I identified a few areas that might position your company for even greater profit.

First, I understand that your staff is stretched thin, as is often the case with startups. In a similar situation, I was able to cut overtime 30% by customizing existing technology to do things that the vendor claimed the program could *not* do—staff got the rest they needed and morale vastly improved. Although I'm an accounting professional, I believe my technology skills might relieve some of your immediate overtime issues.

Second, the accounting program you are currently using for R&D accounting will be cumbersome at best once your volume increases to the levels projected in the 10-K. You are likely already aware of this. There are two technology solutions that offer better scalability and tracking for the intricacies of expense, fixed-asset, inventory, and cost of goods sold. I selected one of these programs for my current company, which allowed for sophisticated data collection used in subsequent business planning and decision-making. The results helped to elevate and even out our monthly cash flow.

Finally, your long-term plans for acquisition growth are impressive. I assisted with due diligence on two M&A projects at Silicon Strategies. In one, I uncovered data that had been overlooked by prior auditors and analysts. This information shifted the strategy for negotiations and saved the company several million in acquisition costs. I believe my skills in this area would be an asset in your future acquisition initiatives.

I plan to attend the NSTI Nanotechnology Conference & Trade Show in San Francisco next month. I'm especially interested in Mr. Warren's presentation on the business perspective of nanotechnology from the venture-capital world. Your assistant, Sharon, mentioned that you will be attending. I'd enjoy getting together for a short visit at the conference. If you would like to call me, I can best be reached at 213-555-5432 between 8–9:30 a.m. EST (5–6:30 a.m. on the west coast) or after 8 p.m. EST. If I don't hear from you, I will contact you to coordinate a convenient time.

I'd enjoy getting together for a brief visit, as I believe it would be mutually beneficial to know one another. If you would like to call me, I can best be reached at 213-555-5432 between 8–9:30 a.m. EST (5–6:30 a.m. on the west coast) or after 8 p.m. EST. If I don't hear from you, I will contact you to further explore these ideas.

Best regards,

Kale Kolburn

**Figure 11.4: An S.O.S. response letter.**

For more ideas on crafting this sort of letter, pick up Jeffrey J. Fox's book *Don't Send a Resume: and Other Contrarian Rules to Help Land a Great Job* (Hyperion).

- An interesting fact you learned in your recent research (be cautious not to reveal insider secrets that competitors have shared with you)

- Industry knowledge you have that will be of value

- Information about an upcoming event or valuable training

- Information about a book or other helpful resource you encountered

- The names of people in your sphere of influence whom the contact might benefit from knowing

- A copy of a relevant article you wrote or a presentation you made

Networking with someone a tier or two above you? You might feel that you need them more than they need you. If so, these "give" ideas might help balance the scales:

- **Enthusiasm:** At the very least, be a breath of fresh air to your networking contact.

- **Card:** Send a tasteful thank-you card.

- **Quote:** E-mail an inspirational or humorous (nothing off-color) quote relevant to the topic of your conversation.

- **An inexpensive thank you:** Send a Starbucks coupon or the like (steer clear of anything expensive to avoid the appearance of a "payoff" for talking to you).

- **Uncertain?:** Ask what you can give to the contact, for instance, "Based on what you know about me, is there anything that I might be able to help you with?" There may, indeed, be something they might think of. One young contact asked this question to a veteran executive, only to learn that the contact would like to know more about his father's work, which later led to a mutually beneficial business deal.

### The Take—INSIDER Info

What do you want to come away with from networking relationships? The goal of focused networking is *not* to find a job lead in every encounter. Instead, it is a process of becoming an INSIDER, an acronym that stands for **I**nformation, **N**ames, **S**upport, **I**deas, **D**ata, **E**nergy, and **R**elationships. Table 11.5 offers more information on these items.

## Table 11.5: Finding the INSIDER Scoop in Networking

| Item | Specifics |
| --- | --- |
| I = Information | Learn more about broad industry trends, opportunities, and issues, as well as companies that are growing or going through challenging times. |
| N = Names | Add new names to your network—find out what's of interest to these people and how you can help them. |
| S = Support | Garner supporters—people who will introduce you to others, endorse you, and be your champion. |
| I = Ideas | Come away with advice or spark new ideas and insights for your search—new strategies to access decision makers, new skills to learn, new companies to learn about, and new leads to follow. |
| D = Data | This is the nitty-gritty data that comes from due diligence on a target company—its financial picture, strategic plans, management team, TOP issues (trends, opportunities, problems, projects), and so on. Fill this information into your Company Profile worksheet. |
| E = Energy | Build momentum by having encouraging encounters with others or taking proactive steps. |
| R = Relationships | Relationships—rapport and bonds—lead to referrals, endorsements, and the insider's edge. |

Finally, throughout your focused networking, remember these tips:

- Always express heartfelt appreciation for the person's time. In this day and age, it's the most precious commodity one can give.

- Offer a *sincere* and *tailored* compliment about the person's career ("Congratulations on your recent coverage in *The Gazette*"…or, "For some time now, I've admired your ability to develop innovative widget programs.").

- Know what INSIDER information you'd like to come away with from each meeting—is it new information, more names, a support of endorsement, insight into an issue, data on a company, deepened relationships, or something else?

- If you're new to networking, get your feet wet by first meeting with people who know and support you.

- Save the most powerful contacts for last.

- Schedule meetings and calls for when your energy is highest.

- Never initiate inquiries about specific job openings, such as "do you have any positions you're trying to fill?" or "are there openings?" This language shifts your position from solution/service provider to supplicant.

- Always offer value to your networking partner.

---

### Be on the Lookout for the Seven Dwarves

Chances are good you will run across a few Disney characters as you network. Talking with Happy and Doc will help balance any conversations with Grumpy and Dopey. The name of the game is to persevere—graciously, assertively, relentlessly, but politely persist. You might even convert a few Grumpies into Happies along the way. But, be cautious not to push too hard in your persisting or the reverse could be true!

---

## Networking for a Confidential Search

How do you go about a search without jeopardizing your current position? Confidential searches are a Catch-22. To uncover more options, it's helpful to let people know that you're looking. The more people who know you're looking, the less confidential your search. To minimize the risk of discovery, use recruiters/ search consultants (*if* your occupational level uses recruiters—not all do). Contact only a handful of well-respected recruiters and make a point of requesting that they take every measure possible to protect both you and your company by keeping your name under wraps. For more information on working with recruiters, see chapter 12.

If a recruiter isn't appropriate for your search, start by upping your networking activity with people who will influence the decision makers at your target companies. Never dine alone! According to networking gurus, there are five networking opportunities a day—breakfast, coffee, lunch, cocktails, and dinner!

Once you've reconnected with your contacts, hand-pick a few whom you trust. The conversation can go this way: "You know, Chris, it'd really take the right opportunity for me to make a move, but your company seems like just the kind of place where I could fit in and make a contribution, especially in helping resolve those supply-chain issues you mentioned. If there's talk of bringing someone new on board, could you let me know before it becomes formally announced?" [end with…] "Again, I wouldn't want my employer to think I'm ready to jump ship, so I'll appreciate your keeping this conversation under your vest." Check in regularly with your contacts and be prepared with a long lead time. Confidential searches generally take longer.

# Step 5: Network Online

Online networking offers an opportunity to connect with people beyond your immediate reach. Some of the more popular venues include blogs, e-lists, online chats, and newsgroups, along with a new breed of virtual connections known simply as online networking sites.

## Blogs

Pew/Internet & American Life Project noted that by the end of 2004, blogs had established themselves as a key part of online culture. In its January 2005 report, Pew reported that 8 million American adults had created blogs and 12 percent of Internet users had posted comments or other materials on blogs. Further, in 2004, Blog readership jumped 58 percent, to 27 percent of all Internet users.

Savvy job seekers are now using blogs to network with corporate recruiters online. Microsoft's Senior Marketing Recruiter, Heather Hamilton, publishes a blog on Marketing and Finance at Microsoft (http://blogs.msdn.com/heatherleigh/articles/90890.aspx).

In a *New York Times* article by Eilene Zimmerman entitled, "Before Applying, Check Out the Blogs (October 3, 2003)," Microsoft's Hamilton was quoted as saying "I have great candidates in process that have resulted from blogging. Personally, I think blogging is going to change the way companies recruit."

To find corporate blogs, you can conduct a search using the blog search engines listed in chapter 10.

Once you identify a target company's blog, determine who the author is and what position the author holds in the company. You can gain volumes of information about the company by reading the blog archives. If the blog is written by a corporate recruiter, you can learn more about upcoming openings before they are posted, ask questions about the opportunities, and position yourself as a candidate. When the position opens, you will have a better chance to land an interview because you have developed a network with important people in the company.

Before posting to a blog, be sure to read the archives and follow the posts for a while to get a sense of etiquette and the best strategy for approach. All posts are published for everyone to read, so use caution regarding confidential or personal information, especially if you're conducting a confidential job search.

## E-lists

E-lists are an automatic mailing list with messages broadcast to the e-mail addresses of everyone on the list. Recipients do not see the names and e-mail addresses of the participants unless a participant chooses to post a comment to the list. (E-lists are sometimes mistakenly referred to as a LISTSERV, which is a commercial product that refers to a specific mailing list server.)

To tap into these virtual venues, inquire with your professional association, trade organization, or university alumni group about which e-list to join. For a catalog of some 50,000 public lists, see Catalist at www.lsoft.com/catalist.html. For private lists, see Topica at www.topica.com/dir/ and Yahoo! Groups at http://groups.yahoo.com/.

If there is a cost to join the list and you are between positions, ask whether there is a discount or free trial for people in your situation. When joining one of these groups, sit back and watch for a bit to get a feel for the culture and etiquette of the group. Watch for intelligent posters—you'll soon see who posts graffiti and who posts artwork. Take note of who seems to be in the know and contact them off-list (not via the e-list, but through their private e-mail address).

Again, as with any networking, take the mindset that it's not just about finding job leads but creating long-term relationships.

## Communities

Yahoo!, Monster, Google, MSN, Microsoft, and many other Web sites offer a variety of networking alternatives, including blogs, newsgroups, forums, discussions, technical chat rooms, user groups, instant messaging, and webcasts.

## Online Chats

Online chats take place on Web sites in areas known as chat rooms. When participating in a chat discussion, your messages are instantaneously relayed to other people in the chat, and their messages are instantaneously relayed to you. Imagine carrying on an e-mail conversation with someone without having to open an e-mail message each time the person responds. Now imagine doing that with 3 to 30 people at the same time. That's online chatting. To participate in an online chat, check out the many career-related chat opportunities at http://chat.yahoo.com/.

## Forums

Forums (also known as newsgroups, discussion groups, discussion forums, or online conferences) are online services or bulletin board services where you can read or respond to messages. A good resource for locating newsgroups is Infinite Ink's Finding News Groups at www.ii.com/internet/messaging/newsgroups/.

Monster.com offers the opportunity to enter forums on some 25 general and targeted advice message boards. From www.monster.com, click on "Career Advice" then click on "Community," and then click on "message board index." Lycos.com (http://discussion.lycos.com) allows you to search for forums, bulletin boards, and groups where people are discussing your favorite topic.

For an interesting peek into what recruiters are discussing, subscribe for free to the forum at Electronic Recruiters Exchange (www.erexchange.com). You can unsubscribe at any time.

Fast Company's "Company of Friends" section (www.fastcompany.com/cof/) allows you to search its groups by interests, country, industry, or name.

## Online Networking Sites

Ever-advancing technology is causing a new genre of online networking sites to sprout up on the Internet. These sites allow you to contact others through a network of connections for the purpose of job search, business leads, and industry information. Most provide you with a profile page and allow you to post your bio. Some of the more popular sites include the following:

- **www.LinkedIn.com:** LinkedIn is currently used by more than 2.8 million professionals across the globe, including 840,000 users in Europe and 240,000 in Asia. Unique to LinkedIn is its service that allows members to post jobs and hire people within their network. It also offers a job search function so that you can search for jobs through your network. This provides you with the opportunity to network with the person posting the position.

- **www.Ryze.com:** Ryze has more than 250,000 members in more than 200 countries. You can join special networks related to your industry, interest, or location. More than 1,000 organizations host networks on Ryze to help their members interact with each other.

- **www.tribe.net:** Tribe offers geographical and topical networking groups and also allows members to post job listings.

- **www.Friendster.com:** Friendster has more than 17 million members and recently began offering free blogs powered by Typepad.

There are other helpful online networking resources. If you've lost contact with former business colleagues, you might be able to find them at www.CorporateAlumni.com, www.zoominfo.com (formerly Eliyon), or www.ziggs.com. When this book went to press, Ziggs was still in beta format but already had an index of more than 2.5 million professionals representing nearly 70,000 companies. Ziggs was developed to allow you to find profiles on professionals, as well as easily create your own professional profile and list it on search engines.

Many job boards also offer networking opportunities:

- **www.monster.com:** To access Monster Networking, from the homepage, click on Network Now. Type in keywords for your search (for example, writing, engineering, sales), enter your ZIP code/radius, and click Get Results to see a list of contacts. You can click on a contact's name to view his or her profile. If you desire to contact this person, select Introduce Me.

- **www.execunet.com** and **www.ritesite.com:** These two executive job boards enable you to post your bio into a member-searchable database and accept or reject invitations to network individually with others.

Online networking sites (some free, some fee-based) can be useful for finding contacts who work in a particular industry, profession, or company. When you're at one of these sites, look for a link that says **Search** or **Find.** From there, search for a specific name or browse contacts in a variety of categories. Most sites provide a kind of Web-map that shows you how many degrees of separation lie between you and your desired contact.

The potential downfall of many online communities, according to LinkedIn CEO Reid Hoffman in a recent issue of *Online Business Networks News,* is that "they attract many 'have-nots' (job seekers, startups seeking funding, small companies seeking customers, etc.) and very few 'haves' (potential employers, venture capitalists with money to invest, and so on)." LinkedIn's infrastructure has attracted many "haves" while protecting them from being deluged with requests. LinkedIn recently announced a partnership with DirectEmployers.com, which gives LinkedIn members access to a database of more than 200,000 jobs and then helps them network their way in.

When this book went to press, zoominfo.com was offering the *Networking* feature of its online subscription database to job seekers for free. With it, you can look up your former employers in order to reconnect with co-workers who might be helpful in your job search.

## Step 6: Stay on the Radar Screen

"It's not what you know, it's who you know." When it comes to job search, that maxim might well be rewritten as "It's not who you know, it's who knows *you!*" Uncovering opportunities requires that you be seen and known by the right people. You can accomplish this through several tactics.

### Write or Make Presentations

Few actions lend more credibility than being published or making presentations!

- **Write articles:** Write an article for a trade journal, association newsletter, or industry Web site. It's often easy to get an article published online because Web sites are incessantly hungry for fresh content. Even if you don't have a home for your intended article, write it anyway. At the least, it can be offered as an informative leave-behind or thank-you gift to networking contacts. One of the easiest ways to write an article is to create a 10-tips list for a common need or problem. An informal survey of how several companies are handling a problem or responding to a trend is another idea for an article topic. This latter strategy gives you a valid reason to call target companies as you research your article. Be sure to ask a friend with editing skills to review your article before submitting it for public consumption.

- **Make a presentation at a conference or meeting:** Public speaking garners immediate visibility *and* credibility. Choose something timely to speak about, and find an audience. Local groups are often looking for speakers on topics of interest to their membership.

 **Attend** *and make your presence known at* **seminars, workshops, meetings, conferences, webinars, or teleseminars that others present:** Going to an event, quiet as a church mouse, doesn't qualify as a radar-screen activity. Take your attendance a step further at these events by asking an intelligent question or offering an insightful comment so that the group notes your presence. You never know who in the room will take notice—it could be a person whose boss is looking to fill a new position, or it could be the boss him- or herself. (*Caution:* Be sure that your question or comment isn't grandstanding and truly offers value to others.)

**Create an e-newsletter:** You thought e-newsletters were just from companies, right? There's no reason you can't create your own. Fill it with brief but interesting content, and send it off to your network on a monthly basis. If your list of contacts gets unwieldy or you'd like to dress up the appearance with e-mail stationery, check out the resources at www.ConstantContact.com, http://EZezine.com, or Microsoft's www.ListBuilder.com.

## Create an Online Presence

No longer reserved for techies with advanced Web programming skills, technology has made it relatively simple to create tools that will give you an online presence. ePortfolios and blogs top the list (see chapter 10 for details on creating and marketing these tools).

### Five Reasons to Have an Online Presence

Kirsten Dixson of Brandego.com helps job seekers develop an online presence and differentiate themselves using sophisticated Web portfolios and blogs. Recognized for her expertise by *Business Week Online*, Kirsten offers five reasons for developing an online presence:

1. Gives you the opportunity to be on the forefront of a technology trend and create a well-organized resource that is related to your area of expertise.

2. Is an excellent platform for you to promote your personal brand online.

3. Builds visibility and credibility.

4. Provides your visitors a "free trial" of your expertise and opens the door for people to contact you with interesting career opportunities.

5. Enables you to distinguish yourself from others with similar skills and abilities.

## Get in Front of People

If ePortfolios and blogs are not your cup of tea, perhaps some of these radar-screen activities that are less technical will suit you better:

- **Serve on an association committee that has visibility:** Involvement in your professional association must go beyond paying membership dues. Get involved—especially in a capacity that will allow you some visibility. Doing remote database work from your home office probably won't give you the visibility you want; serving on the program planning committee or handing out binders at the registration desk of a conference will.

- **Volunteer:** If your schedule permits, inquire about opportunities to volunteer in a capacity that allows decision makers and potential teammates to interact with you and see your abilities in action. Job shadowing has similar benefits. For instance, many pharmaceutical sales wannabes do ride-alongs with experienced reps to better understand the field. If the person's behavior on the ride-along portrays a high-potential candidate, the rep will feel more comfortable about recommending him or her to the sales manager.

- **Do project work:** Related to volunteer work is project work. Be proactive. Request an arrangement to do work on a short-term, contract basis for your target company. Your desire to prove your mettle and skills will impress decision makers.

- **Intern:** Interning is often a good venue for college students or recent graduates to display their wares. Some internships are a gateway to full-time positions. Visit www.internjobs.com or www.internweb.com to explore internship opportunities.

---

### A Radar Screen E-mail Tip

Create a signature line for your outgoing e-mail that provides readers with one-click access to your ePortfolio, blog, or online résumé.

---

## Step 7: Augment with Traditional Job Search Methods

To make sure you cover all the bases, you should include a few traditional/passive job search methods in your targeted/active strategy. An absolute must is to post your résumé at the Web sites of your target companies. In addition, spend a *little* time (not a lot!) searching postings at major career sites and niche sites. Details on these and other traditional strategies are discussed in chapter 12.

# Chapter Wrap-Up

A targeted/active approach can add more interviews to your job search pipeline because it opens you up to opportunities within the hidden job market. This new-economy search strategy will help you develop one of the skills most critical for career success in the 21st century: connecting with a web of fundamental business contacts. These connections are the infrastructure for accessing needed skills and resources while you're on the job, as well as the safety net for new opportunities when you go to access your next position. With the now-undeniable employment trend of spending just a few years at many employers (versus a lifetime with one employer), the targeted strategy and its emphasis on focused networking will serve you well throughout your career.

## 10 Quick Tips to Conduct a Targeted Search and Tap the Hidden Job Market

1. **Get several interviews in the pipeline to increase your options.** Look for both opportunities and openings. An opportunity is an unadvertised situation or position where your skill set can contribute to company/shareholder value. An opening is an advertised position soliciting a predefined skill set to perform a specific task.

2. **Understand the four-stage evolution of a job opening.** In stage one, the employer is on the lookout for top talent, and may create a position just to take advantage of that talent. In stages two and three, there is a clear need for help, yet only insiders are aware of the situation. In stage four, the opening is finally advertised. Opportunities are available in stages one through three of this evolutionary process. Openings are available only in stage four. Competition for the position increases exponentially throughout the four stages.

3. **Conduct a targeted, or "new economy," search—this allows you to uncover opportunities and openings.** In a targeted/active search, the starting point is companies—you identify specific companies you'd like to work for and target both opportunities and openings that align with your Magic F.I.T.™. Conversely, in a broad search, or traditional/passive job search, the starting point is positions—you rely on advertised openings that align with your functional skills. Here, the openings might be available with any number of companies.

4. **Master the seven steps of a targeted search, the first of which is to identify target companies.** In step 1, tap into people, print resources, and the Internet to create a healthy list of companies you would like to work for. Several considerations might help you hone in on specific companies, such as location/commute time, company size, reputation, opportunities available within the company, passion for the company's products/services, relationships with people in the company, company culture, benefits, and so on.

*(continued)*

*(continued)*

5. **Steps 2 and 3—read and research—go hand in hand.** Read your target company's Web site, industry/niche Web sites, company blogs, online news, trade journals, local/regional/national newspapers, analyst reports, industry white papers, popular business books, and so on. Keep a log of contact names that can lead you to decision makers in your target company. Uncover TOP issues (**T**rends, **O**pportunities, **P**roblems/**P**rojects) within your target companies. Find a way to offer a return-on-investment by adding value to the bottom line.

6. **In step 4, talk to people through focused networking—focused, meaning talking with people who have a relationship with hiring managers or knowledge of your target company.** The best approach is not necessarily to contact the hiring manager directly. Often, speaking first with people who are just one or two phone calls away from decision makers will "warm up" your candidacy, give you insider status, and greatly strengthen your standing once you get to the hiring manager. Focus your networking on people inside the target company, industry association leaders, recruiters/employment professionals, company vendors/suppliers/advisors, customers, industry writers, academic thought leaders, and your past/present co-workers, as well as your circle of family and friends. Refer to the ideas in table 11.4 for approaching each of these contacts.

7. **Leverage your strengths in networking, especially when networking is not part of your immediate skill set.** For instance, if you are an excellent researcher, make this the centerpiece of your networking effort. If you are an excellent writer, craft well-conceived letters to your contacts as the first step. If you are more introverted than extroverted, start with online networking or by approaching contacts that are of a like mind. If you love people, but it takes you a while to get to know them, volunteer in places where your target contacts congregate.

8. **For step 5, take your networking online.** Join industry association e-lists; visit or participate in online chats, discussion boards, and blogs; and check out online networking Web sites. In the give-and-take of networking (whether live or online), don't overlook what you can "give" to your contact. In the "take" part of the equation, go for the INSIDER scoop, which is shorthand for Information, Names, Support, Ideas, Data, Energy, and Relationships. Refer to table 11.5 for specifics on each of these items.

9. **Step 6 requires that you stay on the radar screen.** It's not just who you know, it's who knows you! To be seen by the right people, write articles, make presentations, attend (and make your presence known at) seminars/meetings, send out a brief e-newsletter, publish a blog, serve on an association committee that has visibility, volunteer, or do project work.

10. **In step 7 of a targeted/active search, augment with traditional/passive search methods.** Cover your bases by posting a résumé at your target companies' Web sites and searching for relevant postings at career portals and niche sites. Remember that these activities should be fill-in-the-cracks work, not the focus of your search!

## Magical Coaching Questions

Of the seven steps in a targeted/active search, which area is your strength?

_____

_____

_____

_____

How can you leverage that strength to make your job search easier?

_____

_____

_____

_____

Which of the seven steps is an area you'd like to build up?

_____

_____

_____

How will doing so enhance your job search…and your career over the long term?

_____

_____

_____

What steps will you take to make that happen?

_____

_____

_____

Who can help you with this?

_____

_____

_____

*Chapter*

# 12

# Cover Your Bases with Traditional Search Strategies

*"Excellence is to do a common thing in an uncommon way."*

—Booker T. Washington

For decades, job seekers have turned to traditional job search strategies to find new employment: responding to job announcements, sending résumé mailings unsolicited to companies, using employment agencies and recruiters, attending career events, and so on. Surprisingly, the success rate of these approaches is fairly low, often in the single-digit range. To boost the odds of success, job seekers have turned more and more to networking, where approximately 60 percent or more of all new jobs are found. In chapter 11, the concept of *focused networking* was introduced—a new, supercharged networking strategy to connect with people who have both a *relationship* with decision makers and *knowledge* of your target companies. Focused networking is at the heart of a targeted strategy and can yield the highest success rate when compared to other search strategies.

## Why People Continue to Use Traditional Search Strategies

Yet, many people continue to concentrate their efforts on traditional job search strategies instead of targeted search strategies. Why? Here are two key reasons, one stemming from job seekers and the other from employers:

⚝ **Job seekers:** Most job seekers can learn fairly easily the steps of a traditional/passive, or broad, search. However, many job seekers have not received solid training in how to conduct a targeted search or engage in focused networking, making them uncertain about the process. And, for many job seekers, it's much easier to rest in the relative ease and anonymity of posting résumés or expecting an employment agency to do the legwork for you.

**Employers:** The traditional system of soliciting and screening résumés is the mainstay of the corporate recruiting function. Fortune 500 companies report finding approximately 30 percent of their new hires in this traditional sourcing manner.

So it's apparent that the traditional system does work, *to some degree*...more so when the economy is booming and there is heavy competition for talent. However, relying *solely* on traditional search methods to get interviews is a lot like relying on the slot machines in Las Vegas to feed your family. We all know that the house is programmed to win. According to a major manufacturer of gaming equipment, the slots pay off only 2 to 15 percent of the time. Unfortunately, many of the statistics for traditional job search methods are pretty close to Vegas gaming odds. Read on to learn which traditional strategies have the highest rate of return so that you can spend your time wisely.

# The Seven Venues of a Traditional Search

The seven most common venues of a traditional search include the following:

1. Online searches

2. Résumé posting

3. Résumé distribution

4. Recruiters and agencies

5. Classified ads

6. Direct inquiry or mailing

7. Career events

Let's look briefly at each one.

## Venue 1: Online Searches

The past decade has seen tremendous shifts in recruiting, with many employers transferring the bulk of their recruiting budget from newspaper classifieds to online venues. Especially true of larger companies, the trend toward online recruiting continues to increase every year. Gerry Crispin and Mark Mehler, authors of *CareerXroads,* a reference guide to job and résumé Web sites, recently released their annual *CareerXroads Source of Hires Study.* In it, they document where companies look for candidates when it comes time to fill positions:

38 percent of all open positions were filled by internal transfer and promotion, up from 35 percent the prior year (note that this sizeable figure might be reason to accept a stepping-stone position in a larger company where there is a strong probability of being promoted).

61 percent of all external hires were attributed to just two channels—the Internet (29.6 percent) and employee referrals (31.7 percent), up from 60 percent the prior year.

In the early 2000s, the use of Internet sources increased a notable 11 percent, from 20.5 percent in 2001 to 31.8 percent in 2003, with a slight decrease to 29.6 percent in 2004. Conversely, the increase in employee referrals (networking) was less than half that number—only a 5 percent increase—from 23.3 percent to 28.5 percent in 2003, with another increase to 31.7 in 2004. The data represent more than 280,000 positions that were filled in one year—roughly a quarter of the combined companies' total workforce of more than one million. Crispin and Mehler's study was conducted among primarily Fortune 500 companies—not necessarily representative of the entire hiring landscape throughout America, but nonetheless is indicative of trends in how candidates are found (what corporate America does usually filters down to small business and mom-and-pop America).

Where should you apply online? According to Crispin and Mehler's study, these sources accounted for the Internet hires:

- 67.9 percent from company Web sites
- 17.6 percent from niche job sites
- 8.7 percent from Monster.com
- 4.1 percent from CareerBuilder.com
- 1.8 percent from HotJobs.com

It bears noting that smaller companies—those without the resources to underwrite sophisticated recruiting functions at their Web sites—may source a higher percentage of candidates from niche and career sites, as well as from referral networking.

Regardless of the size of your target company, prioritize your online searches (and subsequent résumé posting) in this order:

1. Target company's Web site (jobs/employment page, when available)

2. Niche career sites

3. Major career Web sites, such as Monster.com, CareerBuilder.com, or HotJobs.com

## Vary Your Keyword Search Terms

When searching sites for postings, vary the search terms with "first-cousin" titles. For instance, when searching for positions in Sales, closely related keywords might include Sales Representative, Outside Sales, Sales Consultant, Key Account Representative, or even Marketing Representative.

## Company Web Sites

When targeting large companies, it's likely you'll be able to submit a résumé directly at the company's Web site. Roughly 75 percent of Fortune 500 companies have a Careers button on their home pages. More and more companies are following suit, as they recognize that sifting through their own résumé database can be more cost-effective and expeditious than sorting through résumé databases at mega sites such as Monster.com or CareerBuilder.com.

## Niche Job Sites

Who fills more jobs than Monster? According to the *CareerXroads' Source of Hire Study*, niche boards fill twice as many jobs as Monster.com. Niche job sites specialize in employment for a particular functional area or industry. One of the best resources I've found for a centralized collection of niche sites is John Sumser's Interbiznet.com. The niche sites listed in this section are printed (with permission) from www.interbiznet.com/hunt/archives/030813.html. The lists are ordered by amount of traffic. (For updates, search for Job Board Rankings at www.interbiznet.com/hunt/archives/.)

Review the following lists for sites appropriate to your functional or industry target. Search the sites on a weekly basis for relevant job postings. If the site has a job-alert feature, set up an account to receive e-mail notification of relevant positions.

### Top Executive Sites

- 6FigureJobs: www.6figurejobs.com
- CareerJournal.com: www.careerjournal.com
- ChiefMonster: www.chiefmonster.com
- eKornFerry.com: www.ekornferry.com
- ExecuNet: www.execunet.com
- Futurestep: www.futurestep.com
- MBA Jungle: www.mbajungle.com
- MBA-exchange.com: www.mba-exchange.com
- Netshare.com: www.netshare.com
- Spencer Stuart Talent Network: www.spencerstuart.com

### Industry Niche Sites

- Absolutely Health Care: www.healthjobsusa.com
- Allnurses.com: www.allnurses.com
- AllRetailJobs.com: www.allretailjobs.com
- AirlineCareer.com: www.airlinecareer.com

- CareerBank.com: www.careerbank.com
- ComputerJobs.com: www.computerjobs.com
- ComputerWork.com: www.computerwork.com
- Destiny Group: www.destinygrp.com
- Dice.com: www.dice.com
- Engineering Central: www.engcen.com
- Engineering Job Source: www.engineerjobs.com
- EngineeringJobs.Com: www.engineeringjobs.com
- HealthcareSource: www.healthcaresource.com
- Hcareers.com: www.hcareers.com
- HireBio: www.hirebio.com
- Jobs4HR: www.jobs4hr.com
- Jobscience.com: www.jobscience.com
- JobsInLogistics.com: www.jobsinlogistics.com
- Jobsinthemoney: www.jobsinthemoney.com
- JustTechJobs.com: www.justtechjobs.com
- Lawjobs.com: www.lawjobs.com
- Legalstaff.com: www.legalstaff.com
- Medzilla.com: www.medzilla.com
- NurseTown.com: www.nursetown.com
- Nursing Spectrum: www.nursingspectrum.com
- NursingCenter: www.nursingcenter.com
- SalesHeads.com: www.salesheads.com
- Sales Jobs: www.salesjobs.com
- TaxTalent.com: www.taxtalent.com
- Tech-Engine.com: www.tech-engine.com
- Techies.com: www.techies.com
- Telecomcareers.net: www.telecomcareers.net
- TVJobs.com: www.tvjobs.com

## College Recruiting Sites

- AboutJobs.com: www.aboutjobs.com
- AfterCollege: www.aftercollege.com

- CampusCareerCenter.com: www.campuscareercenter.com
- College Job Board: www.collegejobboard.com
- CollegeCentral.com: www.collegecentral.com
- CollegeGrad.com: www.collegegrad.com
- CollegeJournal.com: www.collegejournal.com
- CollegeRecruiter: www.collegerecruiter.com
- Entryleveljobs.net: www.entryleveljobs.net
- eRecruiting: www.erecruiting.com
- Gradunet: www.gradunet.co.uk
- Historically Black Colleges and Universities—Careers: www.hbcu-careers.net
- Jobpostings.net: www.jobpostings.net
- NACElink.com: www.nacelink.com

## Diversity Sites

- Diversity: www.Diversity.com
- Diversity Search: www.DiversitySearch.com
- Hire Diversity: www.hirediversity.com
- Ihispano.com: www.ihispano.com
- IMDiversity.com: www.imdiversity.com
- LatPro: www.latpro.com
- News Jobs: www.newsjobs.com
- Saludos: www.Saludos.com

## International Sites

- CareerOne: www.careerone.com.au
- Doctorjob.com: www.doctorjob.com
- Gis-A-Job: www.gisajob.com
- Go Jobsite UK: www.gojobsite.co.uk
- Jobnet: www.jobnet.com.au
- Jobpilot.com: www.jobpilot.com
- Jobserve: www.jobserve.com
- JobShark: www.jobshark.ca
- Monster Canada: www.monster.ca

- Monster India: www.monsterindia.com
- Monster Ireland: www.monster.ie
- Monster UK: www.monster.co.uk
- Nixers.com: www.nixers.com
- PlanetRecruit: www.planetrecruit.com
- Reed Executive: www.reed.co.uk
- SEEK: www.seek.com.au
- Stepstone: www.stepstone.com
- Top Jobs: www.topjobs.co.uk
- Totaljobs.com: www.totaljobs.com
- Workthing: www.workthing.com
- Workopolis: www.workopolis.com

## Additional Resources for Niche Sites

If you don't see a niche site listed for your functional area or industry, one of these sites might lead you to additional niche sites:

- **AIRS (Advanced Internet Recruiting Seminars):** www.AirsDirectory.com/directories/job_boards/
- **Riley Guide's Job Banks & Recruiting Sites:** www.rileyguide.com/multiple.html
- **Pam Dixon:** www.pamdixon.com/jobsearch.htm (by Pam Dixon, author of *Job Searching Online For Dummies* [Wiley] … a good collection of information about major career Web sites, as well as niche sites)
- **Pat Kendall:** www.jumpstartyourjobsearch.com (by Pat Kendall, author of *Jumpstart Your Online Job Search* [Prima Publishing], is a good collection of sites for company research, niche sites, diversity sites, freelancing, international sites, and so on)

## Major Career Web Sites

The following major career sites are the heavy hitters when it comes to rich content and a significant collection of job listings. For some time, Monster and CareerBuilder have been jockeying for position as *the* premier career site. When this book went to press, CareerBuilder was in the lead with 400,000 jobs listed at the site and 14.7 million unique job-seeking visitors. Search both of these sites, along with any others that contain a number of relevant job listings.

- CareerBuilder: www.careerbuilder.com
- Monster.com: www.monster.com

- HotJobs.com: www.hotjobs.yahoo.com
- America's Job Bank: www.ajb.dni.us/
- Net-Temps: www.net-temps.com
- Vault: www.vault.com
- Job.com: www.job.com
- 4jobs.com: www.4jobs.com
- Employment 911: www.employment911.com

On sites where this service is available, set up an account to receive e-mail notices about relevant job postings.

# Venue 2: Résumé Posting

As with online searches, post your résumé to company, niche, and major career Web sites.

Post your résumé to *all* of the target companies you identified in chapter 11. If there are relevant job postings at your target company's Web site, comb these ads carefully for keywords and load your résumé with any terms that are applicable to your background. For tips on keywording your résumé, see chapter 8. Further, include a cover letter that is tailored to the target company. Use strategies described in the Solution/Service letter presented in chapter 11 or refer to the sample letters in chapter 10 for more ideas on crafting customized cover letters.

## Convert Your Résumé Before You Post It

Follow the steps in chapter 10 to convert your MS Word résumé into ASCII plain-text format for pasting into e-forms at Web sites.

When searches of niche or career Web sites yield an ideal job (one in sync with your Magic F.I.T.™), submit your résumé. Most niche and career sites allow you to set up an account where you can store more than one version of your résumé and cover letter. When setting up accounts at niche or career sites, limit yourself to sites that offer a significant number of openings relevant to your target. It can be time-consuming to set up and update résumés at a dozen sites.

## Maintaining Confidentiality When Posting Your Résumé

Finally, when posting your résumé online, consider these steps to conduct a confidential search or to minimize the potential for identity theft:

- Use an e-mail address reserved only for your job search. If you're conducting a confidential search, do not include your first or last name as part of the e-mail address. For instance, use mgmt-candidate@yahoo.com instead of johnsmith@yahoo.com.
- Omit certain contact information such as your street address and ZIP code.

- Use discretion in listing your telephone number. Some wary job seekers use an answering service rather than give out home or mobile telephone numbers.

- If you're concerned that your boss will discover your search, camouflage the current employer's name on your résumé. For instance, "Major Manufacturing Company" instead of ABC Manufacturing, Inc.

- Some candidates go so far as to substitute a title for their name on the résumé. For instance, "Manufacturing Management Candidate" instead of John Smith.

- Never, never, never give out your Social Security number or financial information when posting to a general Web site. Some unscrupulous sites actually scam candidates by saying they've been selected for an interview but need to conduct a credit check first, and then proceed to collect bank account numbers or credit-card information. For more information on scams, visit www.idtheftcenter.org/html/scam-alerts.htm. The exception to the rule would be when applying at an established company that you trust. For instance, some Fortune 500 companies request your Social Security number and date of birth, which is used for background checks. This information is supposedly not seen by people in the hiring process until a conditional offer of employment has been extended.

### Avoid Résumé Graffiti

Peter Weddle, author of several employment-related and Internet resources, coined the phrase *résumé graffiti* to describe how applicants indiscriminately submit résumés for jobs that they aren't remotely qualified for. This willy-nilly posting of résumés clogs up résumé databases and has led some sites to build sophisticated prescreening filters so that only qualified applicants can apply. One site, www.InterviewExchange.com, uses a bidding process where job seekers register and receive several hundred points that can then be used to bid on jobs posted at the site. Once a job seeker uses all her points for bidding, a waiting period is required until more points can be received. If a job seeker chooses to bid all of her points for a particular posting, indicating her high level of interest in the position, it communicates to the employer that this isn't a graffiti artist, but a serious candidate.

## Venue 3: Résumé Distribution

Résumé distribution refers to e-mailing recruiters *en masse*. With the click of a few buttons, your résumé can be in the hands of hundreds of recruiters. Let me clarify that by saying your résumé can be in the *e-mail bin* of hundreds of recruiters. Whether the recruiters choose to open the e-mail and add your résumé to their applicant databases is quite another issue, especially when they are inundated with résumés from graffiti candidates.

In résumé distribution, more is *not* necessarily better. Blasting your résumé to thousands of recruiters goes beyond the slot-machine odds noted at the beginning of this chapter; now you're playing the lotto, where your chances, according to probability experts, are roughly 14 million to 1.

Don't get me wrong—résumé distribution can be an effective tool in job search, provided that you follow one important rule: *Think targeted.* This will greatly improve your odds of getting a callback from a résumé distribution. Be sure to use job search savvy when shopping for résumé-distribution services: It's not the total number of database contacts that should impress you—it's the level of targeting available. Does the service allow you to sort by a pinpointed functional area, specific industry, regional area, or, better yet, telephone area code or ZIP code? Some allow you to tailor your distribution to recruiters who work with candidates in a typical salary range, such as $50,000 to $99,000, or $100,000 to 150,000, or $150,000+.

The distribution service should also be able to provide you with a list of the contacts to whom your résumé was sent. If necessary, spend the extra money to receive the complete contact information to facilitate followup. And, be circumspect about cost—many services have add-ons that can quickly add up.

The following services have a record for longevity and integrity in the résumé-distribution market:

- **Resume Machine:** www.ResumeMachine.com
- **Resume Zapper:** www.ResumeZapper.com
- **Resume Blaster:** www.ResumeBlaster.com

My favorite résumé-distribution site is Resume Machine. Not only do they provide distribution services, they also offer posting services. The difference? Distribution means your résumé is e-mailed to recruiters or companies. Posting means your résumé is deposited at Web sites so that it goes directly into an organization's résumé database or applicant-tracking system. Instead of posting your résumé to organizations one by one (a very time-consuming venture), you fill in information once at Resume Machine. This one-time filling in of information will be a little tedious, but that level of precision is mandatory so that data can later be fit into the different configurations of dozens of Web sites. If you come across a résumé-posting service that doesn't break down your résumé data into very small bites, you'll likely not get your money's worth.

Bottom line, the benefit of an *en masse* résumé posting is that you are certain the résumé gets into the database of the recruiter, which is not guaranteed when you distribute your résumé via e-mail.

When using a résumé-distribution service, remember to convert your résumé before e-mailing. Steps for conversion and conversion cleanup are outlined in chapter 10.

## Venue 4: Recruiters and Agencies

Clearly, the preferred strategy for job search is to hook up directly with hiring managers *or* people who can connect you with hiring managers. The recruiting community—both internal human resource recruiters and external recruiters or employment agencies—certainly falls within the category of people who can connect you with hiring managers. Don't overlook recruiters and employment agencies in your search campaign because they often know which companies are hiring. At the same time, recognize that recruiters should not be the foundation of your search strategy, given this statistic from a recent survey by the global human resource consulting firm DBM:

**Only 10% of job seekers found new employment as a result of search firms or agencies.**

Before contacting these resources, understand the difference between search firms/recruiters and employment agencies. Although both are in the business of helping companies with staffing, there are some major differences:

- Employment agencies typically work with entry-level to mid-level positions and often have temporary assignments available. Agencies sometimes take a more proactive role in helping applicants find employment and generally limit their work to a local geographic area. Fees to the agency are usually paid by the company that has engaged them, although occasionally the fee will be split between the candidate and the company. In general, avoid an arrangement where you have to pay. Most agencies welcome walk-in applicants and appreciate it when you initiate contact.

- Also known as executive search consultants (or their informal title of head-hunters), recruiters are engaged by companies to find experienced talent. They are skilled at finding the needle in the haystack. That "needle" might be at the executive or management level, a technical position, a sales capacity, a specialty occupation, or any hard-to-fill position. Location of the recruiter and candidate is rarely an issue—a recruiter in Boston could be tasked with sourcing candidates for a position in Los Angeles. Recruiters don't work with career changers (people moving from one occupational area or industry to another). Likewise, they often won't have time for a candidate if he or she isn't a perfect fit for a job order they are currently working on. In general, recruiters prefer to do the initiating.

If you are in an occupational category or industry where working with a recruiter is appropriate, know these additional facts. Job seekers do not *hire* a recruiter. The company does the hiring (and paying), which means that the recruiter's foremost allegiance is to the client company, not you. Recruiting contracts are either on a contingent or retained basis. A contingency search, typical in low to mid-level searches, means that the recruiter will be paid when the candidate is hired by the employer. A retained search, common in senior-level searches, means that the recruiting firm has an exclusive relationship to present qualified candidates to the company for a contracted period of time. In a retained search, the recruiting firm is paid regardless of whether a candidate is hired.

Recruiters find, or source, candidates through a number of methods. Often, their strategies are not too unlike what the job seeker does to find opportunities. They read and pay attention to the names of potential "A" candidates. They network in online communities where their target candidates congregate. They search the Internet and their own proprietary databases. And they network, often asking company insiders, "Who on your team has a reputation as a top performer?" These referrals carry more weight than an unknown candidate, even if they look great on paper (their résumé). Accordingly, when approaching recruiters, lessen your "unknown" factor in one of these ways:

- Ask a colleague who knows the recruiter to place a call for you to warm up the introduction.

- Mention the name of someone already in the recruiter's sphere—a former candidate the recruiter placed, a hiring manager in one of the recruiter's client companies, a professional association contact, and so on.

- Show the recruiter you've done some research on him or her—for instance, mention that you understand he or she frequently sources candidates for companies such as ABC Company and DEF Incorporated.

- Mention respectable projects that the recruiter will be familiar with, such as "I recently worked on the conference planning committee for the regional meeting of the National Association of Purchasing Managers, and I understand you're a member."

Granted, this strategy requires legwork on your part. It is certainly more time-consuming than the automated résumé e-mailing to hundreds of recruiters via a distribution service, but it will give you better traction. If you plan on sending a mass e-mailing to recruiters or have already done so, follow up with several of them using the preceding strategies, or choose a networking strategy from chapter 11. For instance, search the forum archives at www.erexchange.com and look for posts made by recruiters from your industry. This material will give you a good conversation starter and position you above all the other candidates who approach with a boring, generic line.

## Recruiter Resources

To access listings of recruiters, refer to these resources:

- **The Directory of Executive Recruiters (Kennedy Publications):** Also available online at www.kennedyinfo.com/db/db_der_bas.html, the site allows you free access to the number of recruiters in your industry and then requires a fee if you want to purchase the full contact information.

- **Ken Cole's Recruiting & Search Report:** www.rsronline.com/.

- **Recruiter graduates of AIRS (Advanced Internet Recruiting Seminars):** www.airsdirectory.com/directories/cir/.

- **Resume Distribution Services:** See "Venue 3: Résumé Distribution," earlier in this chapter.

- **Recruiters Online Network:** www.recruitersonline.com/jobs2/ frameset_candidates.php (click on Find a Recruiter).

- **Riley Guide:** www.rileyguide.com/recruiters.html (this amazingly comprehensive site provides free and fee-based directories of recruiters).

- **Top Echelon:** www.topechelon.com/.

- **WorkTree:** www.worktree.com (click Recruiter Links, which then allows you to sort by recruiter specialty, name, city, and state).

Some of the larger recruiting firms include the following:

- **Heidrick & Struggles:** www.heidrick.com

- **Korn/Ferry International:** www.kornferry.com

- **Spencer Stuart:** www.spencerstuart.com

## Agency Resources

You can access a listing of employment agencies via these sites:

- **National Association of Personnel Services' Membership Directory:** www.napsweb.org/MemDir/index.cfm

- **Business.com:** www.business.com/directory/human_resources/ hiring_and_retention/recruiting_services/search_firms/

Some of the larger employment agencies with offices in major markets include the following:

- **Manpower:** www.manpower.com

- **Snelling & Snelling:** www.snelling.com

- **Kelly Services:** www.kellyservices.com

# Venue 5: Classified Ads

Despite the cost efficacy of posting positions online, some employers still advertise with good old-fashioned ink in newspapers and trade journals. Again, don't make this the mainstay of your search strategy. According to surveys by CareerXroads and human resources consulting firm DBM, the odds are slim:

**Only 3–7% of job seekers found new employment as a result of advertisements.**

Review classified ads on Sundays and Wednesdays (or whatever day the paper typically has heavier employment advertising), and scour every issue of your industry's trade journals. Often, your local newspaper will carry its classified ads online. Newspaper Links (www.newspaperlinks.com) will help you find your local paper online. And, depending on your search, these national publications might be of help:

*USA Today:* www.usatoday.com

The *Wall Street Journal:* www.wsj.com

The following strategy will help increase your response rate from newspaper ads:

1. Find a warm contact either inside or closely linked to the company. Call this person to do some due diligence on the company and position. Hone in on TOP issues (**T**rends, **O**pportunities, **P**roblems/**P**rojects).

2. Call the hiring manager (not human resources) about the position. Mention the name of your warm contact, offer one of your sound bites (see chapter 4), and open a dialogue around one of the TOP issues you learned about. Your goals in this step are to learn more about the position, establish a connection with the hiring manager, share a SMART Story or two, and spark enough curiosity about you that the hiring manager will invite you in for a face-to-face discussion.

3. After landing an appointment, follow up with a brief e-mail to the hiring manager and attach your résumé.

4. Submit a résumé through the proper human resources channel described in the ad. Mention in this cover letter that you've already had a conversation with Ms. Jones, the hiring manager, and look forward to continuing the interview process.

When responding to classified ads, do so as quickly as possible. If the human resources department receives enough qualified applicants early in the game and you are late to respond, you might have trouble getting included in the interview pool. Ideally, this means you'll need to connect with your contacts and speak with the hiring manager the very day the ad appears. Sometimes an ad will continue to appear even after human resources has all the qualified candidates they need. This is because newspapers offer a discount for running an ad for an extended period of time.

Finally, if you've come across a "dream job" ad that is several weeks or even months old, respond anyway (using the research and focused networking techniques you learned in chapter 11). It's not all that unusual for a company to have put the hiring process on hold or delayed making a decision because they haven't found the ideal candidate.

## Venue 6: Direct Inquiry or Mailing

Odds with a direct approach or mailing are pretty slim. Surveys by global human resources consulting firm DBM and college career centers indicate the following:

**Approximately 3% of job seekers found employment as a result of a mailing or direct approach.**

Why such poor odds? Most likely because you are an anonymous candidate with no connection to the company. Because they don't know you from Adam, your letter might be received with the same indifference you have when opening your mailbox to find half a dozen unsolicited offers for products that you don't need or want.

What's the antidote to indifference? Take the time to tailor your letter using the merge/field functions in MS Word. Ideally, mention a referral name, as well as evidence that you understand the company's TOP (**T**rends, **O**pportunities, **P**roblems/**P**rojects) issues. Address the letter to a hiring authority. Yes, this will take more time, but it beats throwing your money away on an anonymous campaign.

The odds appear to be better for six-figure professionals when it comes to direct mail, as the following sidebar notes.

### Find Six-Figure Jobs with Targeted Direct (Snail) Mail

Mark Hovind, founder of JobBait.com, specializes in targeted direct-mail campaigns for six-figure executives (do-it-yourself tips can be found at the Web site). Hovind reports that sending résumés and cover letters directly to decision makers is the fastest, most effective way to find six-figure jobs. With targeted direct mail, you can saturate your marketplace and get your résumé in the right place at the right time. Sending 1,000 letters has odds up to 50 percent, and sending 3,000 letters per hundred thousand in salary has odds up to 85 percent. To maximize your odds, use the Dunn and Bradstreet database at ZapData.com to find these decision makers…and make sure you drill all the way down to eight-digit standard industry codes. If you stop short with four-digit standard industry codes, you can easily waste more than half your letters on the wrong target companies.

Some of the same resources mentioned under "Purchase Mailing Lists" in chapter 11 can provide you with company mailing information. One firm, Pro/FileResearch.com, will actually generate letters for you.

In a direct-mail campaign, you'll need a broadcast letter. A sample, reprinted from *Cover Letter Magic*, is provided in figure 12.1.

Here's one last tip on the direct inquiry approach. If your target position is a support-level or common position that is in high demand, cold calling companies may work. Some job seekers use the Yellow Pages to cold call by telephone. Others canvass industrial parks or business districts in person. If you make a good impression in person, this strategy can be effective. Remember to collect business cards so that you can follow up and turn your cold calling into a warmer relationship.

**HAROLD WONG**

555 Benene Drive    http://www.hwong.com    Cellular: (555) 555-5555

Fairmont, CA 95555    hwong@worldnet.att.net    Residence: (555) 444-4444

---

[date]

John Henry, General Manager
Manco Incorporated
555 Bellini Way
Fairmont, CA 95555

Dear Mr. Henry:

Is Manco Incorporated in need of an experienced production/manufacturing professional?

I am targeting a few select companies in the tri-county area that might benefit from my experience with leading-edge manufacturers. John Johnson of NAPM suggested I contact you. Over the past 10 years, I have advanced through production planning, quality assurance, and plant operations positions with Metalistics Mfg. and Perspec Plastics. Since 1996, I have served as assistant plant manager at Perspec. You may have read in *The Fairmont Chronicle* that the plant is slated for consolidation with a Colorado facility next month. Although offered a relocation opportunity, I have opted to remain in Northern California.

Briefly, the skill-set, experience, and performance record I bring to the table include the following:

**Knowledge base:** Experienced in industrial and manufacturing engineering (plastics, sheet metal fabrication, refrigeration systems), production/assembly, quality assurance, safety, and environmental regulatory compliance.

**Management skills:** Performed annual planning functions, including budgeting, monthly forecasting, and controlling of operating expenses. Initiated cost-tracking systems, new inventory models, and other efficiencies that represent more than $1,000,000 in combined savings.

**Supervisory/human resource skills:** Made hiring-termination decisions and supervised up to 65 production team members and six department leaders. Enhanced management-labor relations by empowering staff to make and implement suggestions that saved time, money, and manpower. Applied customer-focused, team-based, and total lowest-cost concepts.

**Conscientious and company-minded:** At both Metalistics Mfg. and Perspec, quickly promoted and entrusted with additional responsibilities based on my attitude and aptitude.

At this time, I am interested in positions such as production supervisor/manager, assistant plant manager, industrial project engineer, or quality assurance manager. Mr. Henry, should you have these or similar opportunities, I would be happy to fax my résumé (or you may download it at my Web site: www.hwong.com/resume.html).

In advance, thank you for your consideration.

Sincerely,

Harold Wong

**Figure 12.1: A sample broadcast letter.**

## Venue 7: Career Events

Job fairs, or career fairs, are another venue to meet employers. Again, don't spend the lion's share of your time here, as job seekers report only single-digit success in landing a position via job fairs:

**Only 3% of job seekers found employment as a result of a job fairs.**

To find out where fairs are being held, do the following:

- Check your local newspaper. Announcements for job fairs are usually placed near the employment ads.
- Check with other in-the-know organizations, such as your professional association, alumni placement office, or local employment agencies.
- Call your target companies and ask what career fairs they attend and recruit at.
- Look online at http://jobsearch.about.com/cs/jobfairs/.
- Google the words "job fair" and your geographic location, such as *job fair, San Francisco* or *career fair, San Francisco* for listings.

When attending these events, go with an agenda. Find out ahead of time what companies will be there. Are they on your target list, and is it even worth going if the attending companies don't fit the company profile you've outlined in chapter 11? Conduct preliminary research on the key companies you want to connect with. When you're at the event, engage employers with intelligent questions about their future plans and current needs. Use your sound bites and SMART Stories™ to convey the value you'd bring to the organization. A handful of solid, connected conversations will be better than blitzing the room. At the end of your conversation, hand-write a few phrases at the top of your résumé to help the employer later jog her memory about who you are and what conversation you had. Gather employer business cards so that you can follow up with people you've met. And, always remember the what's-in-it-for-me (the employer) mantra—it's all about them, not you!

## Chapter Wrap-Up

Smart candidates make targeted search strategies the centerpiece of their campaign, and then use traditional search strategies to cover their bases. By all means, submit your résumé to your target companies. Reinforce this strategy by including a customized cover letter that mentions a warm contact and conveys knowledge of the company's TOP (**T**rends, **O**pportunities, **P**roblems/Projects) issues. Search for and apply to positions that are a good Magic F.I.T.™ at target company Web sites, as well as at niche sites or major career sites. If the position you are targeting is frequently sourced by a recruiter, include recruiters in your strategy. Use other venues—direct-mail campaigns, job fairs, and so on—as a backup to your primary focus on targeted job searching.

# 10 Quick Tips to Cover Your Bases with Traditional Search Strategies

1. **Use traditional job search strategies sparingly—the odds are simply not in your favor.** Spend the majority of your time on targeted search activities (see Tip #10) and use traditional strategies to cover your bases.

2. **Conduct online searches in a strategic manner.** First, search the Web sites of companies you've targeted for relevant postings. Second, search niche job sites—those that specialize in your functional area or industry. Niche sites generate twice the number of hires that Monster.com does. A handy collection of niche sites can be found at www.Interbiznet.com. Third, search major career sites such as Monster.com and CareerBuilder.com.

3. **Post your résumé and a customized letter at each of your target companies' Web sites.** Mention an insider contact in your letter, along with reference to the company's TOP (**T**rends, **O**pportunities, **P**roblems/**P**rojects) issues and how you can be of value with regard to these issues. Roughly 75 percent of Fortune 500 companies provide résumé-posting capability at their sites. Approximately 30 percent of Fortune 500 companies' new hires were sourced via the Internet, most often from their company Web sites, followed by niche sites and major career sites.

4. **When posting to sites that don't have the ability to receive an MS Word version of your résumé, convert your résumé to ASCII text.** This will eliminate formatting glitches. If you're conducting a highly confidential search, don't post your résumé online. To minimize the potential for identity theft, use a veiled e-mail address, such as mgmt-candidate@yahoo.com instead of johnsmith@cisco.com, omit address information (mentioning a regional area is okay), and use discretion regarding which telephone number you'll include on the résumé. You can also change company names to increase your confidentiality. For instance, Leading Regional Technology Company instead of Big Apple Systems Integration, Inc.

5. **Use a résumé-distribution service that not only e-mails your résumé to recruiters but also has the capacity for mass-posting of your résumé to recruiting sites.** Shop wisely for a résumé-distribution service. Beware those that boast the ability to e-mail your résumé to thousands of recruiters. You don't want thousands. You want finely targeted numbers, specifically by functional/occupational area, industry, geography, or telephone area code. Quality is more important than quantity.

6. **Determine whether recruiters or employment agencies are appropriate for your search.** Recruiters might work locally or nationally to source executives, managers, and professionals in "hard-to-fill" occupations. Remember that the recruiter's first loyalty is to the client company and that he or she doesn't proactively market candidates to numerous employers. Employment agencies typically confine their services to a local geographic area, work

with entry-level to mid-level positions, and often have temporary assignments available. Agencies might take a more proactive role in helping applicants find employment. Approximately 10 percent of job seekers find new employment as a result of search firms or agencies.

7. **Review classified ads in your local newspaper, national newspaper (if appropriate), and trade journals.** When responding, find a warm contact either inside or closely linked to the company to learn about the company's TOP (**T**rends, **O**pportunities, **P**roblems/**P**rojects) issues. Then connect with the hiring manager to discuss how you can address those issues and bring value to the bottom line. Your goal is to spark enough curiosity about you that the hiring manager will invite you in for a face-to-face discussion (interview!). Follow up with a brief e-mail to the hiring manager with your résumé, and submit your résumé through proper channels with human resources, mentioning that you've already had a conversation with Ms. Hiring Manager. Approximately 3 to 7 percent of job seekers find new employment through classified ads.

8. **Consider a direct-inquiry/direct-mail campaign.** If your target position is a support-level or common position that is in high demand, cold calling companies by telephone or in person might work. For other job targets, mail a "broadcast letter" that offers a quick thumbnail of your strengths and evidence of how you've contributed to solving problems that are common to your potential employer. Approximately 3 percent of job seekers find new employment with this approach. To improve these odds, take your anonymity factor out of the equation with a warm referral and insight into the employer's TOP (**T**rends, **O**pportunities, **P**roblems/**P**rojects) issues.

9. **Career events can connect you with employers, although only 3 percent of job seekers find employment as a result of job or career fairs.** Find where these events are held by checking the classified section of your paper, inquiring with professional associations or local employment agencies, asking your target companies what career fairs they attend and recruit at, and looking online using keywords "job fair" and your geographic location. Don't just attend the job fair; attend with an agenda. Know what companies you want to have conversations with, use your sound bites and SMART Stories™, and remember the mantra—it's all about them, not you!

10. **Remember, he who places all his bets on long odds usually loses.** For better odds, combine these strategies with a targeted/active approach where you identify ideal companies, read, research, talk with people through focused networking, and stay on the radar screen of people who influence the hiring process.

## Magical Coaching Questions

Which of the seven traditional job search areas do you need to stop doing or spend less time on?

_____

_____

What's the hidden payoff for spending time there? For instance, one of my job search clients recognized that she was spending too much time on attending job fairs because it felt "safer" and less intimidating than networking with connections to target companies.

_____

_____

_____

_____

On what activities will you refocus your time and energy?

_____

_____

_____

Who will help you stay accountable to this new focus?

_____

_____

# Part 4

# Interviews

Chapter 13: Pass Online Prescreens and Telephone Interviews with Flying Colors

Chapter 14: The 4 *C*s of Interviewing—Connect, Clarify, Collaborate, and Close

Chapter 15: Score Points in Behavioral Interviews

Chapter 16: Ace Frequently Asked Questions, Industry-Specific Questions, and Illegal or Awkward Questions

## Chapter

# 13

# Pass Online Prescreens and Telephone Interviews with Flying Colors

*"Patience and perseverance have a magical effect before which difficulties disappear and obstacles vanish."*

—John Quincy Adams

Online screening and assessments are becoming more and more popular with employers. Dr. Charles Handler, recognized thought leader in the development of online screening and assessment technology, shares that companies use these tools to make sure they're hiring the best person for the job. Handler's *Buyer's Guide to Web-Based Screening & Staffing Assessment Systems* offers examples that underscore the financial rewards to employers:

- RadioShack found that the use of staffing-assessment tools for hourly workers was associated with an increase in revenue of about $10 per hour per employee. This translates to an annual revenue increase of more than $12,000 per part-time hourly employee. Given that RadioShack has well over 1,000 part- and full-time hourly employees, the total return on investment (ROI) from this assessment system easily exceeds $12 million a year.

- Neiman Marcus integrated Web-based assessment tools into its hiring process for sales associates and saw a substantial drop in average turnover of new hires and a major increase in average new-hire sales per hour. These changes translate into several million dollars in annual revenue gains.

Sherwin-Williams estimates that its use of automated assessment tools reduced the number of employment interviews conducted each year by more than 5,000.

Look for prescreening and assessments to increase as more surveys like these continue to tout a solid ROI to employers. You'll encounter them during two phases of your application and interviewing process:

**During the application process:** These tools are used early in the staffing process, oftentimes from your home computer when you submit your résumé to the company's Web site. Prescreening assessments ask you to respond to questions about your experience, skills, and qualifications in order to identify whether you meet minimum job requirements.

**During the interview process:** Typically used with professional, technical, and management candidates once face-to-face interviews are under way, these tools are used when companies want a more in-depth evaluation of candidates. Formal assessments are scientifically based tools that look at measurements of personality and intelligence. Other exercises and activities that are loosely grouped under the heading of assessments include culture and work environment inventories, talent and skill measures, knowledge tests, integrity and reliability tests, situational tests, and job simulations. These tests are usually taken at the employer's place of business or at a third-party site (such as a consulting firm specializing in hiring or performance management) designated by the employer.

In this chapter, we look at online prescreening tools, assessments, and telephone interviews in more depth.

# Navigate Online Prescreening Tools

Prescreening tools are typically short, taking from 15 to 30 minutes to complete, and presented at the time you apply for a position posted on a company's Web site. Salary requirements and relocation are often key screening devices, and information about your personality, work experiences, or work values may be collected. Results of the assessments are typically evaluated in conjunction with your résumé. If you appear to be a good match, you'll likely be considered for a telephone screening interview.

## What Are Applicant Tracking Systems?

The technology used to collect screening information is referred to as an *applicant tracking system*, or ATS. Applicant tracking systems enable companies to screen and hire dozens if not hundreds of people quickly. For instance, using an ATS, Citigroup is able to keep up with processing the 25,000-plus résumés it receives weekly, which leads to the hiring of approximately 500 people every week.

An ATS will screen for one or more of the following areas:

- Résumé data
- Automated qualifications screening
- Index of "job fit"
- Biodata and personality questions

When will you encounter these electronic gatekeepers? A survey by Rocket-Hire, a consulting firm that advises companies on employee selections systems, indicates that 54 percent of companies that make less than 150 hiring decisions per year have or are installing an ATS, whereas 95 percent of companies that make between 151 and 500 hiring decisions per year have or are installing an ATS. Clearly, the larger the company, the greater the possibility you'll have to jump through online screening hoops.

## What to Expect from Prescreening Tools

When applying at companies that use an ATS, be prepared to answer questions about these topics:

- Salary requirements
- Geographic preference
- Ability to relocate
- Ability to work days, evenings, weekends, and holidays (you'll see this question frequently when applying with retailers)
- Willingness to travel and what percentage of the time
- Education, including details about your major and GPA
- Number of years of experience in certain occupational areas or with certain products
- Countries in which you are legally authorized to work
- Willingness to work on a performance-based pay structure that includes bonuses and various award incentives
- Willingness to attend ongoing training sessions
- Willingness to complete a background investigation check or credit check as a condition of employment
- Your current status—employed, on a leave of absence, or on a layoff from any company
- Whether you have been discharged (fired) from any employer
- How many work days you have missed in the last 12 months
- Ever been convicted of a crime

✦ Service in the military, along with dates and what branch served in

✦ Eligibility to work in the United States

## Job Fit and Personality Questions

Questions about job fit and personality might look like these examples, which have been adapted from the careers page of a Fortune 100 company:

Compared to others in your current (or most recent) full-time job, which statement best describes your situation

- I receive more promotions than my co-workers.
- I have more responsibility than my co-workers.
- I have more freedom than my co-workers.
- I receive more awards/recognition than my co-workers.
- I have never held a full-time job.

Which statement best describes how you feel about supervision at work:

- I prefer to know exactly what's expected of me.
- I prefer to know the limits of my job.
- I prefer to help my supervisor set my assignments and goals.
- I prefer very little guidance from my supervisor.
- I don't know.

## Personality-Based Questions

According to Rocket-Hire, employers consider biodata, or personality-based questions, to be the most effective form of screening. Here, you'll likely be asked to agree or disagree with statements such as these:

- Working well under pressure is one of my strengths.
- I can do several things at once and still maintain the quality of my work.
- I adapt well to frequent changes on the job.
- When I finish a task, I am usually proud of the result.

Follow the tips in the following sidebar when you encounter prescreening questions online.

## 10 Tips to Prepare for Prescreening Tools

1. Know your basic requirements with respect to salary range and availability for relocation ahead of time.

2. Have a printed version of your résumé nearby to help jog your memory about details, such as the number of years of experience you have in certain skill areas. This way, you'll be sure that your information is consistent.

3. Answer as many questions as possible. If you leave questions blank, it generates a response of "no information" in the final printout that employers see. Too many blanks look suspicious!

4. In general, offer as broad an answer as possible without lying. For example, Home Depot's extensive online screening tool asks about knowledge of different home-improvement areas, from paint to plumbing. If the extent of your knowledge in these areas extends to painting a room in your house or running a snake through a drain, you may be able to make a case for truthfully having knowledge of these areas. If you don't have knowledge of an area that appears to be important to employers, do whatever you can as quickly as possible to gain the knowledge needed. Enroll in a class, research information online, or job-shadow an individual in your target field—control the controllables!

5. Use discretion. Some screening tools require you to indicate a level of knowledge, such as minimal, general, or advanced. Employers understand that it will be tempting to exaggerate your knowledge level. However, don't overinflate your skills. You'll likely be asked for more details in the interview and won't want to compromise your candidacy by coming up short in the live interview.

6. Buy time. If you encounter online screening questions that you'd like to give more thought to, do the following:

   • Print the page, or copy and paste the questions from the Web site into your word-processing program.

   • Go through the full series of online screening pages (you might need to insert *x*'s into the blank textboxes in order to proceed to subsequent pages).

   • Do *not* click the final "submit" button.

   • Sit down and take some time to determine intelligent answers to the questions asked.

   • Go back to the Web site and complete the online screening process.

7. Don't think about falsifying information on screening questions. Most end with legalese to this effect:

*(continued)*

*(continued)*

> *Applicant hereby certifies that the answers to the foregoing questions are true and correct. I agree if the information is found to be false in any respect, including omission of information, I will be subject to dismissal without notice. I authorize you to investigate all information in this application. I hereby authorize my former employers to release information pertaining to my work record, habits, and performance. I understand that additional background investigation may be necessary for certain positions.*

8. Want to do a second take? If you complete the screening questions and realize you didn't provide the best answers, there may be hope. One of my persevering clients figured out a way around the system by revisiting the site and using her maiden name. Her revised, but still truthful, responses landed a face-to-face interview (under her maiden name). If you've already given them your Social Security number, there's not much you can do because systems allow for only one entry per Social Security number. Some systems allow you to reapply after a certain time period.

9. When you encounter requests for your Social Security number online, be discriminating. It might be safe to provide it at larger, well-established companies that have thorough security for your data. Look closely at the employer's Web site name: If there is an s after the http, standing for secure, your data has a greater measure of security. Secure sites will read https://www.websitename.com instead of http://www.websitename.com. If given the option, do not provide your Social Security number for an initial screening. Many larger companies request your Social Security number and date of birth, stipulating that it is used only for background checks and not provided to people in the hiring process until an offer of employment has been extended.

10. Print pages as you go so that you have a copy of the information you submitted.

Once you've made it past the online screening gauntlet, you'll move to the next phase of screening: the telephone interview. See "Make a Great First Impression in Telephone Interviews" later in this chapter for information about this phase of the interview process.

# Ace Formal Assessments

Formal assessments—instruments that offer test-retest reliability and validity—are becoming increasingly popular with employers as a screening device. The Association of Test Publishers notes that business for employment testing companies has increased 10 to 15 percent per year for the last three years. The two most common genres of assessments you might encounter during the face-to-face interview phase are those that measure psychometrics (personality traits) and those that measure cognitive ability (mental ability and aptitude).

Psychometric tests, or the evaluation of psychological attributes, allow employers to gauge your flexibility, sociability, employee relations skills, management style, leadership qualities, fit with a particular organization's culture, and other traits. Instruments that fall under the umbrella of psychometric assessments include the following:

- **Behavioral assessments:** These are built around what psychologists call the "Big Five" personality factors (extroversion, emotional stability, receptivity, accommodation, and self-control). Popular behavioral assessments include 16PF, DiSC®, PIAV (Personal Interests, Attitudes & Values), Predictive Index, Hogan Personality Assessment, The Profile, and the Enneagram.

- **Ethics and integrity assessments:** These assessments help predict whether candidates' attitudes will create good or poor customer relations and a disruptive or harmonious workplace environment.

- **Cognitive ability assessments:** Also known as intelligence or aptitude tests, these assessments are certainly the least entertaining for candidates! They are purposefully difficult and frequently designed so that you cannot finish them in the allotted time. Cognitive assessments can determine what you know, how you think, and how quickly you learn. Common cognitive ability tests include the Wonderlic Personnel Test®, Thurston Test of Mental Agility, Watson Glaser Critical Thinking Index Test, and Profiles International's Style Test.

- **Aptitude assessments:** Similar to cognitive ability assessments, there are also special cognitive ability tests designed to measure aptitude for a variety of fields, such as accounting, banking, computer programming, engineering, finance, insurance, law, mechanical trades, reporting, sales, securities trading, and more. Sales aptitude tests are very common because employers want to make sure they're not hiring a clerk when they need a closer.

For more information on the preceding instruments, as well as favored responses when encountering psychometric assessments and the rights you have as a test taker, see the predecessor to this book, *Interview Magic: Job Interview Secrets from America's Career and Life Coach,* also published by JIST.

# Make a Great First Impression in Telephone Interviews

Quick quiz! Your primary goal in a telephone interview is to

A. Persuade the interviewer you are the right person for the job.

B. Convert it to a face-to-face meeting.

C. Determine whether the position is of interest to you.

If you answered *B*, you're on the right track. *A* is part of the answer—you must convince the person you can do the job, but at this point you don't have to convince them that you're the number-one candidate for the job. *C* is a component of your agenda, but it's not your primary goal in a telephone interview.

The employer has a different goal than you when conducting a telephone interview. It is either to

    A. Establish continued interest in you as a candidate (read: keep you on the list), or

    B. Determine that you don't sufficiently meet the job's specifications (read: cross you off the list).

Let's look at what you can do to keep yourself on the list.

## Set Up Your Phone Zone

Beware the casual call from a recruiter. It is an interview in disguise. "Many candidates don't recognize that interviewing starts before they even agree to be a candidate," reveals Kate Kingsley, president of KLKingsley executive search and former partner of Korn/Ferry International. This is a reminder that *any* conversation with a key employment or networking contact might be a form of an interview.

To avoid getting caught off guard, set up your "phone zone." This should be a quiet space without the potential for interruptions, where you have easy access to the following:

- Résumé
- Three-point marketing message, verbal business card, and mini-bio (from chapter 5)
- SMART Stories™ (from chapter 4)
- Company research
- Questions you'd like to ask the company
- Answers to questions you anticipate being asked
- Computer, notepad, pen, calculator, stickies (write your interviewer's name on a stickie so that you can readily use his or her name in your conversation)
- Appointment book or PDA
- Clock
- Water (should you experience a dry mouth or frog in your throat)

Employers may call at the least expected hour. If necessary, use one of the following phrases to buy time and get centered:

- When you need a few seconds to take some deep breaths, say: "Thank you for calling. May I put you on hold for a moment while I close the door?"

When you need a few minutes to eliminate background noise (at all costs, avoid dogs barking, television noise, kid noise, and so on), consider this response: "I'm so pleased to hear from you. May I call you back in five minutes? I was just finishing up something and I want to give you my complete attention."

When you need a few hours, try this: "Thank you for calling. I'm anxious to speak with you but I'm just walking into (or out for) an appointment. When would be a convenient time for me to call you back?"

When you need better reception quality if you're on a cell phone: "You've caught me on my mobile number in an area where there isn't good reception. May I call you back on a land line? When would be a good time? Actually, now that I think of it, I can be in your area this afternoon or tomorrow morning. Which of those would be better for your schedule?"

When you need some confidentiality if the interviewer has called you at work: "You've caught me at work. May I call you back around the noon hour (or at my next break)?" Or, "It's difficult for me to speak freely here. May we schedule a time to meet at your office?"

## What to Expect During a Telephone Interview

During the telephone screening, which may last between 15 and 45 minutes, interviewers will determine whether

You meet basic qualifications for the job (if they haven't already done so online).

Your answers are consistent with information on your résumé/application.

You understand the position.

You have expressed interest in, and *enthusiasm* for, the position.

You have asked relevant questions.

Depending on the company, you might be screened by a human resource professional, a third-party recruiter, or even the hiring manager. Human resource professionals will typically ask questions that verify you have the "hard skills" to do the job, such as the right degree and certification, number of years of experience in certain areas, and so on. Third-party recruiters or hiring managers will likely ask more in-depth questions. When the telephone interview gets underway, anticipate some of these frequently asked questions:

1. "What are the top duties you perform in your current/most recent position?"

2. "What types of decisions do you frequently make in your current/most recent position? How do you go about making them?"

3. "What is the most significant project or suggestion you've initiated in your career?"

4. "How many years of experience do you have with _____ [the type of product or service you'll be providing at the company]?"

5. "Why are you leaving your current employer?" (or "Why did you leave your last employer?")

6. "What do you know about our company?"

7. "Why are you the best candidate for this position?"

8. "When would you be available?"

9. "Is the salary range for the position within your acceptable range?"

10. "What questions do you have?"

You might encounter several variations on these questions. Refer to chapter 16 for the Magic Words strategy for frequently asked questions. Because employers often consider your reasoning ability and thought process as important as the answer itself, verbalize more than you might normally in a conversation. This will help the interviewer judge your decision-making process and get to know you better.

## Questions to Ask in a Telephone Interview

What questions will you ask to determine whether this position is worth pursuing? Unfortunately, you won't often have a lot of time to ask questions in a telephone interview. The interviewer is more interested in confirming facts than establishing a relationship at this point. There are, however, a few key questions that will help you understand the position:

- "How would you describe the ideal candidate for this position?"

- "What are the top-priority projects or tasks for this position in the next three to six months?"

- "How does this position fit into the company's long-term plans?"

Notice that there are no questions about salary or benefits among these questions. It's more important at this stage that you learn how you can contribute value to the company or department. From the information you uncover, you can begin thinking about how you might approach the position and contribute value to the team or organization.

## A Dozen Must-Do's in Telephone Interviews

There are some unique disadvantages to telephone interviews to be aware of. For instance, you don't have the benefit of making eye contact or reading body language, nor is it as easy to hold someone's attention on the phone as it is in person. These 12 tips will help make your telephone time a success:

- **Gather dashboard data:** You'll need the caller's name and title, company, address, telephone, and e-mail address for your thank-you letter and follow up. Asking for this information shows interviewers that you are alert and attentive to details.

- **Listen like a blind person:** You won't have the benefit of visual clues on the telephone. To truly hone in on what is being asked, consider closing your eyes to block out distractions. Another trick is to *silently* repeat a few sentences that the interviewer says (don't do this for more than a minute or two). This silent-echo technique will help you focus on what's being said.

- **Avoid background noises:** Children, animals, music, lawnmowers, and so on must all be silenced. One recruiter told me of a telephone call with a candidate who had a squawking parrot in the background. Not surprisingly, the candidate didn't win a face-to-face interview.

- **Use SMART Stories™:** Have your SMART Stories™ memorized or at hand. Interviewers will appreciate concise and specific responses to questions. Never omit the "R" in SMART—providing results will definitely set you apart from your competition.

- **Use verbal nods and avoid long pauses:** When face to face, you can smile, use eye contact, and nod your head to show a listener you are interested. Because you can't do these things on the telephone, use an occasional "I see" or "go on" or "I understand" to indicate that you're listening carefully. If you must pause to think of an answer, avoid "dead air" by saying something like, *"That's an interesting question."*

- **Be aware of your voice:** Is it too high? Too soft? Too loud? Tape record yourself to get an idea of what others hear. Listen for pitch, tone, volume, and attitude. Wear a smile and add warmth and enthusiasm to your voice (see "Tips for Adding Warmth and Energy to Your Voice" later in this chapter).

- **Monitor your talking:** Consider shortening the length of your responses a tad for telephone interviews. It's easy to lose a phone listener's attention because he or she might have visual distractions that you're not aware of. If you have a tendency to be a talker, pull back so that you don't dominate the conversation. A stopwatch or a small hourglass that measures one or two minutes of time may be just the thing to help you remember to keep responses crisp and brief.

- **Expect the unexpected:** You might be asked to participate in a role-play or answer questions that surprise you. If you need a few seconds to think on your feet, fill in the gap by repeating some of the interviewer's instructions. For instance, "Very good, let me review the scenario so that I'm clear on what you're describing." And then repeat a few of the steps.

- **Take notes:** Note-taking helps you remember the specifics of your conversation and makes you look like a great listener when you bring up important points from the telephone interview at the subsequent live interview.

- **Ask for a face-to-face meeting:** When the interviewer asks a particularly important question, respond with a request for a face-to-face meeting. "That's an important question, and one that I could answer more completely in person." And, if appropriate: "I have some interesting material that would shed more light on that subject. Is it possible to set up a meeting on Thursday or Friday?"

- **Close with a thank you:** Interviewers are typically busy people with a full plate of responsibilities. Graciously thank them for taking the time out of their busy schedules to speak with you. For instance, "I'm sure that finding the right candidate is an important but time-consuming process. I just want to thank you for taking time from your schedule to speak with me and for setting up our next meeting. I'll look forward to the next steps."

- **Send a performance-based thank you:** Double up with an e-mail thank you (for speed) and a handwritten note (see chapter 10 for a sample of a performance-based follow-up letter, or *Interview Magic*, also by JIST, for additional samples).

## How to Wrap Up the Telephone Interview

At the conclusion of the telephone interview, one of three things will happen:

- **Scenario A—Accepted:** You will be invited for a face-to-face interview. There is no doubt in the interviewer's mind that you meet the criteria for the position.

- **Scenario B—Postponed:** You will be told that the results of your conversation will be reviewed before taking further action. This might not be good news for you. Don't lose heart, though. It might just be that you were the first person interviewed and the interviewers want to hear everyone before making a decision.

- **Scenario C—Declined:** You will be told that your qualifications are not suitable or that there is a lack of specific expertise or knowledge in your background.

### What to Do When You Are Accepted

If it's Scenario A, congratulations! If the interviewer doesn't provide you with an outline of what to expect next, including whether you'll be required to take assessments, follow with this sort of response:

"Thank you. I'm certainly looking forward to it. I wonder if you'd help me with a few things so that I can prepare properly."

In a light, conversational tone, ask some of these questions. Of course, wait for a response before asking each subsequent question.

- "Who will I meet with?" (Write down this information.)

- "And their titles?"

- "Will those be individual or group meetings?"

- "When would you be able to send me a job description?" (Instead of asking "if" you can see the job description, this question presumes that one already exists and that you are entitled to see it.)

- "How long should I schedule for the meeting?"

- "What dates and times do you have blocked out?" (This might give you an idea of how many candidates the interviewer will be seeing.)

- "Is it possible that we could make that appointment for as late [or early] in the day as possible?" (Sometimes candidates start to blur in the interviewers' minds. Making your interview the first thing or last thing in the day might help prevent this phenomenon!)

- "So that I can be prepared and make best use of everyone's time, what will the focus of our conversations be?"

## What to Do if the Decision Is Postponed

If it's Scenario B, try these magic words:

"Thank you for the opportunity to speak with you. This sounds like a position I could really contribute to based on my background in _____ and knowledge of _____ . What would you need from me to ensure that I'm included on your short list of candidates to interview? I'd like the opportunity to meet to discuss how I can contribute to some of the issues we discussed."

## What to Do if You Are Declined

If it's Scenario C, try this last-ditch effort. Muster all the appreciation and enthusiasm you can, with absolutely no trace of pleading, whining, or resentment in your voice:

"Thank you for the opportunity to speak with you. This sounds like an ideal position based on the research I've done in _____ and my knowledge of _____ . Because I'm committed to contributing to your company in some way, whether immediately or down the road, I'd value a chance to meet with you and learn more about where I might fit in best—perhaps there are opportunities at a different level or in a different department. I'd value your guidance on what actions I can take to increase my ability to be a contributor. Or, perhaps there's someone in another department you'd like to direct me to."

Following a successful online screening and/or telephone interview, you'll be invited to a live interview where your competitors could number as many as a dozen. The components of the 4-C strategy to **C**onnect with your interviewers, **C**larify what the actual job is about, **C**ollaborate on strategies for results, and **C**lose the interview are found in chapter 14. During this phase of the interview process, you might also be asked to complete formal assessments, which you read about earlier in this chapter.

# Chapter Wrap-Up

Whether you're facing a battery of online prescreening questions, formal assessments, or telephone screening, relax and recognize that the employer is only trying to make the best possible match. A good match is good for everyone. The employer gets a happier, more productive employee. You get to do work that you're wired to do and enjoy.

## 10 Quick Tips for Managing Online Prescreening and Telephone Interviews

1. When applying for a position at a company's Web site (especially larger companies), be prepared to answer questions about salary requirements, geographic preference, relocation, schedule, education, experience, skill level, legal authorization to work in the U.S., criminal record, work history, military service, and more.

2. Keep a printed version of your résumé nearby to help jog your memory about details so that your responses to online prescreening are consistent.

3. Although it is difficult to study for online prescreening or assessments, you can prepare by being rested, breathing deeply to stay relaxed, and answering questions from the perspective of how the employer would like to see you operate within a work environment.

4. Remember that any telephone call from a recruiter, important networking contact, or employer is a form of an interview. Treat it accordingly.

5. Your goal for the telephone screen is to provide sufficient information and value to the employer so that you are offered a face-to-face interview. If you are not offered one, ask for one.

6. Listen like a blind person.

7. For telephone interviews, operate from a phone zone, a place where you can work in quiet and with concentration (eliminate background noises, including pets, children, radio, music, vacuum cleaners, lawnmowers, and so on). Outfit your phone zone with your résumé, three-point marketing message, verbal business card, SMART Stories™, company research, questions you'd like to ask the company, answers to questions you anticipate being asked, as well as business office paraphernalia (computer, PDA, notepad, pen, pencil, calculator, stickies, clock, water bottle, and so on).

8. For telephone interviews, add warmth to your voice by genuinely caring about the interviewer at the other end of the line. Use verbal nods and avoid long pauses.

9. Monitor your talking. The length of your responses should be a bit shorter than they would be for a face-to-face interview.

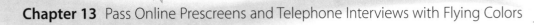

10. Close the phone interview with a warm thank you. Then, send a performance-based follow-up. Be sure to get the person's name and contact information for this purpose.

---

### ⭐ Magical Coaching Questions

If you are applying online, what steps you can take to better prepare yourself for prescreening questions?

_____

_____

_____

With respect to telephone interviews, who can help give you an honest, but humane, appraisal of your telephone voice and manner? _____. Ask this person to rate you in each of these areas:

|  | Never True | | Sometimes True | | Always True |
|---|---|---|---|---|---|
| Telephone voice conveys warmth. | 1 | 2 | 3 | 4 | 5 |
| Telephone voice conveys energy (enough breath taken in to use the diaphragm to project the voice). | 1 | 2 | 3 | 4 | 5 |
| Pronounces words clearly and crisply (for example, _speakin' of makin' a presentation, we wen' tah…_ vs. _speaking of making a presentation, we went to…_). | 1 | 2 | 3 | 4 | 5 |
| Voice has chest (not nasal) resonance. | 1 | 2 | 3 | 4 | 5 |
| Voice is right volume (not too loud or soft). | 1 | 2 | 3 | 4 | 5 |
| Voice is right pitch (not too high). | 1 | 2 | 3 | 4 | 5 |
| Voice is interesting to listen to (not monotonous). | 1 | 2 | 3 | 4 | 5 |
| Speaks at a good pace (not too fast or slow). | 1 | 2 | 3 | 4 | 5 |

---

_(continued)_

*(continued)*

| | Never True | | Sometimes True | | Always True |
|---|---|---|---|---|---|
| Avoids verbal "pollution" (does not litter speech with phrases such as "you know" or terms such as "like" or "okay") or other distractions, such as frequent clearing of the throat. | 1 | 2 | 3 | 4 | 5 |
| Offers "verbal nods" to help telephone listeners know they are being heard. | 1 | 2 | 3 | 4 | 5 |
| Avoids long pauses or awkward silences | 1 | 2 | 3 | 4 | 5 |
| Uses correct speech (avoids slang terms, double negatives, incorrect grammar, and so on). | 1 | 2 | 3 | 4 | 5 |
| Has a good "rate of exchange," allowing for two-way conversation with listener; not overtalking and dominating or, the opposite, undertalking and appearing taciturn. | 1 | 2 | 3 | 4 | 5 |
| Speaks with authority and confidence. | 1 | 2 | 3 | 4 | 5 |
| Communicates thoughts logically and persuasively. | 1 | 2 | 3 | 4 | 5 |

Choose a few items from the preceding list that you'd like to focus on. What steps will you take to improve your competency in these areas?

_____

_____

_____

_____

Chapter

# 14

# The 4 *C*s of Interviewing— Connect, Clarify, Collaborate, and Close

*"Most conversations are simply monologues delivered in the presence of a witness."*

—Margaret Miller

Interviewing is about helping others (the employer) become more successful while also moving your career forward into an ideal state (for example, gaining meaningful employment, adequate remuneration, responsibility, recognition, and so on). To better understand how that happens, we can turn to a coaching framework. The model involves four Cs:

Phase 1: Connect

Phase 2: Clarify

Phase 3: Collaborate

Phase 4: Close

You'll note that interviewers structure interviews roughly in this manner, although perhaps not consciously. At the beginning of the face-to-face interview, they *connect* with you so that you'll be able to relax and be yourself; they'll also be evaluating the subjective chemistry between you and the interview team. They then *clarify* whether you can do the job. In some instances, they ask you to *collaborate* on how to get the job done. And, if they sense that you can get the job done, they *close* the deal.

As a candidate, you can also follow this format, but with a slightly different perspective. Your job will be to

- ★ *Connect* with the interviewer to enhance chemistry.
- ★ *Clarify* the primary deliverables of the job (what needs to be done).
- ★ *Collaborate* on how you would do the job.
- ★ *Close* in a respectful manner that indicates your desire for the position and commitment to the company.

Let's look at how that's done.

# Phase 1: Connect with the Interviewer—How to Create the Right Chemistry

Recall from "Five Phases of a Job Transition" (U=Uncover Phase) in chapter 2, that you will be judged by your interviewers on three dimensions: Chemistry, Competency, and Compensation. This first dimension—Chemistry—is critical. You'll want to connect with the company's mission, its people, and its customers. You'll also want the interviewer to connect with you!

What does it mean to connect with someone? To get clear on this, think about someone in your work world with whom you connect well. When you speak to this person, what is present in the conversation? When you interact, how does this person behave? Chances are good that, in addition to having some things in common, the person you're thinking of respects you, supports you, and is a good listener and communicator. You can do the same in your interview.

## Follow the Six Keys to Connecting

To connect with interviewers, do the following:

1. **Clear the 30-second hurdle with a positive halo effect.** Psychologists divide job interviews into two parts. Dr. Joyce Brothers refers to the first part as the "30-second hurdle"—a crucial half-minute where most employers make up their minds about a candidate based on the halo effect. This phenomenon refers to an interviewer's first impression of you, which can be negative or positive. A positive halo effect can help people think you are even better than you are. A negative halo effect will make it virtually impossible to ace the second part of the interview, which is everything after the first 30 seconds! You can predispose people to like you by wearing an engaging smile, shaking hands firmly, dressing appropriately, and making the person feel that you are absolutely delighted to meet them. You can also put on a halo

by associating yourself with a trusted colleague or friend of the interviewer—this is where networking can really work for you!

2. **Share something in common.** When entering an interviewer's office, notice your surroundings. It might be that you can make small talk about the interviewer's awards on the wall, interesting artwork, pictures of kids, plants, tidy desk, out-of-the-ordinary furniture, and so on. A terrific way to share something in common is to comment on the interviewer's background based on the company research you've done. (Note the openers in the upcoming sidebar.) Another bonding agent is laughter—share it whenever possible.

---

### Be Ready with Openers to Connect with Interviewers

If meeting new people makes you nervous, practice an opener to help you feel more in control. One of these might suit you well:

- "It's so nice to meet you. Congratulations on your latest article. I loved your point about _____ [fill in the blank…using recycled materials, going to a flex-time model, mastering the art of spiel, etc.]"

- "Nice to meet you." Then, if the interviewer's desk is cluttered with family photos, consider saying, "It looks like you've got a budding baseball star there!"

- "I've so looked forward to meeting you. I really enjoyed the presentation you gave at the Widget-Makers Conference last fall."

- "I'm pleased to meet you. I have to tell you that everyone I've met to this point has been nothing but first-class. Your assistant has been especially helpful."

- "Good to see you again. I'll be interested to catch up on what you've been doing since we last spoke."

- [And, if you have no clue about who the person is] "So glad to meet you. I've been looking forward to better understanding your organization and where I can be of value."

---

3. **Respect them.** Acknowledge that interviewers likely have demanding schedules and difficult work. Respect them for the position of authority they have earned. You do not have to agree with them on everything. You do, however, need to recognize that they may see, hear, feel, and interpret the world differently and therefore behave differently than you. Seek to respect others first…it's the fastest way to earn it in return.

4. **Support them.** Make the interviewer's job easier by helping them find the right person for the position. You'd probably like it if *you* were that person, and you should do everything in your power to show that you are! If, however, you're not, consider doing what one new grad did when he recognized he wasn't going to fit the needs of a particular department manager. He

gave the manager the names of two classmates who he thought would be ideal candidates. Talk about making a lasting impression!

5. **Listen with laser accuracy.** It is impossible to connect with others if you don't listen well. Good listening is fueled by curiosity and compassion.

6. **Communicate exceptionally.** Respond with relevance and an attitude of respect. Recognize that your interviewer's learning style, values, and personality will impact your communication.

Something magical happens to a relationship when you listen fully—speakers sense that they are important to you, interesting, valued, and respected. They'll then want to extend to you the same respect. This process is foundational to connecting.

## L.I.S.T.E.N. Like a Laser

To connect with interviewers as you listen, remember these LISTENing tips:

**L—Laser your focus.** Lock out distractions and lock on to the whole question, not just a small piece of it. Remain fully present: Look into the speaker's eyes (alternately shift your focus from one eye to the other to avoid staring). Don't multitask (eat, take a phone call, or answer e-mail) or drift mentally to your next pressing appointment or any other concern that's on your mind.

**I—Investigate.** Be curious. Probe beyond the surface...move beyond listening *to* the speaker to listening *for* (empathetically) the speaker's meaning, motives, feelings, priorities, values, perspective, and needs. Further, ask yourself, "How might this person think? Do they take in information in a sequential/sensing mode or in a conceptual/intuitive mode? Do they make decisions from a logical/thinking perspective or a human relations/feeling perspective?" It's impossible to be a good listener without being genuinely interested in the other person.

**S—Silence your tongue!** Hold judgment and listen with an open mind. Don't take things personally. If what the speaker is saying makes you defensive, irritated, or nervous, there's a greater chance you'll miss the main point. Let the other person finish their sentences. Be comfortable with a little silence in the conversation.

**T—Take brief notes.** If clarification is needed, repeat the interviewer's question or statement. Take time to formulate your response.

**E—Elevate the other person.** Good listeners make the other person feel significant, valued, and respected. Act professionally, but resist the urge to be right, show off, or act brilliant with all the right answers. As a candidate, you're there to be a professional solution. Remember the mantra, "*It's about them, not me.*"

N—**Note the nonverbals.** Mirror the body language of your speaker. Does the speaker's body language indicate stress, confusion, frustration, or boredom? If so, how can you respond to improve the situation? Lean forward slightly to show interest.

## R.E.S.P.O.N.D. with Relevance and Respect

You can also connect with interviewers by RESPONDing well:

R—**Remember your objective.** It is to gain employment by educating the interviewer of *your value*. Everything that comes out of your mouth should be *relevant* to this objective. Single-mindedly stay on course with your responses. Be selective about how much you say. Resist the urge to tell all, over-explain, or apologize for any shortcomings.

E—**Engage the interviewer.** Eye contact, open body language, facial animation, and appropriate gestures are important. Reflect back and confirm your understanding of what is being said. Ask open and closed questions (see "Clarify," later in this chapter). You can also engage interviewers by addressing their different learning styles—such as auditory, visual, and kinesthetic.

S—**Share succinctly.** Know what your point is, and get to it quickly.

P—**Point to benefits.** Benefits are the single greatest influencer in communicating your value—the ability to be of benefit to the employer's bottom line, productivity, problems, and so on. Frame your comments in light of how you will benefit the employer. Occasionally, offer what broadcasters refer to as a tease: *"I'd love to tell you about how our team went from 82 percent to 99.9 percent accuracy in 30 days. Let me set the stage for you. We had a challenging situation where...."*

O—**Offer proof.** Whenever you're making a claim about certain skills, make it stand up in court. For instance, instead of saying "I can help your company be more efficient based on my experience and commitment," substantiate your statement: *"I served on a process-improvement task force that delivered a 30 percent productivity increase for my last employer, and I'm completely confident that similar productivity gains can be achieved here, as well."*

N—**Never drone on.** Two to three minutes seems to be the extent of many people's attention span. After this point, your response has the potential to morph from terrific to tedious. If you're delivering a SMART Story™, consider a pulse check in the middle of your story to keep interviewers awake and interested. For instance, after describing the situation and action in the SMART Story™, ask *"Would more detail be helpful?"* Or, *"I understand you're experiencing something similar in your department."* Or, *"Would you like to hear about scenario A or scenario B?"*

D—**Dedicate yourself to a win-win relationship.** Never manipulate a conversation toward a selfish agenda. Let mutual benefit be your goal.

## Quell the Urge to Over-Tell

Have you ever been around someone who regularly tells you more than you need to know? Or, someone who insists on proving they're right? These people suffer from the social ill of over-telling. You don't want to be one of these people on an interview. Situations that prompt the urge to tell include nervousness, passion about your subject, and uncomfortable silence. It's natural to talk more when you're nervous or passionate about your subject, so be aware and pull back on the reins. Learn to be comfortable with silence—stop talking after you've delivered your SMART Story™ or short response—and wait patiently for the interviewer to ask another question.

Telltale signs of over-telling include seeing a glazed look in the interviewer's eye, a yawn, finger or pencil tapping, boredom, or distraction. Re-engage the interviewer by asking a question. Listen. Then refocus on what's more important to the interviewer. *Make it about them, not you!*

## Check Your Motive and Attitude

Speech coach Brenda Besdansky of SpeakersWorld.com is fond of quoting Louis Armstrong: "It's not the watcha say but the howcha say it." You've likely experienced a horrible *howcha*: a boss delivers bad news in a callous, matter-of-fact way or a friend corrects you with a judgmental, condescending tone, and it just doesn't hit you right. It wasn't *what* was said; it was *how* it was said. Voice tone, inflection, and motive make all the difference in increasing your interviewer's receptivity. Check yourself with the following before-and-after examples to make sure you're in the "after" camp:

### Before

Tone and inflection that doesn't work: whining, begging, manipulating, sarcasm, arrogance, condescension, self-centeredness

### After

Tone and inflection that does work: respect, confidence, deference, concerned curiosity, attentiveness, thoughtfulness

### Before

Motive that doesn't work: "I'll tell them anything they need to hear just to get the job." Interviewers see through this! Or, "I've been screwed in the past, and it's my turn now—you owe me this job." Now honestly, would you invite someone with this attitude to join your team?

### After

 Motive that does work: "I'll explore what they need and promote myself 100 percent if it's a good fit both for me and for them." (If it's not a good fit, you should explore whether the position could be tweaked so that you can still be of value.)

## Use the Mirroring Technique

Mirroring is a neurolinguistic programming (NLP) technique designed to enhance communication. The principle is to match aspects of your interviewer's voice, mannerisms, and body language. For instance:

- If the interviewer greets you with perfect posture in a brisk, business-like tone and says, "Jane Doe, good to meet you," then stand up straighter and respond briskly with "John Dokes, good to meet you!"

- If the interviewer uses hand gestures to explain something, feel free to use hand gestures when speaking.

- If the interviewer leans forward to emphasize a point, subtly lean forward to listen.

- If the interviewer asks questions slowly and softly, respond in a similar volume and pace (but be cautious to not speak too slowly or too softly—you want to convey energy and be audible).

- If the interviewer is cold and businesslike and refers to a lot of technical jargon, data, and source material, cite data and source material in your answers and don't attempt to win him or her over by being warm and fuzzy.

The point is not to mimic the speaker, but to match his or her style without losing your personality in the process. Of course, there are some situations where mirroring would not be called for—for instance, when a speaker is angry or emotional. Also, resist the urge to mirror any behaviors that wouldn't win an etiquette award, such as slouching or scratching!

## Connect with Different Types of Interviewers

Beyond different learning styles, people also have different interviewing styles. In his book, *Hire with Your Head* (John Wiley & Sons, Inc., 2002), Lou Adler teaches interviewers to recognize their default interviewing style, whether emotional, intuitive, or technical. "Interviewers have a tendency to hire in their own image," says Adler. For instance, logic-driven, all-business executives have a tendency to hire logic-driven, all-business candidates. Creative, spontaneous managers have a tendency to hire creative, spontaneous candidates. Instead, advises Adler, it is wiser to hire people who complement the team.

Table 14.1 describes Adler's three interviewer styles. In the right column, I've offered suggestions for what you can do to connect with each type.

### Table 14.1: Traits of Three Interviewer Styles

| Interviewer Style | Interviewer Traits | How You Can Connect |
| --- | --- | --- |
| Emotional interviewer | The emotional interviewer makes decisions based largely on first impressions, personality, appearance, emotional reactions, and feelings about the candidate. Other factors might include academics, personal biases, stereotypes, and racial or gender issues. | Emotional interviewers can be tough to persuade if you miss making a good first impression. If you sense there's been a big disconnect with this type of interviewer, try this line: "I may not be what you initially envisioned as the ideal candidate. I hope you'll keep an open mind. May I share some work examples that point to my ability to deliver the results you need?" |
| Intuitive interviewer | This interviewer makes decisions based on gut feelings and the candidate having a few critical traits. The decision is then globalized, meaning that in the eyes of the interviewer, because the candidate has those traits he or she can do everything and, without those critical traits, nothing. More general factors include character, religion, values, appropriate style, and location where raised. (Note that many people vote in this manner, thinking the candidate belongs to my party, so that makes him or her the best.) This is where interviewers have the greatest tendency to hire in their own image. | You may sense that things are going swimmingly. Be cautious, though, as the interviewer may have to "sell you" to colleagues or home-office people whom you won't have a chance to meet. If so, consider this language: "It seems we've really hit it off. I know I can do the job and deliver the results you're after. I want to make sure, though, that you have the solid documentation you need to support my candidacy with your colleagues. May I share some specific successes that relate to the position?" |
| Technical interviewer | The technical interviewer makes decisions based on the possession of strong skills, experiences, and methodologies. This interviewer does a good job of data collection in the interview, but tends to | When lacking a certain skill that the technical interviewer is looking for, say, "How do you want to see those skills implemented?" Then follow with a SMART Story™ that describes how you did something similar using a related skill set. |

overvalue years of specific experience, degrees held, specific areas of technical competence, and thinking skills. This interviewer has the potential to overlook high-potential candidates who don't yet have the "required" experience.

Emphasize what you accomplished without much experience to demonstrate motivation and ability to learn. Consider saying in a respectful, inquisitive tone, "I've been told by managers that motivation and ability to learn is a better predictor of success than identical experience. I'm sure there are people in the company for which this is true. What have you found to be the case?"

Adler proposes that most interviewers are a combination of emotional plus either intuitive or technical. The best combination is intuitive plus technical, with an emphasis on gathering performance-based answers from the candidate. Your SMART Stories™ will be critical in this process.

There are other methods for connecting with interviewers:

- **Connect with different learning styles:** Auditory (those who learn best by hearing), visual (learn best by seeing or picturing in their minds), and kinesthetic (learn best by doing or feeling it internally

- **Connect with different temperaments** (as outlined in chapter 3, Step 6: "Know Your Personality Type"): Idealists (NF), Guardians/Traditionalists (SJ), Rational/Conceptualizers (NT), and Artisan/Experiencers (SP)

- **Connect with different levels of interviewers:** Hiring manager, boss' boss, human resources, technical people, sales and marketing people, managing directors or finance people, peers, subordinates

For a detailed explanation of how to relate to these styles, temperaments, and levels of interviewers, see the companion book *Interview Magic* (JIST).

## How to Tell if Someone Is Lying

Although interviewers might be watching you for signs of stretching the truth, you can also observe them to gauge their honesty. Intelligence analysts claim that when people are lying, their eyes will look up and to the left. Other signs to watch for include a sudden change in body posture; an increase in the number of verbal delays (such as, "umm," "errr," or "and-ah"); a change in pitch or rate of speech; sudden jiggling of a foot or leg; or facial expressions that are incongruous with the person's words. So, when you ask an important question, such as, "Do you anticipate any reductions-in-force or reorganizations in the next 6 to 12 months?," observe the interviewer closely!

# Phase 2: Clarify *What* Needs to Be Done

Now that you've learned the essentials of connecting with your interviewer, you're ready to *clarify* the "deliverables"—ask lots of questions about *what* needs to be done. Before we proceed, though, let me make one point crystal clear. Out of respect for the interviewer, let him or her take the lead on clarifying whether you can do the job. You don't want to bulldoze your way in and start asking questions out of turn. However, you should be diligent about doing your share of clarifying! As you do, focus on *what the employer needs*—these are the deliverables.

The difference between clarifying and not clarifying the deliverables is like night and day—one keeps you in the dark; the other sheds light on the subject, as table 14.2 illustrates.

### Table 14.2: Differences Between Clarifying and Not Clarifying the Deliverables

| When You Do *Not* Clarify the Needs of the Employer | When You Do Clarify the Needs of the Employer |
| --- | --- |
| You have nothing to aim at! | You can target your responses to show how you can solve or serve (SOS) the employer's needs. |
| When no need is established, there is little incentive or urgency on the part of the employer to hire. | You can help keep momentum going to see the need satisfied. |
| You have no way of knowing whether you are right for the position. | When you are right for the position, you gain more confidence and authority. |

Good consultants, sales professionals, or service people *always* find out what the customer needs.

## Ask for a Job Description

Recall from the section in chapter 13 on telephone interviews that you'll want to request a position description once you pass the telephone screening. This position description might or might not materialize. If it doesn't, be wary. It could mean that the employer doesn't know what they want in the position. When the position description does show up, study it carefully. Some descriptions are well written. Some are outdated. Some aren't even close to the real position. It's your job to clarify what are the real deliverables that the employer needs.

## Ask Big-Picture Questions in the First Interview

Use open questions to gather information. Open questions start with what, how, and why. Some of your questions can also start with who, where, and when. In the first face-to-face interview, ask aerial-mode, big-picture questions to clarify what really needs to be done. Here are a dozen to get you started (do *not* ask all of these questions—choose just a few, or else the interviewer will feel like they are at the Inquisition):

- What do you want to see accomplished in your team/department/company in the next three to six months? What would be the ideal outcome?
- How will you measure success?
- How will this position specifically support that goal?
- How does this position impact the organization overall?
- What do you see as the two or three most important tasks for this position in the immediate future?
- With the ideal person in the position, what can be accomplished?
- Who would you point to as a top performer in this position? What traits make them stand out? What specific actions make them so successful? (Interviewers may be hesitant to let the cat out of the bag and tell you specifically what qualities they are looking for; however, these questions can uncover them for you.)
- What percentage of time would you like devoted to each of the key tasks we've spoken of?
- Who will this position work with internally? Externally?
- To whom would I report?
- Are you saying that the most important issues are _____ and _____?
- How soon do you want to make a decision?
- Do I understand correctly that when this position is filled, you'll be able to _____?(Fill in the blank: get started on the new launch, clean up the backlog, be freed up to do the work you need to do, catch up on your outstanding receivables, and so on.)

Do your best to get a head start on answers to these questions prior to walking into the interview (see "Step 3: Research," in chapter 11, for more details). Note that the questions on the preceding list center on *the position*. This next list will give you insights into *the company*. Again, learn as much as you can *before* your face-to-face meeting. Assuming answers to the following questions aren't a matter of public record, you might want to ask the following:

- How long has the company been in business? Is it publicly or privately held? If privately held, by whom?

- What are the company's major milestones, key products/services, and strengths?

- How many employees are there? Where? Have there been recent layoffs? Are any planned?

- What does the organizational chart look like? Where does this position fit in?

Bring a notepad to the interview containing questions you want to ask and use it to take notes. Beyond this purpose, a notepad can give you something to hold onto during the interview to ease any nervous tension.

### The Right Timing Is Important When Asking Questions

A good interviewer will clarify whether you have what it takes to do the job. Before you can start asking deeper clarifying questions of your own, first answer the interviewer's questions with SMART Stories™ that confirm your competencies. "Dance" with the interviewer—if financial subjects are being discussed, don't switch the subject to team development.

Once the interviewer gets a better sense of your qualifications, he or she will be more open to answering your questions. Look for opportunities at the end of your stories to ask tie-in questions that clarify what needs to be done.

This example illustrates how to ask a tie-in question at the end of a SMART Story™:

> …*Bottom line, we saved more than an hour a day in processing receipts. Is this an area of concern for you, or would you say there are other key challenges your bookkeeping department is facing?*

After the interviewer responds, continue with

> *I'd be curious to hear what you have found that works best.*

## Ask Deeper-Detail Questions in Second and Third Interviews

As you get further into the interview process, you'll have established the rapport, trust, and mutual interest to ask deeper, more probing questions. The more senior the position, the more questions you can and should ask. Whereas general questions are appropriate for the HR department, detail questions are more appropriate for managers.

Be cautious! If you ask deeper-detail questions too early in the process, you could come across as pushy or presumptuous. Save these types of questions for the second or third interviews.

- Questions about the position ("What would the ideal person in this job accomplish on a weekly basis?" "How is it that this position became open? May I ask, did the person leave or get promoted? What results were you most pleased with? What do you need done next? How many people have had this position over the past few years? What do you look for when considering someone for promotion?")

- Questions about current and future challenges ("What stands between where the project/situation is today and where you want to be?" "What have you already done or put in place to achieve those goals?" "What's gotten in the way in the past?" "What if that weren't an issue?" "What is the company's vision for the next 5 to 10 years?")

- Questions about people (to whom would you report, who makes the final hiring decision, who will be your direct reports, whom will you service, who's in charge, and so on)

- Questions about resources ("What resources are in place to support this position/project?" And, for positions that would normally have access to financial information, "What information are you able to share about financial trends?")

- Questions about strategy ("What's your short-term and long-term strategy for this initiative/program?" Or, if you're being hired to help develop strategy: "What opportunities are available to us? How has strategy been developed in the past? How can that process be improved upon?")

- Questions about systems and timeline ("What systems are in place to measure success?" or "Tell me about the infrastructure and technology in place for this project. What's working well? What could be improved upon?" and "Do I understand correctly that you need to fill this position in the next 30 days?")

Listen for important issues and problems that need to be resolved—this is where the ultimate motivation to hire comes from. Avoid trying to note every single need the employer mentions. You'll be better off addressing several key issues than using a diluted, shotgun approach.

Move forward methodically with your questions. Don't jump into explaining how you can solve problems until you have asked enough questions and gathered the key information you need. Solving problems and documenting skills should be reserved for Phase 3, Collaborating.

## Ask Questions Based on Intuition, Tempered by Good Judgment

We've all sensed those red flags that tell us to proceed with caution. Some people see them in their head. Others hear a still, small voice that says, "I don't like the way this sounds!" Others get a tight feeling in their stomach that warns them that something is not right. What does your intuition tell you? Follow it. Trust it. What questions can you ask to probe more deeply?

# Phase 3: Collaborate on *How* to Do the Job

In the *collaborate* phase, your objectives are to

- Focus on *how* the deliverables established in Phase 2 *(clarify)* will be met.

- Offer evidence of meeting prior deliverables using SMART Stories™ and other documentary aids.

- Demonstrate tangibly how you'd do the job.

- Give the employer a glimpse of you doing the job.

To establish how the deliverables will be met, ask questions such as these:

- "What is currently working well?"

- "What didn't work well?"

- "What did the prior incumbent do well?"

- "What would you like to see more of?"

- "How would you prefer to see this handled?"

- "This is how I might approach that, based on my last position and training I recently attended…what have you found works best inside your company?"

- "I read recently in our trade journal how some companies in California had tried a new strategy for that issue…what are your thoughts on that?"

- "I noted that competitors are trying this approach…what do you think about this?"

- "I really admired the way your team approached that situation. Will you be using the same strategy on the next project?"

Use SMART Stories™ to answer behavioral interviewing questions. As you do, occasionally make the "T" in the SMART Story™ a tie-in with a clarifying or collaborating question (see chapter 4 for a review of developing SMART Stories™). This next example shows how you can combine the SMART Story™ format with collaborating. The description that follows picks up near the end of the SMART Story™ as the candidate described her results:

> …The vendor research I did enabled me to source the part for this special order in less than 24 hours, when it normally took a week to satisfy this kind of request.

Here comes the tie-in, which is actually a collaborating question:

> May I ask, how would you prefer to see something like this handled?

> ## The Secret to Being Able to Ask Any Question
>
> Mary Jansen Scroggins, former sales manager with giftware leader Applause and principal of Jansen & Associates, LLC, offers some sage advice for asking questions: "You can ask anything if you ask permission." For instance, preface your clarifying or collaborating questions with one of these permission-based questions:
>
> - "May I ask more about that?"
>
> - "Could I learn more about that?"
>
> - "When would be a good time to ask a question about your product?"
>
> - "Would it be alright if I took a few minutes to explore that?"

## Collaborate Using a Demonstration

To demonstrate tangibly how you'd do the job, consider using one of these methods:

- MS PowerPoint presentation addressing a typical challenge if this is something that would be applicable to the position
- Recent sample of work at your past employer (being careful to protect confidential information)
- Fictionalized case study
- Impromptu whiteboard brainstorm of steps you'd take to tackle a challenge
- Interaction with team members in an actual meeting

## Collaborate by Walking Around

A great way to shift the interview from interrogative question-and-answer to collaborative discussion is to ask the interviewer for a tour. One or more of these areas may be appropriate:

- The office space
- The building
- The grounds
- The production floor
- The warehouse
- The sales office
- A key customer's site
- A vendor's operation
- A retail space where the company's products/services are sold

When walking around or touring, ask lots of questions, take notes, and meet as many insiders as you can (don't forget to note their names and, if it seems appropriate, ask for business cards). This will give you great material for writing follow-up letters or developing leave-behinds (described later in this chapter).

You've mastered the art of connecting, and learned the importance of clarifying and collaborating. Now it's time to understand and apply the art and science of closing.

# Phase 4: Close with Professionalism—How to Wrap Up and Win

In a sales transaction, sales professionals are taught to "close" the sale—this is the point near the end of the sales process where the seller asks the prospect to say "Yes!" In an interview, the *close* is designed to make it logical and easy for the employer to say yes to you.

Closing should never be a manipulative, pressure-packed culmination of the interview. Because the employer holds the decision-making power, it would be inappropriate for you to be pushy or badger them into offering a position. More harm than good would come from such a strategy. It is, however, appropriate to

- Respectfully gain agreement from the employer that you have what they need.

- Close any gaps between what the employer wants and what you can deliver.

- Understand the company's interview process.

- Express your desire for the position—ask for the job!

- Keep up the momentum and communication with the employer.

Let's look at how to do these things.

## Gain Agreement

Using a collaborative tone of voice, gain agreement by presenting the facts, as these examples show:

- "As I understand it, you need *xyz* accomplished in this position. I've outlined my experience and results at my last employer that relate to this goal, and I'm confident I could make a solid contribution here. What's more important, though, is how you view my qualifications. *From your perspective, what do you see as my greatest value to the organization?*"

- "Thanks for providing more details on the company and the position. I'm confident my background will be critical to the success of the priority projects you mentioned. *I'm curious, though, what you sense as my greatest strengths for the position?*"

"I've enjoyed our conversation. May I recap my understanding of what you need? We discussed customer retention as the key focus of the position, specifically improving the regularity of weekly e-mail updates and monthly follow-up, and well as creating and implementing a customer survey mechanism in the next three months. *Are you satisfied that my demonstration of how I'd approach the survey will meet your needs?*"

"We've covered a lot of territory this morning. To highlight, it sounds as though you want someone who can work independently to research and generate potential contacts for the planned giving department. *May I ask which of my experiences you see as most relevant to the position?*"

Notice the key agreement questions at the end of each of the preceding examples. These questions are designed to help the interviewer favorably summarize your candidacy and conclude that you are the right person for the job.

## Close Any Gaps

The interviewer may answer affirmatively to your "gain agreement" questions in an effort to not show their hand. These next questions will help you uncover hidden concerns and gauge where you stand:

"What would it take to assure you that I would be the best person for this position?"

"How could I improve my value even more?"

If the interviewer gives you an honest answer to these questions, do not take it personally. Listen objectively and analytically. Do *not* get defensive or irritated. Instead, problem-solve and close the gaps. You might accomplish this by providing the interviewer a sample of your work product. It might be revisiting a particular subject and offering more details and results in a SMART Story™. It might be that you need more training. If it's something like the latter, ask the following:

"What would you like me to accomplish in the job as a result of that training?"

This focuses the interviewer back on "doing" the job, as opposed to having the right pedigree. If you're able to deliver the result they want, reiterate this ability. Then, commit to immediately starting on the training program (or whatever they want) while in the job.

## Understand the Company's Interview Process

Every company handles its interview process differently. These questions will help you know what to expect next:

Can you tell me about your interview process?

How many steps are in the interview process?

What is the next step? When might we set that up?

## Express Desire for the Position

Express your desire for the position and ask for the job. Too many times interviewers have told me, "They just didn't seem interested in the position. I really want someone who is motivated and excited about working here." If you're blasé in the interview, interviewers will assume you'll be disengaged in the workplace.

Crank up the energy in your voice and try on one of these closing statements:

"I'm extremely interested. Although I'm looking at a couple of opportunities right now, this appears to be the one where I could make the biggest contribution." (*Note:* Find any other opportunity so that you can say this truthfully—even if your "other opportunity" is temporary or part-time, such as hosting a fireworks stand around the Fourth of July or selling Amway part-time. You won't, of course, disclose those opportunities to the interviewer!)

"I can assure you that if you extended a reasonable offer today, I would be on board tomorrow."

"I know beyond a shadow of a doubt that this is the perfect position for me. There may be candidates who have heftier resumes than I do, but no one will give you more enthusiasm, commitment, and can-do attitude."

### A Great Close Wins a Job with *O* Magazine

Michelle Burford helps shape the voice of one of the most influential women in America, that of Oprah Winfrey. In the April 2004 issue of *Christianity Today,* Burford relays her story of applying for a job with *O* magazine. She was not what you'd call a front-runner candidate. Burford put it bluntly to her interviewer: "There are 100 people out there who have a better résumé. But what you'll get with me is a real passion and a real understanding of what she [Oprah] would want to put out there. You won't find anyone who cares more." She was hired two days later, and played a significant role in one of the most successful magazine launches in history.

It might be difficult for you to sound enthusiastic about a position if you're not sure that it's the right one for you. The checklist in table 14.3 outlines 10 areas that will help you determine whether the position is, indeed, a good match. In the column to the right, enter a number between 1 and 10 to indicate your satisfaction level.

### Table 14.3: How to Determine Whether This Is the Right Position

| Factor | Rate Each Item on a Scale of 1–10 (1 = Intolerable; 5 = I Can Live with This; 10 = Dream Job) |
| --- | --- |
| FUNCTIONAL FIT: | Is the position in synch with your favorite strengths? Will it allow you to use your honed skills, acquired knowledge, and wired-from-birth talents? Do you get to use these talents/skills the majority of the time? For instance, if analytical tasks invigorate you, will you spend the majority of your time doing this? Or does the position also require that 50 percent of your time be spent doing tasks that aren't your favorite strengths or talents, such as making verbal presentations regarding the results of your analysis? Remember, work is less taxing physically and emotionally when you're doing something that comes easily. |
| INDUSTRY: | Do you have an affinity for this industry? Is it aligned with a cause or higher purpose for you? Will you enjoy working with the products or services that the industry represents? Is this important to you? |
| INCOME: | Is compensation within industry standards? Will you make what you need to meet your financial obligations and goals? If the offer is lower than you had hoped, will you be able to go to work every day without feeling angry, cheated, or undervalued? Your financial situation may influence your decision—in other words, if you are presently unemployed, how long can you afford to wait? |
| COMPANY AND CULTURE: | Are employees treated fairly? Are team spirit and fair play evident? Does the company do what it says it will do in its policies and other communications? Are staff members viewed as the company's greatest asset? What about company stability in terms of finances and future…has there been a history of downsizing, mergers, or acquisitions? Do trade-journal articles or conversations with competitors or insiders reveal that the company may be in financial trouble? Is the ambiance and social structure in your comfort zone? Is the company's mission statement aligned with your values? If the company expects everyone to work 60-hour work weeks, is this okay with you? Do you like the company's dress code, stated or unstated? |

*(continued)*

*(continued)*

| Factor | Rate Each Item on a Scale of 1–10 (1 = Intolerable; 5 = I Can Live with This; 10 = Dream Job) |
|---|---|
| ADVANCEMENT, GROWTH, AND GOALS: | Will this position be a logical fit for your long-term plans? If this is more of a bridge job than a dream job, will it allow you to still have the time and energy you need to work on action steps toward your dream job? If this is a position toward the end of your career, will it allow you to create the legacy you want? If you're in your early- or mid-career, is this the right stepping stone? Does the company have a policy for promoting from within? Are professional development and training programs offered? Will the company reimburse you for training completed outside the company? |
| LEVEL OF RESPONSIBILITY: | Does the opportunity offer the responsibility you'd like? Will the position give you what's important to you, for instance, an intellectual challenge, leadership opportunities, an impressive title, clout, freedom, independence, the ability to influence change, and so on? |
| CAMARADERIE: | Do you like the people you'll work for and with? If you prefer to be with like-minded people, will this be the case? Or, if you prefer to be surrounded by diversity and divergent opinions, will this be the case? Is the social atmosphere of the department or company in synch with what you want, such as honest communications, a sense of connectedness, trust, teamwork, interaction, autonomy, service, and so on? |
| DIRECT SUPERVISOR: | Does your immediate supervisor have a good reputation? Are employee turnover rates low? Does your supervisor-to-be appear to be committed to professional growth and development, as opposed to stuck in a rut and stagnant? What, if any, red flags or concerns might you have about personality conflicts or your boss' management style? |
| LOCATION AND FACILITIES: | Is the company's distance from your home acceptable? If the opportunity requires an excessive commute, is telecommuting or relocation a possibility? If no, are there measures you can put in place that will help salvage the commute time, such as taking a course that involves audiotapes? Beyond commute considerations, is the location safe? Will your work space be conducive to productivity and creativity? Does the company provide the equipment and support you need to do your job effectively? |

| PERSONAL/FAMILY: | Will the position enhance or complement your personal/ family commitments? Will the schedule or stress level prevent you from giving what you want to your spouse/ partner, children, or other important people in your life? |
|---|---|
| Total Score: | |

Sometimes the question of "Am I compromising or settling for less?" comes into play. A preponderance of low scores to the questions in table 14.3 will help you sort that out. You can also use this system to compare multiple employment offers. And, remember that in the 21st century, saying "yes" to a job offer is not a lifetime commitment. The more important question is, "is it right for now?"

## Keep Up the Momentum and Communication

One of the best things you can do at the close of an interview is to keep the door open for future communications. Here are some secrets to make that happen:

- **Give the employer a "leave-behind."** A leave-behind is an item that you leave with the interviewers at the end of the interview, such as a fact sheet (see the examples at the end of this chapter), a case study, before-and-after photos, a collection of testimonials, a bookmark with an apropos quote, or a meaningful but inexpensive gift, such as one of your favorite motivational books. It's a great closing move and makes a lasting impression when you're no longer in front of the employer. If multiple interviews are part of the process, think about what you can offer at the end of the first and second or subsequent interviews.

- **Ask, "What's the next step?"** Try to arrange the next interview before leaving. Then, in your most deferential tone of voice, offer: "I'd like to be able to follow up with you as additional ideas from our discussion come to mind. Is e-mail or phone contact best for you?"

- **When the interviewer says she will get back to you, ask: "When might I expect your call?** May I ask you to use my mobile number, as that's the best way to reach me."

- **Send a performance-based thank-you/follow-up note like those at the end of this chapter.**

# Measure Your Performance in a Post-Interview Analysis

After you finish an interview, you can do some post-interview analysis on your performance to help you learn and continue to get better with each interview.

| Post-Interview Coaching Questions | Your Answers |
| --- | --- |
| What went right? | |
| What would I change or do differently next time? | |
| What did I learn from the experience? | |

Further, consider rating yourself on a scale of 1 to 10 to measure how effective you were.

| Item | Rating Scale | | | | | | | | | |
| --- | --- | --- | --- | --- | --- | --- | --- | --- | --- | --- |
| I connected with the interviewer (dressed appropriately, arrived early, exuded professionalism, shared commonalities, used LASER listening, and so on). | 1 | 2 | 3 | 4 | 5 | 6 | 7 | 8 | 9 | 10 |
| I made the interview about them (the company's needs and how I could satisfy them), not me (what I want, need, or deserve). | 1 | 2 | 3 | 4 | 5 | 6 | 7 | 8 | 9 | 10 |
| I clarified both the deliverables of the job and how critical this position is to the interviewer/company. | 1 | 2 | 3 | 4 | 5 | 6 | 7 | 8 | 9 | 10 |
| I collaborated with the interviewer on how he or she would like the job done. | 1 | 2 | 3 | 4 | 5 | 6 | 7 | 8 | 9 | 10 |
| I offered a demonstration of how I would do the job; I gave the interviewer a sense of how I would perform in the position. | 1 | 2 | 3 | 4 | 5 | 6 | 7 | 8 | 9 | 10 |
| I offered *complete* SMART Stories™ for behavioral interview questions. | 1 | 2 | 3 | 4 | 5 | 6 | 7 | 8 | 9 | 10 |
| Every word out of my mouth was positive, pertinent, and precise. | 1 | 2 | 3 | 4 | 5 | 6 | 7 | 8 | 9 | 10 |
| I am a known commodity to the interviewer—people within the company or individuals who have strategic alliances with the company know me and recommended me to the interviewer. | 1 | 2 | 3 | 4 | 5 | 6 | 7 | 8 | 9 | 10 |

| I closed the interview by gaining agreement, closing gaps, understanding the company's interviewing process, and expressing desire for the position. | 1  2  3  4  5  6  7  8  9  10 |
|---|---|
| I sent a performance-based thank-you/ follow-up letter within 24 hours. | 1  2  3  4  5  6  7  8  9  10 |

Total Score: _____ out of 100

# The 4 Cs in Second and Subsequent Interviews

Remember to cover each of the 4 Cs on second and subsequent interviews. Table 14.4 outlines some subtle differences of the 4 Cs in first versus subsequent interviews.

### Table 14.4: The 4 Cs in First and Subsequent Interviews

|  | **First Interview** | **Second and Subsequent Interviews** |
|---|---|---|
| Connect | By initial research, commonalities, respect | By continued research, follow through, respect |
| Clarify | Big-picture details | Fine-tuning details |
| Collaborate | Depending on length of interview, surface-level to high-level issues | High-level, confidential issues |
| Close | Establish agreement about mutual interest; close gaps; convey enthusiasm; ask for the job if there is to be only one interview | Confirm mutual commitment; close gaps; convey enthusiasm; ask for the job |

 *Note:* When you're meeting a new individual at second or subsequent interviews, treat the encounter as though it were a first interview and give sufficient time to each of the Connect, Clarify, Collaborate, and Close phases.

# Sample Follow-Up Letters and "Leave-Behinds"

Follow-up letters and leave-behinds are tools that will keep you "in view" and remembered by hiring managers. Adapt the following before-and-after samples as templates for your campaign.

# CHARLES CANDIDATE

555 N. 14th Street                                   Work: (415) 555-5555
San Francisco, CA 94111      charlescandidate@msn.com       Mobile: (415) 555-5556

[date]

Javier Gomez, V.P. Marketing
HI-TECH PARTNERS
55 Market Street
San Francisco, CA 94111

Subject: Promotional Market Manager

Dear Javier:

Thank you for the opportunity to interview for the Market Manager position. I appreciated your time and enjoyed talking with you about the position. The interview confirmed my initial positive thoughts of Hi-Tech Partners and the strategic course you have charted for the company.

As I understand it, your goal is to match the position with someone who can deliver these three key priorities:

- **Offer a strong track record**—With 10 years of experience at two respected Fortune companies, I have demonstrated a solid trajectory of advancement. Highlights with Sony include a #1 ranking among 150 sales managers nationwide, with 45% sales growth; for HP, again a #1 ranking among 24 market managers, based on nearly doubling sales volume over the prior year.

- **Be a visionary leader and change agent**—I am currently sharing a new and aggressive vision with my national account to triple sales. This is being accomplished by tapping the right people for the right position, leveraging team members' strengths, and restructuring elements of the sales team to focus on key deliverables.

- **Deliver results**—Generating record-setting results has been the hallmark of my career. My commitment to you in the first few months would be to understand fully the needs of the business, identify underdeveloped and untapped opportunities, and then create a strategic plan that addresses growth in both core business and new business development. This would be the blueprint for executing initiatives to align the sales team with their inherent strengths, implement sales training, develop licensed and branded promotional premiums, and emphasize conceptual selling to generate more business for your accounts.

Given these experiences and competencies, I'm confident the 50% growth you are targeting for the division is attainable. As my track record shows, I have always exceeded growth expectations and am certain I would do the same for Hi-Tech Partners.

I look forward to speaking with you again soon.

Sincerely,


Charles Candidate

**Figure 14.1: Sample performance-based thank-you/follow-up letter.**

## JOAN E. FONTANELLA

One Wooded Lane                                                                    (206) 543-5432
Seattle, WA 98765              joyjoy@inspring.net              mobile (206) 432-4321

[date]

Ms. Jessica Dupree
Regional Manager
Pharma Pharmaceuticals
555 Research Lane
Paramus, NJ 01234

Dear Ms. Dupree:

I understand you will likely be coming to a decision soon about the new District Sales
Manager for the Western U.S. In addition to technical competencies for the position, you'll
likely want someone with whom you'll be able to work easily…someone who supports you
in your initiatives and values teamwork.

I have earned a strong reputation for supporting my regional managers and working well
with other managers. Illustrating this is the attached letter of recommendation from Allen
Anguiano, Pharmacia Director of Specialty Sales. In it, he writes:

> *"I value sales managers who are proactive drivers, who understand the importance of
> strategic planning, and who are positive, people-oriented leaders…professionals who
> consistently deliver. Joan embodies all of these qualities…and more…. Of my eight
> current direct reports, I would rank her at the top."*

In addition, quotes from other district sales managers include the following:

"[Joan] has always been extremely professional, organized, and willing to do more than her
share." ~ Craig Maleski, DSM

"As a new DSM, Joan was my mentor…. Collaboration is one of her strong suits."
~ Judi Zantilla, DSM

"Joan is an open, supportive co-worker ... her teamwork is appreciated by myself, our other
DM counterparts, and RSD." ~ Hillary Jones, DSM

Jennifer indicated you were tied up in meetings on Friday when I left a voice message. I
would like the opportunity to meet again to review your needs and how I can help achieve
Pharma's goals.

Best,

Joan Fontanella

**Figure 14.2: Sample follow-up letter after second interview.**

**JENNA JONES**

32123 W. Belmont                                      (916) 543-5432
Sacramento, CA 95454                                  jj2000@email.net

[date]

Francine Pinelle
Wholesome Life Products
123 Westmont Street
Sacramento, CA 95454

Dear Francine:

Despite my disappointment in the Sacramento position being put on hold, I am grateful for the opportunity because it introduced me to you!

I deeply appreciate your enthusiasm, time, and commitment toward my application with Wholesome Life Products. Please keep me in mind should other opportunities arise.

I'll look forward to helping you with the school asthma screening project.

Best regards,

Jenna Jones

**Figure 14.3: Sample follow-up letter after not getting the job.**

| | Program Manager |
| South Texas Community College | Division of Continuing Education |
| | Prepared by |
| | Carrie Candidate, M.S. |

## Goal #1:

**Identify, develop, and promote instructional programs that effectively meet the continuing-education needs of individuals and organizations.**

## Strategies:

1. Formulate a task force for planning and implementing the preceding objective.

2. Conduct an employer needs assessment, including design of a survey instrument. Analyze results, draw conclusions, and make recommendations to the task force or management team.

3. Establish employer advisory committees by industries and fields.

4. Identify employee skills, knowledge, and competencies in demand by South Texas employers.

5. Incorporate innovative delivery systems to meet the adult learner needs.

6. Develop a comprehensive marketing and promotion plan to target audiences (for example, direct-mail marketing, advertising, and employer visits to targeted organizations).

7. Based on employer feedback, create and develop flyers and brochures and market to target audiences, including

   - Special-education teachers in the K–12 systems
   - Human resource managers in education and business
   - First-line supervisors in management positions
   - Healthcare professionals
   - Accountants
   - Therapists and social workers

8. Be visible at key community events to promote the Division of Continuing Education.

9. Evaluate return-on-investment in all activities to ensure fiscal goals are met.

**Figure 14.4: Sample leave-behind document describing strategies the candidate would suggest to meet a specific program goal.**

# AIDEN B. CARLISLE

(312) 555-5555                    abc-win@yahoo.com                    (312) 555-5556

### FINANCE / OPERATIONS HIGHLIGHTS

Delivered record cash flow, profit & shareholder value in *every* assignment.
Leveraged national/international sales & manufacturing opportunities.
Orchestrated complex turnarounds in record time.
Funded companies in difficult capital markets.
Created/redesigned systems and infrastructure for startups and existing companies.
Well-versed in diverse industries (high-tech manufacturing, software, consumer products, retail).

**Strengths:**

- Managing P&L, boosting shareholder value (equity, dividends), quickly capturing cost controls & cash-flow gains, building companies into international market leaders, designing process improvements & best practices, optimizing production & logistics, evaluating/implementing domestic & international outsourcing opportunities (China, Hong Kong, Singapore, Taiwan, Mexico).

**Turnaround Strategy:**

- Led restructuring of widget manufacturing company in 5 months…drove $18 million to bottom line in 1 year…reduced monthly burn from $2 million to $500K (Capital Machine, Inc.).

- Led international business preservation strategy, completing 5-year business plan in 1 month…salvaged $5 million credit facility…crafted operations strategies to capture first-year tangible savings of $1 million in manufacturing and production (Kay Emporium, Inc.).

**Corporate Growth:**

- Launched unique patented business platform that transformed startup into an international category leader and drove sales from $4 million to $50 million in 3 years (Cartell, Inc.).

- Executed M&A growth strategy that propelled company revenue from $95 million to $700 million in 2 years (Trim-Co, Inc.).

**Manufacturing & Distribution Operations:**

- Increased manufacturing capacity 900% through consolidation of production and distribution processes—from 500 to 5,000 units per week in 30 days (Cartell, Inc.).

- Conceived operational strategies that accelerated growth of wholly owned centers from 1 to 12 and associated centers from 0 to 1,300 in 12–15 months (Cartell, Inc.).

**Finance/ Funding:**

- Spearheaded $122 million in public and private debt/equity financings throughout career.

- Key in placing $195 million in debt securities (Trim-Co, Inc.).

- Steered company through successful IPO, netting $26 million…led leveraged management buyout 4 years later (TTC Systems).

**Leadership & Team Building:**

- Recruited by Boards for ability to set/execute fast-traction strategies, create a sense of urgency, and build momentum.

- Polished corporate/media interface … at ease working with Boards, staff, key partners.

**Figure 14.5: Sample leave-behind one-page document highlighting accomplishments in key competency areas.**

# Chapter Wrap-Up

You can outperform your competition by wrapping the 4 *C*s methodology around each interview, remembering to do the following:

- **Connect:** Connecting is all about communicating—not just giving out information, but getting through to people.

- **Clarify:** Connecting gets at the *what* and *how* of the "deliverables" to be accomplished in the new position—this empowers you, helping you know what to aim at and how to target your responses.

- **Collaborate:** Collaborating keeps the employer's focus on the most important factor: your ability to do the job. It also helps the employer to start picturing you in the position.

- **Close:** Closing involves a four-step process wherein you'll gain agreement that you have what the employer needs, close any gaps, express your desire for the position or ask for the job, and keep momentum rolling and communication going.

Throughout all phases of the 4 *C*s—Connect, Clarify, Collaborate, and Close—let your personality and natural enthusiasm shine through. ***Employers love to hire people who love what they do (and are competent because of their passion!).*** Recognize that the more connection or rapport you gain with the interviewer, the more you'll be able to clarify and collaborate. The more you clarify and collaborate, the more natural it will be to close.

# 10 Quick Tips to Connect, Clarify, Collaborate, and Close the Interview

1. **Connect by remembering the interview mantra: "It's about them, not me."** Seek to respect others first…it's the fastest way to earn it in return. Recognize that interviewers are people with challenges, deadlines, and stress—help them alleviate their stress by solving and serving. Offer your best case for why you're the right person for the job and able to support the company.

2. **Use the LISTEN acronym,** which stands for **L**aser your focus; **I**nvestigate and be curious; **S**ilence your tongue—hold your judgment and open your mind; **T**ake brief notes and take time to formulate your response; **E**levate the other person; and **N**ote the nonverbals, including your body language and that of your interviewer. It is impossible to connect with others if you don't listen well.

3. **RESPOND well,** meaning **R**emember your objective; **E**ngage the interviewer; **S**hare succinctly; **P**oint to benefits; **O**ffer proof; **N**ever drone on; and **D**edicate yourself to a win-win relationship. And, pay attention to the how-cha's—tone, inflection, body language, attitude, and motive combine to make how you say it just as important as what you say.

4. **Connect with each of the various company contacts.** You may meet with the hiring manager, your boss's boss, a human resources representative, technical people, sales and marketing people, finance people, peers, subordinates, and key customers. Each of these individuals has a different agenda that you'll want to be aware of when formulating your responses.

5. **Clarify the employer's top two or three "deliverables."** Before asking clarifying questions of your own, answer the interviewer's questions. Use SMART Stories™ to confirm your competencies and tie-in to their needs. Once interviewers get a better sense of your qualifications, they'll be more open to answering your questions. Remember to time your questions so that it doesn't look like you're commandeering the interview.

6. **In your first face-to-face interview, ask big-picture questions.** "What do you want to see accomplished in your team/department/company in the next three to six months?" "How will you measure success?" "How will this position specifically support that goal?" "What are your long-range plans and how can this position support those plans?" Ideally, you should ask these types of questions to your networking contacts prior to the interview so that you can arrive prepared and ready to position yourself as a solution. As the interview progresses (either well into the first interview or in a second or subsequent interview), ask deeper-detail questions.

7. **Once you're entirely clear on what needs to be done, Collaborate!** Here, you'll focus on how the deliverables will be met. Discussion might include comments like these: "We had a similar situation at my last employer. The strategy we took involved _____ which worked out well. How would something like this work within your organizational structure?" Or, "I saw a presentation at the last CMIN conference that addressed that very issue. I'm wondering whether we could explore how this might be tailored for your needs."

8. **To demonstrate how you would do the job, TAKE ACTION.** Consider giving an MS PowerPoint presentation to demonstrate your presentation skills, addressing a fictionalized case study to demonstrate your analytical skills, brainstorming marketing strategies to demonstrate your marketing skills, making a sales presentation to demonstrate your closing skills, sitting down at the computer to demonstrate your technical skills, sitting in on an actual meeting with potential co-workers to demonstrate your collaborative skills, transcribing a tape to demonstrate your transcription skills, and so on. Whatever you'll be doing on the job, show the employer how you can do it. The more the employer can visibly see you doing the work, the better.

9. **As the interview comes to the close, make it easy for the employer to say "Yes!, we want you."** Start by gaining agreement that you have what it takes, such as "May I ask what you see as my greatest strengths for the position?" Or, "Are you satisfied that I'd meet your needs in the position?" Close any gaps between what the employer wants and what you can deliver.

10. **Express desire for the position, and ask for the job!** Consider a "leave-behind," such as a fact sheet relevant to the interviewers or a collection of testimonials. Keep the door open for future communications by asking, "What's the next step?" Ask permission to follow up. Send a performance-based thank-you/follow-up note the same day that you interview. If the interview went really well, also consider a quick telephone call a few hours later in the day.

---

## Magical Coaching Questions

What in your background will provide common ground with the interviewer, the company's mission, its people, and its customers?

_____

_____

_____

To clarify in the interview, what big-picture questions will you ask your interviewers? Prioritize the list. Review the list just prior to the interview to keep it fresh in your mind. How will you remind yourself to ask these during the interview?

_____

_____

_____

_____

_____

What deeper-detail clarifying questions will you ask?

_____

_____

_____

*(continued)*

*(continued)*

_____

_____

_____

What clues will you watch for that the interviewer is willing to discuss deeper-detail questions?

_____

_____

_____

Are there any red flags you have about a position you're interviewing for?

_____

_____

_____

Review the collaborating questions in this chapter. What collaborating questions will you ask?

_____

_____

_____

_____

How will you practice asking tie-in questions at the close of your SMART Stories™ to clarify and collaborate? Who can support you in this?

_____

_____

_____

What specific action can you take to demonstrate to an interviewer your ability to do the job?

_____

_____

_____

With regard to closing the interview, what gaps, if any, do you anticipate between what your skills are and what the employer wants done?

_____

_____

_____

If you anticipate gaps, what actions would help close those gaps?

_____

_____

_____

_____

_____

Refer back to the factors in table 14.3. Which is most important to you?

_____

What minimum score do you need for each of the factors before you'd consider taking the job? _____

What is the lowest total score you would accept? _____

Chapter

# 15

# Score Points in Behavioral Interviews

*"There may be luck in getting a job, but there's no luck in keeping it."*

—J. Ogden Armour, Armour Meat Packing Company

The article title in the mountain of morning e-mail quickly caught my attention: "Why Do We Make Stupid Hiring Decisions?" The author, Dr. Wendell Williams, Managing Director of ScientificSelections.com, bluntly addressed his audience of hiring authorities: "Hiring is an emotional issue. No matter whether we admit it or not, use tests or not, or use a professional recruiter or not, we all go through a multi-step psychological decision process to decide who gets hired."

Recruiting professionals, in their quest to source the very best candidate and *not* make emotional hiring decisions, have developed and finely tuned selection systems over the past several decades. The latest advancement in these selection systems is *behavioral interviewing*. It is based on the premise that relevant past behavior is the best predictor of future performance in a similar environment.

Behavioral interviewing helps prevent hiring managers from making emotional hiring decisions or asking questions that don't help them objectively assess job-related skills, abilities, and motivation.

# How to Spot a Behavioral Interview Question

As opposed to a series of disjointed, interrogative questions like you might find in a traditional interview, you will find that behavioral interview questions allow for a structured, logical conversational style. Behavioral questions frequently start with these phrases:

- Tell me/us about a time when you....
- Describe a situation where you....
- Give me/us an example of a time when you....
- How have you handled _____ in the past...?
- When have you been in a situation where you had to...?

Once you've answered the interviewer's anchor question, a series of probing questions might follow:

- What was your specific role?
- Who else was involved?
- How did you decide which task to do first?
- How did the outcome affect the company?
- What might you have done differently?
- How has that experience affected the way you would approach the situation today?

Train yourself to spot these behavioral interview questions, as interviewers will be looking for a particular type of response.

# What Employers Look for in Behavioral Interviews

What are interviewers looking for with these anchor and probing questions? As the term "behavioral interview" implies, they're looking for *behaviors* that are equated with success. They're also after something even more important, the thing that's considered the driver of those behaviors: *competencies*. Competencies are capabilities, skills, and talents that make the behavior easy, enjoyable, and almost addicting. Competencies align with your Magic F.I.T.™—work that you are good at and love—work that gives you "the Tingle Factor!"

## How Employers Link Competencies to Interview Questions

How do interviewers determine what questions to ask? They must first conduct a thorough job analysis to identify relevant knowledge and skills. They will also look at top performers in a similar position and note what capabilities, or competencies, they possess. These competencies might be technical skills (such as proficiency in certain software programs) and performance skills (such as creativity or intuition).

## 50 Common Competencies in Demand by Employers

Because employers are looking for competencies in behavioral interviewing, you'll need to know which competencies are in demand. Following are 50 competencies that employers commonly seek:

| | |
|---|---|
| 1. Analyzing issues | 26. Initiative/motivation |
| 2. Attitude/optimism/passion | 27. Innovation/creativity |
| 3. Building relationships/alliances | 28. Interpersonal skills |
| 4. Building talent resources | 29. Judgment |
| 5. Change innovation | 30. Leadership |
| 6. Change management | 31. Listening skills |
| 7. Coaching/inspiring others | 32. Multitasking |
| 8. Collaboration | 33. Negotiation |
| 9. Communication | 34. Organization |
| 10. Confidence | 35. Planning |
| 11. Conflict management | 36. Problem solving |
| 12. Courage | 37. Process improvement |
| 13. Customer service | 38. Project management |
| 14. Decisiveness | 39. Quality awareness |
| 15. Delegation | 40. Quantitative analysis |
| 16. Detail-orientation | 41. Reliability/responsibility |
| 17. Diversity acumen | 42. Research skills |
| 18. Ethics/integrity | 43. Self-management/self-learning |
| 19. Execution | 44. Sensitivity/intuition |
| 20. Financial acumen | 45. Strategic thinking |
| 21. Flexibility/adaptability | 46. Teamwork |
| 22. Follow-up skills | 47. Technical/technology skills |
| 23. Global perspective | 48. Tenacity |
| 24. Independence | 49. Time management |
| 25. Influencing others | 50. Writing |

Although this list covers many critical competencies identified by employers today, it is by no means exhaustive. If you were to pare the list to just the 10 most commonly sought competencies, you might find these:

1. Analytical skills

2. Communication skills (verbal/written/interpersonal)

3. Flexibility/adaptability

4. Initiative/drive/energy*

5. Leadership skills

6. Planning skills

7. Problem-solving skills

8. Teamwork skills

9. Technical/technology skills

10. Time-management skills

*Initiative (also described as energy or drive) is listed by some recruiting experts as the universal trait of success.*

### NY Times Survey of Desired Skills

Beta Research Corporation, on behalf of the *New York Times Job Market*, interviewed 250 hiring managers in the New York metropolitan area to learn which skills were most in demand. They said the following:

- Ability to work in a team environment (89%)

- Ability to learn quickly (84%)

- Presentation/verbal communications (76%)

- Multitasking (73%)

- Time management (69%)

Skills most in demand for management candidates were the following:

- Leadership (67%)

- Strategic thinking (56%)

Skills most in demand for administration candidates were the following:

- Technical (25%)

- Analytical (24%)

Skills most in demand for entry-level positions were the following:

- Ability to learn quickly (32%)

Further, employers said they were willing to pay more money to candidates with proficiency in the following:

- Multitasking (65%)
- Can quickly learn on the job (64%)
- Possess strategic-thinking abilities (61%)

# How Employers Use Competencies to Develop Interview Questions

Once employers pinpoint job-specific competencies, they can craft questions to elicit responses that will help them evaluate the candidate's past behavior.

There are three steps employers follow to get from competency to question:

1. They identify approximately 5 to 10 key competencies for the position. For example, a management candidate may need the capability to

   - Analyze issues
   - Think strategically
   - Establish plans
   - Drive execution
   - Manage change
   - Build relationships
   - Engage and inspire people
   - Influence others
   - Promote corporate citizenship
   - Demonstrate initiative

2. Behaviors are then defined that describe each of these competencies. For instance, "establish plans" might be defined as *setting clear goals and direction during a project.*

3. From this definition of behavior, questions are teased out to determine whether the person regularly used those behaviors. For instance, they might ask, "Tell me about a time when you established goals and direction for a project."

# Mining Job Descriptions for Competencies

It's wise to prepare for interviews by researching, analyzing, and making an educated guess as to which competencies the employer desires. Job postings and job descriptions can be an excellent source for identifying job-specific competencies. The following example highlights competencies seen in the Skills and Abilities section of an online job posting.

### Position Summary:

Performs all general functions related to the receipt and management of work and service requests using a variety of custom-designed software tools. This includes answering phones, placing outbound service requests, maintaining work management queues, facilitating communication through e-mail, and directing calls to appropriate departments.

### Skills and Abilities:

The successful candidate places primary importance on delivering superior customer service; demonstrates consummate people skills [interpersonal skills] and talent at interacting effectively with people; pursues work with insatiable energy and drive [initiative]; is self-motivated, and thrives on doing a job in a meticulous [detail-oriented] and thorough manner and completes quality work on time; works independently, takes initiative, and demonstrates a desire to achieve; seeks out opportunities to help rather than waiting to be asked; minimizes nonproductive time [initiative] and fills slow periods with activities that will enable preparation to meet the future needs of the company; has excellent attendance [work ethic], is punctual, and has a consistent professional appearance; has superior organizational skills, is flexible, and can adjust to shifting priorities; proficient knowledge of computer programs [technical proficiency] such as Word, Excel, PowerPoint, and various custom-designed software.

In the preceding sample, I have highlighted for you the key competencies in grey and, to help clarify, also set off inserted common competency terms in brackets. Based on this job posting, the employer is looking for the following competencies in its next new hire:

- Customer service
- Interpersonal skills
- Initiative/self-motivation
- Detail oriented
- Work ethic
- Organizational skills
- Flexible
- Technical proficiency

When a candidate's key competencies are evaluated in an actual interview, the employer might use a form similar to the one in table 15.1.

### Table 15.1: Interviewer's Candidate Assessment Form

| COMPETENCIES | Candidate's Competency/Skill Level | | | | | Score |
| --- | --- | --- | --- | --- | --- | --- |
| | 1 (low) | 2 | 3 (average) | 4 | 5 (high) | |
| Customer service | | | ✓ | | | 3 |
| Interpersonal skills | | | | ✓ | | 4 |
| Initiative | | ✓ | | | | 2 |
| Detail oriented | | | | | ✓ | 5 |
| Work ethic | | | | | ✓ | 5 |
| Organizational skills | | | | | ✓ | 5 |
| Flexible | | ✓ | | | | 2 |
| Technical proficiency | | | ✓ | | | 3 |
| **OTHER FACTORS** | | | | | | |
| Experience and industry background | | | | ✓ | | 4 |
| Performance trend over time | | ✓ | | | | 2 |
| Education and credentials | | | | | ✓ | 5 |
| Personality and cultural fit | | ✓ | | | | 2 |
| TOTAL | | | | | 42 out of possible 50 | |

Note how the competencies, along with other factors, are listed in the far-left column. A rating scale of 1–5, with 1 being low and 5 being high, is used for each factor. The far-right column produces scores that can then be totaled. This particular candidate scored 42 out of a possible 50.

# Linking Competencies to Your SMART Stories™

Recall chapter 4, in which you developed numerous SMART Stories™. Near the end of that chapter, we discussed leaving blank the "Tie-in/Theme" section on the SMART Story™ worksheet. Now is the time to link your competencies to your SMART Stories™. To do so, follow these steps:

1. Pull out job postings you've applied to (or a job description for an upcoming interview) and highlight the competencies. To aid in this process, review competency terms from the list of 50 common competencies earlier in this chapter. Are there terms in the list that apply to the job postings/description(s)?

2. Compile a master list of competencies from your job postings/descriptions.

3. Next, read through the SMART Stories™ you've written. What competencies are apparent in each story? Review your newly compiled master list or the 50 common competencies earlier in this chapter if you need help identifying competencies. For each SMART Story™, write out a few competencies in the Keywords and Competencies section (found near the bottom of each SMART Story™ worksheet).

4. Finally, check to be sure that each of the competencies noted in your master list is illustrated in at least one of your SMART Stories™. This way, when an interviewer asks you to "Describe a situation when you demonstrated initiative" (or any other competency), you'll know which SMART Story™ to offer.

Wouldn't it be lovely if the interviewer would tell you what specific competencies he or she was looking for in the ideal candidate? It's not likely to be that easy. Employers are often hesitant to reveal the competencies they are seeking in a candidate. In *Recruiting, Interviewing, Selecting & Orienting New Employees* (American Management Association), author Diane Arthur advises interviewers "not to identify the qualities being sought in the desired candidate." The interviewer's concern, of course, is that candidates will tell them only what they want to hear.

To counter this, consider these magic words:

> I appreciate your need to make a sound hiring decision. I'll, of course, be as honest and helpful as I can because I want to make sure that this is the best fit for both of us. If you'd identify some of the key traits that are important for success in the position, I can better offer examples that will help you judge what type of an asset I can be.

# Why SMART Stories™ Are Critical in Behavioral Interviews

During a behavioral interview, candidates are asked a series of standardized questions to elicit three key pieces of data:

- **Situation/circumstances:** What was the context in which the behavior or action took place?

- **Behavior:** What actions were actually taken in the situation?

- **Result/outcome:** What was the bottom line of the action taken?

These three segments correlate beautifully with the SMART Stories™ you developed in chapter 4. Recall that the SMART acronym stands for **S**ituation and **M**ore, **A**ction, **R**esult, and **T**ie-in/Theme. Here's how the SMART Story™ matches up with the three segments interviewers want to know:

- **Situation/circumstances** equates to the SMART Story's™ **Situation and More.**

- **Behavior** equates to the SMART Story's™ **Action taken.**

**Results/outcome** equates, of course, to the SMART Story's™ **Results.** After explaining results, follow with the **Tie-in/Theme,** where you can engage the interviewer with a relevant "tie-in" comment or question or underscore the theme (competency) of the story (for example, analytical skills).

## Make Sure Your SMART Stories™ Are Complete

Be mindful of delivering solid SMART Stories™. Development Dimensions International, a respected leader in behavioral interview training, teaches interviewers to watch for three common *faux pas* made by candidates:

* **Vague statements:** These are general statements that might sound good, but provide no specifics of what the person actually did.

* **Opinions:** These are personal beliefs, judgments, or feelings about something that, like vague statements, provide no information about what the person actually did.

* **Theoretical or future-oriented statements:** These tell what a candidate would do, would like to do, or would likely do in the future, but not what was actually done in the past.

Table 15.2 provides a comparison of SMART Story™ elements that illustrate some of the common mistakes.

### Table 15.2: SMART Story™ Analysis

|  | Before | After |
|---|---|---|
| Situation and More: | *I was responsible for business development for my district.* [Here, the candidate makes the error of giving a vague statement that doesn't provide the context for the story.] | *I enjoy telling my "how-I-went-bald" story! It started with being given the charge by my senior VP to turn around a two-year history of double-digit declining revenues for the district. At the time, the district was ranked last among 17 for revenue performance and had been through four business development managers over the course of three years.* |
| Action: | *I think it's really important to involve team members in the process.* [The candidate provides an opinion, which is not necessarily wrong—just incomplete.] | *Here's the storyboard. I piloted a new business development program for the district, which included creating sales strategies for a full complement of products and services (commercial* |

*(continued)*

*(continued)*

| | Before | After |
|---|---|---|
| | *I always take the time to find out what's happening in the district, and I've turned around a lot of districts that way.* [This is a vague statement.] | *loans, trust and investment services, cash management services, retirement and depository accounts, government guarantee programs, computerized banking, alliance banking). I scheduled a two-day meeting for the 30 branch managers in the district, and I used a very motivational "All-Star" theme. At the meeting, I created a vision for what could be accomplished, laid out the program, and then used interactive train-the-trainer systems so that they could teach the strategies to 150+ sales reps in the district. I laid down the challenge, telling them that if we reached our goal early, I would shave my head! I had already cleared this with the senior VP.* |
| Results: | *We met our goal, and actually exceeded it, with $16+ million in loan commitments approved.* [This sentence is accurate but lacks impact because no context or comparison is offered.] | *Bottom line, we secured 44 new customers with $16+ million in loan commitments approved, added nearly $4 million in deposits, and secured first-time fee revenue of $162,000 from establishing new international business. We broke all records for loan and deposit growth in the district's 30-year history and boosted the district's ranking from #17 among 17 to #2 in less than two years. And, yes, I was proud to be bald for a time!* |
| Tie-in/ Theme: | [Many candidates completely miss the opportunity to reemphasize the theme of the story or to tie in their response to the interviewer's desired competency.] | *My communication and motivational skills were foundational to this success. By the way, in visiting some of your branches, I had a few ideas about how fee-based revenue could be introduced.* |

Note that the competency themes underscored in this story are leadership, motivation, innovation, strategy, analytical, and communications.

## Be Mindful of the Shape of Your SMART Story™

Make your SMART Story™ bell-shaped. Note the picture of the Liberty Bell below (subliminal message: your SMART Story™ will lead you to freedom to do what you do best).

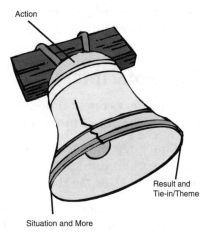

Action

Result and
Tie-in/Theme

Situation and More

**Figure 15.1: The ideal shape for your Smart Story™.**

The bulk of the mass is in the center of the bell. That's where the bulk of your information should be as you tell a story—spend more time on the Action. The lip on either side of the bell is analogous to the beginning (Situation and More) and ending (Result and Tie-in/Theme) of your SMART Story™. Spend less time on the Situation and Results. From the interviewer's perspective, the quality of a behavioral interview response rests in the details (Action) of what you did.

## Vary the Length of Your Responses

Vary the length of your responses. For instance, if you've just answered a question that required a lengthy answer with lots of details, you might not want to provide as many details in your next response. You can gauge whether you're giving the interviewer enough information by tagging one of these questions onto your response:

- Would you like more details on that?

- Is that the kind of information you are looking for?

- Would you like another example?

- Two or three other examples come to mind that address that issue. They speak to times when I did _____ and _____ [fill in these blanks with relevant subject matter]. Would those be of interest to you now, or do you have enough information?

# Chapter Wrap-Up

Given employers' successes with behavioral/competency-based interviewing, it's likely you'll encounter at least a few behavioral questions if not a full-blown behavioral interview in your job search. Welcome this type of interview because it allows you to be judged on your experience more than your interview stage presence. Behavioral interviews are more about substance than style!

## 10 Quick Tips for Behavioral Interviews

1. Behavioral interviewing is very common because it works! Its premise is that past behavior is the best indicator of future performance.

2. Recognize behavioral interview questions by introductory phrases such as "Tell me/us about a time when you...," "Describe a situation where you...," "Give me/us an example of...," or "In the past, how have you handled...."

3. Be prepared for very specific anchor questions, such as, "As an accountant, describe a time when you encountered unethical accounting practices. How did you handle it?"

4. After the anchor question, be prepared for probing questions, such as "What was your specific role?" "Who else was involved?" "How did you decide which task to do first?" "How did the outcome affect the company?" "What might you have done differently?" and "How has that affected the way you would approach the situation today?"

5. Competencies drive behavior. Competencies are capabilities, skills, and talents that make the behavior easy or enjoyable to perform.

6. Employers look at the behaviors of top performers in similar positions to identify competencies. If you want to move forward, model yourself after top performers.

7. There are more than 50 common competencies in demand by employers. Among the most important are initiative/drive/energy and communication skills.

8. Mine job postings and job descriptions to create a master list of key competencies for your target position.

9. Review your SMART Stories™ and note several competencies that are illustrated in the story.

10. Avoid making vague statements, giving opinions, or offering theoretical or future-oriented statements when delivering your SMART Story™.

## Magical Coaching Questions

Practice delivering your SMART Stories™ to a colleague or friend. Use the following form to score yourself.

### Practice Your SMART Stories™

| | 1 (low) | 2 | 3 (average) | 4 | 5 (high) | Score |
|---|---|---|---|---|---|---|
| Avoids vague statements | | | | | | |
| Avoids opinions | | | | | | |
| Avoids theoretical or future-oriented statements | | | | | | |
| Situation and more described | | | | | | |
| Action described | | | | | | |
| Action comprises the bulk of the story | | | | | | |
| Results are specific with numbers | | | | | | |
| Competency theme or tie-in is present | | | | | | |

What are you doing right/well when delivering your SMART Stories™?

_____

_____

_____

*(continued)*

*(continued)*

What part of your SMART Stories™ do you want to enhance?

_____

_____

_____

What is one step you could take in the next 24 hours to make that happen? What will be the benefit of doing so?

_____

_____

_____

## Chapter
# 16

# Ace Frequently Asked Questions, Industry-Specific Questions, and Illegal or Awkward Questions

*"The truth isn't the truth until people believe you, and they can't believe you if they don't know what you're saying, and they can't know what you're saying if they don't listen to you, and they won't listen to you if you're not interesting, and you won't be interesting unless you say things imaginatively, originally, freshly."*

—William Bernbach, American advertising executive

As the preceding quote implies, you'll want to be interesting, original, and fresh in every interview! You can do that by keeping these 5 *D*s in mind:

- **Discover** what the employer truly needs to have done (the deliverables).
- **Document** your knowledge, skills, and experience to capably do the job (talent/competencies).
- **Demonstrate** your ability to do the job with greater profitability to the company than other candidates (value).
- **Display** your ability to motivate yourself and/or others (energy and enthusiasm).
- **Describe** your ability to fit in with the company culture (chemistry).

In this chapter, we'll look at strategies for answering Frequently Asked Questions (FAQs) and Industry-Specific Questions (ISQs), including a *Before* and *After* example for most questions to give you a feel for how, and how not, to respond. (For more *Before* and *After* responses to additional FAQs, "sticky wicket" interview questions, and illegal interview questions, see *Interview Magic*, also published by JIST.)

# Frequently Asked Questions

## Question
**Tell me about yourself.**

## Strategy
Focus on what the interviewers need to know to determine that you're the best investment they could make.

Give the interviewer a quick "READ" on this question, which stands for

- **Relevant:** First, sift everything you say through the relevance filter. Ask yourself, "is the information I'm sharing important to the interviewers? Will the information make them think more or less favorably of me?"

- **Experience:** Provide a quick overview of years of experience or most important companies worked for, along with position titles and responsibility highlights.

- **Academics:** Mention impressive institutions, degrees, certifications, or alumni networks associated with your education.

- **Deliverables:** Translate your experience into value by offering one or two results.

## "Before" Answer
*I graduated from college, went to work in the late '70s for an advertising firm; then went to another firm; then started my own business, which was really great because it met my needs to be flexible and raise my kids, plus be my own boss.*

## "After"—the "Magic Words" Answer
*I'd be happy to. Before I do that, I'm wondering if you'd tell me a little more about two or three key strengths you're looking for in the ideal candidate.* After the interviewer responds, say *Great, it sounds like we're definitely on the same page. You asked about my background.*

*With virtually 20 years of experience, the last seven as a creative director at Smith & Jones Agency, I offer three key strengths that I believe are closely aligned to your needs for the position.*

*First, I'm an excellent **advertising strategist**—my skills in this area have delivered an ROI of 10:1 on marketing funds, which as you know is well above average.*

*Second, I'm an excellent **project manager;** have numerous contacts with artists, copywriters, and printers; and am able to bring projects in on time and on a shoestring budget. It wasn't unusual for me to save $5,000 on printing costs when our total budget was $25,000.*

*Third, I have a strong **creative background.** Many of the campaigns I directed earned national advertising awards. Based on our chats thus far, I'm confident that my skill set would be a close match for what you need.*

*And, I'd love to hear more about what you need for this position. For instance, what do you consider the most pressing projects or issues I'd be tackling in the first 90 days on the job?*

---

## Question

**What types of decisions do you frequently make in your current/most recent position? How do you go about making them?**

## Strategy

This question helps reveal to the interviewer how much responsibility you carry, your analytical skills, how you prioritize your day, what initiative you take, and what you consider to be important decisions. If you are in management, describe your ability to make both big-picture and detail decisions that align with long-term strategy, such as responsibility for $300,000 in buying decisions for a "tween" retailer, as well as details regarding trend, fabric, and color direction. If you are not in a supervisory or management role, avoid the misstep of saying that you don't make decisions, as the *Before* answer illustrates.

## "Before" Answer

*I don't have any supervisory authority, so I really don't make too many decisions.*

## "After"—the "Magic Words" Answer

*Magic*

*As a customer support rep, I make decisions throughout my day, from deciding how to prioritize the processing of Internet orders that are in my e-mail bin each morning to determining whether I need to consult my supervisor on a customer complaint or special order to solving a particular problem related to one of the orders. For instance, just last week there was a situation where the client wanted a one-day delivery on his order. [Tell a SMART Story™ here with emphasis on Action so that the interviewer sees how you go about making decisions.]*

*The most important decision I make each day is to choose the right attitude and remember that work is about meeting the needs of our clients.*

---

## Question

**What is the most significant project or suggestion you have initiated in your career?**

### Strategy

Note the last three words: *in your career.* This should be your biggest, most salient initiative. The interviewer is looking for your drive and energy here—what is the most important idea or project you personally set into motion, and what do you deem significant. Depending on your functional position and years of experience, it might be something like a new company or major project launched, or it may be on a smaller scale, such as an idea you suggested that was implemented and adopted by others. This before-and-after answer suggests how a college student applying for a management-training program might answer the question.

### "Before" Answer

*Since I've been in college and am just starting my career, I can't say that there is anything too significant yet. But, I'm looking forward to doing some significant projects.*

Magic

### "After"—the "Magic Words" Answer

*A number of projects come to mind, such as initiating a college schedule that allowed me to complete my degree in three and a half instead of four years and proposing a philanthropic fund-raiser for my business fraternity that raised $16,000. I'd have to say, though, that the suggestion I'm most proud of is the one I proposed to classmates to identify "best practices" for study groups, which made a dramatic improvement in some people's grades. Let me explain. We were studying best practices in an upper-division management class. I asked the question in class, "what if we were to apply this to how we study?" It turned out that several people were interested, so we agreed to meet outside of class. From that core group of five people, we formed the "Best Practice, Ace-the-Class Study Group." Under my direction, we located and evaluated study groups both on our campus and on six other campuses in the Northeast. From that research, we identified 10 best practices that we put into place. We met twice a week, and I took turns leading the group every other time with another leader. Our group grew and replicated itself, ultimately to 12 separate groups on campus with a total of more than 100 students participating. Most important, we measured progress by our grades. On average, students improved their class grades by one full mark, and we even had some students who started the study groups with Ds who were now making As. I also took the initiative to create a manual so that other groups could easily form and continue without my being there.*

---

### Question

**How would you describe your ideal work environment?**

### Strategy

Ideally, you'd want to describe the company that you're interviewing with—just be careful to not go overboard and look like a sycophant. Research the company (of course, you've already done this!) and offer details.

### "Before" Answer

*I'm really looking for a company that appreciates and rewards its employees...a place where there's a sense of community and people trust one another.*

### *"After"—the "Magic Words" Answer*

*I noted the mission statement on your Web site that says, "To build a great company that values people and inspires excellence in healthcare." I'm very closely aligned with that statement. I want to be part of a culture that inspires excellence—I believe it's the catalyst for innovation and market leadership.* [The prior statement should appeal to the Rational/Conceptualizer.] *That excellence should be applied throughout the organization so that best practices are identified and people know what is expected of them.* [The prior statement should appeal to the Guardian/Traditionalist.] *At the same time, those practices should allow people the freedom to act as needed to fulfill needs.* [The last statement should appeal to the Experiencer.] *I believe people are a company's most important asset, so ideally managers should be committed to matching people to positions that are a good fit. When there's a good fit, employees are naturally motivated and enthusiastic about their work.* [The last statement should appeal to the Idealist.] *And, of course, there should be bottom-line value to everyone, from shareholders and employees to physicians and patients. When all of these elements are in place, there's a naturally occurring synergy that will cause everyone to benefit.*

---

### Question
**Describe your ideal boss.**

### Strategy
The interviewer wants to know 1) if you are manageable and 2) how to manage you. Be brief with your explanation, or you might end up with a disparity between your ideal boss and who will actually be managing you. At the same time, this is an opportunity to convey how you want others to treat you.

### *"Before" Answer*
*My ideal boss would be someone who respects me, sets realistic goals, does not micromanage, and does not keep changing the target every other day.* [The "does nots" in this answer make it too negative.]

### *"After"—the "Magic Words" Answer*
*That's easy, because I've had the privilege of working under ideal bosses.* [Note that this sentence doesn't say that every boss was ideal.] *The relationships were based on mutual respect, shared goals, and open communication.*

---

### Question
**Have you worked under bosses who weren't ideal?**

### Strategy
This question may come after the prior question about your ideal boss. If so, don't be drawn into criticizing a prior boss who wasn't ideal. People will only wonder whether you'll later do the same to someone in their company.

### *"Before" Answer*

*Well, yes. My current boss. That's part of the reason I am looking for a new position. His ethical standards are not what you'd call pure.*

Magic

### *"After"—the "Magic Words" Answer*

*I find it helpful to think in terms of a person's assets and potential. Bosses are human, and each one has certain strengths. I consider it my job to recognize and focus on the positives. Looking in the negative direction often creates dissension. Whatever the case, I like to build my relationships on respect, common goals, and direct communication.*

---

### Question

**That's a good answer. Can you give me an example of someone who wasn't an ideal boss?**

### Strategy

Keep your cool and don't allow any unresolved feelings of anger or resentment to seep into the response, no matter how badly you might have been mistreated by a boss in the past. Be brief and upbeat in your answer.

### *"Before" Answer*

*That would be my current boss. There have been a number of situations where he's asked me to do things that crossed the line of ethics. For instance, when turning in insurance applications, he's asked me to change dates and medical information so that policies would be accepted by the underwriters.*

Magic

### *"After"—the "Magic Words" Answer*

*I've been fortunate to work with some really talented people over the years, and learned something from a variety of management styles. If I were pressed, I'd have to say that one person with whom I worked was challenging because the target goal changed frequently and, though I was committed to communicating with that person, I wasn't kept in the loop. I value keeping communication lines open and think it's critical to helping not only my boss know that I'm on track and delivering results, but those who report to me as well. I find that communicating is critical to keeping people motivated.*

---

### Question

**Why are you leaving your current employer? (or Why did you leave your last employer?)**

### Strategy

Avoid saying anything negative about former employers, or it will look like you are whining or not taking responsibility for yourself. Some of the best reasons for leaving include a desire to

- Learn more (the job provided no opportunity to learn and apply growth)

- Earn more (you needed more salary)

- Grow more (you wanted to take on more responsibility)

- Work more (the job was temporary or part-time, the company cut your hours or had a RIF/layoff, or the company relocated its headquarters/ offices)

- Commute/travel less

Other acceptable reasons include family relocation and personal situations (maternity, accident/illness, caring for a terminally ill loved one, and so on). Any other answer might raise red flags with the interviewer. Avoid telling too many details, but be factual.

### "Before" Answer

*My company has had a series of reductions-in-force recently and my boss told me that I'd better start looking since our department goals haven't been reached lately.*

Magic

### "After"—the "Magic Words" Answer

*My current employer had a reduction in force recently due to lackluster sales. I felt very proud that they valued my work so as to keep me on board. However, given the situation, I felt it was a good time to investigate leading-edge companies where my opportunity for growth is unlimited. I discovered this position through my colleague Frank McGill, who works here in purchasing. I got pretty excited when he told me what you've been doing with your inventory-control processes. I've read a lot about your process and went to a breakout session on the subject at the NAPM conference recently. In my present supply-chain role, I implemented processes and systems that reduced our cycle time by 15 percent. I'm sure this experience would be valuable to your organization.*

### Question

**What prompted each of your departures from previous organizations?**

### Strategy

This is similar to "why are you leaving your current employer?" Here, the interviewer is looking for patterns of why you leave positions. Is it that you get bored after a certain amount of time? Is it that you can't get along with people? Is it that you lose your temper and quit? Is it that you jump ship for any new opportunity that comes along? To answer this question, point to items in the list of acceptable reasons noted in the prior question.

Note that the final sentence in the *After* example allows you to control whom the interviewer calls. If you don't hold favored status with one of your prior bosses, you can steer the interviewer toward someone at the company who will give you a favorable reference.

### "Before" Answer

*In my last position, I was forced out by a power play. Prior to that, I had a boss whom I didn't see eye to eye with. In the position before that, my manager just wouldn't give me more responsibility and I needed more challenge and variety.*

Magic

### "After"—the "Magic Words" Answer

*In my last position, the company moved its offices farther north, so the commute became more than two hours each way for me. Prior to that, I was recruited to start up a new program similar to the one you have here—I'm confident my knowledge of bringing that program from ground zero to self-sustaining will be of interest to you and I'll look forward to giving you more details on that when you're ready. And finally, before that, I had been with the ABC Company seven years and, being a family-owned company, the organizational structure allowed no room for advancement. I can offer you contact persons and phone numbers for each of those employers if you'd like.*

---

### Question

**What do you know about (or expect from) the position?**

### Strategy

This is a chance to show off how you've done your homework on the position. State what you understand to be the key competencies needed for the position, the top two or three tasks, the key deliverables expected in the upcoming 6 to 12 months, to whom the position reports, and how it fits in with or supports the overall company.

### "Before" Answer

*Well, I don't know too much yet—just what the person in the telephone interview mentioned to me. I'd love to hear more.*

Magic

### "After"—the "Magic Words" Answer

*As I understand it, I would support the management and marketing of three product lines. I'd be reporting to the Marketing Supervisor.* [Use "I would" and "I'd be" to help interviewers start to visualize you in the position.] *You need someone who has excellent organizational skills, is detail-oriented, and communicates well to collaborate with a range of departments like R&D, fabrication, packaging, and distribution. Conversations with people inside and outside the company lead me to believe that the key tasks are coordinating production of marketing materials and keeping communication lines open with internal and external partners, including your graphic designers and printer, so that everyone is on the same page about deadlines. From a results standpoint, it sounds as though you'd like to see a system developed to improve internal communications, plus build out the collateral marketing materials for the newest addition to your widget product line.*

*If now is the best time, I can tell you how I tackled some similar projects in my role as Marketing Manager at XYZ Company.*

---

## Question

**What do you know about our company?**

## Strategy

Your response should include both an understanding of the company *and* the industry. Be informed! If it's a public company, research it using Hoovers.com or other resources mentioned in chapter 11. If the company has a Web site, read all the significant pages, especially press releases, bios of key decision-makers, products and services pages, career opportunities pages, and so on. Talk to external company contacts, such as suppliers, vendors, consultants, and customers. Talk to internal company contacts, including those in the department you will be joining and those in other departments. Using the Company Profile Worksheet in chapter 11, highlight TOP issues (**T**rends, **O**pportunities, **P**rojects/Problems).

## "Before" Answer

*I know your company has a reputation as a great place to work. Tell me more.*

*Magic*

## "After"—the "Magic Words" Answer

*I understand from my research that the company is one of the leading regional widget manufacturers, and that your top competitors are Acme Widgets and ABC Widge-co. Vernon Reynolds founded the company 60 years ago and his son has been at the helm since 1990. Under his direction, you've added fiber-optic widgets and expanded your distribution from two states to seven. I've spoken with several people outside the company to learn a bit more, and everything I heard was positive. I'm really interested to learn more about this new device that you'll be launching in the near term. One of the customers I spoke with mentioned that they're anxious to get that item shipped. Is this the most important project that you're working on to date, or is the other initiative involving plastic-coated widgets a higher priority?*

Wait for the interviewer to respond. Then, if appropriate, add a SMART Story™ that describes your background as it relates to the company's goals and working priorities.

---

## Question

**What contribution do you anticipate being able to make in this position?**

## Strategy

If this question is asked too early in the interview process, respond with something along these lines: *I'm committed to offering a solid contribution to the department and company and will be better able to indicate what that contribution will be once I know more about the deliverables for the position. May we revisit this question once we've covered some of the results that you're looking for?*

### *"Before" Answer*

*I plan to make a solid contribution—I always have in the past and will do so in the future.*

### *"After"—the "Magic Words" Answer*

*I anticipate contributing in a way that will make you glad you hired me! Seriously, I'm confident I would do something similar to what I've done in my past positions. For instance, I came in to a situation where* _____ [fill in the blank with some numbers-driven fact, such as our accounting department's month-end close was taking 10 days] *and helped to* _____ [fill in the blank, such as reduce the month-end close to just three days].

---

### Question

**Tell me about a time when you worked with a difficult person.**

### Strategy

Responding to the question affirms that you find some people difficult. Rephrase the question in a way that indicates you don't find people difficult. Avoid the temptation to share horror stories about difficult people you have worked with.

### *"Before" Answer*

*Oh my gosh, could I tell you stories. One manager was on an around-the-world ego trip and wouldn't allow anyone to take credit for their own ideas. One time he took one of my ideas and went directly to his director with it. The director loved the idea and implemented it, and I never got a dime for it. That guy was definitely what you'd call difficult.*

### *"After"—the "Magic Words" Answer*

*I tend to not think of people as difficult. Instead, I view situations as opportunities to problem-solve and learn. For instance, in my last position, there was someone on my team who regularly missed deadlines—I'll call him Ralph, which wasn't his real name. When this happened, it prevented me from generating reports for my supervisor who needed them by the end of each month. Rather than blame Ralph for the report being late, I set up a calendaring system to check in with him five days prior to when I needed the information, and then again one day before I needed the information. Even with this reminder system, he still occasionally missed the deadline. That's when I made an appointment to sit down with him and learn more about what he did.*

*It turned out that he was trying to do the work of two people and was very hesitant to delegate tasks. Together, we collaborated on how I personally could access the information I needed rather than have him pull the numbers for me. That was eight months ago, and I haven't missed a deadline since then. It takes me about 30 minutes to get the data, which is less time than it was taking to send multiple reminders to Ralph. I figure that I can't control how other people will act; however, I can control my choices and actions. Sometimes it's more important to look at who is willing to change than who should change.*

---

## Question

**What do you like about your current position?**

**Tell me about work activities you enjoy so much that you lose track of time.**

## Strategy

This is a loaded question. If you describe tasks that aren't part of the new position, you might appear to be a poor fit. The *Before* answer that follows would backfire if the position you're interviewing for requires extroverted activity and the ability to deal with ambiguity. If asked this question early in the interview, give a brief response and talk about tasks that are aligned with what you know of the position from the job description or pre-interview research.

## "Before" Answer

*I really like having structure to my day. I know exactly what's expected of me so that I can shoot for a daily goal and hit it. Each morning, I come in and download the reports that need to be analyzed and get so engrossed that I don't even realize it when someone walks into my cubicle. I've been known to forget to take a lunch break.*

Magic

## "After"—the "Magic Words" Answer

*It's interesting that some of the responsibilities I enjoy the most are similar to what you've described as key to this position. For instance, I really enjoy a day where there's lots of demands and you never quite know what's going to happen next. I work best when there's business action and I can think on my feet. For example….*

---

## Question

**What do you dislike about your current position?**

**What interests you least about your current position?**

**Jobs have pluses and minuses. What do you consider the minuses to your current position?**

## Strategy

The interviewer will be listening with twofold interest. First, do you point to dislikes about your current position that you'll also have to perform in the target position? If so, this will be a red flag to the interviewer. Second, are you not at a loss to list the things you dislike? If so, you'll be branded as negative. If pressed to list something you dislike, point to some minor housekeeping chore that requires little time, such as "backing up my computer" or "changing my outgoing voice-mail message daily." If you choose the latter, consider saying, "I prefer to just jump in and get started with the day, but I know that it's helpful to customers and my work group to know whether I'm in and when I'll be available to return calls."

### *"Before" Answer*

*I guess I'd have to say the deadlines. Sometimes it feels like herding cats to get everyone moving in the same direction and still meet the client's deadlines.*

Magic

### *"After"—the "Magic Words" Answer*

*I don't think that I can point to anything I particularly dislike about managing creative teams. I feel very fortunate that I've found a career that really suits my strengths and talents. Earlier, you mentioned a need for someone who can handle the stress of deadlines. In my last position, I had as many as six significant projects going on at once, all with tight deadlines. I used MS Project to create a tracking system that kept all the projects on a timeline. Prior to two of the six companies contracting with me, they had missed deadlines and gone over budget. I was able to correct that.*

---

### Question

**What are your strengths?**

**What is your greatest strength?**

**What strengths do you bring to the position?**

**What are your outstanding qualities?**

### Strategy

This would be a prime time to pull out your Three-Point Marketing Message (see chapter 5) and make sure it is tailored to the interviewer's primary needs. Recall the resume and sound-bite examples of Chris Caballero, who had mastered the 3 *R*s of sales: **R**esearch, **R**elationships, and **R**evenue Enhancement. Note how she uses this message in the *After* response.

### *"Before" Answer*

*Colleagues tell me I have excellent communication skills, am a people person, and am a quick learner. I'm sure all of these skills would be of value.*

Magic

### *"After"—the "Magic Words" Answer*

*I have a number of strengths that would be of value to the position. As it relates to what we've discussed, I'd point to three key factors.*

*Number one, I'm an excellent researcher—I've developed qualified business leads using traditional and online research methods.... Approximately 40 percent of those leads were converted into new business.*

*Number two, I'm known for building relationships—I've quickly established loyal and trusting relationships with key accounts, networking contacts, and referral sources.*

*And number three, I know how to deliver revenue increases—throughout my career I have set new records for group and convention business at boutique hotels, as well as major-brand properties like yours. In my last position, I increased overall sales 45 percent and increased the average sale 17 percent.*

*May I ask, what kinds of goals are you targeting for the next three to six months?*

---

## Question

**What is your greatest weakness?**

**In what areas do you feel you need work?**

## Strategy

Avoid describing a personality trait as these are harder to "fix." Pointing to a tendency for perfectionism or impatience with lazy people is a worn-out response—interviewers have heard these a million times. Focus on a new skill that can be learned or dazzle them with the insight that your greatest strength can sometimes be your greatest weakness, as the *After* example shows. This strategy moves the interviewer from focusing on the weakness toward hearing a SMART Story™ that describes how you overcame the weakness.

## "Before" Answer

*I'm a perfectionist and sometimes get impatient with people who don't put in a 110 percent effort.*

*Magic*

## "After"—the "Magic Words" Answer

*I have come to realize that, as a manager, my greatest strength—which is my analytical skill—can sometimes be my greatest weakness if I over-rely on my logical, rational side and don't factor in the human equation. What I've done to counter this is to make sure I ask for input from team members who offer different perspectives. This has worked well to bring a balanced, 360-degree analysis to situations. For instance, there was a situation with XYZ Co. where we needed to make cutbacks. It was clear from a business perspective that at least three people in the department needed to be laid off. I sought input from several of my direct reports before making a final decision, and their thoughts helped me to see some options that would achieve our financial goals without jeopardizing morale and stability. I can offer you more details on how that worked out if you would like. [Then, segue into your SMART Story™.]*

---

## Question

**What is your greatest failure?**

**Describe a situation where you failed to reach a goal.**

## Strategy

The interviewer wants to know if you are human—are you humble enough to admit to failure without blaming someone else for it? And, how do you deal with adversity? If possible, pick a situation that is in the past to distance yourself from a recent disappointment. Avoid a response that veers toward personal issues, such as a failed marriage, bankruptcy, or a child gone astray. Referencing a quote may be apropos:

> *"The difference between average people and achieving people is their perception of and response to failure."*
>
> —John Maxwell in *Failing Forward*

> *"I have not failed. I've just found 10,000 ways that won't work."*
>
> —Thomas Edison

> *"A failure is a man who has blundered but is not capable of cashing in on the experience."*
>
> —Elbert Hubbard

### *"Before" Answer*

*Last quarter, our team didn't make our quota, although I was over quota.* (Although this answer sounds positive, it skirts the heart of the question.)

*Magic*

### *"After"—the "Magic Words" Answer*

*I love the famous quote that says "A failure is a man who has blundered but is not capable of cashing in on the experience." I believe that nothing should be defined as a failure if we learn from it and it gives us more currency of knowledge in the days ahead. For instance, back when I first got out of college, I decided to try my hand as a day trader. I read several books on the subject and opened an online account. To make a long story short, the bottom line was that day trading was not my calling. Although I understood the principles of day trading and made a little money, I didn't meet my financial goals and it wasn't something I thoroughly enjoyed. What I learned from the experience is that I excel at things I am passionate about. That's why my career path over the last four years has been in training and development—it's what I'm passionate about. And obviously, that's benefited the people I serve in the business world. For instance, the last program I wrote and implemented at SDS Corporation helped boost productivity among call-center representatives by nearly 15 percent. I'm anxious to learn more about what you consider the top priorities for your training and development department.*

### Question

**Tell me about a difficult problem you've had to deal with.**

### Strategy

Don't stress over this question. What you want to convey to the interviewer is how you go about solving problems. Provide a SMART Story™ that details your thought processes, methods, and mindset for managing the problem. Choose a story that doesn't involve a problem with difficult people, as it might appear you are criticizing others.

## *"Before" Answer*

*My work is full of difficult problems, including a workload that only the Bionic Man could manage, customers who are demanding, and computer equipment and software so outdated that tech support no longer provides support for it. Once, I had to get a report out and the system kept crashing….*

Magic

## *"After"—the "Magic Words" Answer*

*I have a formula for challenging situations. First, I take the attitude that "every problem is perfect"—meaning, the problem has surfaced so that I or others can make some change for the better. Second, I step back and get some perspective on the situation. Third, I generate ideas about how to solve it, which often involves collaborating with others, and then prioritize the options. If the solution is something that needs approval from my supervisor, I present the options and recommendation to her. Finally, I implement the solution. Let me give you an example.*

*When I worked as a service technician for ABC Electronics, my quota required making 15 service calls a day. This was a challenging task in itself, yet I always made my quota, even if it meant working well into the evening. Then, after ABC merged with XYZ, we were given the additional responsibility of selling maintenance contracts. In the past, I had joked that if I had to depend on sales for a living, my family would starve. So, you can well imagine that at first, I wasn't selling any maintenance contracts. My quota was seven contracts a day.*

*I recognized that I needed to follow my advice about every problem being perfect, so I started thinking about what needed to be done. First, I asked my supervisor if there was sales training support. She said there wasn't a budget for it. I then went to one of my co-workers who was selling contracts left and right, and he gave me some good pointers. I also bought some of Zig Ziglar's books on sales and motivation, and those helped as well.*

*I realized that the biggest problem wasn't with the quota—it was with my mindset. I changed my thought process from, "I'm taking these people's hard-earned money" to "this will be a valuable service for a number of people." When that attitude was in place, coupled with some tips from my co-worker, things started to turn around. The first week, I sold four contracts; the second week, I was up to 10; and, by the end of the quarter, I was hitting quota regularly. This put me in the top 20 percent for sales among a team of 30 technicians.*

*What I learned from this is that sales had been difficult because I thought it was difficult. Once I changed my thinking, everything else changed. I just had to believe there was an answer, find resources to help, and then put it into action.*

---

## Question

**Solve this scenario: Production is down 65 percent due to a 90 percent turnover rate and, in the next six months, we want you to double production from two years when we were at record productivity. How would you solve this problem and meet our goal?**

### Strategy

This is the "impossible scenario" question. Beware of providing an answer that implies you can solve the issue, or you'll look either inexperienced or unrealistic. It's best to describe the process you would go through and then relate a SMART Story™ that is similar to (but not as Herculean as) what the interviewer wants accomplished.

### "Before" Answer

*I don't think it can be done.*

### "After"—the "Magic Words" Answer

*First, I'd work with the management team to ensure that SMART goals were in place, meaning* S*pecific,* M*easurable,* A*chievable,* R*ealistic, and* T*ime-Sensitive. Then I'd analyze the key components to productivity—people, systems, and equipment. From there, I'd compare what's happening to best practices in the industry. If turnover were one of the main issues, I'd address recruiting, training, and working conditions.*

*I'd also invite input from the production floor, as I've achieved double-digit increases in productivity in the past based on great suggestions from my team. Then, I'd write and implement a plan. I can give you an example of how I led a similar turnaround for XYZ Company a few years ago. The results were similar to what you're after, although it took us a bit longer.*

---

### Question

**What opportunities have you created for yourself in your current position?**

### Strategy

This is a question designed to gauge your initiative (recall that initiative is typically the single best indicator of success). Offer a SMART Story™. Be cautious that your story doesn't paint you as someone who is self-serving or opportunistic. Employers love self-starters, so make sure you have a good example for this answer. And, if you don't have an immediate answer, what *can* you do to create opportunity for yourself in your current position?

### "Before" Answer

*The structure of my current department doesn't really allow for many changes. I suppose I'd have to say that just doing my job well has led to me getting high marks on my most recent performance evaluation.*

### "After"—the "Magic Words" Answer

*I always look for opportunities. When I started work at my current employer, we had monthly staff meetings. I noticed that people often used these as venues for grousing, which impacted the morale and productivity of the meeting. I went to my boss privately and suggested something that was done at my prior employer. The suggestion involved having weekly meetings where each staff member came to the meeting with one opportunity idea. There was to be no criticism of the idea or comments about why something would not work. Then, at the end of the meeting everyone voted secretly on the idea they thought was best. At the end of the month, our boss chose one of the four ideas for the month and implemented it.*

*This really changed the dynamic of our meetings. People got charged up about what was possible instead of focusing on negatives. My boss liked the idea and put me in charge of leading the portion of the weekly meeting where we discussed the opportunity ideas. Because I took the initiative on this, I was then selected to take the lead on some of the ideas that were chosen for implementation. I can give you an example if you'd like. [Then lead into a SMART Story™ if the interviewer says yes.]*

---

## Question
**Tell me about a time when you persuaded others to take action.**

## Strategy
Whether or not you're applying for supervisory/management positions, employers want to know how well you influence others. Pick a situation that will be significant because you might not get another question like this. Use a SMART Story™ that illustrates a benefit to the company/team and not just you, as the following *Before* answer shows.

## "Before" Answer
*I wanted some time off to travel but had used up all my personal time. I convinced a couple of co-workers to trade several shifts with me so that I could get the time I needed.*

## "After"—the "Magic Words" Answer
Consider this example for a support-level candidate:

*In my role as secretary to the production supervisor for an organic baby-food processor, I noted that we could be doing a better job of communicating with growers about projected harvest dates. Frequently what would happen is the growers would report their picking schedules, with produce available during the second week of July. Production would then schedule a full crew for that Monday; but in reality, the produce wouldn't be ready until Wednesday or Thursday. We had to pay workers for coming in and then send them home. I thought that there had to be a solution to this, but didn't immediately think of anything. A few weeks later, I had jury duty, which required that I call in every night to learn whether I had an assignment. I wondered, why not do something similar for our growers and production crews? I suggested it to my supervisor. At first, he just listened and said he'd think about it. A week later, I approached him about it again and told him that I'd done some research on how a hot line could be set up for growers and then a general information line for employees who would be grouped into Team A, B, and C. When the harvest was heavy, all teams would be called in. I also spoke with the Field Liaison to get his input on how this could work. And, I penciled out a potential savings of 7 percent on labor if we didn't have to call in people and then send them home. My supervisor took this to our operations*

*manager and the system was approved with some modifications. At the end of the season, we achieved a 12 percent reduction in labor, which translated to a five-figure savings. I felt quite proud that I had a part in that.*

---

## Question

**That is an excellent answer. Could you also give me an example that didn't have such a positive outcome?**

## Strategy

A skilled interviewer will ask this question to get a balanced perspective, especially if you're acing every question with particularly positive responses. Don't be tempted to don a Superman cape. It is appropriate to share stories that didn't have a neat-and-tidy Hollywood ending. You will be more suspect if you can't admit to things occasionally not going well. Offer a SMART Story™, then wrap up the response with ideas outlined in the *After* example that follows.

### "Before" Answer

*I really can't think of any.*

### "After"—the "Magic Words" Answer

*Benjamin Franklin said, "The things which hurt, instruct." I can offer an example of how things didn't turn out and what I learned from the event. [Offer a SMART Story™. Then close with something like this:] When things don't go well, I follow the advice that Dr. John Maxwell presents in his book* Failing Forward.

*I first look at the cause. Was it the situation, someone else, or myself?*

- *Was it a failure or just falling short?*
- *What successes are contained in the failure?*
- *What can I learn from what happened?*
- *Am I grateful for the experience?*
- *How can I turn this into a success?*
- *Who can help me with this issue?*
- *Where do I go from here?*

---

## Question

**How would you go about solving the following problem: _____?**

## Strategy

This question probes your decision-making process. The problem presented will be something related to the position, such as reducing the time to do a task, cutting costs, increasing productivity, or improving morale. Describe gathering input from important parties yet without relying totally on others to make the decision. If possible, relate the question to your past experience so that the interviewer sees your experience with this issue.

### *"Before" Answer*

*Yes, I've solved that kind of problem before. I analyzed the situation, put a plan into place, and executed the plan. As a result, we went from a product development cycle of 12 months to 7 months.*

Magic

### *"After"—the "Magic Words" Answer*

*That's an interesting challenge. I encountered something similar in my current position a few months ago and I can share with you how I approached it and what worked for our company. Bottom line, as Director of Product Development I was able to reduce the time it took to get a product to market from 12 months to 7 months by working more closely with my counterparts in engineering, manufacturing, and marketing. Here's what I did to make that happen.* [Offer a complete SMART Story™ with emphasis on the action to reveal your decision-making process.] *Of course, there might be some adjustments necessary to fit this process to your organizational structure, and I'd be happy to hear your thoughts on this.*

---

### Question

**Why do you work?**

**Why do you do what you do?**

**Why are you a _____?**

**What are you most passionate about?**

### Strategy

These questions are all related. The interviewer wants to know both your motives and how to motivate you! Consider linking this answer to the Fulfillment statement you wrote in chapter 3 (see "Step 4: Define Fulfillment"). Remember that fulfillment is what transforms your position from paycheck to purpose. Purpose produces passion, and passion fuels perseverance, enthusiasm, creativity, productivity, and income to peak levels. You can also point to items from your list of Things That Matter (see chapter 3, "Step 3: Think About the Things That Matter").

### *"Before" Answer*

*Well, it's pretty obvious, I guess, since everybody needs to pay the bills!*

*Or, I work because I enjoy a sense of accomplishment.*

### "After"—the "Magic Words" Answer

*I am a Financial Manager because it's a great venue for my values of order, structure, ethics, and financial integrity. When a company has its financial house in order, it is in a position to thrive and prosper, which means that its shareholders, employees, and customers will also prosper. I take great pleasure and pride in helping make that happen.*

---

### Question

**How do you handle criticism?**

### Strategy

The underlying question here: "Is this person teachable?" Explain how you've openly received criticism and what you learned from it. Point to an example in the past so that it doesn't appear you made a recent mistake, and choose something that isn't related to character.

### "Before" Answer

*I take criticism in stride.*

### "After"—the "Magic Words" Answer

*It used to be that I would get annoyed by criticism. It wasn't until I took a different perspective on the subject that I realized it could help me improve and be better at what I do. I especially appreciate it when criticism is constructive, delivered with a respectful attitude, and with the intent to bring benefit to the team. For instance, when I first started at BBB Company, my boss sat in on a meeting that I had with one of our vendors. After the meeting, he first shared with me what went well and what I'd done right. Then, he shared with me what I could do to be even better. Specifically, it was about having better access to the paperwork around the vendor's history so that I could have more leverage in the negotiations. He then helped me visualize how doing that would enhance the negotiations. He was right, and s ince that time I've been thorough about preparing for meetings and visualizing a positive outcome.*

*I've used a similar technique in mentoring my staff, where I sandwich the areas for improvement between what they've done well and how the change will enhance their success.*

---

### Question

**How do you learn best?**

### Strategy

This question is a little different from the prior question about your favorite teacher. Now, the interviewer wants to know how you learn best. Review the three primary learning styles outlined in chapter 14 (see "Connect with Different Types of Interviewers") so that you understand your own learning style. Then, give an example of how you learned something faster using that style.

### "Before" Answer

*I think I learn best through trial-and-error. If people just explain something to me, it doesn't seem to stick as well as when they let me have some hands-on practice.*

Magic

### "After"—the "Magic Words" Answer

*I have a friend who is a trainer, so she has helped me understand that there are different learning styles. The three most common are auditory, visual, and kinesthetic. Because I'm committed to learning things as efficiently as possible, I explored and found that my natural style was visual. Let me give you an example of how that helped me learn a new program.*

*Some time ago, my boss had asked me to learn PowerPoint. I taught myself by carving out some personal time in the evenings to go through the tutorials. Knowing that demonstrations, diagrams, and pictures were helpful to me, this worked out well. Within a week, I was producing PowerPoint presentations that incorporated advanced features such as tables, images, and animations. My boss asked me to share some of what I'd learned with other users in our office.*

---

### Question

**How does this position fit into your long-term career plans? (or Where do you see yourself in 5 to 10 years?)**

### Strategy

Some people have a clear picture of where they want to be in five years. Some do not. Rather than share a future vision that might not complement what the company needs, consider framing your response in a broad, noncommittal manner. Who can tell the future?

### "Before" Answer

*I'd like to be in your position in five years.* [This might be a good answer if the interviewer is your potential manager and is looking to groom a successor so that he, too, can climb the corporate ladder. However, unless you know it to be the case, this response can be a bit of a risk, not to mention a cliché.]

Magic

### "After"—the "Magic Words" Answer

*I don't have a crystal ball, but I can tell you what's most important to me for the future. I want to continually add to my skills, take on new challenges, and contribute value to the company. I'm not certain what shape that will take, but I believe it will involve using my strengths in the areas of _____, _____, and _____.* [These should be strengths that are required in the position for which you're interviewing.] *I know that this position often branches out into either _____ or _____. At this point, I'd be open to either track, depending on where the company might need me most. In the meantime, I like preparing for "planned happenstance"—meaning that I will develop myself in a manner that attracts opportunities.*

---

## Question
**Why are you the best candidate for this position?**

**Why should we hire you?**

## Strategy
This question will often be asked at the end of the interview. It's a great time to pull out your Three-Point Marketing Message and link it to important deliverables you've uncovered during the course of the interview.

## "Before" Answer
*I'm an excellent case manager who is great with people. I have the degree and certifications you're looking for, and this sounds like a great place to work, with people I can really connect with. I'd be more committed than anyone.*

*Magic*

## "After"—the "Magic Words" Answer
*As a case manager with more than 15 years of experience, I have a unique combination of counseling, teaching, and client advocacy work with high-risk youth—all of which you've indicated as important to the position. I've outlined a number of specific successes in each of those three areas during the course of our conversation.*

*Beyond those successes, I'd have to say that I have a heart for working with this population. If you don't mind me sharing a personal story...ten years ago, I had a nephew who committed suicide. Had there been services available to him like your organization is offering now, he might still be alive. That experience has motivated me to become great at what I do. I have letters from parents who've thanked me for making a difference in their child's life, and that is my greatest reward.*

*Given my experience and commitment, I don't think there's anyone who can bring you more knowledge, resources, or passion for seeing your clients succeed.*

---

## Question
**The salary range for the position is $\_\_–\_\_,000. Is that acceptable to you? Have you made more than this?**

## Strategy
This question frequently comes in a telephone interview or first interview. If you answer, "yes" to the first question but ask for more when salary negotiations roll around, you will appear insincere or dishonest. To your "yes," add the phrase "provided the actual job is consistent with the job description I was given." This will give you some latitude because positions oftentimes have more responsibility than what's found in the formal job description.

## "Before" Answer
*Yes, that's fine. No, I've not made more than this.*

### *"After"—the "Magic Words" Answer*

*Magic*

[If the salary range is within your range:] *Although salary isn't the most important factor in a job, I'm interested in fair compensation for the value I contribute. Your salary range aligns with my research, provided the actual job is consistent with the job description I was given. That range is consistent with my past experience.*

Or, *That salary range is about 15 percent lower than what my research shows. Actually, I'm wondering whether I could learn more about the position first. It's been my experience that if I'm the right person for the position, we'll be able to come to agreement on the terms. And, yes, I have made more than this in the past. Salary isn't the most important factor in a job for me, although I'm interested in fair compensation for the value I contribute.*

---

### *Question*
**What questions do you have?**

### *Strategy*
This is a great time to check your notepad that contains the clarifying or collaborating questions you'll want to ask from chapter 14. If there are questions you have that haven't yet been covered, this is the time to ask them.

### *"Before" Answer*
*No, I don't. You've been very thorough.*

### *"After"—the "Magic Words" Answer*

*Magic*

*Actually, we've really covered a lot of ground already. Most of the questions I have here on my list were already answered. I do have just a couple more that I'd like to discuss. Could you tell me....*

---

## 10 Quick Tips for Responding to FAQs

Let these 10 tips guide you in responding, remembering that answers should always be

1. **Positive:** Videotape yourself or write out your responses and analyze them for any shades of negativity. Listen for the howcha's (see "Check Your Motive and Attitude" in chapter 14). Prior to the interview, empty your mind and heart of clutter, cares, and concerns—put them in an imaginary box if need be. Then, picture your future self, confidently and enthusiastically doing the work of your dreams. Now infuse your voice with energy, optimism, interest, and respect.

*(continued)*

*(continued)*

Absolutely no accusing, making veiled inferences, whining, blaming, criticizing, or complaining allowed! For each response you practice, ask yourself the following:

- How might this be worded in a more positive light?

- Is what I'm saying building or busting my case?

- Is my response making the interviewer more confident and certain I can do the job?

Never reveal feelings of discouragement in an interview, even if you sense that the interview isn't going well. You have nothing to gain; interviewers won't hire out of pity. They want to hire winners, and winners persevere with positivity!

2. **Pertinent:** Choose the most relevant story or information for your response. Resist the urge to over-tell or share information that does not add to your qualifications.

3. **Precise:** Be brief, succinct, and specific. Avoid rambling, as this Before example shows:

   *Before:* We had a problem with employees leaving. Actually, they would stay for just a short amount of time because we were hiring a lot of college students. That caused some interesting generational communication issues, actually, but I can tell you about that later if you'd like. So, my boss formed a team and we put in place a number of programs during the time I was there that significantly helped our retention numbers.

   *After:* I was asked to serve on a four-member team tasked with improving employee retention. We developed and implemented programs that improved our retention from 75 percent to 92 percent over an 18-month period. I can tell you more about my specific role on the team if you'd like.

4. **Profit-Oriented:** Everything you say (and everything you do once you're on the job) should be about contributing value, and therefore profit, to the company.

5. **SMART and Bell-Shaped:** When it comes to behavioral questions, respond with a SMART Story™, one that outlines the Situation and More, Action taken, Result achieved, and Tie-in to the

interviewer's question or a competency Theme. Remember to make your SMART Story™ bell-shaped (see chapter 15).

6. **Bulleted:** When you're giving a lengthy response (such as a SMART Story™), deliver it in bullet points or with numbers. It will help the interviewer to follow along. And, if ever you sense you're losing or "snoozing" the interviewer, stop and ask a question to engage him or her!

7. **Perceptive:** Don't let your professional guard down when the interviewer seems chatty or informal. Many candidates have lost job offers by misinterpreting interviewer casualness as a signal that the interviewer is befriending them. (One pharmaceutical candidate lost points—and the job offer—when an interviewer used this tactic. The candidate got carried away describing how much time and effort she was putting into planning her wedding. This personal information caused the interviewer to be concerned that the candidate wouldn't be able to give her full attention to an important product launch.)

8. **Timed:** A response lasting one to two minutes, or a little longer if you're answering a behavioral question, is fine. If you need to talk longer, break up the response with a question midway:

   * "Am I giving you the details you need?"

   * "Would you like an example of that?"

   * "What have you seen to be the case in your organization?"

9. **Fresh:** Don't backtrack! You can occasionally reference a story that you've already given, but avoid reusing stories multiple times as it may confuse (or bore) the interviewer. This is why it's important to have plenty of SMART Stories™.

10. **Interactive:** Avoid yes-no answers—they don't encourage conversation. Occasionally use a "menu" approach where you offer the interviewer two or three options and ask which one they'd like to hear more about. For instance, in response to the question, "What are your greatest strengths?" you might say, "I've been complimented by supervisors for the ability to conceptualize, strategize, and execute. Is one of these more important than another for this position? If so, I'd be happy to start there with an example of how I've used that skill."

# Master Your Industry-Specific Questions (ISQs)

You've just learned a number of frequently asked questions (FAQs) that might be asked of any candidate. But that's rarely where the interview ends. Hiring managers want to make sure you have the industry knowledge and depth of experience needed to perform and excel in the job. To determine this, they will ask Industry-Specific Questions (ISQs), many of which will be behavioral interview questions (see chapter 15 for tips on managing behavioral interviews).

## 10 Quick Tips for Answering ISQs

To prepare for ISQs, follow these tips:

1. **Ask!:** Network with people in your industry to learn at least 5, and preferably 10, Industry-Specific Questions that might be asked in an interview.

2. **Be SMART:** Whenever possible, offer a SMART Story™ to give the interviewer a behavioral, fact-based response. Vary the length of your responses (see chapter 15 on behavioral interviews).

3. **Occasionally preface responses with a Philosophical comment:** State your philosophy or position on a subject. For instance, "I believe that _____ [mention whatever relevant issue is at hand] is one of the top five factors for successful widgetry."

4. **Occasionally preface responses with an Overview statement:** Make an overview or umbrella statement. For instance, "With 10 years of experience at ABC Company, I have solid skills in the full widget-making lifecycle, including R&D, testing, marketing, sales, distribution, and customer service. To answer your question more specifically, I can point to a time when…."

5. **Occasionally preface responses with an Enthusiastic remark:** Convey enthusiasm, excitement, and passion. For instance, "Absolutely! That's one of my favorite responsibilities. (Or, "I am well-versed in that!") The situation that readily comes to mind is this…."

6. **Occasionally preface responses with a Tease:** Tell them the result at the beginning of the story to hold their attention. For instance, "I can recap how I led a cross-training initiative at ABC Widget Co. that saved $90,000 in overtime costs and improved productivity 7 percent. Here's what the situation looked like…."

7. **Anticipate:** Prepare to shine, even when you don't have the exact experience an interviewer is looking for. See Tips 8 through 10 (Assistance, Observations, Research) for options.

8. **Describe assistance:** Describe how you have assisted with elements of a successful product launch using a SMART Story™ format. "Recently, my current employer launched a new over-the-counter drug that exceeded its projections by 17 percent. My role in the project was as assistant product manager…." After stating the results, tie in the story to your history of continually taking on larger challenges with success and the confidence you have in managing this new responsibility.

9. **Describe observations:** Use a SMART Story™ format to reference how you observed a successful person handle the situation, along with what worked and what you would do differently to improve the situation. "What comes to mind is how I have observed my current company's product manager handling the launch of a new in-home security device. Although I didn't participate directly in the project, I closely observed her actions because of my passion for product management…."

10. **Describe research:** Describe how you would theoretically handle it using the SMART format. Consider introducing your response with, "I anticipated that would be important to you, so I did some research to enhance my knowledge on that topic. Here's how I would handle it."

# Field Illegal and Awkward Interview Questions

Beyond FAQs and ISQs, you'll also need to be wary of illegal and awkward interview questions. Let's look at illegal questions first.

## How to Spot Illegal Interview Questions

Today's employers are pretty savvy about what they can and cannot legally ask in a job interview. However, this doesn't mean that you won't be asked illegal questions, so it's best to give thought ahead of time to your answers. The following table outlines illegal and legal questions for a variety of categories.

### Table 16.1: Illegal and Legal Interview Questions

| Category | Illegal Questions | Legal Questions |
| --- | --- | --- |
| National Origin/Citizenship | • Are you a U.S. citizen?<br>• Where were you/your parents born?<br>• What is your native language? | • Are you authorized to work in the United States?<br>• What languages do you read/speak/write fluently? (Legal to ask only when relevant to the performance of the job.) |

*(continued)*

*(continued)*

| Category | Illegal Questions | Legal Questions |
|---|---|---|
| Marital/Family Status | • Are you married, single, divorced, separated, engaged, or widowed?<br>• With whom do you live?<br>• Do you plan to have a family? When?<br>• How many children do you have? How old?<br>• What are your child-care arrangements?<br>• Does your husband support your decision to work? | • What's your marital status?<br>• Would you be willing to relocate if necessary?<br>• Is there any reason that you will not be able to come to work every day, on time? (This question is acceptable if it is asked of all candidates.)<br>• Would you be able and willing to travel as needed for the job? (This question is legal if it is asked of all candidates.)<br>• Would you be able and willing to work overtime as necessary? (This question is legal assuming it is asked of all candidates.) |
| Age | • How old are you?<br>• When did you graduate?<br>• What's your birth date? | • Are you over the age of 18?<br>• Are you old enough to work? |
| Affiliations | • What clubs or social organizations do you belong to? | • List any memberships in professional groups or other organizations that you consider relevant to your ability to perform this job. |
| Religion | • What religion do you practice?<br>• Are you a member of a particular church?<br>• The job requires that you work on Fridays, Saturdays, and Sundays. Will your religion cause a problem with this schedule? | • The position requires that you work Fridays, Saturdays, and Sundays. Will you be able to work these days? |
| Disabilities | • Do you have any disabilities?<br>• Please complete the following medical history.<br>• Have you had any recent or past illnesses or operations? If yes, list | • Do you need an accommodation to perform the job? (This question can be asked only *after* a job offer has been made.)<br>• Are you able to perform the essential functions of |

them and give dates when these occurred.
- What was the date of your last physical exam?
- How's your family's health?
- When did you lose your eyesight? How?
- Have you ever filed a workers' compensation claim?

this job? (This question is fine after the interviewer has thoroughly described the job.)
- Can you demonstrate how you would perform the following job-related functions?
- As part of the hiring process, after a job offer has been made, you will be required to undergo a medical exam. (This must be a condition of employment for all entering employees in that position. Exam results must be kept strictly confidential, except that medical/safety personnel may be informed if emergency medical treatment is required. Supervisors may also be informed about necessary job accommodations, based on exam results.)

| | | |
|---|---|---|
| Medical History | • Please complete the following medical history.<br>• What current or past medical problems might limit your ability to do this job?<br>• Do you smoke?<br>• Have you had a history of mental illness? | • Are you able to perform the essential functions of this position? (This can be asked only after the interviewer explains the position.)<br>• Our smoking policy is this… can you adhere to it? |
| Arrest/Prison Record | • Have you ever been arrested?<br>• Have you ever pled guilty to a crime?<br>• Have you ever been in trouble with the law? | • Have you been convicted of a felony within the past seven years?<br>• Do you have a valid driver's license? |
| Military | • Were you honorably discharged?<br>• Tell me about your military record.<br>• Have you served in the military of countries other than the United States? | • In what branch of the Armed Forces did you serve?<br>• What type of training or education did you receive in the military? |

*(continued)*

*(continued)*

| Category | Illegal Questions | Legal Questions |
|----------|-------------------|-----------------|
| Credit | • Do you have any credit problems?<br>• Have you recently filed for personal bankruptcy?<br>• Is your salary presently subject to legal attachment or wage garnishment? | • If hired, would you allow us to order a credit report to confirm statements made on your employment application (provided you receive a copy)? |

Be aware that it is also illegal for employers to ask

- For photographs before hiring
- For references from clergy before hiring
- Questions of females that are not asked of males

## A Skillful Three-Point System for Responding to Illegal Questions

Now that you know how to spot illegal questions, how will you respond to them? Basically, you have three options:

- Flat-out tell the interviewer, "That's an illegal question—you're not allowed to ask me that." You might as well tell the interviewer, "You're stupid" or "You're breaking the law"—neither of which will rack up any points for rapport and relationship building. Consider that it's quite possible the interviewer is simply untrained and unaware of the illegality of the question.

- Directly answer the illegal question, but run the risk of ruining your candidacy.

- Leverage the question as an opportunity to sell your character and strengths.

Obviously, the latter option is the only viable choice. Use this three-step process to leverage questions to your advantage:

1. **Avoid** a direct answer if the illegal question has the slightest chance of hurting your candidacy.

2. **Address** the underlying concern.

3. **Accentuate** a positive character trait or skill in your answer.

Let me illustrate. The interviewer asks: *Are you married?* Although illegal, it seems a fairly innocuous question. No harm in answering, right? Actually, it depends on the interviewer's perspective—something you're not necessarily privy to. A "no" answer might be interpreted as "he is unable to make a commitment or not ready for responsibility." A "yes" answer might be interpreted as "she is too busy with family to put in overtime." Either way, you lose.

Note the following *Before* and *After* responses to the question, "Are you married?"

### Before

> Yes, I am married, and happily so for 20 years. We have four kids, with two in college, so you can imagine that my tuition bills are pretty hefty.

The *Before* response focuses wrongly on the candidate's needs. Mentioning college tuition might backfire when it comes time for salary negotiations, as employers want to pay based on your value, not on your economic situation.

### After

> I am in a solid relationship and am blessed to have someone who supports me wholly in my career. Some people may wonder whether my personal life will restrict the amount of travel or extended hours necessary for the position. I can assure you there won't be a problem. My last position required 50 percent overnight travel, and I thrive on that sort of schedule. I give the company 18-hour days when I'm traveling, as I find that quiet time in the hotel at night is perfect for getting a jump-start on planning or preparing for presentations.

Note how the *After* response follows the three-point Avoid—Address—Accentuate strategy. The first sentence ("I am in a solid relationship…") avoids a direct answer to the question. The next two sentences ("Some people may wonder…") addresses the underlying concern. And the final two sentences ("My last position required…") accentuates a positive.

## How to Manage Awkward or "Sticky-Wicket" Questions

We've covered how to respond to FAQs, ISQs, and illegal or borderline-illegal questions. Now let's look at just a few more questions that are perfectly legal for the interviewer to ask, but could prove to be sticky wickets for you.

### Difficult Question

**"Why have you been unemployed so long?"**

### The "Magic Words" Answer

Avoid blaming the economy or the state of your industry. Be upbeat and optimistic as you say something like this: "I've taken the time to find something that would be the right fit and, in the meantime, kept busy by sharpening some of my industry knowledge through Web-based courses. I had offers for a couple of opportunities, but they weren't a good fit. With respect to the right fit, I've specifically targeted situations where I can leverage my strengths in a _____ (fill in the blank with the type of company) where I could play a role in setting policy and driving results. I also wanted an environment that would be a good fit. I'm confident that will be the case here. You mentioned, for instance, that you need someone who can…."

## Difficult Question
**"You have a gap on your resume between your last two employers. What did you do during that time?"**

### The "Magic Words" Answers
Honesty is usually the best policy, provided you don't give more details than absolutely necessary. For instance, if the gap was several months to one year, it's acceptable to mention that you were, for instance,

- Taking maternity leave
- Caring for children
- Caring for a terminally ill family member
- Taking time off for travel abroad
- Planning or getting settled after a move
- Taking time to pursue studies

If the time was spent entirely in a longer-than-hoped-for job search, be ready to point to some other concurrent activity, such as

- Taking some industry-relevant classes
- Volunteering in an activity related to your profession
- Taking care of family responsibilities

Consider using this "lottery" analogy to describe your excitement to get back to work. "Many people say that if they won the lottery they'd retire to Tahiti. I can tell you that I'd be climbing the walls if I couldn't work. I love the pace and the energy that I draw from work, and I'm excited that this opportunity looks like such a good match for my skills."

## Difficult Question
**"Why was your employment period with this company such a short time?"**

### The "Magic Words" Answers
If the employer was the reason, you might say that the company was undercapitalized and reduced its force. If this wasn't the case, you might say that the position changed significantly after you came on board and didn't offer the level of responsibility that was originally intended. When preparing your answers, recall the options for leaving an employer listed earlier in the chapter—to learn more, earn more, grow more, work more, and commute/travel less.

### Difficult Question
"Why aren't you making more at this point in your career?"

### The "Magic Words" Answers
This might be an opportunity to find out what salary range the employer has in mind. "I recognize that my current salary isn't what it should be, and that's one of the reasons that I'm sitting here with you today! The contributions I've made to my past employer have resulted in tangible cost savings [or profit increases], and I'm confident I can do the same for you. With that in mind, what salary range did you have in mind for someone with my skills?"

### Difficult Question
"Have you ever been fired?"

### The "Magic Words" Answers
The employer's concern is whether you were dismissed for lack of performance or an inability to get along with people. Use the preemptive strike here—find a way to bring this up early on and on your own terms. For instance, when the interviewer is walking through your resume, you might say, *"By the way, I want you to know that the reason I left the position that ended in 1999 was because I was asked to leave. Here's what happened…."* (Don't blame or complain about anyone.)

If you messed up, say so without degrading yourself or offering excessive details. Talk about the lessons learned from that experience: "I made the mistake of not following through on an important order—it cost the company some business. I learned an important lesson, which is to always…. I wanted to bring this up so that you didn't think I was trying to hide something."

If you were fired because of a change in management, speak to this without belittling the management: "There was a change in management, which led to me and a number of my colleagues being let go."

If it was a personality clash: "I've been fortunate to work with a number of fine supervisors over the years, and I've had excellent relationships with all of them, save one individual. I'm disappointed that there wasn't an opportunity to work further on the relationship. You'd probably like to hear some other people's perspectives on this as well, and I'm happy to provide you some references from that employment period." (Then, be sure to let your references know that someone might be calling about this.)

### Difficult Question
"Tell me about a situation where you had a strained relationship with a boss or co-worker."

*Magic*

### The "Magic Words" Answers

The question presumes that you had a strained relationship. Do not admit to strained relationships, and never badmouth or criticize anyone. "I'm happy to report that I can't tell you about a situation where relationships were strained." The word "strained" implies you couldn't or wouldn't take the initiative to resolve a problem. There might have been a situation where another individual was difficult to be around on a regular basis, but that doesn't mean *your* relationship was strained. You can use a similar response strategy to the question, "Have you worked under bosses who weren't ideal?" earlier in this chapter.

### Difficult Question

**You don't have the degree we're looking for. Or, why didn't you complete your college degree?**

*Magic*

### The "Magic Words" Answers

"I can understand your concern about that. Tell me, though, what is it specifically you want to have accomplished as a result of that degree?" After you get some specific deliverables from the interviewer, you can then describe how your experience will allow you to meet those deliverables. Also, if a specific degree is very important to the interviewer, explore whether you could start the training while employed with the company.

Here's another tack you can take with this answer. "I understand that good academic training is important, but I also look at people who didn't complete high school, like the Wright Brothers, Albert Einstein, Steve Jobs of Apple, and Henry Ford. It was Ford who said, 'Whether you think you can do a thing or not, you're right.' I not only think I can do this, I know I can do it. And, although you may have candidates with more impressive degrees on their resumes, I'm confident that no one will give you better hands-on experience, insight into these issues, or passion toward carrying them out than I will."

### Difficult Question

**What is the biggest work-related mistake you've made?**

*Magic*

### The "Magic Words" Answers

Point to something early in your career, rather than a recent mistake. Employers won't buy it if you tell them you haven't made any mistakes. No one walks on water! Here's an example: *"I'd have to say that my biggest work-related mistake was not putting contingency plans in place when I planned a presentation to be given by a well-known author. I didn't follow up to confirm 24 hours in advance, and the author had gotten the date mixed up on her calendar, so she didn't show up and couldn't be reached. I had a room of 400 people waiting for this person, and she never made it. I had egg on my face, and learned a very critical lesson that day, which is to never assume anything and always double-check everything and always, always, always have a backup plan! To prove I learned my lesson, I can tell you that the last special event I planned, I did have a backup speaker!"*

## Difficult Question
**What would you do if your supervisor asked you to do something that went against your ethics?**

*Magic*

## The "Magic Words" Answers
Dialogue with the interviewer and do your best to toss this question back into the interviewer's court. Ask questions such as, "Is there a particular situation you can cite that would help me get a better understanding of this?" "Can you tell me what your concern is?" "Has this been an issue in the past?" "How would you prefer I handle the situation?" Your response might include something to this effect: "I would clarify what it was the supervisor needed done. If it appeared to be out of line with company policy, I would bring this up in a nonjudgmental way, as my loyalty would be toward making sure the company remains out of anyone's legal crosshairs." Note that this is a situation where you would *not* want to offer a SMART Story™ because doing so might slander a prior colleague.

---

### 10 Quick Tips for Responding to Illegal or Awkward Questions

1. **Reconcile yourself to the fact that you will probably have to answer illegal questions.** Give interviewers the benefit of the doubt—perhaps they are stressed or haven't been trained in legally compliant interviewing practices. Correcting them or showing that you know more than they do about legal questions will probably not win you any points (unless you're applying for a human resources position where you should know these types of laws).

2. **The best option for answering illegal or awkward questions is to follow the three A's: Avoid, Address, and Accentuate.** Avoid a direct answer if the question has the slightest chance of hurting your candidacy. Address the underlying concern. Finally, accentuate a positive character trait or skill in your answer.

3. **Remember to add a SMART Story™ to your Avoid-Address-Accentuate response when appropriate.**

4. **To improve your chances of acing the interview, follow this rule of thumb: Apply only for positions you can manage.** Anything else will cause you to fall short on the job, damaging your self-esteem and work record. For instance, if for health reasons your energy level isn't up to working 60-hour work weeks, don't apply to a company that expects those hours.

5. **Don't say more than you need to.** Do not tell employers anything they are not legally authorized to ask!

*(continued)*

*(continued)*

6. **Resist any urge to reveal information that might cause a future inconvenience to the employer, such as the possibility of starting a family or requiring surgery in the next year.** No one knows what tomorrow holds! However, if you are pregnant and don't plan to return to work after delivery, don't apply for a full-time, permanent position. If you know you are scheduled for surgery soon, wait until you've recuperated to apply for a full-time, permanent position.

7. **The 10 areas that often lead to illegal or awkward questions include national origin, age, marital/family status, affiliations, religion, disabilities, medical/personal history, arrest/prison record, military service, and credit history.** Which of these might be problematic for you?

8. **Write a personalized list of illegal or awkward questions that you dread being asked.** Practice the Avoid-Address-Accentuate strategy for illegal questions. Practice putting a Positive-Pertinent-Precise spin on awkward questions (see "10 Quick Tips for Responding to FAQs" earlier in this chapter).

9. **Prepare for reference and background checks by lining up references who will speak about you with enthusiasm and support.**

10. **If you have any concerns about potential skeletons in your closet, pay to have a reference/background check on yourself so that you'll know what employers might learn.** With respect to your rights in reference/background checks, employers must obtain prior authorization from you and, if they base a decision not to hire you on negative background information found during the check, are obligated to provide you the results and give you the opportunity to dispute the findings.

# Chapter Wrap-Up

Regardless of the interview question, remember the mantra you've heard throughout this book:

**It's about them, not you.**

Please be clear on this philosophy: It is *not* because I am encouraging you to be misleading or superficial. It is because every successful professional knows that if you first find the "what's in it for them" in a business relationship, people will open up, cooperate, and support you. Once this is in place, you can then decide on the *what's in it for you.*

Throughout the interview, weave in language you developed from chapter 5, including your

- **Three-Point Marketing Message**—a theme of knowledge, skills, or abilities relevant to the position

- **Benefits and Buying Motivators**—how you can bring more productivity and profitability to the company than your competitors might

---

## Magical Coaching Tips

Do some practice interviewing with a colleague or friend. Practice just 5 to 10 questions at a time. Videotape or audiotape your sessions. Then, review the tape and evaluate your responses using the following form (see "10 Quick Tips for Responding to FAQs" earlier in this chapter for details on each column heading). Give yourself a checkmark if your response addresses the column heading. Note that the SMART and Bell-Shaped columns (marked by asterisks) apply only when behavioral-based questions are asked.

For Industry-Specific Questions, identify two or three industry contacts you will approach (for ideas on identifying contacts, refer to "Step 4: Talk to People in the Know Through Focused Networking" in chapter 11):

1. _____

2. _____

3. _____

Ask the following questions to contacts who have been on recent job interviews:

- What are five industry-specific or technical questions you were asked in your recent interviews?

- What responses did the interviewers react favorably to?

Ask the following questions to contacts who are experienced in interviewing and hiring:

- What five industry-specific or technical questions do you regularly ask when interviewing candidates?

- What competencies or knowledge are you probing for with those questions?

- What were some of the A+ responses to those questions by people you hired?

- What constructive criticism could you give me if I were to answer that question in this manner [then, share your answer]?

On a separate sheet of paper or your computer, itemize and develop your answer strategy for 10 ISQs you might be asked on an interview.

*(continued)*

*(continued)*

| Question | Positive | Pertinent | Precise | Profit | SMART* | Bell-Shaped | Perceptive | Timed | Fresh | Interactive |
|---|---|---|---|---|---|---|---|---|---|---|
| Example: Tell me about yourself. | | ✓ | ✓ | | ✓ | | ✓ | ✓ | ✓ | |

*Part*

**5**

# Salary Negotiation and Job Success

Chapter 17:   Negotiate Your Salary: The Secrets to Knowing and Receiving What You're Worth

Chapter 18:   10 Tips for a Great Start in Your New Position

## Chapter 17

# Negotiate Your Salary: The Secrets to Knowing and Receiving What You're Worth

*"In the business world, everyone is paid in two coins: cash and experience. Take the experience first; the cash will come later."*

—Harold S. Geneen, Accountant, Industrialist, and CEO

A salary negotiation can resemble a high-wire act, a back-and-forth dance across delicate territory where one false step can spell disaster. Not only that, you're expected to perform this dance during the life-changing period of career transition, when you might already be experiencing new emotional highs and lows and when your entire future depends on your negotiation—or so it seems.

Well, take a deep breath and go back to the core message that you've worked to communicate in every step of your job search: "It's all about value." To effectively negotiate your compensation, you must first understand your value, learn about the value of the position, and base your negotiation on the value you can deliver to the organization. In this chapter we examine the high-wire dance from first to last steps and give you ideas, strategies, and language you can use to negotiate a compensation package that rewards you fairly for your contributions.

# Preparing for the Salary Dance

Be prepared to negotiate salary from day one of your job search! Don't wait to learn how to deal with this issue until you are interviewing or until you are offered a position. Questions about salary often arise in the first telephone screen or even earlier, with a question about your salary requirements included in an ad or online posting. Learn how to deal with these requests so that you don't harm your future negotiating position, box yourself into a lower salary, or eliminate yourself from consideration right at the start.

## Research Comparable Salaries

Every good high-wire artist spends much more time practicing the act than performing it. Similarly, you will want to put a great deal of time and effort into preparing to negotiate your salary before you actually attempt it "live." First you must lay the groundwork by putting together some hard numbers about average compensation for someone with your skills, qualifications, years of experience, industry focus, and geographic location. Negotiating without this information is like taking to the high wire without carefully checking to be sure your wire is secure: There is no support for your position and your negotiations will soon collapse. With this information, you have a secure base of knowledge that will give you confidence as you negotiate.

With abundant resources available on the Web, in the library, and through your network, there's no need to rely on just one source for comparable salary data. It's unlikely that you will be able to identify a precise salary for the exact job you are considering, but the more information you have, the more confident you'll feel about negotiating your salary based on "fair market value."

### Salary Tools and Surveys

The Internet abounds with tools and resources that will give you detailed information about salary ranges for specific professions in specific geographic areas. Additional resources are available in print publications, both books and periodicals, that you can find at your local library. Your reference librarian can help you find the most precise and most comprehensive sources for your particular field and level. Here are a few to get you started:

- **JobSmart.org Gateway** (www.jobsmart.org): This Web site is a gateway to hundreds of salary surveys available on the Internet.

- **Salary tools:** The following sites are a good place to start; you can easily find many more by entering the word "salary" into your favorite search engine.

  workindex.com/salary/
  www.careerbuilder.com
  www.monster.com
  www.salary.com
  www.salaryexpert.com
  www.salarysource.com
  www.wageweb.com

- **Professional associations:** If you are a member of one or more professional associations, contact them directly to ask about salary surveys. Or use the *Encyclopedia of Associations* as a reference to find associations relevant to your field, and then call or go to their Web sites for more information.

- **U.S. Department of Labor,** *Occupational Outlook Handbook:* This resource is a treasure-trove of career information including salary ranges. Explore www.bls.gov/oco/ to find data for your profession.

- **Federal government salary tables:** If you are interested in a job with the federal government, you can review salary ranges for every grade and profession at this site: www.opm.gov/oca/04tables/index.asp.

- **The Riley Guide to Employment Opportunities and Job Resources on the Internet:** This exceptional site includes a comprehensive resource list for salary information (www.rileyguide.com/salary.html) and a separate section on executive compensation (www.rileyguide.com/execpay.html). You will find links to dozens of helpful sites; there is also a review of one of the fee-based salary reports you can purchase on the Web.

## Internet Postings and Want Ads

During your job search, as you review online job postings or print classified ads, you will find that many include salary information that you can add to the data you are collecting. The large job boards such as Monster.com and CareerBuilder.com are also a quick source for some hard salary numbers.

## Network Contacts

Include questions about salary as part of your networking interviews. Of course, you would not want to ask your contact how much he or she makes! But you can inquire about salary ranges and, in general, what you might expect at that company. This phrasing will allow you to ask without stepping into the forbidden territory of someone's personal financial situation:

- "Tell me, what is an average salary for someone with my experience at your company? What would a top performer earn?"

- "How does your company determine its salary ranges?"

- "What does your company pay for Java programmers with five years of experience?"

- "I've been at the same company so long, I'm out of touch with salary ranges. Can you help me out with some general information about your company?"

Be sure to talk to your friends who work at large companies. Most large organizations have fixed salary ranges based on job grade, and these tables are often published in an employee handbook.

## Recruiters

Recruiters are an excellent source of salary information. They are usually looking for "tight-fit" candidates within very specific salary ranges. During any contact you have with a recruiter, ask for a "market check" on your salary expectations. You might also ask whether the recruiting firm has conducted any salary surveys for your profession.

## Put It All Together

Relying on multiple sources means that you will have a wide range of data that, together, should give you a fairly accurate picture of the "going rate" for your profession. Table 17.1 shows a sample of comparative salary data developed by a Web designer.

### Table 17.1: Research on Comparative Salary Data

| Source | Low Range | Median | Upper Range |
| --- | --- | --- | --- |
| Salary tool: workindex.com/salary/ (national averages) | $46,027 | $54,704 | $58,315 |
| Salary tool: www.salary.com (national averages) | $45,662 | $54,269 | $57,853 |
| Salary tool: www.salaryexpert.com (New York/statewide average) | $37,383 | $47,798 | $56,517 |
| Salary survey: American Institute of Graphic Artists | $40,000 | $48,000 | $56,700 |
| Print ad: Flash Designer/ Graphic Artist (Kansas City Star) | $32,000 | | $40,000 |
| Online ad: Production Artist (New York) | $57,000 | | $66,000 |
| Network contact: president, Kansas City Ad Club | $40,000 | $45,000 | $50,000 |
| Network contact: Acme Corporation, job grade 8 | $45,000 | $47,500 | $50,000 |
| Average | $42,965 | $49,544 | $54,423 |

Keep in mind that these figures do not include benefits, which can vary widely depending on your employer, or performance bonuses, which can drive up your compensation significantly. In most cases, benefits offered by a company are fairly uniform, whereas bonus payments vary widely and are open to negotiation. Later in this chapter, we discuss negotiating strategies for all of the components of your compensation—salary, benefits, commissions, bonuses, and perks.

Follow the "Magical Coaching Tips" and "10 Quick Tips for Salary Negotiations" at the end of this chapter to research your own comparative salary data.

## Develop Your Salary Targets

Now that you know what the "going rate" is for people in your profession, you can begin to develop your target salary ranges for your next position.

Compare your data to your current or most recent salary, taking into consideration the number of years of experience you have, your level of expertise, and the current job market for people in your profession. As you develop your salary targets, don't forget about projected bonuses or long-term benefits that you might be losing if you leave your current job.

### Supply and Demand

The rules of supply and demand come into play during salary negotiations. If your expertise is in short supply, the demand is stronger and you have more negotiating power. On the other hand, if the market is flooded with people of comparable skill, you will have less room to maneuver in the salary dance. In the fast-growth 1990s, salaries, perks, and bonuses grew astronomically, sometimes to unreasonable heights. With the economy in flux since 2000, some salaries, particularly at the executive level and for technical jobs, have fallen a bit, and perks such as signing bonuses and lucrative buyout clauses are less common.

After analyzing all of your findings, develop your target compensation in three ranges:

- **Your "reality" number:** The lowest salary you will accept; the bottom line you need to pay bills comfortably and work toward your long-term savings and lifestyle goals.

- **Your "comfort" number:** An amount you can accept and feel that you are being adequately compensated for your value; a reasonable and realistic goal.

- **Your "dream" number:** Your ideal salary and/or the level of compensation commanded by top performers in your target positions.

The higher your value to the employer, the more likely you will be able to achieve your "dream" number. What can you do to move yourself up the value chain? Is there a specific skill or expertise that would make you a more desirable candidate? Can you make the case that you are a "star performer" and therefore worthy of higher compensation? Remember, it's not about what you want, need, or deserve (in other words, how long you've been paying your dues); it's all about value.

Use the "Magical Coaching Tips" worksheet at the end of this chapter to identify your own reality, comfort, and dream numbers. Armed with this information, you are prepared to negotiate your salary based on fair market value.

# How to Deflect Salary Questions Until the Offer

**"Send resume with salary requirements to..."**

How often have you seen an ad with this phrase? Or, even more intimidating, "Resumes without salary requirements will not be considered." At what point should you share your requirements and start the salary dance?

In a nutshell, the time to discuss salary is after a firm job offer has been made. Before you receive an offer, you have no negotiating power, and you are more likely to harm than help yourself with a too-early discussion of salary. Think of it this way: Hiring is like shopping. The employer will first peruse a large number of candidates, "try on" a few via interviews, and then make a selection. At that point, the employer has switched from "shopper" to "buyer," and this switch gives a powerful boost to your ability to negotiate.

To preserve your negotiating power, learn to deflect questions about salary until you have received an offer. Here are some strategies.

## In Cover Letters

There are several ways you can handle the salary question in your cover letters:

- **Ignore.** Make no mention of salary. In a nutshell, the time to discuss salary is after a firm job offer has been made. Before you receive an offer, you have no negotiating power, and you are more likely to harm than help yourself with a too-early discussion of salary. In all likelihood, ignoring the salary issue now will not harm your chances of being selected for an interview.

- **Defer.** "I will be happy to discuss salary considerations during an interview." Remember that it's in your best interest not to discuss salary until a job offer has been made, so you might not want to make this offer.

- **Address without revealing anything.** "My salary requirements are open; I am more interested in the challenges and opportunities of this position and expect that your company pays a competitive salary." This response might be seen as evasive, but it does indicate that you read the ad and are at least responding to the company's request.

- **Share a range.** "Based on my understanding of the fair market value of this position, I anticipate a salary in the $85,000 to $95,000 range." Or, "My current compensation is in the high forties, and I anticipate this would increase 10 to 15 percent in a new position." The only problem with this response is that the employer now knows what you expect and can initiate negotiations at that level...or below.

## During a Telephone Screen Interview

In many cases the first stage in the interview process is a telephone screen to determine whether you have the right mix of skills, experience, and achievements to warrant an interview. This interview might be with a recruiter or hiring manager, but often it is administered by a human resources screener armed with a predetermined list of questions. As discussed in chapter 13, your objective is to pass the screen and earn an invitation for an in-person meeting. Try not to screen yourself out by revealing salary information at this point; refer to the next section for specific language you can use to bring the conversation back to your qualifications and your fit for the position.

### Recruiters: The Exception to the Rule

With recruiters, it's okay to reveal salary information. Because recruiters are seeking candidates who fit their client company's specifications to a "T," they need to know whether your salary expectations are in line with what the company is offering. Most recruiters will not continue the conversation if you are not forthcoming about your current salary and your expectations. Feel free to share this with them, along with any factors that might influence your request, such as a forthcoming bonus or a two-year salary freeze at your company.

## During In-Person Interviews

The purpose of an interview is for both you and the employer to explore your fit with the company and the position. In the early stages of these explorations, you don't have a complete view of the opportunity and its challenges, and the company has not had a chance to learn enough about you to switch from "shopper" to "buyer." As a result, salary discussions at this point are premature.

As a savvy job seeker, learn to deflect the question and redirect the discussion toward your qualifications. Here are a few suggestions for turning the question around without appearing difficult, stubborn, uncooperative, or manipulative. Remember the *howcha's:* How you say this will be as important as what you say. Strive for politeness and objective curiosity.

- "Salary is important, but it's not my first consideration. I am more interested in finding the right position, where I can make a real contribution. I'm very interested in what you've told me so far; can we continue that discussion?"

- "I want to be fairly compensated for the value I bring to the company. I'd like to learn more about the challenges you're facing and how I can help."

- "I've always been compensated fairly based on my contributions; I anticipate this would be the case at Widget Products, too. Can you tell me more about your current challenges? So far I'm excited about the position, and I'd like to learn more."

- "To tell you the truth, I don't have enough information about this position yet to be able to determine a meaningful salary. Can you tell me more about the scope of the position and your performance expectations?"

You get the idea. Address the question but stay focused on what's really important—whether you are a good fit for the position and the company.

Because interviewing can be stressful, candidates sometimes lose their composure and blurt out a response when asked a direct question such as "What are your salary requirements?" If this happens to you, don't be too hard on yourself! The interviewer has probably asked this question dozens if not hundreds of times and knows how to keep pressing to get the information from you. You, on the other hand, are probably much less experienced at interviewing and are concerned with making a great impression. You don't want to get into a stand-off with the interviewer or refuse to answer the question. So, just in case you feel compelled to provide an answer, prepare and practice a statement that includes salary ranges, rather than hard numbers, and is based on your research:

- "I understand that fair market value for this position is in the $80,000 to $95,000 range. Is that what you expect?"

- "I've always been paid competitively based on my contributions to the company. Most recently I've earned in the low seventies, and I would expect a 15 to 20 percent increase for this challenging role."

- "My research tells me that your company pays $22,000 to $25,000 for this level. I am comfortable with this range."

## Never State a Range Below Your Reality Number

When stating ranges, never mention a figure that is below your reality number. Keep in mind that while you are focusing on the upper end of your range, the employer hears and homes in on the lower number you recite. It's likely you'll receive an offer that is closer to the lower end of your range than the higher.

# When an Offer Is Made

Congratulations! You've accomplished your goal in the interview process and earned a job offer. The employer has switched from "shopper" to "buyer," and the salary dance has fully begun. If you prepare diligently for all possibilities, you'll be able to negotiate the high-wire maneuvers with confidence and ease.

## The Employer's First Move

The first move might come as a question from the employer: "So, what will it take to bring you on board?" or "We'd like to make you an offer. What salary range were you thinking of?"

## Your First Move

Be careful! In your relief at getting the offer, it's tempting to jump right in and share your research and your target ranges. But it's better to keep your cool and remember the strategies for deflecting salary discussions that you practiced earlier in the process. For the most beneficial outcome, you must "deflect" one more time so that the employer, and not you, is the first to associate a salary number with your job offer. These responses will help:

- "Thank you! I'm excited about the opportunity! Based on the value I can bring to meet the challenges we discussed, what do you think is fair compensation for this position?"

- "I'm glad we agree that I have the right mix of skills and experience to really make an impact in this position. In what salary range do you see me?"

- "Thank you. I appreciate your confidence in me. We've discussed some significant challenges, and I'm looking forward to tackling them. What figure did you have in mind?"

Next comes your first real move in the salary dance. When the employer comes back with a number or a range, your initial response is critically important.

## The Moment of Silence

In every case, whatever the number, whether high or low, your first response should be to repeat the number, thoughtfully and non-judgmentally. Then stop talking. This is called the Moment of Silence. Bite your tongue, and let the employer make the next move.

### Repeat the Top End of the Range

When the employer states a range, your repetition of the number should be the top end of the range. Let's say the employer answers, "Well, our range for this position is $47,000 to $52,000." Your thoughtful response: "Fifty-two thousand dollars…." Your goal is to plant the top end of the range in your listener's mind, rather than the minimum amount offered.

During the silence, you'll be calculating silently to compare the number to your reality, comfort, and dream numbers. This can be particularly difficult if the numbers are presented in a different format—hourly, weekly, or monthly, for example, when you've calculated annually. During this Moment of Silence, you will need to determine whether this is a reality, comfort, or dream number so that you can make your next move with confidence.

How else can the Moment of Silence help you? The employer, now in "buyer" mentality, does not want to lose you. If you don't jump at the offer immediately, it's possible the hiring authority will come right back with a higher figure: "Well, I guess we could go to $55,000." Without saying a word, you've just earned a five percent raise!

If the employer does not respond with a new number, it's your turn to make a move. What you say next will depend on how closely the offer matches your expectations.

## Be Sure You Are Clear About the Parameters of the Job

At this point in your discussions you should have an excellent understanding of the position scope, challenges, and performance expectations. But before you start to negotiate your compensation, it is essential to clear up any questions that remain about the following:

- Job description
- Job functions
- Reporting relationships (who you'll report to and who will report to you)
- Start date
- Employment status

    - Full-time employee eligible for full benefits

    - Part-time employee with perhaps partial benefits

    - Exempt status, where you will be exempt from certain hour and pay laws and thus not be eligible for overtime pay (usually applies to professional and administrative positions)

    - Non-exempt employee, where you will usually be paid an hourly wage and will be eligible for overtime pay for hours beyond those stipulated in your job description (usually applies to assembly, production, customer service, and other nonprofessional positions)

    - Independent contractor, where you will not be considered an employee and therefore will not receive company benefits; with this status, you will be responsible for paying self-employment taxes

### Independent Contractor or Employee?

Many employers are hiring workers as independent contractors instead of employees. The distinction has important tax and employment benefits consequences. Those who should be classified as employees but aren't may lose out on Workers' Compensation, unemployment benefits, and, in many cases, group insurance (including life and health) and retirement benefits. In general, a worker is an employee when the business has the right to direct and control the worker. For instance, if the business provides training in required procedures and you receive extensive instructions on how work is to be done, this suggests that you may be an employee. For more information, visit the IRS Web site: www.irs.gov/faqs/faq-kw68.html.

All of these factors can have a significant impact on your compensation and working conditions and therefore will affect the way you react to the salary that has been offered.

## Agree on Base Salary Before Benefits or Bonuses

You might also be wondering about benefits, performance bonuses, and perks that you will be entitled to or that you can negotiate. Although these must be factored into your decision, at this point you need to come to an agreement on base compensation (salary) for a clearly defined position. Then you can tackle the additional issues one by one as you work your way through the negotiation.

Many companies are proud of their benefits packages and might try to use them as a lever to persuade you to accept a lower salary. Only you can determine the compensation level that makes sense for you, your family, your career, and your current circumstances. Keep in mind that if you accept a lower salary now, it will affect your compensation going forward with the company, because most salary increases are given as a percentage of current salary.

# What to Say When the Offer Is Just Right

You've done your research into fair market rates for this kind of position, and you have a full understanding of the job scope and expectations. The interviewer offers you a salary that is in the comfort or dream range and is eminently fair given the parameters of the position. It's a great company to work for, and the job will advance your long-term career goals. There's absolutely no reason you can't accept on the spot.

> That sounds terrific, Ms. Williams. My research tells me that that is a very fair market value for this position. I appreciate your confidence in me and am excited about delivering the results we've discussed.

Next, you'll move on to discussion of your complete compensation package, including bonuses, benefits, and perks...and here you can certainly negotiate, even if you haven't negotiated the base salary figure.

### To Counter-Offer, or Not to Counter-Offer?

News flash! Counter-offers are *not* compulsory. Some companies lay their "best and final" offer on the table when they offer you the job. Because you've done your homework, you will know when an offer is good. In some circumstances, when the job market is very tight—the demand for your expertise is low and the supply of candidates is high—you will have little if any negotiating power. Don't be overconfident or greedy; if the offer is attractive and meets your needs and expectations, take it!

# How to Initiate a Counter-Offer

In cases where the employer has not laid his best offer on the table (or his best offer isn't matching up to your reality number), you'll have some work to do.

## What to Say When the Offer Is Too Low

You have paused for a Moment of Silence, and perhaps the employer has upped the original figure that was offered. In any event, the offer is below your reality number and/or below what you consider to be fair compensation for the position. Here's how to reply.

Express appreciation for the offer:

> Mr. Martinez, I'm flattered that you think I'm the right person for the job, and I'm excited about meeting these challenges.

Clarify job parameters:

> Let me be sure we both have the same understanding about the position. This would be a full-time, exempt position as Warehouse Manager for your Columbus facility. I would be reporting to the Operations Director and be responsible for a staff of 10 hourly employees. I would be expected to manage the implementation of new barcoding software in the first six months and lead some vigorous cost-cutting programs to achieve at least 10 percent cost savings in the first year.

Be sure you have accurately summarized the position. Wait for the interviewer's assent and clear up any differences before you proceed.

> Do I have that straight?

Make a persuasive case for a higher salary, based on the *value* you can bring to the position. Mention the employer's *most pressing problem,* as uncovered during the interview process, and your ability to solve it.

> As we discussed, I have the right skill set to make an immediate impact in this position, and I am confident of my ability to deliver 10 percent cost savings or even more in the first year, based on my track record with Acme Corp. And, as you know, I've led successful software implementations of this type twice, and I project a smooth process completed in four to six months. Based on my contributions, and what I understand to be fair market value for this type of position, a salary in the *X* to *Y* range would be more appropriate. What can you do in that range?

## Other Ways You Can Initiate a Counter-Offer

Here are some other options for language to use when responding to an offer that is too low. The goal is to engage in dialogue, so you want to avoid being confrontational, acting insulted, or being scornful. Such an attitude will harm or even sabotage the negotiation; and even if you don't lose the offer, you will damage your relationship with a future co-worker.

"I've talked to peers in the industry and researched salaries on several well-respected Web sites, and to be honest, I'm a little disappointed. I expected an offer in the *X* to *Y* range, based on fair market value. What flexibility do you have?"

"Quite frankly, I'm disappointed. Is there any room to negotiate?"

"I have a real problem; can you help me?"

## Language to Avoid

Keep in mind that employers are not really interested in what you want, need, or deserve; their fundamental concern is "What can you do for me?" Therefore, steer clear of language that communicates your wants or needs or expresses any sense of entitlement.

| "Before" You-Centered Language | "After" Employer-Centered Language |
|---|---|
| I really need more. | I'm extremely interested, but I must confess I'm disappointed in the proposed salary. Fair market value indicates 15 percent more for a position with this level of responsibility and 25 percent more for someone with my ability to contribute. What flexibility do you have? |
| Are you sure you can't do more? | How might the position be modified or upgraded to warrant more? |
| I can't make a move for less than *X*. | While salary is not my only concern, it is important. I'm eager to contribute and confident of my ability to do so. How can we structure the compensation so that I'm rewarded for meeting established goals? |

## Three Possible Responses from the Employer

Now it's the employer's move. He has three options, and your next step will depend on what he does.

### 1. Employer Stands Pat

I'm sorry, but that is what we've budgeted, and we consider it to be a very fair salary for the position.

Don't give up yet! Perhaps you can negotiate performance bonuses that will bring the amount up to your reality or comfort level. Maybe the benefits are terrific or you can negotiate some additional perks. Unless the number is totally out of the question, I recommend that you table the base salary discussion and continue negotiating other aspects of your compensation.

> OK, I understand your position. I do feel confident of my ability to achieve these goals for the company, so maybe we can build in some performance bonuses that will make us both happy. And what is the benefit package like? It might be I've overlooked something in my calculations.

## 2. Employer Ups the Offer a Bit but It's Still Below Your Expectations

> Well, I guess we could go to *X*.

Follow the pattern of your initial response—be polite and enthusiastic, reiterate key challenges, and express your confidence in achieving results for the company.

> I appreciate your flexibility. You know, we talked about the problems you're having with personnel and team issues in the warehouse. I know that is affecting your productivity. I have a very consistent history of building strong teams in environments just like this, and I have full confidence in my ability to do the same here at Acme Widgeters. I've calculated that a 5 percent productivity boost would improve your bottom line by $100,000 in the first year alone. Based on this kind of contribution, don't you agree that a salary in the *X* to *Y* range is fair?

You can continue in this vein as long as the employer is receptive and you are able to document specific areas where you can help the company. It's always helpful to tie specific dollar benefits to your contributions; this will help the employer see that hiring you will deliver more value than cost to the company.

When you are satisfied that you have negotiated base pay that is appropriate for your value and meets your expectations, accept enthusiastically and move on to phase two, where you negotiate details of your total compensation package, including performance bonuses, benefits, and perks.

## 3. Employer Counter-Offers an Attractive Salary That Is in Line with What You Can Deliver to the Company

You don't have to negotiate further; you can move on to discussing your total compensation package, including performance bonuses, benefits, and perks.

> That sounds terrific. I appreciate your flexibility and feel confident in my ability to deliver the results we've discussed.

# Negotiating Additional Elements of Your Compensation Package

Once base salary is settled, you can discuss and negotiate additional components of the compensation package. Company benefits might or might not be negotiable, but your package can also include performance bonuses and additional perquisites (commonly known as "perks") that offer much more room for creativity and flexibility.

You want to be absolutely clear about all the parameters of your compensation package, such as bonuses, raises, overtime, benefits, health insurance, stock options, 401(k) or other retirement plans, profit-sharing plans, performance evaluations, vacation policy, sick days, tuition reimbursement, and so on.

### Practice Negotiating

If negotiating isn't something you do on a regular basis, find ways to practice. For instance, ask for payment terms on a dentist bill, suggest to a shop owner a discount on an item you're interested in purchasing, or request a donation from an organization for a charitable cause. It might be as simple as asking a sibling for help with something, such as hosting a family get-together that normally would be held at your place. Any of these situations will give you practice asking for what you need and finding ways to compromise so that both parties have their needs met.

# Get the Offer in Writing and Think It Over

Your job offer and initial negotiation might take place during a final interview. If that's the case, most likely you will discuss and come to tentative agreement about a general salary figure, as described in the preceding sections. During this discussion, you might agree to some performance bonuses or a commission structure, and the employer might reference the company's benefits package and perhaps some other types of compensation and rewards.

You've conducted a professional negotiation and come to tentative agreement on your basic compensation. Now is the time to get the offer in writing and take it home to think it over.

A formal written offer is standard operating procedure at some companies. Within a reasonable period of time, typically two to five days, you will receive a package of materials that includes a description of the job and detailed information on salary, benefits, bonuses, and total compensation.

Carefully review the material to be sure it reflects everything you discussed with the hiring manager. Undoubtedly, there will be items you'll want to negotiate further. Write down any questions you have and make notes about further requests or changes. Then contact the hiring manager and set up a time to discuss the package in person. Don't ask for a meeting to talk about "compensation"; instead, ask to get together to answer a few final questions to help you in making your decision.

## Negotiate Face-to-Face

Do not attempt to negotiate or counter-offer your compensation package by e-mail or phone. An in-person meeting is the most productive and professional setting and will allow you to review and resolve every item and come to complete agreement. Obviously, if you are living in a different city, you might not be able to conduct this meeting in person, and in that case opt for a phone meeting rather than an e-mail dialogue. At the end of every phone conversation, be sure you recap what was discussed; then follow that up in writing (e-mail is fine) to confirm the discussion. You don't want to leave room for error. Misunderstandings can cause hard feelings and jeopardize the job offer or your future working relationships.

What should you do if the company does not make its offer in writing? You should ask for it at the conclusion of your initial negotiation. Recap what you discussed, corroborating the job details and compensation to be sure you and the hiring manager are in agreement. Then ask for a written offer so that you can mull it over or discuss it with your spouse. Hesitancy or refusal might be a red flag signaling uncertainty about hiring you, so be wary!

During the interim period and final negotiations, continue to be positive, poised, and professional. Be responsive to the company's needs, stress your enthusiasm, ask when they need to have your response, and meet every deadline. The impressions you make during the negotiation phase of a job offer will make a lasting impression on the people you'll be working with every day, so be sure it is a positive impression!

As you prepare your notes for the next phase of negotiations, analyze the total compensation package—salary, bonuses, benefits, and perks—against your needs, goals, and researched information. Overall, how does the package compare to your reality, comfort, and dream numbers? Use the "Magical Coaching Tips" worksheet to evaluate this or multiple job offers.

## Bring All the Decision-Makers to the Table

Be sure all the decision-makers are present at the meeting. It is a frustrating experience to try to negotiate with someone who does not have the authority to make a decision. If you sense or know that your contact is not the final authority, push to have the decision-maker present at the meeting. You don't want to offend your contact, but you do want to be sure that matters are resolved with a minimum of back-and-forth discussion between your contact and the decision maker. Try phrasing it as a convenience—"Would it be more convenient if I we include the hiring manager in our discussion?" or "This is an important commitment for me, and I will have quite a few questions. To keep it as convenient as possible, should we include Ms. Chow in our discussions?" You can't force the issue, but give it your best shot.

The saying is that "everything is negotiable," but that might not be true. Some companies offer fixed benefit plans that are the same for every employee; others refuse to adjust salaries outside of a range; still others provide a comprehensive pay/benefits package in their first offer and do not wish to negotiate or "haggle" over details. But unless you ask, you will never know whether an item is negotiable. Be creative! You know what's important to you and what will keep you motivated.

When asking for more, be careful not to appear greedy or entitled. Compare the phrasing in these examples and see how simply wording your request more politely creates a more positive, professional image.

| Before | After |
|---|---|
| I couldn't consider less than four weeks of vacation. | I realize you don't have any flexibility on the salary, but I wonder if you'd consider an extra week's vacation. That would mean a lot to me and would enable me to visit my family on the other side of the country. |
| These health benefits are worthless to me. Can I get cash instead? | Because I have full coverage through my spouse, I won't need to take advantage of your health insurance benefit. Is there a chance this could be swapped for a cash benefit? |
| I want you to pay for my MBA. | I've just begun my MBA studies and I'm excited about the added expertise I'll be able to offer you as a result. My current company covers the tuition and the two days per month of class time. Is that something I could continue here? |

Throughout your negotiations, stay upbeat and positive about the job and the company. Be sure all of your questions are answered, and if you have negotiated any changes to the original written offer, ask for a revised offer letter.

Close the meeting by expressing your enthusiasm! Ask the employer when a firm answer is needed. Tell them you want to review everything carefully once more and discuss the opportunity with your spouse. Assure them you'll be back in touch as soon as possible. And be sure to keep your promise!

## Evaluate the Offer or Multiple Offers

Analyzing a job offer is a complex process that involves emotion as well as logic. The job and company must be a good FIT for your career goals, skills, interests, and personal style. You should be excited about the challenges, satisfied with the compensation package, and confident that you have the ability to achieve the stated goals. A little bit of trepidation is normal!

Use the "Magical Coaching Tips" worksheet at the end of this chapter to ask yourself several questions that will help you evaluate the offer or compare this offer to another offer.

If you already have a job offer from another employer (Company X), it's acceptable to let the first employer (Company Y) know and to use this as leverage. For instance, *"I'm evaluating a second offer at this time. To be honest, Company Y is my first choice, although the base salary you're proposing is 10 percent less. I'm wondering what room there might be to get closer to, or even match, that 10 percent difference."*

Another situation that often arises is that you've received a job offer from Employer A while you're waiting to be called back for a second interview by Employer B, who happens to be your first-choice employer. If this happens, contact Employer B and say, "I wanted to touch base on your timeframe for this position. It happens that I have an offer from another employer that I'll need to make a decision about and yet my preference is to make a commitment to your company. Is it possible we might meet soon?"

## Accept and Finalize Your Agreement

When you've made the decision to accept a job offer, confirm it in writing as soon as possible, and always within the time you promised. Your professional, positive, enthusiastic acceptance will set the right tone as you start your new position. Your acceptance letter might look something like figure 17.1.

# Chapter Wrap-Up

Hiring costs money, and companies want a return on that investment. They are not looking for seat warmers, cubicle fillers, or office decorations; they want people who will add value to the company and improve its bottom line. Be confident of your value and assured in your negotiations. Such an attitude will enable you to dance across the high wire with ease and arrive safely at your career destination.

## 10 Quick Tips for Salary Negotiations

1. **Communicate your value during interviews and through salary negotiations.** Enter negotiations as a confident optimist—if you expect more, you'll be more likely to get more.

2. **Memorize responses to deflect salary discussions until the employer has shifted from "shopper" to "buyer."**

3. **Be prepared**—learn the fair market value for your talents by researching the low, median, and high range for similar positions.

4. **Identify your reality, comfort, and dream number salary range.**

5. **Base your salary requests on what you bring to the company and what you will achieve—not on what you need, want, or deserve.**

6. **First, agree in principle on base compensation. Then, explore and negotiate bonuses, benefits, and perks.** Know what "throwaways" you are willing to

Jayne Smythe
123 West 53rd Street
Airtown, NY 12345
(917) 543-2100
jaynesmythe@msn.com

[date]

[Certified Mail; return receipt requested]

Name, Title
Company
Street Address
City, State, ZIP

Dear Ms. _____:

It's been a pleasure meeting with you and other members of the Widget Manufacturers, Inc. team. This letter confirms that I agree to be employed by _____ [name of company] as a _____ [position title] beginning _____ [start date].

As compensation, I agree to accept an annual salary of $_____ payable in _____ [monthly, weekly] installments in the sum of $_____. Additionally, I understand that I will receive _____ [state benefits agreed to].

Upon termination of our agreement for any reason other than gross negligence on my part, I shall be entitled to receive my bonus and salary for the remaining period of the quarter in which my termination occurs.

If any terms of this letter are unclear or incorrect, please reply in writing within three days of receipt of this letter. I can be reached at (917) 543-2100 should you need anything from me prior to my start date.

I am thoroughly looking forward to joining the team and making a valuable contribution to the organization.

Sincerely,

Jayne Smythe

**Figure 17.1: An acceptance letter.**

concede. When you are willing to give something away (tuition reimbursement, for example), it makes you look flexible. In other cases, offer a concession in exchange for something that is of importance to you.

7. **Frame any counter-offer requests in employer-centered language instead of you-centered language.** Express your requests without anxiety, anger, or attitude, but in a manner that is positive, poised, and professional.

8. **Get the offer in writing.** If you can't, draft and submit your own letter outlining your understanding of the position. Evaluate offers on multiple planes—salary, job duties, future potential, location, commute, schedule, company culture, and so on.

9. **Be willing to walk away.** Consider what the consequences will be of accepting a salary and benefit package below your reality number.

10. **Don't cut off other options until you have actually started work.** Wait to share the good news with your broader circles of contacts until you are actually on board. And, remain courteous and professional…don't forget that you will be working with the people with whom you are now negotiating.

---

## Magical Coaching Tips

### When Researching Salary
Using table 17.1 near the beginning of this chapter as a guide, develop your own comparative salary data.

### My Research on Comparative Salary Data

| Source | Low Range | Median | Upper Range |
|---|---|---|---|
| Salary tool: workindex.com/salary/ (national averages) | $ | $ | $ |
| Salary tool: www.salary.com (national averages) | $ | $ | $ |
| Salary tool: www.salaryexpert.com (New York/statewide average) | $ | $ | $ |
| Salary survey: professional association or other source | $ | $ | $ |
| Print ad/source: | $ | $ | $ |
| Online ad: | $ | $ | $ |
| Network contact | $ | $ | $ |

| | | | |
|---|---|---|---|
| Network contact | $ | $ | $ |
| Average | $ | $ | $ |

### When Developing Your Salary Target

Develop your own salary range of reality, comfort, and dream numbers.

| | Current Salary | Reality Number | Comfort Number | Dream Number |
|---|---|---|---|---|
| Base | | | | |
| Bonus | | | | |
| Commissions | | | | |
| Projected raise | | | | |
| Stock options not yet vested | | | | |
| Benefit/retirement plans not yet vested | | | | |
| Other | | | | |
| Total | | | | |

### When Evaluating an Offer or Multiple Job Offers

When evaluating an offer, ask yourself some of these questions as you weigh the pros and cons of each unique opportunity.

| | Offer #1 Negative Neutral Positive - o + (Circle one) | Offer #2 Negative Neutral Positive - o + (Circle one) |
|---|---|---|
| **The Job** | | |
| Is the job a good fit for my professional strengths? | - o + | - o + |
| Will I be doing what I love to do most of the time (or will I be doing a lot of tasks that frustrate me or burn me out)? | - o + | - o + |
| Will the work challenge me? | - o + | - o + |

*(continued)*

*(continued)*

| | Offer #1 Negative Neutral Positive | | | Offer #2 Negative Neutral Positive | | |
|---|---|---|---|---|---|---|
| | **- o +** (Circle one) | | | **- o +** (Circle one) | | |
| Do I have all the training and education I need to do the job well? If not, will the company provide it? | - | o | + | - | o | + |
| Will I have the resources necessary to do the job well? | - | o | + | - | o | + |
| Did I feel good rapport with co-workers? | - | o | + | - | o | + |
| Do I like my boss? (Also analyze the individual's behavioral style, managerial style, record of promoting staff, ability to mentor, grasp of his or her job, and relationship within company hierarchy.) | - | o | + | - | o | + |
| Are there opportunities for advancement? Realistically, how long will this take and how straightforward is the process? | - | o | + | - | o | + |
| Will I be compensated adequately for my efforts? | - | o | + | - | o | + |
| Can I earn bonus pay for performance? | - | o | + | - | o | + |
| Is there potential to increase my salary in the near future? | - | o | + | - | o | + |
| Are the benefits adequate for me and my family? | - | o | + | - | o | + |
| Is there anything that's missing that I consider important? | - | o | + | - | o | + |
| Are performance expectations achievable? | - | o | + | - | o | + |
| Does the level of challenge frighten or stimulate me? | - | o | + | - | o | + |
| Will I be excited about going to work most days? | - | o | + | - | o | + |

| | Offer #1<br>Negative<br>Neutral<br>Positive<br>- o +<br>(Circle one) | | | Offer #2<br>Negative<br>Neutral<br>Positive<br>- o +<br>(Circle one) | | |
|---|---|---|---|---|---|---|
| **The Culture** | | | | | | |
| What hours am I expected to work? What are the unwritten "rules" for arrival and departure times? Is evening and weekend work the norm? | - | o | + | - | o | + |
| What social opportunities exist? Are these congruent with my interests? | - | o | + | - | o | + |
| What does the atmosphere feel like? Is it friendly, brisk and businesslike, laid back, casual, formal? How does this match with my style? | - | o | + | - | o | + |
| Is there a lot of deadline pressure? Will I perform my best under these circumstances? | - | o | + | - | o | + |
| Is the level of intensity about right for me? | - | o | + | - | o | + |
| Is the balance of individual and team work right for me? | - | o | + | - | o | + |
| What kind of political currents do I sense? Am I comfortable with those? | -<br>- | o<br>o | +<br>+ | -<br>- | o<br>o | +<br>+ |
| Is the job highly structured or unstructured? Is this what I prefer? | - | o | + | - | o | + |
| What has the negotiation been like? Has it been courteous and professional, or do I get a sense that the company begrudges paying me what I'm worth? | - | o | + | - | o | + |
| What is the average tenure of people in my department? | - | o | + | - | o | + |
| Is the leadership team in my area new or well established? How do I feel about that? | - | o | + | - | o | + |

*(continued)*

*(continued)*

| | Offer #1 Negative Neutral Positive - o + (Circle one) | Offer #2 Negative Neutral Positive - o + (Circle one) |
|---|---|---|
| **The Company** | | |
| Is the company growing or downsizing? | - o + | - o + |
| What are its future plans? How do I feel about those? | - o + | - o + |
| Does it seem to be seizing market opportunities, or are competitors leaving it in the dust? | - o + | - o + |
| How stable is the executive team? | - o + | - o + |
| What is the public image of the company? Do my interviews confirm or refute it? | - o + | - o + |
| Is the company an industry leader or struggling to keep up with the competition? | - o + | - o + |
| Has the company had financial or legal woes recently? What is the status? | - o + | - o + |
| How competitive are its core products? What is on the horizon? | - o + | - o + |
| What are the most significant market challenges the company faces? | - o + | - o + |
| How has the company handled downsizing in the past? | - o + | - o + |
| Is the location and commute acceptable? | - o + | - o + |

When evaluating multiple job offers, look at the number of positives circled in each column. Depending on how you weight each item, it's likely that the column with more positives (+) is the better of the two offers.

## Chapter 18

# 10 Tips for a Great Start in Your New Position

*"My will shall shape the future. Whether I fail or succeed shall be no man's doing but my own. I am the force; I can clear any obstacle before me or I can be lost in the maze. My choice; my responsibility; win or lose, only I hold the key to my destiny."*

—Elaine Maxwell, American writer

Congratulations on your new position! You worked hard, challenged yourself, took some calculated risks, and clinched a deal. You are probably breathing a sigh of relief because the stress and uncertainty associated with job search are over. However, don't start coasting! As an "A" player, you'll want to convince your new employer that they made a good decision in investing in you.

Now is the time to prepare for your first days on the job. To do so, we'll look at five tips for each of the two key areas:

- Results
- Relationships

Keep in mind that the better you do in this position, the more success you will have. The more success you have, the more valuable you will be to other employers. The more valuable you are to other employers, the more in demand you will be. And, when you're in demand, any future job search will go that much faster and more easily.

# Your Results

Harvard Business School associate professor Michael Watkins studies leadership and negotiation. In his book *The First 90 Days: Critical Success Strategies for New Leaders at All Levels* (Harvard Business School Press), he speaks of a *break-even point*—the point at which new leaders have contributed as much value to their new organizations as they have consumed from it. Watkins reports that the average time it takes for a midlevel manager to reach this point is 6.2 months. Whether you're an entry-level employee or a seasoned professional, I challenge you to beat the averages. Deliver results!

## 1. Set Goals and Create Value

One of your early priorities will be to sit down with your boss to clarify what he or she wants accomplished. Because you asked crystal-clear clarifying questions during the interview (chapter 14), you probably have a general idea of the boss' agenda. To confirm this, ask the following questions:

- What are the priorities you'd like me to focus on in the coming 60 to 90 days?

- What strategy and systems should be applied to each of these priorities?

- What resources are in place or need to be in place to support successful outcomes?

- What specific results do you want to see?

- How will my results be evaluated?

Commit this conversation to paper (or e-mail) to prevent any misunderstandings. Some companies create formal written goals for each new employee. If your company does not do this, create your own written record and save a copy. It doesn't have to be long or detailed. Simple will suffice, as this e-mail illustrates:

> To: Your New Boss
>
> Subject: Confirming 3-Month Priorities
>
> Dear _____ , [boss' name]
>
> Thanks for a great meeting this morning. I appreciate the time you took to outline the priorities that you have for me in the next three months. Specifically, I will look forward to
>
> * identifying a minimum of 50 new prospects for the widget line
>
> * making face-to-face contact with a minimum of 20 purchasing managers
>
> * cleaning up the prospect database so that data is clean and accurate
>
> Should your priorities change, please let me know. I'll be sending you weekly updates each Friday to report on progress and inroads made. In the meantime, I am excited to get started!
>
> Best,
>
> Your Name

In your first weeks on the job, concentrate on the direction of your progress, not the velocity. Yes, it's nice to "hit the ground running," but it's more important that you be running in the right direction.

Recall that every employer wants one thing from you. That one thing is value. To provide value, you must generate results that will make your employer a better, stronger, more productive, and profitable company.

To create value, ask your boss the following:

- What would I need to do to blow the lid off of your expectations for me in the next 90 days?

- I want to be sure I'm creating value for you on this project. What should I be aware of to be as productive and profitable as possible?

## 2. Underpromise; Overdeliver

International business guru Tom Peters coined the phrase "Underpromise; Overdeliver," now repeated in mantra-like fashion in businesses from Bangalore to Boston. Here's how the principle works: If you think it will take you three business days to complete a task, promise that you will have it done in four (underpromise). Then, deliver it in three (overdeliver). Or, if you can manufacture 110 widgets in one month, commit to 100 (underpromise). Then, manufacture 110 (overdeliver).

While underpromising helps you manage others' expectations of you, overdelivering enhances the positive feelings and trust that co-workers or customers will have toward you.

## 3. Do Homework

It seems there are a zillion things to learn when you're starting a new job. At some point, your brain will go into overload and shut down until it is ready to absorb more information. To speed up your learning curve, go the extra mile the first few weeks on the job. Take materials home with you to study in the evening (provided that this does not violate company policy). Of course, be diligent about returning them the next morning. These materials might include policy manuals, instructional binders, client files, and other nonconfidential materials. While studying, make notes and jot down questions that come to mind. You'll impress your boss when you say, "I noticed in the files that one of our key customers had a significant dip in volume recently. What was the reason for that?"

In addition, take copious notes throughout the day from conversations with your boss and others, and then review these each evening, as well.

If you're feeling overwhelmed at the amount of knowledge to absorb, ask your boss or a trusted co-worker how to prioritize the information.

## 4. Jump-Start Momentum with an Early Win

Momentum is crucial to your credibility. It will help others see that you're on the right track and cause you to feel as though you're making headway. Review the priority projects (see "Set Goals and Create Value" at the beginning of this chapter) and choose one of the goals your boss is passionate about. Then identify action steps associated with the goal. Determine which of these action steps will best leverage your success (or ask your boss' advice) and go for it!

Be sure to communicate your wins in writing to the right people (save a copy for your personal files). Do so without bragging and give credit to others whenever and wherever possible. For instance,

> Dear _____ [boss' name]:
>
> I know we'll cover this in our regular Friday meeting, but I couldn't wait to share this "win" with you. Your instincts about ABC Company were right on. I followed up and landed a meeting with the Director of Purchasing. Because you mentioned that this would be a tough account to break into, I'm especially pleased. Thanks again for your help. I'll look forward to hearing your thoughts on my meeting strategy when we speak on Friday.
>
> Your Name

## 5. Show Initiative

Recall from chapter 15 on behavioral interviewing that initiative (also described as energy or drive) is often listed as the universal trait of success. Here are a few ideas to help you show initiative:

- **Envision life from your boss's perspective.** What does it appear he or she needs help with most? Ask whether you can offer assistance with this.

- **Review your formal job description.** Are there tasks on it that you have not yet learned about? What initiative can you take to learn them on your own?

- **Do not wait to be asked to do something that you know needs to be done.**

- **Observe the corporate culture and analyze how others please your boss.** If your co-workers take action without asking permission, do the same. Just be sure that your actions are in line with organizational policy and norms.

- **Ask what else you could be doing.**

### Expect Bumps in the Road

No matter how excited you are about a new position, there will always be a few challenging moments along the way. Let those "bumps" serve their perfect purpose. What might that purpose be? Ultimately, it is to grow you, to allow you to learn or practice some new skill, or to build your character.

Recall the Big Five personality factors mentioned in chapter 13 (in the "Psychometric Assessments" section). People who score well in each of these factors tend to have fewer, or smaller, bumps in the road. One factor that can derail your career faster than any other is "agreeableness." This term reflects your ability to work collaboratively, your compassion in providing advice, your sensitivity to others' needs, and your diplomacy.

The next time you encounter a challenging moment, ask yourself, "What new skill or character trait does this bump in the road allow me to learn or practice?"

# Your Relationships

Beyond performance, the second area where you'll want to make a great impression is in your relationships. "A" players know that achieving results means little to nothing if you aren't also creating goodwill along the way. Remember that one of the themes throughout this book has been to think of others first, with the mantra "it's about them, not me." Now let's look at what you can do to build those critical relationships.

## 6. Act "As If"

Your relationship with yourself is a good place to start! Why? Because it is critical that you adopt the persona or image required for success, even if there are areas that you feel insecure about. Remember that this is a wonderful opportunity to start afresh! Make the most of it by sowing new empowering thoughts, habits, and actions.

We talked about acting "as if" in chapter 6, with attitude, actions, vocabulary, dress, posture, habits, self-talk, and mindset all playing a part in your success. If you're nervous about stepping into a position of increased responsibility or a position where there is much to learn, you must act as if you are fully capable of doing the job, or else you will undermine others' confidence in you. As you project confidence, be sure to avoid appearing arrogant or a know-it-all.

## 7. Find an Inside Guide

Look for someone inside the company who can serve as a confidant. Similar to a mentor, but not that formal, an inside guide is someone who can give you advice and share insider tips on corporate culture. This person should *not* be someone who evaluates you. Instead, look for someone who is a level or two above you and doing well in the company. To recruit your guide, you might say something like this:

*Jane, you stand out to me as someone who is really doing well. While I'm new to the company, I wonder if you would consider helping me learn my way around and offer some advice so that I can quickly get up to speed on the corporate culture.*

Consider meeting weekly with this person for coffee or lunch.

## Acting "As If" Worksheet

These questions will help you act "as if":

What new attitudes and ways of thinking do you need to adopt?

_____

_____

What assumptions or limiting beliefs do you need to drop?

_____

_____

What new work strategies do you need to apply? For instance, do you need to learn how to delegate more, be more adaptable and open to new ways of doing things, be more attentive to detail, take more initiative, or handle stress better?

_____

_____

If you are used to working in a team but now must work independently (or vice versa), what new work habits do you need to adopt?

_____

_____

## Find an Insider to Learn the Ropes

Ellen, a regional sales manager for a pharmaceutical company, used this strategy when she found herself promoted from the field to the corporate office for a special project. Although she had excelled in field sales management, she had never worked inside the corporate offices and was unsure about protocol. Ellen asked a director-level person to meet with her informally. These weekly lunches helped her assimilate quickly, and also led to many new networking contacts at the director and vice president level.

## 8. Ask for Feedback and Welcome Criticism

On a fairly regular basis, ask your boss for feedback. Don't wait for a formal evaluation to find out where you stand. Questions you might ask include the following:

- What strengths do you see me using regularly?
- What areas can I improve on?

↗ What else could I be doing to "hit a homerun"?

↗ What skills have I acquired or improved on recently?

In addition to feedback, welcome criticism from your co-workers. As unpleasant as criticism might feel, you *want* people to be able to tell you when you could be doing something better or differently. This is one way to become aware of your "blind spots." The fewer your blind spots, the greater your chances for success.

People with healthy self-esteem can accept criticism without reacting defensively. The following before-and-after example illustrates the difference between reacting defensively versus welcoming criticism:

| **Before** | **After** |
| --- | --- |
| Do you really think I was coming across that way? I wasn't intending that at all. If anything, I thought she was the one who sounded rude. And I've noticed you sounding the same way before. | *Thanks, Margie, for bringing that to my attention. I wasn't aware I was coming across that way, and your suggestion will help me be more effective in my communications. Are there any other tips you should share with me?* |

If someone continually doles out negative versus positive criticism, examine whether there is any truth in their statements. At the same time, recognize that their critical comments might stem from anger about some other issue that you have no control over. Silently forgive them and steer clear of them as best as possible.

## Build Your Team

If you are stepping into a position with supervisory responsibilities, you will have additional team-building considerations. Without alienating anyone, you must first assess your team members. For instance, does each member have the "hard skills" and experience needed to deliver desired results? Is each member in the right role? Does each one have the "soft skills" necessary to go from good to great? This assessment might be accomplished best through individual meetings, giving each one a chance to report on self-perceived strengths, current assignments, and ideas for the future. You can then determine whether restructuring the team is warranted. From there, you can begin establishing goals and implementing systems to facilitate those goals.

## 9. Hold Back

As a new employee, listen and think twice before making any kind of comment or suggestion. As an example, one new adjunct professor attending her first faculty meeting repeatedly commented about the inefficiency of a particular process for signing up to teach evening classes. Even after the dean explained to her that the process had recently been improved through automation and that future enhancements were already in the works, the new employee continued to make critical comments. Meanwhile, the more senior professors looked on in amusement, realizing that the new professor had just shot herself in the foot. It would be highly unlikely that the dean would grant her any of the cherry teaching assignments. Moral of the story: Before making suggestions, assume that there are legitimate reasons for systems or processes. Ask in a curious tone of voice what those reasons are before challenging them. The second area you will want to hold back on is asking for favors. Don't ask for any until you have performed some yourself.

## 10. Continue to Network

Insiders will judge you personally before they will be able to judge you based on your performance results. Therefore, it's critical that you score some early relational wins. Look for every opportunity to promote your brand with your boss, co-workers, superiors, customers, and companies your company does business with.

Finally, remember the relationships that helped you get where you are. Touch base with all your job search networking contacts and let them know where you landed. A quick e-mail will suffice, but consider a handwritten note to those who were especially helpful to your success. Use this sample e-mail as a guide:

> Dear Jason:
>
> This is a brief note to update you on my recent _____ [interview, job search, transition] and thank you for your support. I am very pleased to have accepted a position as _____ [title] with _____ [company name], where I will be _____ [brief description of what you will be doing, such as heading up their new business-development efforts in the bio/pharma markets or supporting the operational efforts of the organization]. The opportunity allows me to do what I do best: _____ [use wording that supports your brand, developed in chapter 5, such as creating relationships that drive revenue].
>
> I look forward to keeping in touch about developments in your work-life. If there is anything I might help you with, please do not hesitate to give me a call.
>
> Best regards,
>
>
> Your Name

## Chapter Wrap-Up

As you start your new position, be intentional about your results and your relationships. Schedule some time with yourself on a monthly or biweekly basis to assess how you are doing in both of these areas. On a daily basis, remember to deliver value, value, value! It's the secret to 21st century career security.

In closing the pages of this book, my wish for you is that you be enthusiastically engaged in work that brings value to others. And may it bring you radical rewards!

# Appendix A

# Magic Job Search Tips

## Magic Career-Choice Tips

### Five Magic Tips to Live the Life of Your Dreams
*Contributed by Sue McCullough, BA, JCTC*

1. Relax, close your eyes, and visualize what life would be like if you were living the life of your dreams.

2. Open your eyes and answer each of the following questions with one or two words: How did you feel about your envisioned life? What was your lifestyle and living environment like? What was fun, enjoyable, or exciting? What did you bring to this lifestyle that was uniquely you?

3. Rank the words in order, with 1 being the highest priority. The top five words describe your life's passion and values.

4. Determine what action you'll take this week to bring your passions and values into your life. Be open to possibilities that arise.

5. Make life choices based on whether your life's passion and values would be satisfied.

## Yes, You Can Turn Personal Interests Into a Career
*Contributed by JoAnn Nix, CPRW, JCTC, CCMC, CEIP, CBS*

Does this statement sound familiar? "I know my real passion. If I could earn a great living doing it, I'd be ecstatic!" The good news is that you can turn your personal interest into business ownership and a rewarding career. It's not as difficult as you might think. Following are some initial steps:

1. Make a list of your personal interests and rank them according to preference.

2. Share your list with friends and ask for ideas in transforming your interest into business ownership and a rewarding career. Ask people whether they have contacts in the business you are exploring.

3. Conduct extensive research using Google.com or other resources and gather information about entrepreneurs who own similar businesses. Contact them and schedule meetings. Create a list of key exploratory questions for your meeting.

4. Read books depicting successful entrepreneurs who turned their passions into rewarding careers. Incorporate their ideas into your action plan.

5. Join organizations focused on your personal interests. Hire a small-business consultant or career coach and read business books.

6. Consider a volunteer or internship position to gain needed experience.

7. Always think positive thoughts and live your dreams!

## Uncovering Your Hidden Passions
*Contributed by Cathy Alfandre, CCMC*

Think back to different events you have attended in the last two to three years (weddings, reunions, graduations, holiday gatherings, cocktail parties, anything!). During the course of these events, you met a variety of people and found out what they do for a living. Try to remember: Which jobs or professions interested you most? Think of the people who, when they told you about their work, you wanted to ask lots of questions. Then ponder the following:

- What was the work?

- What, specifically, about the work did you find interesting, even fascinating?

- Even if you know that you would (or could) never actually do that job, what are the appealing characteristics? For example, does it involve public service, or public speaking, or artistic expression, or technical expertise, or…?

Try to remember 5 to 10 different people. Jot down everything you can remember about their jobs. Then look for common themes and insights into your hidden interests and desires.

# Magic Job Search Strategy Tips

## 10 Job Search Truths

*Contributed by Freddie Cheek, M.S. Ed., CCM, CPRW, CRW, CWDP*

1. Everyone has problems—most overcome them with creativity, resourcefulness, and effort.

2. Some things are beyond our control—so learn to let go.

3. Life is a journey and not a terminal activity—don't just plan for this job; think where it can lead.

4. Live in the real world—be practical about goals and objectives.

5. Expect change and embrace it—every tomorrow offers the possibility of being better.

6. You cannot rewrite your past (if only…)—you must accept where you are now and move forward.

7. No one can commit as much time to your job search as you—be your own best administrative assistant.

8. The greatest opportunities are the ones you create—they are the best fit for you.

9. There is no magic bullet—just hard work!

10. **Perception is reality!** If you come across as qualified and a viable candidate for the job, you will be treated as such.

## Go Backwards to Go Forwards

*Contributed by Deborah Wile Dib, CPBS, CCM, CCMC, NCRW, CPRW, CEIP, JCTC*

Every job seeker has moments when the tough work of job search seems overwhelming. To prevent being overwhelmed, or at least reduce its impact, conduct your job search as you've always conducted your jobs—with a support team in place and mental confidence nurtured by past successes. Build energy and confidence by relating job search activities to your successful "job-doing" activities. Ask yourself these questions about your previous jobs:

- What was my toughest project?

- How did I plan strategy and resources?

- Did I give it 100 percent effort?

- Did I do it alone?

- How did I handle stagnation?

- Was failure ever an option?

- How can I think of my job search in that way?

- If I do, what might happen?

Just as dancers and athletes have powerful "muscle memory" that works automatically, you have a "business memory." Comparing your job search to your previous jobs helps put you in a place of business thinking. When you start to think in business terms, your "business memory" will kick in. This will give you the stamina, adrenaline, and sheer guts you need to keep your momentum strong and keep your message confident.

## Stress Management for Career Success

*Contributed by Beth B. Kennedy, MS, LMFT*

It is exciting to think about a new career and the joy it can bring to your life! It is also important to remember that with any change—good or bad—comes stress. Stress can be motivating, but too much can impede your success. The key to reaching your career vision is to realize the importance of stress management. Every day you need to ask yourself, "What am I doing today to manage my stress?" The most stress-resilient people do this without thinking. Simple, doable strategies work best. Are you getting regular exercise? Are you writing in a journal at least once a week, sharing your anxieties, expectations, and excitement? Are you focusing on what you can control and not dwelling on the past? Are you eating healthy? Are you including some of the interests that truly relax you, such as yoga, reading, gardening, cooking, dancing, or time with friends?

Take time every day to ask, "What can I do for myself?" Daily stress-management strategies will recharge your energies and lead to a balanced, successful career!

## Answer the Tough Questions Before the Interview

*Contributed by Deborah Dib, CPBS, CCM, CCMC, NCRW, CPRW, CEIP, JCTC*

A great personal brand tells an employer-enticing story about vision, innovation, solutions, and bottom-line/profit-building performance. It demonstrates personality and work style. It proves a chemistry and culture "fit."

Analyzing your performance in the following six critical areas of impact will help you write a branded résumé and prepare branded interview responses that will build momentum, attract offers, and power your career.

**1. Gap Analysis—Reality Check**

- What do employers in my target market need and want?
- Do I have it?

**2. Skills—Benefit**

- What are my top skills?
- What have I done that links my top skills with bottom-line performance?

**3. Differentiator**

- What do I offer that my competition can't?
- What have I done for my company with my differentiation?

**4. $$**

- How have I created profit or saved money for my company?
- What is the best thing I have done that predicts that I can do this for my next company?

**5. Chemistry**

- What is my emotional appeal (intangible)?
- How have these skills impacted success in my past jobs?

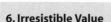
**6. Irresistible Value**

- Why hire *me*?

- What is the one thing that could make me the leading candidate?

## Seven Steps to a Successful Job Search Plan
*Contributed by Beverly Harvey, CPRW, JCTC, CCM, CCMC, MRW*

A successful job search requires a solid plan, including these elements:

1. Consider the various job search strategies that will work for you, and then create a multi-faceted plan.

2. Set up your job search in phases and assign a timeline to each phase. Determine how much time you have to spend on daily and weekly job search activities and budget your time accordingly.

3. Take stock of your resources and inventory (computer, printer, printer cartridges, résumé stationery and envelopes, networking business cards, notecards for follow-ups and thank-yous, a calendaring system, professional wardrobe, and so on). Note that business cards are a must in your networking, and you can obtain them free at www.vistaprint.com.

4. Develop a job search budget. In addition to resources and inventory, consider the cost of distributing your résumé through online vehicles, membership in professional organizations, networking expenses, travel expenses, relocation expenses, hiring a career coach, and so on.

5. Develop a system for keeping track of your contacts, activities, appointments, follow-ups, newly acquired contacts, and information.

6. Document all of your activities.

7. Review your job search progress weekly to determine the effectiveness of each activity and budget job search time toward activities that generate the greatest return. You should allot the highest percentage of your time to networking and informational meetings because they have been proven to generate the best returns.

## Use All Avenues for an Effective Search
*Contributed by Louise Garver, CMP, MCDP, CPRW, CEIP, JCTC*

Are you tapping multiple strategies to win job interviews? If not, consider the following results from a recent survey on recruiting trends conducted annually by Kevin Wheeler, President and Founder of Global Learning Resources, Inc. Recruiters were asked to choose the most effective source of finding candidates from a list of choices. The top five most effective sources remain consistent from the preceding year's survey:

1. Employee referrals (34.7 percent, a 3.3 percent decrease from the preceding year)

2. Networking (18.7 percent, a 3.9 percent decrease from the preceding year)

3. Internet job board postings (12.4 percent, a 4.7 percent increase over the preceding year)

4. The organization's own Web site (9.3 percent, a 4.2 percent increase over the preceding year)

5. Internet searching (6.7 percent, a 0.3 percent increase over the preceding year)

## Working Hard or Working Smart?

*Contributed by Susan Guarneri, MS, NCCC, MCC, CPRW, CCMC, CEIP*

Spend more time on activities that will lead to success. Draw a pie chart and label the slices of the pie with your various job search activities, such as in-person networking, online networking, online job search, researching companies, and job fairs. If you are spending most of your time on online searches, make that the largest slice of the pie, followed by the activity that comes in second for your time, and so on.

Next, compare those slices of the pie to statistics on how people best find jobs. If you're not spending the majority of your time on what works, adjust your focus. Re-slice your pie to reflect best-practice job search activities (see the preceding tip, "Use All Avenues for an Effective Search"), and then "eat" your pie, one slice at a time!

## Job Search Activity Tracker

*Contributed by Freddie Cheek, M.S. Ed., CCM, CPRW, CRW, CWDP*

When you are conducting an aggressive job search, you must keep track of all of your activities. An effective tool is an index-card system that will allow you to track what you do and when.

This system avoids duplication of effort, prevents you from forgetting to get back to contacts, makes company information immediately accessible, and enables you to respond intelligently when prospective employers call.

On the card, record the following: company name, address, and phone number (look up missing details); company contact name; job opening; and all your contact activity dates for résumé submission, follow-up call, interview, and so on). Tape on the back a copy of the ad or a brief description of the opening.

When you find a new posting, check your cards to see whether you have already responded. You can also pull the cards that require a follow-up call. And best of all, when an employer calls, instead of wondering which job is being discussed, politely ask the caller to wait while you get a pad and pen and reach for your card box. You will have the company info, date you responded, and job description right in your hand. You can then reply to questions with answers that fit that job.

## Positive Job Application Responses

*Contributed by Freddie Cheek, M.S. Ed., CCM, CPRW, CRW, CWDP*

When completing a job application, how can you answer questions that deal with problem areas? Here are some appropriate comments:

- **No degree or diploma:** In the area for additional educational information, list any job-specific courses, on-the-job training, and new skills you have obtained.

- **No car or driver's license:** State that you have a thorough knowledge of public transportation and experience getting around town.

- **No work experience:** List your volunteer activities, work-related jobs you did for family (paying bills, budgeting, purchasing, and so on), and recent and relevant training.

- **No professional references:** State any personal or school references who will verify your dependability, honesty, trustworthiness, excellent attendance, solid interpersonal skills, and anything else special.

- **Reasons for leaving past jobs:** Seeking a more challenging position, looking for greater responsibility, wanting a job that better fits your education/training (mention classes), seeking a job utilizing your best skills (list them), or desiring an opportunity to advance (state management abilities). You can also mention the following: caring for a family member (no longer an issue), education, relocation, layoff, and so on.

- **Do not volunteer the following information:** Being fired or arrested, pay was too low, work was too hard, problems with co-workers or boss, hated job, work was beneath you, got bored, ill a lot, or disabled.

## Avoid Costly Direct-Mail Mistakes

*Contributed by Mark Hovind*

When it comes to creating a direct-mail campaign, one of the biggest mistakes job seekers make is not drilling down deep enough in the database to get a precise mailing list. This wastes more than half the cost of mailing letters! For example, the Dunn and Bradstreet database has five levels of precision that use Standard Industry Codes, or SICs. It starts with main divisions such as Construction, Manufacturing, and so on, and gets more precise the deeper you drill down. The next four levels are two-digit, four-digit, six-digit, and eight-digit SICs.

The biggest bang for your buck comes when you're targeting the eight-digit SIC level instead of the four-digit or six-digit level. The eight-digit SIC level has 14 times as many choices as the four-digit level. For example, let's say you are targeting plastic injection molding companies with sales over $5 million. If you stop at the four-digit level, the best you can do is a category called Plastics Products, at SIC 3089 with 2,310 different companies. The plastic injection molders are in this category, along with others that are not your intended target, such as boot and shoe, celluloid, flowerpots, synthetic resin, and more. But when you drill down to the eight-digit SIC level, you will find the 528 Plastic Injection Molding companies at SIC 30890609. Because these are your intended targets, you have just saved 77 percent of your mailing costs.

There is a Do-It-Yourself page on JobBait.com that explains a lot more—including links to the D&B database, cost estimates, how to clean up your mailing list, what kind of paper works best, and how to reduce the risk of ghosting (the reverse-image effect caused when toner transfers from one printed surface to another after a letter is folded—much like paint that is not quite dry).

## AA: The Survivor's Door to Career Opportunity

*Contributed by Barb Poole, CPRW, CRW, BS, CCMC*

Attitude and Acceptance! It is important that you make things happen, instead of waiting for them to happen. Focus on today and what you can do. This might mean letting go of old attitudes and accepting that the way you look for work might have to change. It might mean taking a "survival position."

*(continued)*

*(continued)*

When should you accept a survival position? When these factors are present:

- The position is related to the field you are exploring.

- The position is with a company that you feel comfortable working for.

- The position is simply a financially feasible situation.

Why take a survival position?

- It's often easier to network inside a company.

- Sometimes positions are available only to internal employees.

- There is potential to prove your worth to the company. Things change—someone might quit or retire, creating the perfect fit for you.

- Contract or temporary positions often turn into full-time jobs.

By changing your attitude and accepting contract, temporary, and entry-level positions, you allow doors to open. Remember the old adage, "If life gives you lemons, make lemonade." You can forget your ego and do your best work while you help to create better opportunities!

# How to Transform a Job Fair into a Job Offer

*Contributed by Gail Frank, NCRW, CPRW, JCTC, CEIP, MA*

Career fairs can streamline your job hunt, let you practice interviewing, and help you conduct research on career opportunities. To transform a job fair into a job offer, follow these steps:

### Step 1: Homework

Many job seekers visit a job fair "to see what's out there." Wrong! Prepare for a fair as if it is a personal interview. That means upfront research. Know who is there.

Carry a portfolio with laser-printed, professionally prepared résumés. Dress professionally and simply. Don't bring bulky bags. Keep your right hand free to shake hands.

### Step 2: Your Plan of Attack: Working the Job Fair

Approach the company representative, offer your hand, and introduce yourself. Tell them you are interested in working for them, and why. Ask about their hiring process. Ask how to get an interview. Ask the names of the decision maker or head of the department (very important).

Get business cards from people you meet (very important). Don't overstay your welcome, but communicate your qualifications and your interest level.

### Step 3: Post-Fair Job-Winning Tricks

Now you have names of HR managers, names of all the "decision makers"/department heads, and a good understanding of what the companies need.

Send résumés to department heads at each company, with a personalized letter summarizing qualifications for that specific job, your interest in it, and a willingness to meet. Copy the HR managers whom you met at the fair. Do not expect them to contact you, so promise to follow up. And do it.

## Two Heads Are Better Than One: Structured Brainstorming
*Contributed by Christine Edick, PCCC, CCMC, JCTC, CEIP*

Here is a tip that puts the saying "two heads are better than one" to good use. Gather your career management team, friends, or colleagues to conduct a structured brainstorming session. Here's how it works:

You address the group with a specific issue, such as "I would like to work for Microsoft but don't know how to get my foot in the door." You allot yourself five minutes to explain everything you have done up to this point. While you are talking, everyone in your group remains quiet and takes notes to respond to you later.

When your five minutes is up, the group then takes 15 minutes to offer their ideas. Each person in the group contributes one idea at a time, without discussion, such as "Who do you know who works for Microsoft?" or "Have you attended any job fairs at Microsoft?" and so on. After each person has contributed, the cycle repeats so that each person contributes a second or third idea until 15 minutes has gone by. During this time, you are writing down the ideas and the person who contributed each idea.

After this exercise, you should have 20 to 50 ideas. Pick three to five that you can do immediately and commit to implementing them in the next few days or weeks. The person who gave you that idea will be your support. Repeat this brainstorming throughout your job search to generate ideas whenever you are stuck.

# Magic Networking Tips

## Networking Memory Jogger
*Contributed by Freddie Cheek, M.S. Ed., CCM, CPRW, CRW, CWDP*

Some of the best networking opportunities are professional affiliation meetings, job fairs, school events, conferences, and community gatherings. The problem is that you meet so many people, and hopefully collect so many business cards, that it is difficult to sort them out after the fact. You are left with a pocket or purse full of cards that all jumble together.

Take a tip from sales professionals and use the back of each business card. While you are taking a break or sitting at the table or listening to the speaker, make notations on the back of each card. Note any discussion points, the person's description, any reminders (where they went to school, mutual friends, and so on), and any details that will jog your memory later. Also, be sure to note the date and event.

If you write, e-mail, or call that person at a later date, you can mention some information you discussed, a point you have in common, or at least when and where you met. That way, you will remember the contact and help him or her remember you.

For the cards of those who might be more important to your search, dog-ear one corner of the card to help you remember to quickly follow up.

## Finding Time to Network

*Contributed by Wendy Terwelp, CCMC, RPBS, IJCTC, CEIP*

Network, network, network! Nearly 85 percent of all job seekers land positions through networking. "Well, I don't have time," you say. You don't? Even if it means getting hired? Here are some quick tips:

1. Read your local business journal during lunch and jot down at least five new contact names each day. By the end of the week, you will have 25 new names or companies you can target for your career search.

2. Combine networking with things you already do. Take five minutes before your event or activity to rehearse your sound bites and list people you plan to speak with and why.

3. If you're already going to a business function you can: a) Wear a name badge that communicates your brand (people will be intrigued!); b) Jot down one unusual or interesting thing about each new person you meet on the back of his/her business card; and c) Jot down what action you plan to take (how you will follow up).

## Get to the Hiring Manager

*Contributed by George Dutch, CMF, CCM, JCTC*

I met recently with a savvy professional who had conducted 35 "informational interviews" with contacts in Toronto's social services sector. Not one of those meetings generated a job offer. That's because almost none of her contacts had the authority or power to hire her. They were good people, but they were not hiring managers!

What is a hiring manager? The person you would report to in any organization... the person who has the final say on whether or not you will get hired. This is typically the person who will work with you every day, the person who must answer for your on-the-job performance, the person whose own career is somewhat dependent on that performance.

Managers are busy managing plans, priorities, projects, programs, budgets, schedules, equipment, and machinery—but they are not always trained to hire, nor do they necessarily enjoy hiring or do it very well. Your goal in job search is to make the hiring process easier for them.

If you don't know how to get in front of hiring managers, or how to develop and convincingly deliver your value proposition, GET HELP! Nothing else will increase your chances of getting hired for better jobs faster.

## Get Known to Get Results

*Contributed by Meg Montford, MCCC, CMF, CCM*

Since the demise of job security, YOU are in charge of your own career. Think of it as if you were in charge of your own company: CEO of Me, Inc. (Branding Guru, Tom Peters, first labeled this workplace shift in 1997.) Just as entrepreneurs are advised to build businesses by integrating four key actions—publishing, public speaking, networking, and creating a Web site—these actions can work for you!

To close a business deal (in other words, get a job!) as CEO of Me, Inc., do the following:

- **Publish:** Write expert articles to attract interest in you, your personal brand. Research what your target market (potential employer) reads, and then submit articles to both print and online publications. Get acknowledged!
- **Present:** Develop expert presentations using the above approach. Contact event organizers to offer your speaking skills. Professional groups welcome presenters who don't charge fees. Get seen!
- **Network:** Meet and greet hiring authorities where they hang out: civic organizations, non-profit boards, fund-raising events, the golf course.... Get involved!
- **Create a Web site:** Put your résumé on its own Web site, and then list the URL on business cards used for networking purposes. Get connected!

Visibility builds credibility. Become a commodity a company must have!

## Professional Associations = Networking Benefits
*Contributed by Louise Garver, CMP, MCDP, CPRW, CEIP, JCTC*

Where can professionals and executives establish contacts with others who have similar interests and career goals? Where can they learn about the latest industry news and what other businesses are doing?

The answer: at the local chapter of their professional association. Professional associations can provide you with an opportunity to network and make valuable industry contacts—whether in your industry or a new one. By attending association-sponsored seminars, workshops, or conferences, you will have access to a new group of contacts that you would never have known. Your new contacts can lead you to positions that might never be advertised or enable you to gain a distinct advantage over the competition.

## A Question to Stimulate More Leads
*Contributed by Joan Cousins, MS, MFA, JCTC*

One of the best ways to gain the inside scoop on an employer or a specific job opening is to talk with a current or recent employee. If you don't know someone, ask friends, relatives, and business associates for names. But how you phrase the question will substantially affect your results. Note the phrasing of this question:

"Who do you know who works at Desirable Employer?"

Because this question presumes your contacts know someone, they will automatically scan their minds the way they search their houses for misplaced car keys. Their attitude—"I know it's got to be here somewhere!"—will turn up far more names of current and recent employees. Your contacts will also feel more satisfied because they were actually able to help you.

Avoid the question people typically ask:

"Do you know someone who works at Desirable Employer?"

*(continued)*

*(continued)*

This question asks your contacts to sort people they know into two categories: (1) Yes, he/she works at the organization or (2) No, he/she does not. You are far more likely to leave empty-handed when you ask a question that requires a simple "yes" or "no" answer.

By reframing this one question, you will create more leads and fewer dead ends.

## Beating the Avoidance Factor for Networking Events

*Contributed by Bonnie Kurka, CCMC, CPRW, JCTC, FJST*

The thought of attending a networking event for many creates a variety of responses, from a bad case of the "butterflies" to panic attacks. Some people avoid them altogether. Here are some simple networking tips to ease the jitters.

1.  Wear something eye-catching or unusual, but tasteful, like an unusual brooch for women or an interesting tie for men. This provides an ice breaker for someone to come up to you and comment on it.

2.  Watch for someone else wearing the "ice breaker" brooch or tie. Go up to them and make a comment.

3.  Plan some general comments and open-ended questions and rehearse them ahead of the event. Hearing your own voice say the words will help you repeat them when you're nervous.

4.  Have a prepared response to the question: "What do you do?" Be sure to end it with a question for your listener.

5.  Go with the goal of meeting and conversing with just two or three people. There is no way you can get to know 200 people in one evening. Try to meet few people well enough that you can make a lunch date or follow-up appointment.

## Getting the Scoop on a Company

*Contributed by Don Orlando, MBA, CPRW, JCTC, CCM, CCMC*

It's an interviewer's favorite question: "How much do you know about our company?" Beyond visiting the corporate Web site and Googling the company, there is another, much more powerful source: your target company's customers.

No one knows an organization better than its customers. Customers can help you answer two critical questions: Is this a company I'd like to work for? If it is, what info would help me get off to a great start?

If you are unsure of whom a company's customers are, visit the corporate Web site. Then speak with the person in that organization most likely to know about the company that interests you. For example, if you want to work for a business-supply company, look for an organization that uses lots of supplies. Then call the person who buys those supplies, the purchasing manager.

When you contact a customer, explain that you're interested in joining a company that serves them. Because the person you are calling might later become your customer, you want to know what your target organization does well and where they might improve.

Imagine the power of your answer, backed up by the company's own customers, when the interviewer asks that favorite question.

### Magic Job Search Words: Follow-Up! Follow-Up! Follow-Up!

*Contributed by Debra Feldman*

Many otherwise savvy businessmen and businesswomen flunk job searching—essentially handing over prime opportunities to their competition—all because they do not complete the follow-up phase. It is not enough to simply prove that your unique talents and abilities match the employer's expectations. Don't depend on the hiring manager to keep the dialogue going forward. Promote her action on an offer by demonstrating that you a) really want this opportunity more than anyone else; b) are persistent despite formidable obstacles; and c) voluntarily take initiative to complete tasks. Assume that the decision-maker is busy and has other priorities. Stay top-of-mind with reminders about how you can reduce costs or make more money to balance the expense of adding you as the newest member of the team.

# Magic Interviewing Tips

### Power Your Voice to Power Your Career

*Contributed by Deborah Wile Dib, CPBS, CCM, CCMC, NCRW, CPRW, CEIP, JCTC*

The world of work today is increasingly virtual—a series of e-mail, voice-mail, and teleconferencing interactions that happen as often or more often than face-to-face meetings.

When you are heard on the phone, does your voice make an immediate impression of confidence and ability? Does it radiate enthusiasm and vigor? If not, you might be hurting your chances for that new job, promotion, or speaking gig.

Whenever you speak in a faceless situation, put the same passion and vitality into your words as you would in a face-to-face meeting. A first impression by phone counts as much as a face-time first impression.

Confidence and passion attract—employers love to hire leader-like, confident people. So speak clearly and speak confidently, whether on a live call, a teleconference, or even a voice mail. And be sure that your outgoing message on your home phone, work phone, and cell phone are clear and professional! No kids, no dogs, no funny jokes, no music.

Make your voice work for you, not against you.

### Test the Telephone Interviewer's Focus

*Contributed by Dale Kurow, M.S.*

Unlike face-to-face interviews, in which you have visual clues, you are functioning blind in a phone interview. You need to become comfortable speaking without visual feedback or reinforcement.

Think like a consultant and ask consulting-type questions after you have been talking for a while uninterrupted. For example:

"Have I touched on the areas you wanted to cover?" Or "Would you like me to elaborate?"

*(continued)*

*(continued)*

Asking these questions will provide valuable clues about the interviewer's focus and help you tailor your future responses.

And, recognize that you'll encounter a number of "gatekeeper" questions as part of the phone interview drill. These are preliminary or screening questions designed to weed out weak or inappropriate candidates. Caution: Don't be so specific with your responses that you eliminate opportunities at this early stage.

## What Language Does the Interviewer Speak?
*Contributed by Christine Edick, PCCC, CCMC, JCTC, CEIP*

Telephone interviews are conducted to screen candidates out. Because you do not have the advantage of watching someone's body language, you need to be acutely aware of their communication style (their neurolinguistic programming style, or NLP). The four NLP styles are visual, auditory, kinesthetic, and auditory digital.

The person with a visual NLP style hears words such as "see, look, picture, and envision." The auditory person uses words such as "tell, hear, talk, and shout." Individuals with the kinesthetic style love words like "feel, handle, touch, and hug." The auditory digital people respond to words such as "think, facts, compute, logical, and rationalize."

Paying attention to keywords, key phrases, and common characteristics is important. If you are not sure which NLP style the interviewer is, make your point by using several of the learning styles throughout your conversation and seeing which one resonates with the listener. Example: "How does that look to you?" or "How does that sound to you?" or "How does that feel to you?" or "Does that make sense to you?"

Having the ability to listen and speak in all communication styles will help you create instant rapport.

## Do-It-Yourself Interview Practice
*Contributed by Billie Ruth Sucher, MS, CTMS, CTSB*

If you don't have someone to practice interviewing with, and you're not in a position to hire a professional interview coach, consider this do-it-yourself strategy. Start with seven index cards, making one card for each of the following words: who, what, when, where, why, how, and how much, representing these questions:

- Who am I?
- What do I want?
- When can I begin work?
- Where am I looking?
- Why hire me?
- How will others speak of me, both positive and negative?
- How much money am I worth?

On the cards, record your responses to these seven questions, using bullet points for key ideas. Next, position a chair in front of a mirror and seat yourself. Draw one of the cards, ask yourself a question, and "read" your response, observing yourself in the mirror. Rest assured, the 15th time you practice the question and response, you will find yourself getting much more comfortable and confident. As your confidence builds, dispense with the chair, stand up, smile, and practice your responses without reading from your cards. Make a mental note of how you look, sound, and feel as you do these exercises. Practice pays in many ways!

## Hidden Agendas in Interviews

*Contributed by George Dutch, CMF, CCM, JCTC*

Behind every hiring decision is an agenda: a problem to be solved, a challenge to overcome, or an issue to deal with. This agenda represents a target for you to hit. Sometimes the target is set up by the employer, for example, sales are low; we want a producer. Sometimes the target is hidden.

An interview is a two-way street. It's a dialogue, not a test. As the interviewee, it is your responsibility to identify the hiring drivers. The best way to do so is to probe with questions, such as the following: What is your vision for your organization? Where does this position fit into your vision? What are the major obstacles to achieving your goals and objectives? What is the top priority you want addressed by this position in the next year? What type of person do you need here? What makes a person successful here?

In every interview, the employer is hoping you will be the solution to a set of challenges or problems. Those challenges represent a target. One of your main goals in an interview is to find that target and hit the bull's-eye!

## You're Hired!

*Contributed by Carol Nason, MA, CPRW*

One of the three most frequently asked questions in an interview is "Why should we hire you?" This question was asked in the final interviews of Donald Trump's *The Apprentice*. Knowing how to answer this question can be just what it takes to put you in first place.

If the question is asked, you can use a prepared answer twice in your interview. Use it first to answer the question, and use it again to give a strong closing to the interview. If the question is not asked, you can still use it for the closing.

Your answer should describe how well qualified you are for this position. Now take it one step further and describe why you are better than any of the other candidates.

To prepare this answer, sort out your skills and accomplishments into two categories. The first category would be a summary of your skills that serve as qualifiers for this position. The second category would be a summary of your complementary skills. Show how these additional attributes can enhance your performance and make you more valuable to the company than any other candidate.

## Seduce the Hiring Manager

*Contributed by William G. Murdock*

The book just jumped off the shelf, *The Art of Seduction*, by Robert Greene (A Joost Elffers book), and no, I'm not going to be vulgar or sexy.

Greene's book is a great read, and it really is about the art of seduction. But what caught my attention, at least at first, was a small section of purple pages, about a third of the way into the book, titled "The Seducer's Victims: The 18 Types." As I looked at the 18 types of "victims," I quickly concluded that this was a book about how to sell to the various personality types, be those types Myers-Briggs or DiSC. With more than 18 years of sales, I was hooked.

Greene's basic point boils down to this: In order to seduce a woman, you must, in essence, find what is missing from her life and become it. I quickly concluded that this advice was, indeed, Step Three of a standard five-step sales process, called "Needs Assessment."

To the chase. Getting hired is often a process of "selling yourself" to the hiring manager, and the rules of seduction apply–to "seduce" the hiring manager, you must find out what is missing from their career, and be able to fulfill it.

How would you make a hiring manager tell you what's missing from their career—a very, very personal revelation? You simply go through the back door and ask this way: "Mr. Smith, as you look over your past five years of employment and add up all your successes, if there were one thing you could add to your résumé, what would it be?" Regardless of the response, you have just found that manager's pain—what is missing from their career. Show them how to solve that issue, and the job is yours!

## Paint the Complete Picture

*Contributed by Louise Kursmark, MRW, CPRW, CEIP, JCTC, CCM*

When discussing your career activities and achievements, both in your résumé and during interviews, be sure that you provide background and context so that your reader/listener truly understands what you did and why it was important.

Consider the difference in meaning and impact between these two statements—both relating strong sales accomplishments:

**Before:** "In my position as Sales Manager for the Northeast District, I led my team in exceeding our goals every quarter for three straight years. It was a real team effort, and we all worked hard to make sure we were successful."

**After:** "When I took the job as Sales Manager, the Northeast District was in disarray due to a major restructuring. Half of the sales team had quit, and the other half was demoralized. I was able to rebuild the team, restore their enthusiasm, and lead them to unprecedented success— we were the only district in the company to beat our goals every quarter for three straight years, and we took more than 25 percent market share from our two top competitors."

## Park Your Baggage at the Door

*Contributed by Jean Cummings, M.A.T., CPBS, CPRW, CEIP*

If you are getting interviews but not offers, you might be bringing in an attitude. Ask yourself the following questions:

- "Am I ambivalent about this job?"

- "Am I worried that this interviewer is going to be like my last boss, who didn't appreciate my work?"

- "Am I worried that this organization is going to take advantage of me and not compensate me fairly?"

If you were recently laid off, consider the following:

- "Do I have feelings of anger, sadness, disappointment, or self-doubt that might be getting 'picked up' by the interviewer?"

So what do you do if you resonate with any of these issues? Try practicing a mock interview with an intuitive person you trust or an executive recruiter and see what attitudes they notice. Then try visualizing the new organization as a place you once worked that you loved, a place in which you felt treated fairly, appreciated, and recognized. That way, when you go into the interview, your prevailing attitude will temporarily be a positive one. You will come across "up," energetic, and interested. If you have the time and interest, consider getting coaching to help you understand your attitude better and gain some resolution. But, in the short term, park your baggage at the door and see the results!

## Delta Force Positive

*Contributed by William G. Murdock*

Sadly, those who get the job are not necessarily the "best qualified" candidates, they are just the "last ones standing" after an elimination process. The question then becomes, how can you avoid the "negative" elimination? Answer: Delta Force Positive.

The first step comes with the realization that you are of little importance to those doing the interview. Oh, sure, they are smiling and asking all kinds of questions about you and your skills. But, in fact, they care only about themselves, their departmental needs, and their mission. Once you understand this, you're on the road to victory.

Delta Force is one of the most elite commando units our military has—very deadly and very effective. I call this tip Delta Force Positive because, while you are being graded negatively in the interview, you are going to counterattack with positive strategies and simply derail the interviewer. My advice: Empower your boss.

Recruiters, HR professionals, and hiring managers are trained to make you talk 80 percent of the time while they talk only 20 percent of the time. Your job is to turn the tables, and the easiest way to make them talk about themselves is to ask them "empowering" questions about their department, their mission, their careers, and themselves.

Here are three samples of Delta Force Positive questions:

*(continued)*

*(continued)*

1. What three things are you doing now to make this company (department) be even more successful? What do you need to achieve these goals?

2. During your time with this company, what has made you most proud?

3. What three things does this company bring to the table that makes its products or services more valuable than the competition?

Consistently guide the conversation away from yourself and toward those issues and goals that management embraces, and force those you are interviewing with to speak in positive and proactive terms about themselves, their company, and mutually shared goals and values. Turn the tables. Force the conversation onto a positive platform, and then back up your questions with examples from your career where you've made a positive difference. The results will be stunning.

## Show It, Don't Tell It

*Contributed by Louise Kursmark, MRW, CPRW, CEIP, JCTC, CCM*

Wondering how to set yourself apart from other, equally qualified candidates? Take the initiative to demonstrate (not just talk about) what you can do for the company. Consider these ideas:

- After an interview, analyze the most significant challenges you learned about. Prepare a report of your analysis along with specific solutions. Send your report to the hiring manager with your thank-you note.

- During the interview, ask the hiring manager whether he or she would like to see you work through a business problem, one that you've identified as critical to the job at hand. Indicate that you'll show them exactly how you would perform if you were on the job. Use a white board or flip chart to walk them through your thought processes, all the way to your conclusions.

- Ask if you can sit in on a planning meeting, during which you can contribute ideas and solutions that relate to the issues at hand. Not every employer will be willing to allow you inside before you're hired, but just making the offer demonstrates your initiative.

With these strategies, you'll be more credible and memorable than other candidates.

## Handling the Questions from Hell

*Contributed by Harriette Royer, MS, and Dr. Lauren Vicker*

Interviews are stressful, but when the prospect of being asked a certain question makes you hyperventilate, you need a strategy for questions from hell, like these:

- What were you doing from 1999 to 2001? (You were in a rehabilitation program.)

- Why did you leave that job? (You were let go.)

- Is there any part of this job you would not be able to perform? (Yes, you have a disability.)

- Are your grades a reflection of your ability? (No—your GPA was embarrassingly low.)

The question has been asked… now what do you do?

1. You're in charge of telling the story the way you want it to be heard. Before you speak, collect your thoughts.

2. First, acknowledge the issue behind the question in a concise, straightforward manner. Never disparage or blame anyone.

3. Next, describe what you learned or gained from the situation and how it has helped/improved you.

4. Finally, connect your learning to the current position.

5. Remember, everyone, including the interviewer, has had unfortunate experiences. The reason for the question is to assess your ability to accept personal responsibility, not to uncover negative information about you.

Example:

**Question:** Why did you leave that job?

**Answer:** I was asked to leave. Let me explain. Shortly after I was hired, it was clear that my skill set didn't match the needs of the department. I offered to get more training but the manager was unwilling and decided to release me. Since then I have taken great care to pursue opportunities that match my abilities—like this position—and I have been more assertive about getting regular feedback on my performance.

## What to Do if You Don't Like Your Interviewer
*Contributed by Jean Cummings, M.A.T., CPBS, CPRW, CEIP*

The shocking truth is that a decision about a candidate in an interview is based primarily on how the applicant looks (appearance, body language) and sounds (voice). Ideally, hiring decisions would be made on how well someone could do the job, and interviewers do try to get at that information. However, there is a subtext that is unspoken but makes a critical difference: how likeable are you to that particular interviewer?

If *you* like the interviewer, the unspoken messages will probably be positive and work in your favor. But, what if you don't like the interviewer?

Here is a golden secret: Before you go into the interview, imagine that the interviewer is a trusted colleague, someone you have worked well with, respected, and liked a lot. Then, when you go into the interview, visualize that colleague. If you are able to imagine that the abrasive, superior, or threatening person in front of you is that person you really like, your tone of voice, facial expressions, body language, and responses will all be affected. The interviewer will pick up your friendly, positive attitude from the way you look and sound and will be more likely to hire you!

## Don't Choke on Your Words

*Contributed by Billie Ruth Sucher, M.S., CTMS, CTSB*

Many questions will be asked during the interview. How you respond will help you—or hurt you—so try this three-step approach for maximum success.

This strategy will be easy to incorporate in the interview process because it parallels one of our favorite pastimes—eating! During the interview, first remember to listen carefully to the question asked (take a bite); next, process the question a few seconds (chew it up); and finally, when you're ready, speak with confidence.

Practical experience suggests that swallowing a bite before it's properly chewed can cause us to choke—just like we can do on our words if we speak before we think!

## Want the Job? Then Ask for It

*Contributed by Linda Matias, CIC, NCRW, JCTC*

**Visualization Approach:** In this method, speak as though you are already part of the team by using words such as "we," "us," and "our." Doing so will allow the interviewer to visualize you in the position. Here's how it might sound:

"As a team member of The International Federation of the Intercups, I would provide our clients with thorough information regarding their accounts, and would handle all inquiries and discrepancies with confidentiality."

**Summation Approach:** Lay out all the facts—the exact reasons there is a match between you and the employer. For example:

"Throughout our conversation today, I have learned about the dynamics of your company, its culture, and the responsibilities of the position. I'm glad to see that your requirements match my experience to the letter—from my ability to manage corporate accounts to my ability to cultivate new business. I look forward to participating in the rest of the interview process and optimistically anticipate being a part of your team."

**Straightforward Approach:** This approach is simple and clear-cut. For instance:

"I'm interested in the position. Have I provided all the information you need to offer me the position?"

## The Reverse Interview: Noteworthy Questions the Job Candidate Can Ask

*Contributed by Edie Rische, NCRW, JCTC, ACCC*

Company-focused questions (rather than self-centered, candidate-focused questions) from you—the prospective employee—can have strategic impact and help you gain a competitive edge over other candidates. It's all about what you can do for the company. Notice how the following forward-thinking examples assume ownership of the position:

- What tasks would you like me to achieve within the next six months?

- What major concerns could I address immediately?

- Which of my skills would ease your worries?

- How does this department fit into the company's five-year plan?

These questions exhibit courage and personal security:

- May I make a suggestion that could very well improve this department's productivity (quality control, cost control, and so on)?

- Is it possible to negotiate a more comprehensive job description for myself that could eliminate duplicated tasks and reduce staffing expense?

And finally, these closing questions reflect confidence and assertive communication:

- Can I anticipate a second interview?

- When can I expect to hear back from you?

- How many candidates are you seriously considering at this time?

Questions like these can make a lasting impression on the interviewer and give you more control in the interview.

# Magic Salary-Negotiation Tips

## Successfully Navigating the Salary-Negotiation Minefield
*Contributed by Donna Srader, M.A.*

Salary negotiations can be stressful, but there are steps you can take to ensure effective and professional discussions.

1. Always research the salary range for the position, industry, and geographic location. Knowledge is power.

2. Never state your salary goal before an offer is made. And, if possible, never be the first to state a dollar amount, even after an offer.

3. When asked about salary, smile confidently and return the question. "What is the salary range at XYZ Company for an entry-level trainer with my experience, education, and skills?"

4. Once the interviewer states a salary range, respond appropriately:

   - "That is very close to the range my research suggested."

   - "My research suggested a slightly higher range in this geographic location (or industry). Do you have any idea why the discrepancy?"

   - "Well, that is certainly worth considering. However, because I have additional experience to contribute, I was looking for a slightly higher range."

5. Recognize salary limits and don't price yourself too high or too low. Be knowledgeable about your worth to the company and what you can contribute. Be reasonable in your salary expectations, whether you are a new graduate, career changer, or highly experienced candidate.

## Magic Tip: Salary Negotiations for Dual-Career Couples

*Contributed by Michelle M. Fleig-Palmer, MBA, CCM*

Juggling two careers while moving to a new town? When you are negotiating benefits for a job that involves relocation, remember to ask for career assistance for your spouse/partner.

First, negotiate contacts. Ask whether the organization can arrange a small networking meeting for your partner with people in his/her career field. A meet-and-greet for your partner, preferably before your move, will help your partner begin networking in pursuit of job opportunities. For example, an applicant was recruited by a company in a small town in Ohio. His wife is an artist. The company paid for a breakfast where the wife was introduced to other artists in that town. This breakfast provided the wife the vital connections she needed to establish herself as an artist in the new community.

Or you could ask someone to take your partner to several community events. For example, if your partner is a businessperson, the local Chamber of Commerce often hosts networking events.

Second, ask for job search help. Your partner will need to polish his/her résumé, cover letter, interviewing skills, and so on. Job search coaches, such as the contributors to the Magic Tips in this book, can provide valuable career assistance to your partner. Many organizations will pay for these services as part of the benefits package offered to you.

Third, "get it in writing." Have the organization provide a letter detailing the specific benefit (networking and/or job search assistance) that will help your partner continue his/her career in the new community.

# Magic Resume and Career Marketing Document Tips

## The Value of an ePortfolio

*Contributed by Beverly Harvey, CPRW, JCTC, CCM, CCMC, MRW*

An ePortfolio does the following:

- Markets the full depth and breadth of your experience, education, talents, skills, and accomplishments.

- Enables you to build an online presence and promote your brand, which is becoming essential as more and more recruiters conduct Google searches on prospective employees.

- Can be accessed by the interviewer during an interview and provide a project history, technical skills list, charts, graphics, pictures, publications, and other examples of your work and qualifications.

- Positions you as a cutting-edge candidate who understands the marketplace.

- May increase your visibility in your industry or field and may lead to unsolicited job offers, as well as other career-enhancing opportunities such as recognition as an "expert" by online and print publications, speaking engagements, and training instructor opportunities.

- Demonstrates your knowledge of technology and familiarity with various types of computer technology and applications.

- Can help bridge the gap during the initial stages of an out-of-state or long-distance job search.

- Provides the reader who has selected your résumé from a database to follow the link to your ePortfolio and read a much more appealing and in-depth presentation.

## Don't Reinvent the Wheel with Every Résumé

*Contributed by Donna Srader, M.A.*

Everyone knows that résumés for entry-level positions should be one page in length. But job seekers should first create a basic document without concern for its length that details all the information that might be included in a résumé. This includes transferable skills and accomplishments for career changers and academic projects and relevant courses for new graduates.

Once you have developed all the sections you might possibly need for all the types of résumés you might write, construct concise, straightforward accomplishment statements. Now use this document to create a targeted, one-page résumé specific to a job, a company, or an industry. Save time and effort by copying and pasting information and devising effective formats for targeted résumés that emphasize your contributions and gain the attention of prospective employers.

## Document Your Successes!

*Contributed by Jean F. West, CPRW, JCTC*

Are you in the habit of keeping a running journal of your work projects and accomplishments? Do you save "atta boy/girl" e-mails and kudos from supervisors, customers, clients, or vendors with whom you work? In this age of career self-management, it is important to get into the habit of documenting your successes. Along with the journal, keep a folder to save samples of your work, e-mails, letters, awards, and so on.

Three immediate uses and benefits of this recordkeeping are the following:

1. **Annual reviews:** Before your next performance review, send your boss a one-page résumé-style report documenting your contributions to the company during the last year.

2. **Résumé updates:** This report can also be used to update your résumé on a regular basis so that you are ready for new opportunities.

3. **Define your brand:** A regular assessment of your accomplishments will help you define and refine your personal brand, which is the expertise you are known for in your field. Building and promoting your personal brand is another wise career self-management practice.

# Get Résumé Credit for Volunteering

*Contributed by Gail Frank, NCRW, CPRW, JCTC, CEIP, MA*

Take credit for all of your life accomplishments. Just because you were not paid, do not relegate your volunteer experience to the end of your résumé.

A potential employer doesn't care whether any of your experience allowed you to be paid very well, very poorly, or not at all. They care about, "What's in it for me? How will this help *my* business?" That is the unspoken question your résumé must answer. Follow these three principles for using volunteer experience in your résumé:

1. **Take the Relevancy test:** Include volunteer experience on your résumé where it provides a specific example of a skill you have or a wonderful personal trait, such as creativity or team leadership, when those traits are valued in the position you are seeking.

2. **Don't just list it:** Explain it! Instead of listing

   Little League Coach
   PTA member

   Try this:

   Coached Little League team to its first winning season in six years through improved morale, an added sense of fun, and enhanced skills.

   Spearheaded quarterly PTA Bake Sale, which raised funds for desperately needed new band uniforms.

3. **Position it correctly:** Consider folding your volunteer experience into the résumé body. Place it before/after/alongside paid work experience. Title the section "Professional Experience," instead of "Work Experience" or "Work History."

# Special Reports: Share Your Wisdom and Stand Out

*Contributed by Christine Edick, PCCC, CCMC, JCTC, CEIP*

A special report is a multi-page document that describes some simple but essential "how-to" information. Whatever your profession, you probably have some insight about how to make a process run more smoothly, efficiently, or profitably. A special report shares that wisdom with potential employers.

A well-crafted special report has much more impact on potential employers than the typical résumé because it does the following:

- Emphasizes your potential contributions.

- Positions you as an expert.

- Is an interesting new format and therefore more likely to be read than a résumé.

- Has substantive value.

A special report has five main elements:

- A benefit-oriented title and subtitle

- An introduction

- Quality information beneficial to the reader, usually in the form of three to five "tips" or "mistakes to avoid."

- Author information: name, phone number, and e-mail address on each page and information about the author at the end

- A nice binding or presentation folder

Many hiring executives believe résumés inflate responsibilities and hide failures. But in a well-prepared report, you are speaking the language of the industry; you are communicating information that works to produce results. This document gives "take-it-to-the-bank" ideas focused on improving the bottom line or solving a nagging problem.

## Pull Quotes: How to Let Others Toot Your Horn

*Contributed by Jan Melnik, MRW, CCM, CPRW*

Cover letters remain as important as ever in a focused job search, but getting your typical four- or five-paragraph letter to stand out from the crowd can be a challenge. The best remedy is to do what no one else can—use the strategy of "pull quoting" to distinguish your candidacy and link your demonstrated accomplishments to the needs identified by the hiring authority. This requires having copies of previous performance evaluations handy—along with letters of commendation and recommendation. Cull through these documents looking for specific and quantified examples that prove what you have done to address actual problems, produce superb results, or effectively lead a team. Then incorporate, at most, two to three sentences that capture the essence of your initiative or achievement and build them into your cover letter.

Optimal placement is usually after the first two paragraphs. Paragraph one is where you immediately tell the reader the position you're interested in and prominently note any referral source. The second paragraph should compellingly present matches between the requirements of the position and your credentials. Wrapping up that paragraph can segue to the pull quotes (using anywhere from one to three different quotes) with a variation of the following closing sentence:

*You might find the following extracts from several performance evaluations (or letters of commendation) useful in evaluating my candidacy (full documents will be presented upon request):*

*"Mr. Miller's talent in bringing alliance partners to the table is unprecedented. He singlehandedly leveraged our two most recent acquisitions and positioned us for continued double-digit growth into the next decade. His value as a negotiator, rainmaker, and consensus-builder cannot be overstated." —L. Johannsen, COO, Abernathy Mineral Resources, Inc.*

*"For more than seven years, we were fortunate to have the leadership skills of Don Miller in our organization. He uniquely combines innate industry knowledge, networked connections, and an ability to rapidly bring together the right people to forge an incredibly productive team." —D. Stephens, President, Tilcon-Tomasso*

Set the pull quotes as individual paragraphs and indent a few spaces in from both left and right margins for maximum impact. This pull-quoting technique ensures that your cover letter will be like no other—and quickly draws the reader's eye to the real value you can bring to an organization.

# Cover Letter Band-Aids: Fix All Those Boo-Boos

*Contributed by Gail Frank, NCRW, CPRW, JCTC, CEIP, MA*

Avoid common cover letter mistakes:

### 1. Overly Stilted Language

**Before:** "Salary should be commensurate with experience."

**After:** "Salary is negotiable based on the exact responsibilities of the position."

### 2. Overly Formal Tone

**Before:** "Allow me to introduce myself" or "Dear Sir/Madam" or "Cordially Yours."

**After:** Replace with a name, or "Dear Hiring Professional." End with "Sincerely" or "Thank You."

### 3. "Me, Me, Me"

**Before:** "Seeking upwardly mobile, challenging position utilizing my skills in…" Remember, the cover letter is supposed to be about what you can for them, not what they can do for you.

**After:** "If your department needs a seasoned customer service manager who can create and deliver training to new representatives…."

### 4. Too Generic

**Before:** "I am submitting my résumé and application for the job you advertised in the local newspaper…"

**After:** "A recent *Wall Street Journal* article states that you are entering the global market. At my previous company I led similar efforts and successfully built sales in Europe and South America…."

### 5. Too Passive/Weak Ending

**Before:** "I look forward to speaking with you about a position at your company." This often-used phrase gives all the power to the reader and strips you of any ability to follow up. Keep control while showing enthusiasm and persistence.

**After:** "I would like to talk with you and see whether I can help your company with its marketing efforts. If I don't hear from you, I'll give you a call next week."

# Tell 'Em What They Want to Know

*Contributed by Deborah Wile Dib, CPBS, CCM, CCMC, NCRW, CPRW, CEIP, JCTC*

Employers who read cover letters don't want to know what you want. They want to know that *you* know what *they* want!

To send an interview-attracting cover letter, you must make a case for employment, and that case cannot be made in a vacuum. You must know something about the company and the company's industry. Before you write your cover letter do the following:

1. Know the current state of the industry and the company (research and network to get this information).

2. Have some ideas of how you can help with emerging problems or situations (positioning, staffing, accelerated growth, loss of market share, and so on).

3. Match your previous accomplishments to the issues you see, and make a case for how these have prepared you to make new contributions.

Once you have done your due diligence and planning, write a letter that succinctly shows your knowledge, your background, your contributions, and your ideas for momentum in the new company. Be a resource, not a supplicant. You'll be interviewing from a position of strength.

Knowledge is power—get it and use it.

## The Resignation Letter: How to Write It and Never Have to Say You're Sorry

*Contributed by Arnold Boldt, CPRW, JCTC*

Especially if you're leaving under less than desirable circumstances, it's wise to use the "KISS" approach: Keep It Strictly Simple. Although you might feel that your resignation letter is the perfect place to defend your point of view, settle a score, or voice your opinion(s) on hot-button issues, think again. It might not be worth jeopardizing any termination benefits (medical insurance, severance salary, and so on) or any hope of a decent reference just to prove your point. Furthermore, burning bridges in this way might backfire down the road because in this age of frequent career changes, you just never know who your next boss will be!

If you truly believe you have a legal case, consult a reputable attorney. Never commit to writing angry thoughts or accusations; these can be retained on file indefinitely and might later haunt you! Instead, keep a personal journal (not online!) or confide in a trusted friend.

Stating that you are leaving because you have found a more challenging career opportunity might be interpreted by your employer to mean that you are bored with your current job. If you write that working there has been pleasant, and then later decide to sue, you might have a more difficult time proving your case. Be clear, concise, and neutral. Try to leave nothing up to the reader's interpretation when writing your resignation letter.

## Slam-Dunk References: Understanding References vs. Employment Verification

*Contributed by Gail Frank, NCRW, CPRW, JCTC, CEIP, MA*

Many people confuse the terms "reference" and "employment verification." "Employment verification" is when the potential employer contacts your previous places of employment to verify that you worked there. This is different from a professional "reference," where someone is willing to discuss your work and vouch for your ability to do a good job.

*(continued)*

*(continued)*

### Who Makes a Good Reference?

Years ago, it was acceptable to provide both "personal" and "professional" references. Today the credibility and relevance of personal references has disappeared. Forget the longtime family friends. Forget the priest or rabbi. Concentrate only on people who can attest to and give specific examples of your work, work ethic, and work style.

You want to offer three or four references. Try for a mixture of people above you (bosses, project leaders, managers), people next to you (peers, colleagues, co-workers), people below you (employees, mentees, support staff), and people outside (vendors, customers). Each of these people will view your skills and contributions differently, and can offer refreshing insight to a new employer. Also strive to present a mixture of work projects, different jobs, and community projects.

# Magic Career-Management Tips

## Ground Rules with Your New Boss
*Contributed by Don Orlando, MBA, CPRW, JCTC, CCM, CCMC*

You've won the job! Now you can devote all your energy to doing well. Two simple steps can make that happen more easily.

1. Set up a "ground rules" meeting with your boss—on your very first day. Every supervisor has a preferred way of doing business. And every employee will find out those ground rules. Too many learn "the way we do things here" in the midst of an important first project. Avoid that stress. Take the time to ask your boss how he or she likes to work. How much decision-making authority will you have? How will your performance be measured? In your boss' view, to whom should you be introduced? This no-stress meeting is a great way to focus your first weeks.

2. As time goes by, document which problems you solved, because that's what you were hired to do. What was the problem? What did you do to fix it? What were the results? Then, a few weeks before your performance review, send your list of problems solved to your boss. You can ask him or her to think of these proofs of performance as a way to judge how you can take on more responsibility—and earn more money.

## Take the Pulse of Your Career Health with an Annual Check-up
*Contributed by Louise Garver, CMP, MCDP, CPRW, CEIP, JCTC*

Once upon a time when we could expect lifelong employment with the same organization, cost-of-living raises, and predictable advancements, little time and effort were spent on refocusing careers. An in-depth annual career check-up is today, in many ways, as important as your annual physical. Rate your responses to the following questions on a scale of 1 to 10, with 10 being the highest score. If your total is less than 55, it might be time to reevaluate your career direction and create new plans.

- How vital is your position to the success of your organization?

- Is your industry/field expanding and experiencing increased demand in today's market?

- Is your job currently meeting your needs for meaningful and challenging work?

- Are you given sufficient opportunities for advancement and professional growth?

- Is your current work allowing enough time for family, relationship, and lifestyle needs?

- Are you receiving pay and benefits appropriate to your financial goals?

- Generally, are your relationships with your boss, co-workers, clients, and customers positive?

# Magic Tip Contributors

The following members of Career Masters Institute (www.cminstitute.com) contributed to the Magic Job Search Tips in the appendix. Please feel free to contact these members should you need additional help with your career, including focusing and creating an orchestrated strategy for your search, developing resumes and other campaign materials, preparing for interviews, and putting a strategy in place for ongoing career management.

You will notice that most of the contributors have one or more credentials listed after their names. The careers industry offers extensive opportunities for ongoing training, and most career professionals take advantage of these opportunities to build their skills and keep their knowledge current. If you are curious about what any one of these credentials means, contact the career practitioner directly. He or she will be glad to discuss certifications and other qualifications as well as information about services that can help you in your career transition.

**Cathy Alfandre, MBA, MILR, CCMC**
Catherine A. Alfandre LLC—Career
Fulfillment Coaching
P.O. Box 453
Easton, CT 06612
Phone: (203) 445-7906
E-mail: cathy@cathyalfandre.com
www.cathyalfandre.com

**Arnold G. Boldt, CPRW, JCTC**
Arnold-Smith Associates
625 Panorama Trail, Bldg. One, Ste. 120C
Rochester, NY 14625
Phone: (585) 383-0350
E-mail: Arnie@ResumeSOS.com
www.ResumeSOS.com

**Freddie Cheek, M.S. Ed., CCM, CPRW, CRW, CWDP**
Cheek & Associates
406 Maynard Dr.
Amherst, NY 14226
Phone: (716) 835-6945

E-mail: fscheek@adelphia.net
www.CheekandAssociates.com

**Joan Cousins, MS, MFA, JCTC**
Creative Career Focus
1480 West St.
Pittsfield, MA 01201
Phone: (413) 443-1154
www.joancousins.com

**Jean Cummings, M.A.T., CPBS, CPRW, CEIP**
A Resume For Today
123 Minot Rd.
Concord, MA 01742
Phone: (978) 371-9266
Toll-free: (800) 324-1699
E-fax: (978) 964-0529
E-mail: jc@AResumeForToday.com
www.AResumeForToday.com

**Deborah Wile Dib, CPBS, CCM, CCMC, NCRW, CPRW, CEIP, JCTC**
The Executive Power Group: Executive Power Coach, Executive Power Brand, Advantage Resumes of New York
77 Buffalo Ave.
Medford, NY 11763
Phone: (631) 475-8513
E-mail: DebDib@executivepowercoach.com
www.executivepowercoach; www.executive-powerbrand; www.advantageresumes.com

**George Dutch, CMF, CCM, JCTC**
JobJoy: The Career Transition Company
750–130 Slater St.
Ottawa, ON
Canada K1P 6E2
Phone: (613) 563-0584
Toll-free: (800) 798-2696
E-mail: jobjoy@sympatico.ca
www.GeorgeDutch.com

**Christine Edick, PCCC, CCMC, JCTC, CEIP**
A Career Coach 4 U
2691 N. Vista Heights
Orange, CA 92867
Phone: (714) 974-6220
E-mail: christine@acareercoach4u.com
www.acareercoach4u.com

**Debra Feldman**
JobWhiz
21 Linwood Ave.
Riverside, CT 06878
Phone: (203) 637-3500
E-mail: DebraFeldman@JobWhiz.com
www.JobWhiz.com

**Michelle M. Fleig-Palmer, MBA, CCM**
University of Nebraska–Lincoln
512 W. 28th St.
Kearney, NE 68845
Phone: (308) 865-8574
E-mail: mfp@bigred.unl.edu

**Gail Frank, NCRW, CPRW, JCTC, CEIP, MA**
Frankly Speaking: Resumes That Work!
10409 Greendale Dr.
Tampa, FL 33626
Phone: (813) 926-1353
Fax: (813) 926-1092

E-mail: gailfrank@post.harvard.edu
www.callfranklyspeaking.com

**Louise Garver, MA, JCTC, CMP, CPRW, MCDP, CEIP**
Career Directions, LLC
143 Melrose Rd.
Broad Brook, CT 06016
Phone: (860) 623-9476
E-mail: careerpro@cox.net
www.resumeimpact.com

**Susan Guarneri, M.S., CCM, NCC, NCCC, LPC, CCMC, CPRW, CEIP, IJCTC**
President, Guarneri Associates/CareerMagicCoach
6670 Crystal Lake Rd.
Three Lakes, WI 54562
Phone: (866) 881-4055
Fax: (715) 546-8039
E-mail: Resumagic@aol.com
www.resume-magic.com

**Beverly Harvey, CPRW, JCTC, CCM, CCMC, MRW**
President, Beverly Harvey Resume & Career Services
P.O. Box 750
Pierson, FL 32180
Phone: (386) 749-3111
Fax: (386) 749-4881
E-mail: beverly@harveycareers.com
www.harveycareers.com

**Mark Hovind**
JobBait.com
4933 W. Craig Rd. #102
Las Vegas, NV 89130
Phone: (702) 648-6616
E-mail: Mark@JobBait.com
www.JobBait.com

**Beth B. Kennedy, MS, LMFT**
Benatti Training & Career Development
35 James St.
Beverly, MA 01915
Phone: (978) 771-7170
E-mail: BBK771@yahoo.com

**Bonnie Kurka, MS, CPRW, JCTC, FJST, CCMC**
Resume Suite
Phone: (877) 570-2573
E-mail: bonnie@resumesuite.com
www.resumesuite.com

**Dale Kurow, M.S.**
Career & Executive Coach
175 W. 76th St., #14D
New York, NY 10023
Phone: (212) 787-6097
E-mail: Dale@dalekurow.com
www.dalekurow.com

**Louise Kursmark, MRW, CPRW, CEIP, JCTC, CCM**
Best Impression Resume and Career Services, Inc.
9847 Catalpa Woods Ct.
Cincinnati, OH 45242
Phone: (513) 792-0030
E-mail: LK@yourbestimpression.com
www.yourbestimpression.com

**Michael S. Levy, CPRW, CEIP, CBPA, MCDP, PHR**
Career Designers Services, LLC
1102 Westbury Pointe Dr., Ste. 102
Tampa, FL 33511
Phone: (813) 655-1461
E-mail: careers@careerdesigners.com
www.careerdesigners.com

**Linda Matias, CIC, NCRW, JCTC**
CareerStrides
80 Davids Dr., Ste. One
Hauppauge, NY 11788
Phone: (631) 387-1894
E-mail: linda@careerstrides.com
www.careerstrides.com

**Sue McCullough, BA, JCTC**
A Win-Win Resume
44 Snapdragon
Irvine, CA 92604
Phone: (949) 786-9015
E-mail: Sue@BeYourPassion.com
www.BeYourPassion.com

**Jan Melnik, MRW, CCM, CPRW**
Absolute Advantage
P.O. Box 718
Durham, CT 06422
Phone: (860) 349-0256
Fax: (860) 349-1343
E-mail: CompSPJan@aol.com
www.JanMelnik.com

**Meg Montford, MCCC, CMF, CCM**
Abilities Enhanced
P.O. Box 9667

Kansas City, MO 64134
Phone: (816) 767-1196
E-mail: meg@abilitiesenhanced.com
www.abilitiesenhanced.com
Blog: www.careerchaos.com

**William G. Murdock**
The Employment Coach
7770 Meadow Rd., Ste. 109
Dallas, TX 75230
Phone: (214) 750-4781
E-mail: bmurdock@swbell.net

**Carol Nason, MA, CPRW**
Career Advantage
95 Flavell Rd.
Groton, MA 01450
Phone: (978) 448-3319
E-mail: nason1046@aol.com
www.acareeradvantageresume.com

**JoAnn Nix, CPRW, JCTC, CEIP, CCMC, CPBS**
A Great Resume Service, Inc.
5704 McClure Rd.
Van Buren, AR 72955
Phone: (800) 265-6901
E-mail: info@agreatresume.com
www.agreatresume.com

**Don Orlando, MBA, CPRW, JCTC, CCM, CCMC**
The McLean Group
640 S. McDonough St.
Montgomery, AL 36104
Phone: (334) 264-2020
Fax: (334) 264-9227
E-mail: yourcareercoach@aol.com

**Barb Poole, CPRW, CRW, BS, CCMC**
President, Hire Imaging
1812 Red Fox Rd.
St. Cloud, MN 56301
Phone: (320) 253-0975
Fax: (320) 253-1790
E-mail: eink@astound.net
www.hireimaging.com

**Edith A. Rische, NCRW, JCTC, ACCC**
Write Away Resume and Career Coaching
5908 73rd St.
Lubbock, TX 79424
Phone: (806) 798-0881
E-mail: earische@cox.net
www.writeawayresume.com

**Harriette Royer, MS**
Career Catalyst
23 Hobart St.
Rochester, NY 14611
Phone: (585) 436-9174
E-mail: royer@frontiernet.net

**Donna Srader, M.A.**
Career Center, The University of
Texas at Dallas
P.O. Box 830688, MC 16
Richardson, TX 75083-0688
Phone: (972) 883-2943
E-mail: donna.srader@utdallas.edu
www.utd.edu/student/career

**Billie Ruth Sucher, M.S., CTMS, CTSB**
Billie Sucher & Associates
7177 Hickman Rd., Ste. 10
Urbandale, IA 50322
Phone: (515) 276-0061
Fax: (515) 334-8076
E-mail: betwnjobs@aol.com

**Wendy Terwelp, CCMC, RPBS, IJCTC, CEIP**
Opportunity Knocks of Wisconsin, LLC
11431 N. Port Washington Rd., Ste. 101
Mequon, WI 53092
Phone: (262) 241-4655
E-mail: consultant@knocks.com
www.knocks.com

**Dr. Lauren Vicker**
Professor & Chair,
Communications/Journalism Department
St. John Fisher College
3690 East Ave.
Rochester, NY 14618
Phone: (585) 385-8205
E-mail: lvicker@sjfc.edu

**Jean F. West, CPRW, JCTC**
Impact Resumes
413 Walnut St., #5206
Green Cove Springs, FL 32043
Phone: (888) 590-2534
E-mail: jean@impactresumes.com
www.impactresumes.com
Blog: http://jeanwest.typepad.com/
impact_resumes/

*Appendix*

# B

# Worksheets to Catalog Professional History

Use the worksheets in this appendix to catalog your professional history, including the information in the following list. This information will help you write your résumé.

- Qualifications
- Professional experience
- Education
- Computer skills
- Professional organizations
- Community involvement
- Awards and honors
- Publications
- Presentations
- Patents
- Personal information
- Endorsements

# WORKSHEETS TO CATALOG PROFESSIONAL HISTORY

## QUALIFICATIONS

Refer to chapter 7 for instructions on using and writing a qualifications summary. Choose from these suggested items:

**Title/functional area:** _____

_____

**Subcategories of functional area or core competencies:** _____

_____

_____

**Industry:** _____

_____

**Number of years of experience:** _____

**Expertise, strengths, specialization:** _____

_____

**"Combination" accomplishment or highlights of accomplishments:** _____

_____

**Advanced degree, certification, licensure:** _____

_____

**Language skills, international business skills:** _____

_____

**Technical/computer skills:** _____

_____

**Personal profile/management style:** _____

_____

**Affiliations:** _____

_____

**Employers, schools with name recognition:** _____

_____

## PROFESSIONAL EXPERIENCE

A.  **Your most recent employer**

Company name: _____

Company's location:  City _____ State _____

Month/Year you were hired: _____ / _____

Month/Year you left: _____ / _____ (list "Present" if still employed)

Your most recent title: _____

List any prior positions with the company (if applicable): _____

_____

Company annual sales (if public): $_____

Indicate whether company is regional, national, or international: _____

Distinguishing characteristics of company (such as "the nation's leading   manufacturer of widgets," "the world's 2nd largest distributor of high-tech components,"  "the region's dominant real estate brokerage," etc.):

_____

_____

Briefly describe your scope of accountability, listing items in order of importance.

1. _____

    _____

2. _____

    _____

3. _____

    _____

4. _____

    _____

5. _____

    _____

6. _____

    _____

**Contributions / Impact Statements:** What did you do to help the company become more profitable, operate more efficiently, or solve specific problems? Be specific about how you did it and what the "before" and "after" facts are. Refer to chapter 9 for ideas on developing impact statements.

1. _____

_____

2. _____

_____

3. _____

_____

4. _____

_____

5. _____

_____

6. _____

_____

7. _____

_____

**B.  The employer prior to your current (or most recent) employer**

Company name: _____

Company's location:  City _____ State _____

Month/Year you were hired:  __ / __

Month/Year you left:  __ / __

Your title: _____

List any prior positions with the company (if applicable): _____

_____

Company annual sales (if public): $_____

Indicate whether company is regional, national, or international: _____

Distinguishing characteristics of company:

_____

Briefly describe your scope of accountability, listing items in order of importance.

1. _____
   _____

2. _____
   _____

3. _____
   _____

4. _____
   _____

5. _____
   _____

6. _____
   _____

**Contributions / Impact Statements:**  What did you do to help the company become more profitable, operate more efficiently, or solve specific problems? Refer to chapter 9 for ideas on developing impact statements.

1. _____
   _____

2. _____
   _____

3. _____
   _____

4. _____
   _____

5. _____
   _____

6. _____
   _____

**C.** **The employer prior to company listed under "B."**

Company name: _____

Company's location:  City _____ State _____

Month/Year you were hired:  _____ / _____

Month/Year you left:  _____ / _____

Your title: _____

List any prior positions with the company (if applicable): _____

_____

Company annual sales (if public): $_____

Indicate whether company is regional, national, or international: _____

Distinguishing characteristics of company:

_____

Briefly describe your scope of accountability, listing items in order of importance.

1. _____

   _____

2. _____

   _____

3. _____

   _____

4. _____

   _____

**Contributions / Impact Statements:**  Refer to chapter 9 for ideas on developing impact statements.

1. _____

   _____

2. _____

   _____

3. _____

**D.** **The employer prior to company listed under "C."**

Company name: _____

Company's location: City _____ State _____

Month/Year you were hired: _____ / _____

Month/Year you left: _____ / _____

Your title: _____

List any prior positions with the company (if applicable): _____

_____

Company annual sales (if public): $_____

Indicate whether company is regional, national, or international: _____

Distinguishing characteristics of company:

_____


Briefly describe your scope of accountability, listing items in order of importance.

1. _____

_____

2. _____

_____

3. _____

_____

4. _____

_____

**Contributions / Impact Statements:** Refer to chapter 9 for ideas on developing impact statements.

1. _____

_____

2. _____

_____

3. _____

_____

**E.   The employer prior to company listed under "D."**

Company name: _____

Company's location:  City _____ State _____

Month/Year you were hired:  _____ / _____

Month/Year you left:  _____ / _____

Your title: _____

List any prior positions with the company (if applicable): _____

_____

Company annual sales (if public): $_____

Indicate whether company is regional, national, or international: _____

Distinguishing characteristics of company:

_____

Briefly describe your scope of accountability, listing items in order of importance.

1. _____

   _____

2. _____

   _____

3. _____

   _____

4. _____

   _____

**Contributions / Impact Statements:**  Refer to chapter 9 for ideas on developing impact statements.

1. _____

   _____

2. _____

   _____

3. _____

   _____

## EDUCATION

Education can include university, community college, vocational trade school, or night classes. Refer to chapter 8 for complete instructions on presenting education.

A.   Name of institution: _____

      Location (city and state): _____

      Dates (year started to year completed): _____ to _____

      Your major: _____

      Did you complete a degree? Yes _____ No _____

      If yes, what degree? (For example, "Master of Arts in Education Administration")

      _____

      _____

      If you are a recent graduate, consider including a list of important or relevant coursework:

      _____

      _____

      Second school (if applicable)

      Name of institution: _____

      Location (city and state): _____

      Dates (year started to year completed): _____ to _____

      Your major: _____

      Did you receive a degree? Yes _____ No _____

      If yes, what degree? (For example, "Bachelor of Arts in Communications")

      _____

      _____

B.   Seminars or conferences relevant to your career (seminar title, date, location, sponsoring organization): _____

      _____

      _____

      _____

C.   Credentials and licenses: _____

      _____

      _____

## COMPUTER SKILLS

List software, hardware, operating systems, or programming languages with which you are familiar. Examples might include standard office-computing programs (such as MS Office with Word, Excel, PowerPoint, and Access), contact management software, Web design and development tools, graphics programs, programming languages, or industry-specific programs. _____

_____

_____

_____

_____

_____

## PROFESSIONAL ORGANIZATIONS, COMMUNITY INVOLVEMENT

Be sure to mention any leadership positions, such as president, treasurer, or committee chairperson, as well as the names of your professional affiliations and community organizations.

_____

_____

_____

_____

_____

## AWARDS, HONORS

This section can include awards from college (if recent), work, or community service.

_____

_____

_____

_____

## PUBLICATIONS, PRESENTATIONS, PATENTS

Include publications, professional writing, formal presentations, and patents.

_____

_____

_____

_____

## BIO BITES, PERSONAL INFORMATION, ADDITIONAL DATA

Do **NOT** include your birth date, height, weight, marital status, religion, or political affiliation. Do consider including items such as the following.

**Interests/Hobbies**—Concentrate on those related to your profession or of general interest (for instance, if you coach a Babe Ruth baseball team and are looking for a position in sporting good sales, say so; or, if you are a jogger and clock 20 miles a week or compete in races, say so!): _____

_____

_____

**Special Abilities**—These skills should relate to your target position (for instance, if you are in sales, special abilities might include public speaking, making formal client presentations, serving as a television or radio spokesperson, networking, negotiating contracts, and so on): _____

_____

_____

_____

**Language(s)**—Fluent, business vocabulary, or conversational skills: _____

_____

**Professional Profile**—Think in terms of the employer's point of view and what is needed in an employee (for instance, if you describe yourself as "dependable," provide evidence of the characteristic, such as "Dependable—perfect work attendance record for past 5 years"): _____

_____

_____

_____

_____

## ENDORSEMENTS

_____

_____

_____

_____

_____

# Index

## A

accomplishments, 231–246
  buying motivators, 232–235
  career management file, 243–245
  fit, 246–247
  impact-mining, 245
  impact statements, 232–235, 246–247
  performance appraisals, 242–243
  strategies, 235–241
    challenge, action, and result (CAR) technique, 239–241
    comparison, 236–238
    numbers, 235–236
    return on investment (ROI), 238–239
  summary, 268
action steps, 27–28, 41, 174–177
Adams, John Quincy, 341
affiliations, 202–203
  keywords, 228–229
  worksheet, 518
affirmations, 162–163
agencies, 329–331
agility, 171
Albom, Mitch, 7
American Society for Training & Development, 6
American Society of Association Executives, 281
Analyze phase of transitions, 25
anecdotes, 105
annual reports, 293
applicant-tracking systems, 342–343
Armour, J. Ogden, 391
ASCII resumes, 253–257
assessments, 83–92, 346–347
  America's Career InfoNet—Skills Profiler, 87
  The Birkman Method Preview Report, 86
  Campbell Interest and Skill Inventory, 86, 88
  Career Leader, 85
  Career Liftoff Interest Inventory, 87
  Career Orientations Inventory, 89
  Career Temperament Report, 90
  Clifton StrengthsFinder, 87
  The Golden Personality Type Profiler, 89
  The Keirsey Temperament Sorter-II, 86, 90
  Knowdell Motivated Skills Card Sort, 87
  MAPP Career Motivational Appraisal, 84
  Myers-Briggs Type Indicator, 89
  O*NET OnLine Skills Search, 87
  O*NET Work Importance Profiles, 88
  Self Worth Inventory, 88
  16 PF Personal Career Developmental Profile Plus Report, 84
  Strong and MBTI Career Report, 85
  Strong Interest Inventory Profile, 88
  Values Arrangement List, 89
  Values Preference Indicator, 89
  Work Behavior Inventory, 90
assets, 10
associations, 281, 314, 518
attitude, 150–151, 170, 173
awards, 518

## B

Barron-Tieger, Barbara, 82
behavioral interviews, 108–114, 391–404
  competencies, 392–398
  questions, 392
  SMART Stories, 398–401

benefits, 441, 455
Bernbach, William, 405
BizWeb, 213
blogs, 255, 258–260, 309, 314
bone-marrow people, 167–170
bonuses, 455
brands, career, 121–146
  benefits, 121–122
  business cards, verbal, 128–133
  communicating, 147
  elements of, 122–123
  image, 138–142
  Mini-Bio, 133–137
  perception, 141
  role models, 138–141
  sound bites, 123–137
  three-point marketing messages, 124, 133
  verbal branding, 123–137
  visual branding, 137–146
  wardrobe, 143–146
    men, 145–146
    women, 143–145
Branton, Nancy, 83
bridge positions, 11
Bridges, Bill, 20
Buckingham, Marcus, 9
budget, 44–45
buoyancy, 149–184
  actions, 174–177
  characteristics, 150
  control, 164–173
    agility, 171
    basics, 165–167
    bone-marrow people, 167–170
    energy, 172–173
    finances, 173
    gratitude, 171
    negative emotions, 173
    positive thoughts, 170
    support, 169–170
    time management, 171–172
  gauging, 151–155
  inspiration, 156–164
    affirmations, 162–163
    future focus, 160–162

    identity, 164
    inner action, 156–158
    perspective, 163
    rewriting thoughts, 156–158
    value, 162–163
  leverage, 182
  listening, 179–180
  mindset, 150–151
  perseverance, 177–178
Burns, Reginna K., 51
business cards, 26, 128–133
buying motivators, 103, 129–131, 232–235, 441

**C**

career destiny questions, 4
career DNA, 8–10
career events, 335
career explorers, 25, 83, 94
career hunters, 25
career management file, 243–245
career needs, 65–69
  The Things That Matter to Me checklist, 67–69
career-choice tips, 477–478
career-management tips, 504–505
Carnegie, Dale, 37, 121
category headings, 195–208
  affiliations, 202–203
  contact information, 196–197
  credentials, 201–202
  education, 201–202
  focus statements, 197–198
  key features, 198–199
  licenses, 201–202
  objective, 197–198
  professional experience, 200
  qualifications summary, 198–199
  single items, 203
  skills, 200–201
  supporting material, 203–206
clarifying (interviews), 366–369
  first interviews, 367–368
  job descriptions, 366
  second interviews, 368–369
classified ads, 321–322

Clifton, Donald O., 9
closing interviews, 372–377
coaching, 93–95, 100
collaborating (interviews), 370–372
companies, identifying, 278–285
    Internet, 281–283
    location, 283
    mailing lists, 283
    people/networking, 279–280
    print resources, 280–281
    prioritizing, 284
    profiles, 284–285
    public records, 283
competencies, 392–398
    common, 393
    interview questions, 395
    job descriptions, 396–397
    SMART Stories, 397–398
Conference Board's Consumer
    Research Center, 5
connecting (interviews), 358–365
    attitude, 362–363
    interviewers, 363–365
    listening, 360–361
    lying, 365
    mirroring, 363
    motive, 362–363
    openers, 359
    over-telling, 362
    responding, 361
contact information, resumes, 196–197
controllables, 164–173
    agility, 171
    basics, 165–167
    bone-marrow people, 167–170
    energy, 172–173
    finances, 173
    gratitude, 171
    negative emotions, 173
    positive thoughts, 170
    support, 169–170
    time management, 171–172
Coolidge, Calvin, 16
counter-offers, 455–457

cover letters, 261–266
    salaries, 450
    tips, 501–503
Covey, Steven, 6
credentials
    keywords, 227–228
    resumes, 201–202
Crispin, Gerry, 213
criticism, 474–475

**D**

date of birth in resumes, 206
date-stamping resumes, 207
de Purucker, Gottfried, 156
decision making, 94–95
Deming, W. Edwards, 253
designed purpose, 9
DiCaprio, Leonardo, 138
Dietschler, Mary Ann, 145
direct mail, 332–334
distribution, resumes, 327–328
Dreyfuss, Richard, 23

**E**

e-forms, 254–257
e-lists, 309–310
e-mail addresses (networking), 296
e-resumes, 253–257
Edison, Thomas, 273
editing resumes, 248–249
education
    keywords, 227–228
    resumes, 201–202
    worksheet, 517
80/20 Principle, 174–175
Eller, Dean, 167
employers
    buying motivators, 103, 129–131,
        232–235, 441
    FAQs about, 410–412
    identity, 72–74
endorsements, 519
Enelow, Wendy S., 268
energy, 172–173

ePortfolios, 257–258, 498–499
executive profiles, 268
experience, 29, 31, 33, 35–36, 200
Express phase of transitions, 26

**F**

Farr, Mike, 275
*Fast Company* magazine, 7
feedback, 474–475
finances, 173
fit, 51–56, 246–247, 344, 375–377
focus statements, 96–97, 197–198
    keywords, 214–220
Forbes, Malcolm, 51
formats, resumes, 187–195
    choosing, 194–195
    chronological format, 187–190,
        194–195
    functional format, 187, 191–195
formatting resumes, 247–248
forums, 310–311
Fowler, Gene, 211
Fox, Jeffrey J., 305
Frankl, Viktor, 160
frequently asked questions, *see* questions, FAQs
fulfillment, 70–72
functional areas, 59–61
future focus, 160–162

**G**

Gallison, Steve, 4
Gatewood, Jean, 168
gauging buoyancy, 151–155
Geneen, Harold S., 445
goals, SMART, 28–43
    attainable, 29–41
        assessments, 30–32
        job search factors, 29–30
        length of search, 33–35
        strategies, 35–41
    measurable, 29
    relevant, 41
    results, 470–471
    specific, 28
    time-specific, 41

Grandma Moses, 9
gratitude, 171

**H**

Hammerstein, Oscar, 58
Handler, Charles, 341
Hanks, Tom, 138
hard skills, 105
Hierarchy of Needs model, 66
high-yield career, 11
holding back, 475–476
homework, 471
honors, 518

**I**

identity, 72–75, 164
image, 138–142
impact statements, 232–235, 246–247
impact-mining, 245
independent contractors, 20, 454
industries and interests, 61–65
    Industry checklist, 62–63
initiative, 472
inner action, 156–158
inside guides, 473–474
inspiration, 156–164
    affirmations, 162–163
    future focus, 160–162
    identity, 164
    inner action, 156–158
    perspective, 163
    rewriting thoughts, 156–158
    value, 162–163
internships, 314
interviews, 76, 179, 290–291, 357–389,
    405
    clarifying, 366–369
        first interviews, 367–368
        job descriptions, 366
        second interviews, 368–369
    closing, 372–377
    collaborating, 370–372
    connecting, 358–365
        attitude, 362–363
        interviewers, 363–365
        listening, 360–361

lying, 365
mirroring, 363
motive, 362–363
openers, 359
over-telling, 362
responding, 361
leave-behinds, 379–384
postmortem analysis, 377–379
salaries, 451–452
second, 368–369, 379
telephone, 347–353
accepted, 352–353
closing, 352–353
declined, 353
expectations, 349–350
impressions, 347–348
phone zones, 348–349
postponed, 353
questions, 350
salaries, 450–451
tips, 350–352
tips, 489–497
Investigate phase of transitions, 26
ISQs (industry-specific questions),
430–431

### J

James, William, 170
job descriptions, 224–225
job fairs, 335
job satisfaction, 5
job situations, 11–12
job success, 3–22
career destiny questions, 4
visualization, 6–8
work-life synergy, 5
Johnson, Samuel, 223
Jung, Carl, 76

### K

Keirsey Temperament Sorter-II, 82
key features, resumes, 198–199
keywords, 211–230, 321
affiliations, 228–229
credentials, 227–228

education, 227–228
focus statements, 214–220
job descriptions, 224–225
licenses, 227–228
objectives, 214–220
offline resources, 212–213
online resources, 213
positioning, 214
professional experience, 223–226
qualifications summaries, 220–223
skills, 226–227
supporting material, 228–229
title statements, 215
King, Martin Luther, Jr., 3–4
Kingsley, Kate, 348
knowledge, 10, 105
Kursmark, Louise M., 268

### L

leave-behinds, 379–384
letters, follow-up, 379–384
letters of recommendation, 207
leverage, 182
licenses
keywords, 227–228
resumes, 201–202
listening, 179–180

### M

Magic F.I.T., 10, 51–100, 131, 278
career needs, 65–69
coaching, 93–95
commitment statements, 58
elements of, 57
finalize, 95
focus statements, 96–97
fulfillment, 70–72
functions, 59–61
identity, 72–75
industries and interests, 61–65
online assessments, 83–92
personality types, 76–82
salary ranges, 82
steps, 98–99

Magical Coaching Questions, 49–50, 100, 120, 148, 183–184, 210, 230, 251–252, 270, 317–318, 338, 355–356, 387–389, 403–404, 441–442, 464–468
marital status in resumes, 206
Maslov, Abraham, 66
Maxwell, Elaine, 469
methods, 277–278
Miller, Margaret, 357
mindset, 150–151
Mini-Bio, 133–137
momentum, 472
motivation, 29, 31, 36–37, 96, 106
Murray, Bill, 23
Myers-Briggs Type Indicator, 76–82

### N

nature, 9–10
negative emotions, 173
networking, 279–280
    approaching, 298–303
    confidential searches, 308
    e-mail addresses, 296
    INSIDER information, 306–308
    on-the-job, 476
    online, 309–312
    referral incentives, 297
    tips, 485–489
    voice mails, 297
networking resumes, 21, 268
never-ending networkers, 20
non-negotiables, 4

### O

objectives, 197–198
    keywords, 214–220
obstacles, 30, 32, 40–41
Occupassion, 4, 10, 25
offers, job, 452–456
    counter-offers, 455–457
    multiple, 461–462, 465–468
    written offers, 459
online searches, 320–326
opportunities, 52–54, 273–276

options, career, 92
Orchestrate phase of transitions, 26

### P

partners (job search), 18–19
performance appraisals, 242–243
perks, 458–459
perseverance, 177–178
persistence (job search), 16–18
personal data in resumes, 206, 519
personality types, 76–82
perspective (job search), 13–16, 163
photographs in resumes, 207
planning (job search), 19–21, 23–50
    macro plans, 20–21
    micro plans, 21
    options, 43–44
    resources and budget, 44
    SMART goals, 28–43
    support team, 45–47
    transition phases, 24–28
portfolios, online (ePortfolios), 257–258, 498–499
positive thoughts, 170
post-interview analysis, 377–379
posting resumes, 326–327
PowerPoint resumes, 268
preparation (job search), 18
prescreens, 341–347
    applicant tracking systems, 342–343
    formal assessments, 346–347
    job fit, 344
    personality, 344
    topics, 343–344
process (job search), 10–12
professional experience
    keywords, 223–226
    resumes, 200
    worksheet, 511–516
profit (job search), 12–13
proofreading resumes, 249–250
public (job search), 19
publications, 518
purpose (job search), 8–10

## Q

qualifications summaries, 198–199
  keywords, 220–223
  worksheet, 510
questions
  awkward, 435–440
    co-workers, 437–438
    degree, 438
    ethics, 439
    fired, 437
    mistakes, 438
    resume gaps, 436
    salary, 437
    short periods of employment, 436
    unemployment, 435–436
  behavioral interviews, 392
  career destiny, 4
  coaching, 49–50, 93–94, 100, 120
  FAQs, 406–429
    boss, 409–410
    co-workers, 414
    company-specific, 413
    contributions, 413–414
    criticism, 424
    current position, 415–416
    decision-making, 407
    employers, 410–412
    expectations, 412
    future, 425
    learning, 424
    motivation, 423–424
    opportunities, 420–421
    personal, 406–407
    persuasion, 421–422
    problems, 418–419, 422–423
    productivity, 419–420
    projects, 407–408
    salary, 426–427
    strengths, 416–417
    value, 426
    weaknesses, 417–418
    work environment, 408–409
  illegal, 431–435
    responding, 434–435
  industry-specific, 430–431

interviews, 108–114, 367–369
personality, 344
salary, 450–452
success stories, 107–108
telephone, 350
topics, 343–344

## R

radar screen, 175
ranges, salary, 452
Really Simple Syndication (RSS) technology, 260
recommendations, 207
recruiters, 329–331, 451
reference list, 207–208, 266–268, 503–504
relationships, 469, 473–476
research, 26, 289–293
  salaries, 446–448
resignation letters, 503
resources, 44–45
  offline, 212–213
  online, 213, 291
  people, 279–280
  print, 280
results, 469–473
  goals, 470–471
  homework, 471
  initiative, 472
  momentum, 472
  underpromise; overdeliver, 471
  value, 470–471
resumes, 187–210
  category headings, 195–208
    affiliations, 202–203
    contact information, 196–197
    credentials, 201–202
    education, 201–202
    focus statements, 197–198
    key features, 198–199
    licenses, 201–202
    objective, 197–198
    professional experience, 200
    qualifications summary, 198–199
    single items, 203

skills, 200–201
supporting material, 203–206
chronological format, 187–190, 194–195
date of birth, 206
date-stamping, 207
distribution, 327–328
editing, 248–249
formatting, 247–248
functional format, 187, 191–195
length, 226
letters of recommendation, 207
marital status, 206
networking, 268
personal data, 206
photograph, 207
posting, 326–327
PowerPoint, 268
proofreading, 249–250
putting it together, 208
reference list, 207–208
salary, 207
tips, 498–504
return on investment (ROI), 102–103, 109
rewriting thoughts, 156–158
Roosevelt, Eleanor, 23
Rushnell, SQuire, 179

**S**

salary
negotiating, 30, 32, 39–40, 82, 445–467
comparing, 448
counter-offers, 456–457
face-to-face, 459–461
multiple offers, 461–462, 465–468
offers, 452–456
perks, 458–459
questions, 450–452
ranges, 452
recruiters, 451
research, 446–448
targets, 449
tips, 497–498
written offers, 459

resumes, 207
Santos, Judy, 168
satisfaction, 5
Scheferman, Heather, 168
Schweitzer, Albert, 3
search engines, 281–282
second interviews, 368–369, 379
Seligman, Martin, 170
Shakespeare, William, 8, 231
single-item categories in resumes, 203
skills, 10, 29–33, 35, 37–38, 105, 226–227
computer, 30, 32, 38, 518
keywords, 226–227
occupational, 226
personal, 226
resumes, 200–201
social, 30–31, 37–38
Slaten, Shandel, 16–17
SMART Stories, 108–114, 124–126, 133, 172
behavioral interviews, 398–401
cataloguing, 117
collaborating, 116
competencies, 397–398
rating, 118–119
writing, 114–119
soft skills, 105
Solutions Or Services (SOS) responses, 105, 130
sound bites, 123–137
special reports, 268, 500–501
Stanley, Thomas J., 58
stepping-stone positions, 11
strategies, 30, 32, 39
challenge, action, result (CAR) technique, 239–241
comparison, 236–238
numbers, 235–236
presenting accomplishments, 235–241
return on investment, 238–239
strategy tips, 479–485
stress, 55
success stories, 26, 105–108
cataloguing, 117
collaborating, 116

rating, 118–119
writing, 114–119
support team, 30–31, 38, 45–47, 169–170, 175
supporting material
 keywords, 228–229
 resumes, 203–206

**T**

*T+D* magazine, 6
taglines, 135
targeted searches, 276–314
 identifying companies, 278–285
  Internet, 281–283
  location, 283
  mailing lists, 283
  people/networking, 279–280
  print resources, 280–281
  prioritizing, 284
  profiles, 284–285
  public records, 283
 networking, 293–308
  approaching, 298–303
  confidential searches, 308
  e-mail addresses, 296
  INSIDER information, 306–308
  online, 309–312
  referral incentives, 297
  voice mails, 297
 radar, 312–314
  online presence, 313
  presentations, 312–313
 reading, 285–289
 research, 289–293
 traditional methods, 314
team-building, 475
telephone interviews, 347–353
 accepted, 352–353
 closing, 352–353
 declined, 353
 expectations, 349–350
 impressions, 347–348
 phone zones, 348–349
 postponed, 353
 questions, 350

salaries, 450–451
tips, 350–352
10 Quick Tips lists
 acing online assessments, 91–92
 answering ISQs, 430–431
 behavioral interviews, 402
 capturing your value, 119–120
 communicating your career brand, 147
 conduct a targeted search and tap the hidden job market, 315–317
 connect, clarify, collaborate, and close the interview, 385–387
 cover letters, 266
 cover your bases with traditional search strategies, 336–337
 creating e-resumes, cover letters, and other career marketing documents, 269–270
 focusing on your Magic F.I.T., 98–99
 getting your job search plan together, 47–48
 managing mindset, 182–183
 managing online prescreening and telephone interviews, 354–355
 prepare for prescreening tools, 344–346
 responding to FAQs, 427–429
 responding to illegal or awkward questions, 439–440
 resume editing, 248–249
 resume formatting, 247–248
 resume keywords, 229–230
 resume proofreading, 249–250
 salary negotiations, 462–464
 structuring your resume, 209–210
 talking to new people, 294–295
 writing accomplishments and finalizing your resume, 250–251
three-part/three-point marketing message, 26, 124, 133, 426, 441
Tieger, Paul D., 82
time availability, 30, 32, 40
time management, 171–172
title statements (keywords), 215

traditional searches, 319–340
  agencies, 329–331
  career events, 335
  classified ads, 321–322
  direct mail, 332–334
  online, 320–326
  recruiters, 329–331
  resume distribution, 327–328
  resume posting, 326–327
transitions, phases of, 24–28
  Analyze, 25
  Express, 26
  Investigate, 26
  Orchestrate, 26
  Uncover, 27–28

### U–V

Uncover phase of transitions, 27–28
underpromise; overdeliver, 471
value, 12–13, 101–105, 162–163
  benefits, 103–105
  buying motivators, 103
  capturing, 119–120
  conveying, 102–106, 121–146
  results, 470–471
  return on investment (ROI), 103
  Solutions Or Services (SOS)
      responses, 105
values, 10
verbal branding, 123–137
  business cards, verbal, 128–133
  elements of, 122–123
  Mini-Bio, 133–137
  sound bites, 123–137
  three-point marketing messages, 124,
      133
visual branding, 137–146
  image, 138–142
  perception, 141
  role models, 138–141
  wardrobe, 143–146
      men, 145–146
      women, 143–145
visualization, 6–8
volunteering, 176, 314, 500
Vonnegut, Kurt Jr., 176

### W

wardrobe, 143–146
Washington, Booker T., 319
Web sites, 322–326
  AccuData America, 283
  AltaVista, 213
  America's Career InfoNet—Skills
      Profiler, 87
  American City Business Journals, 283
  The American Society of Association
      Executives, 281
  Ask Jeeves, 213
  The Birkman Method Preview Report,
      86
  Bizjournals, 291
  BizWeb, 213
  Blogarama, 260
  Blogger.com, 259
  blogharbor.com, 259
  Bloglines, 260
  BlogTree, 260
  Bloomberg, 291
  Bureau of Labor Statistics, 64
  Campbell Interest and Skill Inventory,
      86, 88
  Career Leader, 85
  Career Liftoff Interest Inventory, 87
  Career Orientations Inventory, 89
  Career Temperament Report, 90
  CareerLifePotential.com, 83
  careers, major, 325–326
  CEO Express, 291
  Clifton StrengthsFinder, 87
  CNN.com, 289
  CoachMaryAnn.com, 145
  company, 322
  Corporate Information, 291
  CorporateAlumni.com, 311
  craigslist.com, 282
  D&B's ZapData, 283
  diversity, 324
  Dunn and Bradstreet, 291
  ExecuNet, 311
  executives, 322
  Feed Reader, 260

Feedburner, 260
FeedDemon, 260
*Forbes,* 282
*Fortune,* 282
Friendster, 311
The Golden Personality Type Profiler, 89
GoLeads, 283
Google, 213, 282, 288, 292
The Great Place to Work Institute, 282
Hoovers, 291
*Inc.,* 282
InfoUSA, 283
international, 324–325
JobBait, 283
JobSmart.org, 282
The Keirsey Temperament Sorter-II, 86, 90
Knowdell Motivated Skills Card Sort, 87
LinkedIn, 311
Lycos, 213
MAPP Career Motivational Appraisal, 84
Microsoft, 288
Monster, 311
Myers-Briggs Type Indicator, 89
National Institutes of Health Small Business Office, 64
Netscape Search, 213
Newsgator, 260
niche jobs, 322–323, 325
O*NET OnLine Skills Search, 87
O*NET Work Importance Profiles, 88
*Occupational Outlook Handbook,* 61
Pluck, 260
Pro/File Research, 283
ReachCC.com, 37, 137
recruiting, 323–324
Resume Blaster, 328
Resume Zapper, 328
ResumeMachine.com, 61, 328
RiteSite.com, 311
Royal Dutch Shell, 288
Ryze, 311

salary tools, 446–447
Search Systems, 283
Self Worth Inventory, 88
Siemens, 288
16 PF Personal Career Developmental Profile Plus Report, 84
Strong and MBTI Career Report, 85
Strong Interest Inventory Profile, 88
SuperPages.com, 283
Tribe, 311
TypePad, 259
Values Arrangement List, 89
Values Preference Indicator, 89
VistaPrint.com, 44
Weddle's, 281
Work Behavior Inventory, 90
Yahoo!, 213, 282
Zacks, 292
Ziggs, 311
ZoomInfo, 311
Weddle, Peter, 281, 327
White, E. B., 187
Williamson, Marianne, 6
Winfrey, Oprah, 167, 374
wisdom workers, 20
work-life synergy, 5
worksheets
    Acting "As If," 474
    Actions for Focus, 22
    Affirmations, 162
    Bone-Marrow, 168
    Catalog Professional History, 509–519
    Company Profile, 286–287
    Controlling the Controllables, 166–167
    Data Bits, 197
    Daypop, 260
    Draft Your Fulfillment Statement, 71–72
    80/20, 174–175
    Electronic Recruiter Exchange, 260
    The Essence of My Work Identity, 75
    Focus Statement, 97
    Functional Preferences, 61
    Future Focus, 161

Image, 142
Industry Preference(s), 64
Inspirational Triggers, 159–160
Interests, 65
My Plan B Goal, 44
My Plan C Goal, 44
My SMART Goal, 42–43
My SMART Story, 118
My Support Team, 45–46
My Verbal Business Card, 132
Not Knowing, 181
Reframe Your Perspectives, 16
Salary Figures, 82

SMART Story, 117–118
Technorati, 260
The Things That Matter to Me, 69
Value = Profit, 13
What I Can Accomplish in My Next
    Position, 75
Winks, 180
Your Resume Outline, 208
written offers, 459

## X–Z

Zigler, Zig, 149
Zimmerman, Eilene, 309